"Putman's book is a biblical, the Christmas story as presented in is simple: to help Christians gain a better understanding of Jesus and his work on the cross from the biblical nativity stories. Putman succeeds splendidly. Pastors, scholars, and students alike will benefit from this clear, well-organized, solidly biblical, theological, and practical treatment of the subject of the virgin birth of Christ. A worthy addition to your library."

—**David Allen**, distinguished professor of practical theology, Mid-America Baptist Theological Seminary

"The narratives of Jesus's conception and birth continue to fascinate Christians and interpreters. But over the years, some modern readers have challenged these stories and have failed to reckon with both the biblical text and biblical theology. In *Conceived by the Holy Spirit*, Rhyne Putman guides the reader in matters of exegesis, theology, and history. He leads us to think clearly in light of Christian orthodoxy, and he prepares us with answers to objections we may face. Our redeemer is the virgin-born King whose coming was foretold in ancient days and whose incarnation is the wonder that makes angels and saints sing with joy."

—**Mitch Chase**, associate professor of biblical studies, The Southern Baptist Theological Seminary

"More than an adorable myth attached to the Christmas story, the virgin birth of Jesus Christ is an essential and exciting Christian doctrine. In this new and important volume, Rhyne Putman tells us why—through Scripture and Christian history—this beautiful truth has animated the church's gospel witness. Long an underemphasized, under-covered aspect of the incarnation, Putman helps recover this doctrine for a new generation. Written with clarity and conviction, *Conceived by the Holy Spirit* is an essential book for every pastor's library."

—**Daniel Darling**, director of the Land Center for Cultural Engagement, Southwestern Baptist Theological Seminary

"The virgin birth of Jesus is a theological bedrock for the Christian faith. Only the virgin-born, sinless Son of God could have died as an atoning sacrifice to pay the penalty for the sins of mankind. And Jesus alone fits that description. I am grateful for this book because it sets forth both the beauty and necessity of Jesus's virgin birth in a refreshing, compelling manner."

—**Steve Gaines**, senior pastor, Bellevue Baptist
Church, Memphis, Tennessee

"In *Conceived by the Spirit*, Dr. Putman shows how the incarnation put Jesus's divine nature on display for all to see. His thorough and accessible walkthrough of the virginal conception teaches us that this event was much more than fodder for Christmas carols. In the Son of God's conception by the Spirit, Jesus is revealed as God and as the fulfiller of all Old Testament messianic promises. Further, in an age of deconstruction, Putman shows us the importance of theological retrieval of central Christian truths. May we, like our brothers and sisters before us, praise Jesus as 'born of the Holy Spirit and the Virgin Mary.'"

—**Tony Merida**, pastor of preaching and vision,
Imago Dei Church, Raleigh, North Carolina

"Rhyne Putman's *Conceived by the Holy Spirit* offers a robust and compelling exposition of the crucial, yet often overlooked, doctrine of the virgin birth. Putman uses his skill as a scholar and seasoned churchman to walk readers through a biblical, theological, historical, and missional treatment of this neglected doctrine. As they walk the road to Bethlehem with him, Putman shows not only biblical-theological foundation for the virgin conception, but also leads readers to marvel at their virgin-born King—the Son of God who became man."

—**Christine E. Thornton**, assistant professor of Christian
thought, Southeastern Baptist Theological Seminary

"Rhyne Putman has delivered a biblical and theological work on the significance of the virgin birth of Jesus that is simultaneously substantive and accessible. His careful treatment of the nativity texts and the history of the church's theological interpretation makes this a marvelous resource for anyone wishing to deepen their understanding of the incarnation."

—**Trevin Wax**, vice president for research and resource
development, North American Mission Board

CONCEIVED

by the

HOLY SPIRIT

CONCEIVED *by the*

HOLY SPIRIT

THE VIRGIN BIRTH IN
SCRIPTURE *and* THEOLOGY

RHYNE R. PUTMAN

B&H
ACADEMIC
BRENTWOOD, TENNESSEE

for Annie,
my one and only daughter.

My soul magnifies the Lord
because he gave me you.

May King Jesus always be
the true treasure of your heart.

CONTENTS

Acknowledgments   xiii

Abbreviations   xv

Introduction: Reading the Christmas Story Like Jesus   1

Part One: The Virgin-Born King in the Biblical Story

1   That You May Know with Certainty (Luke 1:1–4)   15

    Answering Objections: The Virgin Birth Came from
      Pagan Mythology   23

2   The God Who Keeps His Covenants (Matthew 1:1, 17)   29

    Answering Objections: The Genealogies of Matthew and Luke
      Cannot Be Reconciled   39

3   The Son Who Chose His Own Parents (Matthew 1:2–16)   45

4   Forerunner to the Virgin-Born King (Luke 1:5–25, 57–80)   57

5   The Virgin-Born King Announced (Luke 1:26–38)   69

    Answering Objections: The Virginal Conception Was
      Only a Metaphor   78

    Answering Objections: God Violated Mary   80

6   My Soul Magnifies the Lord (Luke 1:39–56)   83

7   The Virgin-Born Savior (Matthew 1:18–21, 24–25)   95
    Answering Objections: Jesus Was Illegitimate   99

8   The Virgin-Born King Is God with Us (Matthew 1:22–23,
    Isaiah 7:14)   105

9   In the Fullness of Time (Luke 2:1–7)   123
    Answering Objections: Luke Invented the Census   126

10 The First Witnesses to the Virgin-Born King (Luke 2:8–17)   137

11 Born Under the Law (Luke 2:21–24)   149

12 Come Thou Long Expected Jesus (Luke 2:25–38)   159

13 The Virgin-Born King Manifested to the Nations
    (Matthew 2:1–12)   171

14 Out of Egypt I Called My Son (Matthew 2:13–23)   185
    *Answering Objections: Matthew Invented the
        Slaughter of the Innocents*   189
    Answering Objections: Luke Contradicts the Flight to Egypt   199

15 The Boy Grew Up and Became Strong (Luke 2:39–52)   203

16 The Word Became Flesh: The Virgin-Born King
    in the Other Gospels   213
    *Answering Objections: The Virgin Birth Contradicts
        the Preexistence and Incarnation of Christ*   220

17 Born of a Woman: The Virgin-Born King in the Letters of Paul   229

18 The Serpent Crushed (Genesis 3:14–15; Revelation 12:1–17)   239

Part Two: The Virgin-Born King in Christian Theology and Practice

19 The Church Fathers Who Saved Christmas:
The Virgin-Born King in Early Christology 253

20 One and the Same Son: The Unity of the Virgin-Born King 271

21 The Fittingness of the Virgin Birth: The Virgin-Born King
as the Revealer of God 283

22 Veil'd in Flesh the Godhead See: The Virgin-Born King
and the Doctrine of the Trinity 293

23 And Heav'n and Nature Sing: The Virgin-Born King
in Creation and Science 305
Answering Objections: "Mary Should Have Had an Abortion" 315

24 Born to Give Them Second Birth: The Virgin-Born King
as the New Adam 319

25 Joy to the World: The Two Advents of the Virgin-Born King 331

Conclusion: Come Let Us Adore Him 341
Appendix 1: A Harmony of the Nativity Stories 347
Appendix 2: Marian Dogma and the Sufficiency of Scripture 351
Bibliography 371
Name Index 389
Subject Index 393
Scripture Index 399

ACKNOWLEDGMENTS

With the mother of our Lord I happily confess, "My soul magnifies the Lord, and my spirit rejoices in God my Savior" (Luke 1:46–47). In addition to every spiritual blessing he has provided in Christ, God has also shown such kindness and favor to me with the people he has placed in my life. A project like this one would never have been conceived and carried to completion without people like these.

I must begin by thanking the incredible team at B&H Academic, especially Madison Trammel, Michael McEwen, and Audrey Greeson.

Every pastor needs friends like Stephen McDonald, Tim Walker, Keith Whitfield, and Malcolm Yarnell. Special thanks also go to Matt Emerson, Robert Foster, Adam Harwood, Andrew Hollingsworth, Stan Norman, Charles Quarles, Jeff Riley, Brandon Smith, Bob Stewart, Bill Warren, and Tyler Wittman for their guidance and insight.

With Mt. Zion Baptist Church, God has provided us with a wonderful church family that has shown incredible kindness and love to the Putman family. What I love most about this church is its love for the community and the nations. Not only does this church generously give to Southern Baptist mission efforts, indigenous pastors, and orphan care projects around the world, but this rural church also participates in multiple local and international mission activities every year.

Thank you to the Andrews, the Boozers, Elaine Brent, David Carwyle, the Cobbs, the Claytons, the Cooks, the Couches, the Cupps, the Davises, the Dedricks, the Diggs, the Distrettis, Peggy Dunn, the Easons, the Faulkners, the Fosters, the Frenches, the Gays, the Gibsons, the Gills, the Hansens, the Haugheys, the Harrises, the Hicks, the Johnstons, the Killians, the Kinerds, the Loyds, the Masseys, the Mathernes, the Mays, the Millers, the Newsoms, the Otwells, the Parsleys, the Perkins, the Poes, Tammy and Hannah Rainwater, the Reynolds, the Roberts, the Russells, Ava Jean Slatton, the Screens, the Songers, the Smiths, the Stidmans, the Walkers, Shelby Willcockson, the Willises, and the Wrights. Terry and Melanie, thank you for adopting the Putmans! Jannie, thank you for reading parts of this book and giving feedback.

I serve alongside some incredible people at Williams Baptist University and New Orleans Baptist Theological Seminary. I am especially grateful for Taylor Baker, Tonya Bolton, Tracy Henderson, Mary Elizabeth Ryan, Marvin Schoenecke, and Mike and Gabby Dixon, without whom I wouldn't be able to balance administrative responsibilities and academic life.

In the busyness of ministry and academic life, I have received unflinching support from my wife Micah, my son Ben, my parents Glen and Diane Putman, and my in-laws Collin and Marcia Elder. God has blessed me far beyond what I deserve with a loving family like this one.

I have dedicated this book to my daughter Annie. One of my favorite things is coming home to her enthusiastic greeting after a long day at the office. Never in my wildest imagination did I think I would enjoy being a girl-dad so much! Every day I pray that God would grow this little girl who loves ponies, princess dresses, and coloring with her daddy into a godly woman who cherishes King Jesus above everything else. I hope this book helps you on that journey.

Soli Deo Gloria
Rhyne Putman
March 17, 2023

ABBREVIATIONS

Ant.	Josephus, Flavius. *Antiquities of the Jews.*
IT	*Inschriften griechischer Städte aus Kleinasien*
JETS	*Journal of the Evangelical Theological Society*
NIDNTTE	Moisés Silva, ed. *New International Dictionary of New Testament Theology and Exegesis.* 2nd ed. 5 vols. Grand Rapids: Zondervan, 2014.
NPNF	*Nicene and Post-Nicene Fathers*, Ser. 1. Edited by Alexander Roberts, James Donaldson, Philip Schaff, and Henry Wace. 14 vols. Peabody, MA: Hendrickson, 1994.
NT	New Testament
OT	Old Testament
Prot. Jas.	*The First Gospel of James* (*Protoevangelium of James*)
Rev. Magi.	*Revelation of the Magi*

Introduction

Reading the Christmas Story Like Jesus

I believe . . . in Christ Jesus . . . who was born of
the Holy Spirit and the Virgin Mary.
—THE OLD ROMAN SYMBOL (C. AD 200)

Every Christmas season, people from every walk of life—true follow-ers of Jesus, nominal Christians, agnostics, pagans, and even some atheists—openly celebrate the symbols and key components of the gos-pel story. However, many who celebrate Christmas have forgotten (or never really learned) the profound significance of this story. Through their songs and traditions, many unwittingly pronounce the incarnation of the Second Person of the Trinity, his fulfillment of the law and God's promises, God's zealous desire for the nations, Christ's saving death in the place of sinners, his resurrection from the dead, his glorious second coming, and his eternal reign from the throne of David.

The theological meaning of Christmas may be largely forgotten in our secular age, but the widespread celebration of this event is still

1

a type of common grace. The name of Christ is uttered frequently by those who do not yet know its saving power. The hymns and carols of the season may fall on spiritually deaf ears, but they openly pronounce the humble means by which God the Son entered our world of time and space. Nativity scenes in the public square are visual reminders that the Word became flesh and dwelt among us. To borrow an expression from Flannery O'Connor, Christmas, as celebrated by Western culture, "is hardly Christ-centered" but "is most certainly Christ-haunted."[1]

This study is a biblical, historical, theological, and practical exploration of the Christmas story. My aim is to help Christian disciples reflect on the various ways the biblical nativity stories shape our understanding of the person and work of Jesus Christ, the virgin-born king. These accounts reveal Jesus of Nazareth as

> Israel's long-awaited Messiah,
> the seed of Abraham,
> the eternal heir of David's throne,
> the dawn from on high,
> Immanuel,
> the Son of God,
> the Lord of all creation,
> the Savior of his people,
> the Word made flesh,
> truly God,
> truly human,
> conceived by the Holy Spirit,
> and born of the virgin Mary.

Contemplation on these aspects of Jesus's identity should be more than an intellectual exercise. I remain convinced that thoughtful engagement

---

[1] Flannery O'Connor, "Southern Fiction," in *Mysteries and Manners: Occasional Prose*, ed. Sally and Robert Fitzgerald (New York: Farrar, Straus, & Giroux, 1957), 44.

with these stories and their impact on the Christian tradition will also grow us in our obedience, maturity, and devotion to Christ.

Nativity Stories and the Virginal Conception

We usually associate the word *nativity*, from a Latin term meaning "born" or "native," with the birth of Christ. (The familiar French word *noël* translates the same Latin term.) Nativity or infancy stories, then, are accounts of the events surrounding Jesus's conception, birth, and early childhood. The New Testament (NT) only includes two such accounts: those told in the first two chapters of Matthew (Matt 1:18–2:23) and the first two chapters of Luke (Luke 1:5–2:52).

These Gospels present two distinct but complementary accounts of Christ's nativity. Matthew and Luke recall separate events leading up to and following Jesus's birth. Matthew's story focuses on Joseph's response to God's announcement. Luke's account tells the of story of Mary's humble obedience. Matthew and Luke place different theological emphases on the events that unfold. Despite all their differences, both authors share a common conviction that Jesus Christ entered the world through a virgin's womb to be our Savior. Both authors are convinced that God has come near to us in Christ. Both believe God desires to rescue Jews and Gentiles through Christ.

Although we often use the shorthand term "virgin birth" to describe the miraculous event that occurred in the incarnation of Jesus, this term is, strictly speaking, imprecise. Neither Matthew nor Luke says anything unusual about Jesus's birth. It appears that his birth was completely natural, especially in a time before c-sections or epidurals.

The real spectacle of Jesus's entry into the world was the way Mary conceived Jesus in her womb without a human father. We call this miracle Jesus's "virginal conception" (not to be confused with the Roman Catholic doctrine of Mary's "immaculate conception"). Jesus was, as Scripture and the creeds profess, "conceived by the Holy Spirit" and "born of the virgin

Mary." Through the miracle of his virginal conception, Christ revealed *God to us* and initiated his mission of reconciling us to God.

The NT does not explicitly mention the virginal conception outside Matthew and Luke's first few chapters. Other texts describe Jesus as coming into the world, being born of a woman, taking the form of a servant, etc. But after Matthew and Luke, nothing else is said about how Jesus came to reside with us. This has led many skeptics to suggest that this doctrine was a later fabrication, not part of the original gospel witness. Yet the pieces of the puzzle that Matthew and Luke leave behind fit together with other pieces crafted by Mark, John, Paul, and the other writers of the NT. When snapped together, these fragments form a cohesive picture of Christ, the virgin-born Messiah, the crucified one, and the risen Lord.

How the Nativity Stories Have Been Understood

Throughout history, believers from every Christian tradition have celebrated this virginal conception as the outward "sign" of Jesus's uniqueness as the Son of God, the Word made flesh, and the second person of the Trinity. The virgin birth did not *cause* Jesus to become God—the Son is God in eternity—but the virgin birth did put his divine nature on display for all to see. His conception also signaled that God was about to fulfill his promises and bring salvation to his people.

The doctrine of the virginal conception met with widespread approval in the early Christian church. The first Christian theologians vigorously defended this doctrine against its vocal opponents. These theologians considered this doctrine to be part of the "rule of faith," the one true body of Christian teaching handed down by the earliest followers of Jesus. We know that by the end of the second century, Christians were required to affirm the virgin birth (along with other key doctrines like the resurrection) before they could be baptized as followers of Jesus.[2] The major

---

[2] Hippolytus, *Apostolic Tradition* 21.

creeds and confessions of the church professed that Jesus was "born of the virgin Mary."

Medieval Christians used stories about Jesus's conception to promote the virtues of virginity and chastity. For many medieval Christians, the virgin birth served an important purpose in their doctrines of original sin and the atonement. Along the way, this doctrine also became the basis for devotion to the Virgin Mary in Roman Catholic, Eastern Orthodox, and other "high church" traditions.

Yet the doctrine of the virgin birth has always had its detractors. Some heretical groups claimed Jesus was the natural-born son of Joseph, whereas others claimed he was not born a human being at all. Other anti-Christian writings from the second century accused Christians of making up a story about the virgin birth to cover up an illicit affair between Mary and a Roman soldier.

Following the so-called Enlightenment, many critical biblical scholars in the eighteenth and nineteenth centuries reinterpreted the virgin birth as a pagan or Jewish myth from a pre-modern, pre-scientific era. In the first "quest of the historical Jesus," scholars sought to separate the "Jesus of history" from the "Christ of faith."[3] They proposed that NT miracle stories, including accounts of Christ's virginal conception and resurrection, said more about the faith of early Christians than what happened in the life of the man Jesus of Nazareth. Some of these scholars were Deists who rejected supernatural religion and revelation. Others simply presumed a form of atheism.

The virginal conception also played a pivotal role in the Fundamentalist-Modernist controversy of the early twentieth century. For the modernists or liberal Protestants enthralled with new "higher critical" approaches to the Bible, this doctrine was an optional article of faith likely based on a corruption of earlier and purer forms of the gospel

---

[3] See Hermann Samuel Reimarus, *Reimarus Fragments*, ed. Charles H. Talbert, trans. Ralph S. Fraser (London: SCM, 1970); David F. Strauss, *Das Leben Jesu*, 2 vols. (Tübingen, 1835).

message.[4] For the fundamentalists, the predecessors of modern evangelicals, the virgin birth served as a litmus test for evaluating one's views on the inspiration, authority, and inerrancy of the Bible. The virginal conception was deemed to be one of the five "fundamentals" of the faith that every orthodox Christian should affirm.[5] Many of the great evangelical texts about the virgin birth from the early twentieth century were primarily apologetic defenses of biblical authority, not true theological explorations of the nativity stories themselves.[6]

The influence of modernity waned over the next century. The sexual revolution that gripped the West in the 1950s and 1960s caused many inside and outside the church to rethink their positions regarding sex, marriage, gender roles, and children. The postmodern heirs of liberal Protestantism have expressed some appreciation for the biblical nativity stories, especially in their efforts to recast Mary as a feminist icon. But like their modernist ancestors, they still question the historical and theological value of these texts. Many progressive theologians see themselves as liberators of a Christian tradition rooted in patriarchy and sexual oppression.

Like our twentieth-century forerunners, contemporary evangelicals must defend the truthfulness and historical value of the biblical nativity stories. But our exploration of these texts must be more than a defense of their truthfulness. That is only the first step. These stories are first and foremost Christological texts that reveal who Jesus is (the person of Christ) and what he has done and will do (the work of Christ). To give the virginal conception of Jesus the proper consideration it merits in Christology, we must recover its place in the whole biblical story, its

---

[4] The clearest declaration of this liberal Protestant position on the virgin birth came in Harry Emerson Fosdick's 1922 sermon "Shall the Fundamentalists Win?"

[5] See General Assembly of the Presbyterian Churches U.S.A., "The Doctrinal Deliverance of 1910."

[6] See James Orr, *The Virgin Birth of Christ* (New York: Charles Scribner's Sons, 1907); J. Gresham Machen, *The Virgin Birth of Christ* (New York: Harper & Row, 1930).

relationship to the creeds and confessions of the church, and its connection to other Christian doctrines.

Reading the Christmas Stories Like Jesus

Matthew and Luke give us a unique picture of Christ as the virgin-born king. The rest of the NT may be silent about how Jesus was conceived, but these accounts have massive implications for how we read the entire apostolic witness to Christ. Like a tsunami after an earthquake, the after-effects of the Christmas story reverberate throughout the entire Bible.

Followers of Jesus must read the biblical nativity stories differently than their skeptical counterparts. Our approach to Scripture is shaped and formed by Christ himself in Luke 24:13–49. Though they did not know it at the time, the Emmaus disciples were enrolled in a master class in biblical interpretation taught by the primary subject matter of Scripture, the resurrected Lord. "Beginning with Moses and all the Prophets," Jesus "interpreted for them the things concerning himself in all the Scriptures" (Luke 24:27).

The risen Lord began class with a strongly worded rebuke: "How foolish you are!" (Luke 24:25). Jesus confronted these disciples for their mindless inattention to Scripture and his teaching. Like many of their contemporaries, they were still waiting for an earthly messiah to send their Roman military occupants packing. But had they been paying closer attention, they would have recognized that Jesus came to proclaim the good news of the kingdom of God, not an earthly kingdom.

Jesus's message had not changed after the resurrection. Jesus had always called students of Scripture to pay closer attention to biblical texts. "Have you never read in the Scriptures?" (Matt 21:42). "You are mistaken, because you don't know the Scriptures or the power of God" (Matt 22:29). He told his disciples that "many prophets and kings wanted to see the things you see but didn't see them; to hear the things you hear but didn't hear them" (Luke 10:24). He repeatedly said that "the Scriptures must be fulfilled" (Mark 14:49). Jesus had even harsher words for the unbelieving biblical scholars of his day: "You pore over the Scriptures because you think you have eternal life in them, and yet they testify about me" (John 5:39). From Jesus's instruction on the Emmaus road, we can draw out four implications for our study of the Christmas story in the NT.

First, we desire to read the nativity stories from the same worldview as the authors who wrote them. We do not read these texts simply to understand what ancient people believed about God, as if we were simply studying museum relics from a bygone era. We read these texts to know the God of whom they spoke! Faithful interpretation involves closely listening and submitting to the voices of Spirit-inspired authors in Israel and in the early church.

In the case of the nativity stories, we listen carefully to the Evangelists and ask what they want us to take away from these stories about Jesus's birth. We aren't attempting to discredit them or disregard what they present as gospel truth. Instead, we are asking questions like these: What were the Evangelists trying to do with their words? What do these stories teach us about who God is? How do these texts invite us to know Christ more? We read the nativity stories in submission to the God who inspired them, wanting to hear his voice and obey.

Second, we recognize that the triune God is behind every word of Scripture—including the nativity stories. All Scripture was "inspired" or "breathed out" by God (2 Tim 3:16). This one God exists as three distinct eternal persons: God the Father, God the Son, and God the Holy Spirit. Through what we call *progressive revelation*, God gradually revealed himself in different ways at different stages in the history of Israel and the church. We call this revelation "progressive" because we know more about God at the end of Rev 22:21 than we do in Gen 1:1.

But the unfolding progress of God's self-disclosure does not entail any change in his essence. The same God who revealed himself to be Father, Son, and Holy Spirit in the NT was also Father, Son, and Holy Spirit in the Old Testament (OT). The God who is three-in-one promised to bless Abraham and make him the father of many nations. The triune God spoke to Moses from a burning bush and freed the people of Israel from bondage in Egypt.[7] The same triune God gave David victory over his enemies and spoke through Israel's prophets. The triune God caused a virgin to become pregnant with Israel's Messiah. Even if the people of Israel did not yet know God as Father, Son, and Holy Spirit, the unchanging God who spoke to them and through them was an undivided unity of three persons carrying out an inseparable work and mission.[8]

Third, we understand that the Bible tells one big, cohesive story that culminates in Christ. In the era of Marvel and *Star Wars* films, audiences have grown accustomed to complex "cinematic universes" in which the characters of one story share an inhabited world with characters from other stories set in the same fictional universe. The small details in one story can have ripple effects and callbacks in other stories. Although this can be an exciting feature in contemporary fiction, it is not an original literary idea. It originates in the real-world universe depicted in Scripture.

The biblical canon, written over a 1500-year period by dozens of authors, describes the same "universe" under the same central character: the triune God. The Bible is a library of sixty-six books written in different genres: history, law, prophecy, music, letters, wise sayings, and more. But for all its diversity, the Bible tells one cohesive, overarching, and true story. This story culminates in the story of Jesus of Nazareth.

Old Testament prophets "inquired into what time or what circumstances the Spirit of Christ within them was indicating when he testified in advance to the sufferings of Christ and the glories that would follow" (1 Pet 1:11). With their respective nativity stories, Matthew and Luke highlight Jesus's role in fulfilling these prophetic promises. Matthew quotes the OT more than any other Evangelist because he is trying to

---

[7] The Bible makes the same kinds of claims. Jude, for instance, asserts that "Jesus saved a people out of Egypt and later destroyed those who did not believe" (Jude 1:5).

[8] Scott R. Swain provides seven helpful axioms to guide how we read the Bible through a trinitarian lens in *The Trinity and the Bible: On Theological Interpretation* (Bellingham, WA: Lexham, 2021).

demonstrate to his original Jewish audience that Jesus is the Messiah they have been waiting for. Luke's use of the OT is more subtle. Rather than quoting the OT at length, Luke employs the literary and historical features of the Hebrew Bible to show readers that Jesus's story is the continuation of Israel's story.[9] Luke's nativity story reads like a series of events from the OT, in part because he is trying to demonstrate that the same God at work in Israel was still at work in the life of Jesus.

Finally, we believe that the aim of faithful biblical interpretation is to know and experience Christ. This is true whether we are reading the law of Moses or the Gospels, Proverbs or Paul, the Prophets, or the Psalms. In the words of John Calvin (1509–1564),

> This is what we should in short seek in the whole of Scripture: truly to know Jesus Christ, and the infinite riches that are comprised in him and are offered to us by him from God the Father. If one were to sift thoroughly the Law and the Prophets, he would not find a single word which would not draw and bring us to him.[10]

The encounter with the risen Lord changed the Emmaus disciples forever. When they realized that they had been speaking with Jesus the whole time, their confusion and doubt turned into exuberant joy. "Weren't our hearts burning within us while he was talking with us on the road and explaining the Scriptures to us?" (Luke 24:32) This is the kind of "heartburn" followers of Jesus gladly welcome. We study these texts because we want to encounter our Lord.

This book has two parts: "The Virgin-Born King in the Biblical Story" and "The Virgin-Born King in Christian Theology and Practice."

---

[9] See Nils Dahl, *Jesus in the Memory of the Early Church* (Minneapolis: Augsburg, 1976), 84; Richard B. Hays, *Echoes of Scripture in the Gospels* (Waco, TX: Baylor University Press, 2016), 191–95; C. Kavin Rowe, *Early Narrative Christology: The Lord in the Gospel of Luke* (Berlin: Walter de Gruyter, 2006), 32–34.

[10] John Calvin, "Preface to Olivetan's New Testament," in *Calvin: Commentaries*, ed. Joseph Haroutunian (Louisville: WJK, 1958), 70.

Part one offers a biblical-theological assessment of Matthew's and Luke's nativity stories and explores their connection to the rest of the NT. The study of these texts takes a "horizontal" approach to these narratives—laying them side by side in an attempt to present them in a chronological sequence. Part two explores the development of the virgin birth tradition and its larger impact on the church's teaching about the person and work of Christ, the Trinity, creation, salvation, and last things.

We want to grasp what Matthew and Luke were trying to do with their respective stories about Christ's conception, birth, and childhood. We desire to see how these narratives "fit" with the message of the whole Bible. But more than this—we want to receive these stories like the angels gave them to the shepherds—as "good news of great joy that will be for all the people" (Luke 2:10). We want to explore the unique contribution the nativity stories make to our overall picture of Jesus, the virgin-born king and risen Lord.

— Part One —

The Virgin-Born King
in the Biblical Story

1

That You May Know with Certainty

Luke 1:1–4

"We have learned . . . the plan of our salvation . . . from
those through whom the Gospel has come down to us,
which they . . . by the will of God, handed down to us in
the Scriptures, to be the ground and pillar of our faith."
—IRENAEUS OF LYONS (c. AD 130–202)[1]

There is a scene in the original *Back to the Future* film where "Doc"
Emmett Brown tried to explain to Marty McFly how his time-
traveling DeLorean worked. Doc told Marty that if he wanted to witness
an important moment in history, all he needed to do was to turn on the
time circuits and punch in the date and time he wanted to visit.

---

[1] Irenaeus, *Against Heresies* 3.1.1.

15

Doc Brown used the birth of Christ as an example of how the machine could work and punched in the numbers "12 - 25 - 0000" to show Marty how to get there.

This blink-and-you'll-miss-it sight gag reminds us that Jesus (probably) was not born on December 25 and that there was no year zero on the Gregorian calendar we still use today (After all, the man who invented a time machine was a physicist, not a biblical scholar or a historian). But who would not want to take Doc Brown up on his offer? Who would not want to travel to that familiar manger scene and witness Jesus for himself?

At the heart of the Christian faith is the belief that God became a man and dwelt among us as a historical figure at a real moment in human history. If Jesus did not actually say and do the things ascribed to him in the NT and he is not the person the authors of the NT claim him to be, then those of us who "have put our hope in Christ . . . should be pitied more than anyone" (1 Cor 15:19).

But many skeptics contend that the Jesus whom Christians confess in their creeds and praise in their hymns is a legendary figure who never truly existed, at least in the way that the NT presents him. Critical scholars often claim that the Gospels tell us more about theology than history, more about what early Christians believed than what actually happened in the life of Jesus. This is nowhere more apparent than in their treatments of the nativity stories of Matthew and Luke. Even some scholars who affirm the resurrection of Jesus cast serious doubt on the truthfulness of these stories, charging them with being later additions to the gospel traditions.

But how can we know what happened two millennia ago? What reasons do we have to be confident that Jesus is who Christians claim him to be?

Although we cannot hop in a DeLorean and travel back in time to the moment Jesus was born, the four Gospels give us the best tool any historian can have for learning about past events like Jesus's birth: eye-witness accounts.

We have many good reasons to take Luke and Matthew at their word when they tell us about Jesus's life and childhood. Despite what modern skeptics may claim, they did not invent these stories or steal all their ideas from pagan mythology.

In the introduction to his Gospel, Luke does something truly unique among the four Gospels of the New Testament. He writes an opening statement, like a letter, to his recipient, Theophilus. He explains why he wrote a Gospel and how he went about writing it. Luke faithfully reported what was told to him as a historian. He then carefully crafted his arrangement of these accounts as a master storyteller. As a theologian, Luke connected the dots between Jesus's early life and Israel's God. Finally, as a pastoral leader, Luke wanted believers to follow the faithful example of men and women like Mary, Joseph, Zechariah, Elizabeth, Simeon, and Anna, whose lives were characterized by their obedience to the God revealed in Christ.

Though the experience of Luke would have been different from Matthew or John, who followed Jesus during his ministry, Luke's opening statement gives us a window into the way each gospel account took shape. What Luke reveals applies to all four Gospels: these are credible witnesses to and reports of the life of Jesus.

The Evangelists who wrote the Gospels had another, not-so-secret agenda. They wanted their readers to believe that "Jesus is the Messiah, the Son of God" and "have life in his name" (John 20:31). Despite what some skeptics might claim, the missionary purpose of the Evangelists does not rob them of their ability to inform us about the historical Jesus. After all, all human histories are interpretations of events written with the purpose of informing and persuading. The Gospels just happen to tell the story of the man their authors believe to be the hope of humanity. They staked their lives on the truthfulness of these accounts and asked us to do the same.

Why Luke Wrote a Gospel

Many have undertaken to compile a narrative about the events that have been fulfilled among us, just as the original eyewitnesses and servants of the word handed them down to us. So it also seemed good to me, since I have carefully investigated everything from the very first, to write to you in an orderly sequence, most honorable Theophilus, so that you may know the certainty of the things about which you have been instructed. (Luke 1:1–4)

Though the Evangelist who wrote the Third Gospel does not identify himself by name, all the evidence points to "Luke, the dearly loved physician" (Col 4:14) who traveled with Paul on his later missionary journeys. Though Luke never names himself in his Gospel or the book of Acts, Paul names him on multiple occasions throughout his letters (2 Tim 4:11; Phlm 24). Luke left his fingerprints all over the books he wrote. In Acts 16, the language describing Paul's missionary team suddenly shifts from the third person ("they") to the first person ("we"): "We stayed in that city for several days. . . . We went outside . . . we expected to find a place of prayer" (16:12b–13). Whoever wrote the books of Luke and Acts was with Paul on his last missionary journey.[2]

Luke addressed both of his books to Theophilus, whose name (or alias) means "friend of God" or "God-lover." Theophilus may have been the wealthy patron who footed the bill for Luke's travels and writing ministry. He may have been a code name for a group of believers. Perhaps Theophilus was a Roman official whom Luke was trying to convert. On this side of heaven, we will likely never know.

The precise identity of the Gospel's author and audience is less important than his plainly stated objective. The Evangelist aims to write an organized account of Jesus's life and ministry that will strengthen

---

[2] See also Acts 20:6, 8, 13–16; 21:1–25; 27:1–8, 13–44; 28:1–16. Second-century sources like Irenaeus (*Against Heresies* 3.14.1) and the Muratorian Fragment also identify Luke as the author of the Gospel and the book of Acts.

the faith of his readers. The word Luke uses for "account" (*diēgēsis*) is not "just a tale or a story," but a "*technical term* for the well-ordered, polished product of *the historian's work*: the narrative of the events in the form in which the historian who writes no chronicle, nor rough notes, wants to give it to his readers for the special purpose he has set himself."[3] The author of Luke's Gospel is convinced that he is doing the work of a true historian.

How Luke Acquired the Nativity Story

Luke walks his readers through his process as a researcher and a writer. If the apostles Matthew and John really wrote the Gospels associated with their names, their writing process would have been somewhat different from Luke's because they followed Jesus during his adult ministry. Tradition tells us that John Mark (see Acts 12:12, 25) wrote down Peter's experiences with Jesus in the Gospel of Mark.[4] But Luke was a second-generation follower of Jesus who apparently became a believer at some point during Paul's ministry.

Luke admits that he depended on information "handed down" by "eyewitnesses" and "servants of the word" (Luke 1:2). When he tells us that "many have undertaken to draw up an account," he simply means other Gospels have already been written. Most biblical scholars agree that Luke probably had a copy of Mark's Gospel at his disposal when he was writing his own. Luke also has a lot of material in common with Matthew's Gospel that is not found in Mark, so it is possible that Luke knew about Matthew's gospel or at least shared a common source with Matthew.[5]

---

[3] W. C. van Unnik, "Once More St. Luke's Prologue," *Neotestamentica* 7 (1973): 14–15 (italics mine).

[4] Irenaeus, *Against Heresies* 3.1.1; Eusebius, *Church History* 3.39.15.

[5] We do not know if that was a written source, an oral tradition, or a personal source. See James D. G. Dunn, *Jesus Remembered* (Grand Rapids: Eerdmans, 2003), 147–60.

Matthew and Luke may have written their nativity stories independently of one another, but these stories share important common details:[6]

1. When both stories began, Joseph and Mary were betrothed to one another but had not had sex or moved in together yet (Matt 1:18; Luke 1:27, 34).
2. Joseph was in the lineage of King David (Matt 1:16, 20; Luke 1:27, 32; 2:4).
3. An angel announced the birth of a child (Matt 1:20–21; Luke 1:30–35).
4. Mary would not conceive this child through sexual intercourse (Matt 1:20, 23, 25; Luke 1:34).
5. Mary conceived a son by the power of the Holy Spirit (Matt 1:18, 20; Luke 1:35).
6. The angel commanded the boy to be named Jesus (Matt 1:21; Luke 1:31).
7. Jesus, whose name means "the Lord saves," would be the Savior (Matt 1:21; Luke 2:11).
8. Joseph and Mary were married before Jesus was born (Matt 1:24–25; Luke 2:5–6).
9. Jesus was born in Bethlehem (Matt 2:1; Luke 2:4–7).
10. Jesus was born during the reign of Herod the Great (Matt 2:1; Luke 1:5).
11. Jesus was raised in Nazareth (Matt 2:23; Luke 2:39).

Although there is significant overlap in their details, these stories are independent of one another. Luke's Gospel emphasizes events from Mary's life whereas Matthew's account highlights Joseph's role in the nativity story. Luke's story begins before the conception of John and Jesus. Matthew's story begins when Joseph discovered Mary's pregnancy.

---

[6] Raymond E. Brown, *The Birth of the Messiah: A Commentary on the Infancy Narratives in the Gospels of Matthew and Luke*, rev. ed. (New York: Doubleday, 1993), 34–35.

Many scholars have also observed how much the first two chapters of Luke read like an OT story, with many Hebrew-like qualities in the Greek text. Some scholars have suggested that much of Luke 1–2 was originally written by an earlier Hebrew or Aramaic source and then later translated into Luke's Greek.[7] It's even possible that Mary or one of Jesus's siblings wrote the story down for Luke. Whether Luke wrote this section himself or it was "handed down" by "eyewitnesses" and "servants of the word" (Luke 1:2), the nativity story was not a later addition to the Gospel of Luke. All early manuscript evidence for this Gospel indicates that Luke 1–2 was an original part of the Gospel, uncorrupted and virtually unchanged in its transmission.[8]

Luke *"carefully investigated everything from the very first [the beginning]"* (Luke 1:3). Luke may have been a medical doctor by trade (Col 4:14), but he was also a historian. We can assume that much of the original material in Luke's Gospel was a product of his research, including his version of the Christmas story. When investigating "everything from the beginning," Luke traced the tradition back to a time before he was born. He then wrote these stories out in an orderly manner.

Luke (or the earlier source that was "handed down" to him) likely discovered the stories about John's and Jesus's births from interviews or correspondence with members of Jesus's own family. Jesus's mother and brothers were part of the Jerusalem church (Acts 1:14). Depending on how early we date this Gospel, Mary may have still been alive when it was composed. If she were alive, she herself could have been the direct source for these accounts in Luke. I am personally convinced that this Gospel was written no later than the mid-60s AD.[9] Were Mary alive when the Gospel was composed, she probably would have been in her

---

[7] Stephen C. Farris, "On Discerning Semitic Sources in Luke 1–2," in *Gospel Perspectives: Studies of History and Tradition in the Four Gospels*, ed. R. T. France and David Wenham (Eugene, OR: Wipf and Stock, 2003), 2:201–37.

[8] See Machen, *The Virgin Birth of Christ*, 62–168 (see introduction, n. 6).

[9] See Jonathan Bernier, *Rethinking the Dates of the New Testament: The Evidence for Early Composition* (Grand Rapids: Baker, 2022), 54–66, 77–84.

eighties. Even if she had already died, Jesus's brothers and sisters could have relayed her experiences to Luke.[10]

Whether Luke acquired this information directly from Jesus's family or an older source, the account of Jesus's birth is shared from Mary's perspective. As the NT scholar Charles Quarles observes, the mother of Jesus is the common denominator in every episode of Luke's nativity story.[11]

- Only Mary would know whether she had never been sexually involved with a man.
- Only Mary would have knowledge of a private visitation from Gabriel.
- If Mary spent three months with her cousin Elizabeth, she would have been very familiar with the circumstances surrounding John's birth.
- Although Mary was not present with the shepherds when the angels visited them, Luke explicitly tells us that the shepherds "reported the message they were told about this child" to Mary and Joseph (Luke 2:17).
- She was present when Simeon and Anna blessed the child in the temple.
- Like any other parent, Mary would remember the time when her child went missing in a large city.

Luke also tells us that she "was treasuring" all these things in her heart (Luke 2:19). Years after the incident with Jesus in Jerusalem, Jesus's mother still "kept all these things in her heart" (Luke 2:51). It is reasonable to conclude that the author knows what Mary "treasured" because

---

[10] Raymond E. Brown, *The Virginal Conception and Bodily Resurrection of Jesus* (New York: Paulist, 1973), 61.

[11] Charles L. Quarles, "Why Not 'Beginning from Bethlehem'?," in *Memories of Jesus: A Critical Appraisal of James D. G. Dunn's Jesus Remembered*, ed. Robert B. Stewart and Gary Habermas (Nashville: B&H Academic, 2010), 175.

she still treasured these things all these years later when she reported the events herself.[12]

Answering Objections: The Virgin Birth Came from Pagan Mythology

Since the second century, critics of Christianity have claimed that the story of Jesus's virginal conception was borrowed from pagan mythology (see Justin Martyr, *Dialogue with Trypho* 67). Nineteenth- and twentieth-century scholars affiliated with a movement known as "the history of religions school" obsessively sought out parallels between biblical stories and ancient pagan myths. Unsurprisingly, the doctrine of the virginal conception was one of their favorite targets. These religious scholars avowed that the Gospel authors derived their accounts of Jesus's virginal birth from similar stories of divine births in Babylonian, Buddhist, Greco-Roman, Hindu, and Zoroastrian myths. (George Lucas made a similar claim after he depicted Darth Vader as born of a virgin—conceived by midi-chlorians—in *Star Wars Episode I: The Phantom Menace*.)

No serious biblical scholar today lends much credibility to this thesis. Even among those who reject the virgin birth of Jesus, there is consensus that the comparisons between the NT accounts and these pagan myths are superficial and far-fetched. The Gospels are thoroughly Jewish in character, not Greek (as the repeated references and allusions to OT Scripture in the nativity stories demonstrate). Unlike the Gospels, ancient myths did not usually involve real-world personalities, places, or events. Pagan myths about divine conceptions were usually sultry stories about the gods coming down to earth and

---

[12] See Brandon D. Crowe, "The Sources of Luke and Acts: Where Did Luke Get His Material (and Why Does it Matter)?" in *Issues in Luke-Acts: Selected Essays*, ed. Sean A. Adams and Michael W. Pahl (Piscataway, NJ: Gorgias, 2012), 73–95.

sleeping with human women. These myths certainly do not celebrate the modesty and personal holiness of the mothers within them.

These pagan myths and the biblical nativity stories are, as Thomas Boslooper put it, "as different as . . . monotheism is from polytheism . . . and as different as the polygamous and incestuous pagan society was from the Christian teaching on morals and marriage" (Boslooper, *The Virgin Birth*, 186). The authors of the NT Gospels intend to provide us with an entirely different kind of storytelling—not based on heroic archetypes or pagan myths. They report eyewitness accounts of a Jewish man who purportedly did otherworldly things in the opening decades of the first century just as the Hebrew Scriptures had prophesied. These accounts are ripe with historical details that correspond to what we know about first-century Israel and the Roman Empire.

See Joseph Campbell, *The Hero with a Thousand Faces*, 3rd ed. (Novato, CA: New World Library, 2008), 255–70; Thomas Boslooper, *The Virgin Birth* (Philadelphia: Westminster Press, 1962), 135–86; Machen, *The Virgin Birth of Christ*, 317–79.

The Meaning of Luke's Nativity Story

The nativity stories recorded in Matthew and Luke are noticeably different from the material that follows in the rest of the Gospels. Throughout most of the Gospels, Jesus is the primary figure speaking and acting in the story. But the nativity stories are built around his supporting cast: his nuclear and extended family, angelic messengers, shepherds, wise men, people waiting on God's redemption, and a jealous tyrant. The nativity stories contain no sermons or parables (though Luke's nativity story includes four songs of praise).[13] But these nativity stories simply chronicle

---

[13] See Luke 1:46–55 (Mary's *Magnificat*); 1:67–79 (Zechariah's *Benedictus*); 2:14 (the heavenly army's *Gloria in excelsis Deo*); and 2:28–32 (Simeon's *Nunc dimittis*).

the unusual circumstances and means through which God brought his Son into the world.

In some ways, Luke's nativity story resembles OT history books more than the rest of the Gospel and the book of Acts. His nativity serves as a "continuation" of Israel's history. Luke wants to convince his readers that the same God who is at work in the lives of Abraham, Isaac, Jacob, and the prophets was still at work in Israel in his day. This story has reached its dramatic climax in the life of Israel's virgin-born Lord.

When Luke says these events have been "fulfilled among us" (Luke 1:1), he means that Jesus has fulfilled promises God made to Israel in their recent history. This statement foreshadows the way Luke will use the OT in his own writing, especially in the nativity story. After Luke 1–2, the Evangelist quotes from and alludes to the OT over thirty times, culminating in what Jesus said on the road to Emmaus in Luke 24:13–49. But unlike Matthew's nativity story, Luke does not quote directly from the OT as often as he discerns patterns and echoes from OT stories in the life of Jesus. Luke alludes to OT texts in ways those immersed in the texts would easily detect.

Luke's story may borrow richly from the storytelling features of the OT, but he also looks ahead to the life and ministry of Jesus as the new stage in God's redemptive plan for humanity. The Third Gospel presents a remarkably consistent view of Christ's identity and mission, from the nativity to the ascension.[14] Luke builds on the promises made to Israel but also anticipates the eventual inclusion of the Gentiles among the people of God (something that would have been important to him as a Gentile follower of Jesus). Even when Luke tells stories from the time of Jesus's infancy, he is preparing readers for the Christian mission to the Gentiles recorded in the book of Acts. In describing Jesus as the ruler of an eternal kingdom (Luke 1:33), Luke's nativity story also lays the

---

[14] See Paul S. Minear, "Luke's Use of the Birth Stories," in *Studies in Luke-Acts*, ed. Leander E. Keck and J. Louis Martyn (Philadelphia: Fortress, 1980), 111–30.

groundwork for the emphasis he places on Jesus's teaching about "the kingdom of God."[15]

We Can Have Confidence in the Christmas Story

In a postmodern age where individuals will frequently demand their right to live out their "own truth," the idea of a true story that makes demands on all our lives is often met with hostility and aggression: "It's fine if you want to tell me that *you* believe in Jesus, but don't tell me what I should believe!"

The early church met similar resistance in the first-century Roman Empire. In their world of live-and-let-live religion, Roman polytheists hardly batted an eye at new religious groups who followed a new god. But these early Christians really stirred the pot when they claimed there was only one true God and that this God became a baby in a virgin's womb, was building his kingdom, was crucified, and was raised from the dead on the third day. Early Christians made a pointed political statement when they declared "Christ . . . is Lord of all" (Acts 10:36). If Christ is Lord, Caesar is not. If these audacious claims about Jesus were true, then everything else Romans believed about the world was false.

New Testament authors had to answer the same kinds of objections Christians get today. As Peter wrote, "We did not follow cleverly contrived myths when we made known to you the power and coming of our Lord Jesus Christ; instead, we were eyewitnesses of his majesty" (2 Pet 1:16). The stories about Jesus the earliest Christian communities shared and eventually wrote down into the Gospels were not fabricated myths but true accounts for which early Christians were prepared to die.

The authors of these books staked everything on the truthfulness of their claims. The apostle Paul went on to say that if Jesus has not really been raised from the dead, then our entire way of life is beyond worthless.

---

[15] See Luke 4:43; 6:20; 8:1, 10; 9:2, 11, 27, 60; 10:11; 12:32; 16:16; 18:24; 21:31.

If Jesus is not alive, Paul asserted, people should look on us with pity for being duped (see 1 Cor 15:12–19). The same could be said of the unique way the Gospels tell us Jesus came into the world. If Christ was not conceived of a virgin as the Scriptures have asserted to us, then the records we have about Jesus lose credibility and reliability as accurate sources for his life and ministry.

But Luke here provides us with good reasons to take these stories seriously. Despite what modern skeptics and critics may claim about his Gospel, Luke never implies that the stories of Jesus's birth, miracles, resurrection, and ascension were mere legends created to prove a theological point. Instead, Luke wanted Theophilus to know things about Jesus's life with "certainty" (1:4). Luke expresses his commitment to getting the facts right. Either he was telling Theophilus and his other readers the truth about Jesus, or he was being intentionally deceitful and malicious. Luke does not leave us the option of believing that this story was merely a pious fiction written with the best of intentions.

2

The God Who Keeps His Covenants

Matthew 1:1, 17

Think of the [OT] Scriptures as the loftiest and noblest
of holy things, as the richest of mines which can never be
sufficiently explored. . . . Here you will find the swaddling
clothes and the manger in which Christ lies, and to which the
angel points the shepherds. Simple and lowly are the swaddling
cloths, but dear is the treasure, Christ, who lies in them.

–MARTIN LUTHER[1]

[1] Martin Luther, "Preface to the Old Testament" (1545), trans. Charles M. Jacobs, in *LW* 35:236. See also Richard B. Hays, *Reading Backwards: Figural Christology and the Fourfold Gospel Witness* (Waco, TX: Baylor University Press, 2014), 1–16.

For many modern readers, the opening seventeen verses of Matthew's Gospel read like a phone book—a long, boring list of names from a genealogy. Readers may be tempted to overlook this section and jump straight into the "action" of the Christmas story. To do so, however, is to ignore the important setup for everything that follows. This genealogy is more than a list of hard-to-pronounce names (and some of them are real dingers). With this list, Matthew is telling a story!

The genealogy is a carefully crafted history of Israel's monarchy pregnant with implications for the life and ministry of Jesus. It is also part of Matthew's larger case that Jesus is the long-awaited Messiah promised in the Scriptures. This genealogy demonstrates that, for Matthew, the good news of Jesus presumes the whole OT story.[2]

Matthew introduces his largely Jewish audience to Jesus with three titles that would have carried great significance for them: the "Messiah," the "Son of David," and the "Son of Abraham." By using these titles, Matthew reminds us of the way Jesus embodied and fulfilled the various covenants God made with Israel, Abraham, and David.

A covenant may be defined as "a solemn commitment guaranteeing promises or obligations undertaken by one or both covenanting parties."[3] A covenant is like a binding, lasting contract made between two parties with serious repercussions if it is broken. But unlike business-oriented contracts, which are established to produce some type of mutual benefit for all the parties who are involved, covenants are person-oriented promises that seek to establish a lasting personal relationship between those

---

[2] N. T. Wright, *The New Testament and the People of God* (Minneapolis: Fortress, 1996), 384–36; Chris Bruno, Jared Compton, and Kevin McFadden, *Biblical Theology According to the Apostles: How the Earliest Christians Told the Story of Israel* (Downers Grove: InterVarsity, 2020), 12–14.
[3] Paul R. Williamson, "Covenant," in *Dictionary of the Old Testament: Pentateuch*, ed. T. Desmond Alexander and David W. Baker (Downers Grove: InterVarsity, 2003), 139.

who make them. Fulfilling the obligations of a covenant is more than a business arrangement, it is an act of love.[4]

In the Old Testament, God made a series of such commitments to his creatures—promises made to all of creation like the Noahic covenant (Gen 9:1–17) and covenants with entire nations like the Sinai covenant (Exod 19–24). But the covenants God made to Abraham and David were personal covenants that involved their family lines. With the genealogy that opens his Gospel, Matthew depicts Jesus as the end of their lines and the culmination of all the promises that God made to them.

The Messiah You Weren't Expecting

Matthew opens his Gospel with this headline: "An account of the genealogy of Jesus Christ" (Matt 1:1). The phrase rendered "account of the genealogy" here could also be translated as "book of the genesis" or the "book of origin."[5] Matthew's original readers would have recognized this phrase from the Greek title of the first book of the Bible. Just as Genesis told the story of the beginning of God's work in the world, Matthew told a story of a new beginning for the world in Jesus the Messiah.[6]

Matthew calls Jesus the "Christ," "Messiah," or "anointed one" (*Christou*) that Israel had been waiting for. To be clear, "Christ" is not Jesus's last name but the title of his office (like "Mr. President" or "Your Majesty"). The title "Christ" or "Messiah" translated the Hebrew word *mashiach*, which describes a king or a priest who is anointed with oil for special service to the Lord and Israel.[7] Across the OT, there were several

---

[4] Peter J. Gentry and Stephen J. Wellum, *Kingdom Through Covenant: A Biblical-Theological Understanding of the Covenants* (Wheaton, IL: Crossway, 2012), 140–45.

[5] Charles L. Quarles, *Matthew*, EBTC (Bellingham, WA: Lexham, 2023), 106–7.

[6] Wright, *The New Testament and the People of God*, 385.

[7] See Exod 28:41; Lev 4:16; 6:22; 1 Sam 9:15–16; 12:3, 5; 24:6; 24:10; Ps 2:2.

lowercase-m "messiahs" who were anointed to serve Israel.[8] But the term "Messiah" later came to be associated with the Jewish hope for a king in the line of David who would restore Israel to the prominence it once had as a united kingdom (see Zech 9:9–10; 12:7).

Though a remnant returned to the land after years in exile (587–538 BC), the nation of Israel never returned to its former glory. The people of Judea had foreign rulers like Persia, Alexandria, and Greece. In the ancient world, empires tossed Israel around like a game of hot potato, as this little Middle Eastern province regularly changed imperial ownership. Following the Maccabean revolt in the mid-second century BC—an event celebrated in the Jewish festival of lights or Hanukkah—the people of Israel had a brief window of independence under the Hasmonean Dynasty. But the eighty-year history of the Hasmonean dynasty was plagued by political corruption, spiritual compromise, and civil war. When Jesus was born around 4 or 5 BC, the people of Judea had been living under the thumb of Roman rule for nearly a half century. Many in Israel longed for a Messiah who would liberate them from the oppression of worldly powers, much like the revolt led by Judas "the Hammer" Maccabeus against the Seleucid Empire in the second century BC.[9]

The baby in the manger would have been a major disappointment to those looking for a political savior. What Israel—and for that matter, Rome—needed more than anything else was not a more moral Caesar. They needed someone who could deliver them from sin and death. Throughout his Gospel, Matthew argued that Jesus was the Messiah God promised in the OT, even if he was not the messiah of popular expectation. God's Messiah did something greater than defeat a temporary

---

[8] There are no lower and uppercase letters in Hebrew. This is a rhetorical way of differentiating anointed individuals from the future anointed Messiah-King. This list of "lowercase-m" messiahs includes anointed priests (Lev 4:5, 16; 6:22), anointed kings (1 Sam 16:6; 24:6), and other people who find God's favor (1 Sam 2:10).

[9] See N. T. Wright, *Jesus and the Victory of God* (Minneapolis: Fortress, 1996), 481–86; Wright, *The New Testament and the People of God*, 307–20.

earthly kingdom and set up a temporary dynasty. He launched the king-dom of heaven—the rule of God over the hearts of his people—on earth. Through his cross and resurrection, this virgin-born Messiah took the wrath of God on himself and defeated death and the satanic powers of this age.

The Abrahamic Covenant: When God Makes a Great Nation

The turning point of the original book of Genesis came when God called Abraham to leave his pagan family behind in Haran and go to a new place in Canaan (Gen 12:1–5; Josh 24:3). He promised to make Abraham's family a "great nation" (Gen 12:2). God made a covenant with Abraham and promised this old man with no children that he would have more descendants than there are stars in the sky (Gen 15:5). Then God gave him a son through a miraculous conception (Gen 21:1–7).

Matthew's designation of Jesus as a "son of Abraham" was, in part, a way of identifying Jesus with the nation of Israel. In Jesus's world, being a child of Abraham was a badge of honor reserved exclusively for the Jewish people. God had adopted the nation of Israel to be his people. Israelites had ownership in "the glory, the covenants, the giving of the law, the temple service, and the promises" (Rom 9:4). Peter addressed Jewish men as "the sons of the prophets and of the covenant that God made with [their] ancestors" (Acts 3:25). As a son of Abraham, Jesus was "born under the law" (Gal 4:4) and "came to his own" people (John 1:11).

But Jesus is not just another one of Abraham's descendants. Jesus was the one God promised to Abraham when he said, "All the peoples of the earth will be blessed through you" (Gen 12:3; Rom 4:16–17). Through Jesus, God would bless the whole world. Paul makes this point emphati-cally clear: "Now the promises were spoken to Abraham and to his seed. He does not say 'and to seeds,' as though referring to many, but referring to one, **and to your seed**, who is Christ" (Gal 3:16). Abraham may not have fully understood all that this promise entailed, but he looked to its future fulfillment with expectation and hope. In Jesus's own words, "Abraham rejoiced to see my day; he saw it and was glad" (John 8:56).

The Davidic Covenant: When God Builds a House

Politicians are often concerned about leaving a legacy, doing something that will last long after they are gone. John F. Kennedy avoided nuclear conflict with Cuba and made his countrymen dream of landing on the moon. Ronald Reagan called for the end of the Cold War when he said, "Mr. Gorbachev, tear down this wall!" Good leaders want to leave a positive legacy while they can. The same was true for King David.

During a time of peace, David approached the prophet Nathan with a serious concern. The king was living in a luxurious palace whereas the ark of the covenant that housed God's presence was exposed to the elements in a tent. David wanted to build a temple for God. David's motives were godly, and his logic was simple: if Israel's king had a house, then Israel's God needed one too. Without much prayerful consideration, Nathan's first response was overwhelmingly positive: "Go and do all that is on your mind, for the LORD is with you" (2 Sam 7:3). But God rejected the construction project that David hoped would be his legacy.

Yet God was faithful to David and had something better for him: "I took you from the pasture, from tending the flock, to be ruler over my people Israel. I have been with you wherever you have gone, and I have destroyed all your enemies before you. I will make a great name for you like that of the greatest on the earth" (2 Sam 7:8b–9). David would not get to build a house for God, but God would build a "house" for David.

> When your time comes to be with your ancestors, I will raise up after you your descendant, who is one of your own sons, and I will establish his kingdom. He is the one who will build a house for me, and I will establish his throne forever. I will be his father, and he will be my son. I will not remove my faithful love from him as I removed it from the one who was before you. I will

appoint him over my house and my kingdom forever, and his throne will be established forever. (1 Chr 17:11–14)[10]

The "house" that God promised to build for David was not the earthly temple of David's imagination but an eternal family dynasty. The coming son of David is a "child . . . born for us" and a "son . . . given to us" (Isa 9:6–7). Isaiah did not believe this future descendant of David would be a mere man. Instead, he said he would be "Mighty God" and "Eternal Father." This coming king was depicted as a ruler unlike any other in history. He would be both a descendant of David according to the flesh *and* the God of Israel.

Our Dwelling Place in Every Generation

So all the generations from Abraham to David were fourteen generations; and from David until the exile to Babylon, fourteen generations; and from the exile to Babylon until the Messiah, fourteen generations. (Matt 1:17)

Many people note how short this list is for a genealogy that covers such a long period of time: Aren't several names missing? Unlike modern genealogies that strive for completeness, Matthew's genealogy was never intended to be an exhaustive list of Jesus's relatives. How do we know this?

1. The word often translated "fathered" (or "begot") can refer to siring a child physically but can also mean "was the ancestor of" or a "legal heir."[11]

---

[10] See also 2 Sam 7:12–16. The account in 2 Samuel alludes to Solomon's shortcomings as a king and the judgment that awaits him in 1 Kgs 11:14–40.

[11] D. A. Carson, "Matthew," in *Matthew and Mark*, EBC, rev. ed. (Grand Rapids: Zondervan, 2010), 9:198; Machen, *The Virgin Birth of Christ*, 186 (see introduction, n. 6).

2. There are significant gaps in the record. For example, only four generations are listed in the four-hundred-year period between Perez and Amminadab. Rahab, the Canaanite prostitute who hid Israel's spies, was likely the ancestor of David's great-grandfather Boaz, not his biological mother.

3. Matthew also purposely strikes the three generations between Joram (Jehoram) and Uzziah (Azariah) from the record because of their disobedience to the Lord (Matt 1:8; 1 Chr 3:11–12).

4. Matthew's genealogy is significantly shorter than the genealogy recorded in Luke 3. Between David and Jesus, Matthew lists twenty-eight generations. Luke lists forty-three generations in the same time frame.

The Evangelist is selective about which names he includes because he is more interested in showing Jesus's legal or royal pedigree than providing a genetic history. Jesus is, at least according to Matthew, Joseph's legal (not biological) son.[12]

Matthew also has a theological purpose in the way he organizes this list of names from the royal family tree of Jesus and David. Notice that he sorts these names into three groups of "fourteen" generations (Matt 1:17):

1. From Abraham to David (1:2–6a)—a seven- or-eight-century-long period with thirteen generations, fourteen male names, and three female names.

2. From David until the exile (1:6b–11)—a four-century long period with fourteen generations, fourteen unique male names, and one female.

---

[12] Legal sonship would have been sufficient to be counted in an ancient ancestry (see Gen 48:5–6). Esther is called the "daughter" of Mordecai even though she was his adopted niece (Esth 2:7, 15). Even modern genealogies still include adopted children. See Darrell L. Bock, *Luke 1:1–9:50*, vol. 1, BECNT (Grand Rapids: Baker, 1994), 108. Bock notes that the precedent for including non-biological children in one's genealogy is established in the practice of levirate marriage (Deut 25:5–10).

3. From the exile to Jesus (1:12–16)—a six-century-long period with thirteen generations, thirteen unique male names, and one female name.[13]

Matthew's clever arrangement provides a helpful way of teaching the major periods in the history of Israel. If you can remember these three periods, you have a pretty good grasp on the basic plot of the Old Testament! The period from Abraham to David tells the story of Israel's rise as a kingdom. The period from David to the exile tells the story of its decline. The period of the exile to Jesus tells the story of Israel's expectation for the Messiah-King.[14]

But why "fourteen"? What is the meaning behind Matthew's numerical pattern? Though we do not have definitive answers, biblical scholars have offered two plausible explanations. One possible suggestion is that Matthew uses the number "fourteen" as a multiple of seven, a number frequently associated with "fullness" or "completeness" in the Bible (even the Hebrew words for "seven" and "completeness" have very similar spellings). In the creation account of Gen 1–2:3, God created the world in six days and "rested" on the seventh day. This "rest" does not mean God took a nap. It means that he came to indwell the world he created.[15] Following Matthew's math, three generations of fourteen equal six sevens. Perhaps the Evangelist is making the case that the new "genesis" of Jesus Christ began after three generations (six sevens) on the "seventh day" when God came to rest with his people as Immanuel—God with us (Matt 1:23).[16]

---

[13] This count is based on Marcus Borg and John Dominic Crossan, *The First Christmas: What the Gospels Really Teach About Jesus's Birth* (New York: HarperOne, 2009), 87.

[14] Patrick Schreiner, *Matthew, Disciple and Scribe: The First Gospel and Its Portrait of Jesus* (Grand Rapids: Baker, 2019), 69.

[15] See John H. Walton, *The Lost World of Genesis One: Ancient Cosmology and the Origins Debate* (Downers Grove: IVP Academic, 2009), 72–77.

[16] See R. T. France, *The Gospel of Matthew*, NICNT (Grand Rapids: Eerdmans, 2007), 31–32.

Another possibility is that Matthew used a common Jewish practice of assigning numerical values to letters called *gematria*. The numbers
associated with the three Hebrew letters of David's name add up to fourteen (*dalet* [4] + *vav* [6] + *dalet* [4] = 14). If Matthew used this ancient
technique, his threefold use of "fourteen" was meant to remind us of Jesus
fulfilling the promise made to David.[17] From the time of Abraham to
David, God was preparing to make a covenant with David. From the
time of David to the exile, God was faithful to the covenant he made
with David—even when David's descendants were not. From the time of
the exile to the birth of the Messiah, God never forgot the promise that
he made to David.

Either way we interpret this number, Matthew is clear on this point:
The God who always keeps his covenant promises brought each phase
of Israel's history to its appropriate conclusion. God called Israel to be
his people with Abraham. God kept his promise to David, even during
the downfall of the monarchies in Israel and Judah. During the exile to a
foreign land, God kept his promise to restore his people.

---

[17] See W. D. Davies and Dale C. Allison, Jr., *Matthew 1–7*, ICC (New
York: T&T Clark, 2004), 163–65; Grant R. Osborne, *Matthew*, ECNT (Grand
Rapids: Zondervan, 2010), 60–61.

Answering Objections: The Genealogies of Matthew and Luke Cannot Be Reconciled

Those comparing Matthew and Luke's genealogies of Jesus (Matt 1:1–17; Luke 3:23–38) may notice some significant differences. Matthew's list moves forward from Abraham to Jesus. Luke's much longer list backtracks from Jesus to Adam (and then God). Matthew and Luke's lists diverge after David, with Matthew following the lineage of Solomon (Matt 1:6b) and Luke following the line of David's son Nathan, who was presumably named after the prophet (Luke 3:31; cf. 2 Sam 5:14; 1 Chr 3:5; 14:4). Both lists of names include Shealtiel and Zerubbabel in their divergent Davidic lines.

Matthew 1:2–17
41 names

Abraham	Solomon	**Shealtiel**
Isaac	Rehoboam	**Zerubbabel**
Jacob	Abijah	Abiud
Judah	Asa	Eliakim
Perez	Jehoshaphat	Azor
Hezron	Joram	Zadok
Ram	Uzziah	Achim
Amminadab	Jotham	Eliud
Nahshon	Ahaz	Eleazar
Salmon	Hezekiah	Matthan
Boaz	Manasseh	Jacob
Obed	Amon	**Joseph**
Jesse	Josiah	**Jesus**
David	Jeconiah	

Luke 3:23–38

77 names (in reverse order)

God	Phalec	**Obed**	Joshua	Naggai
Adam	Ragau	**Jesse**	Er	Esli
Seth	Saruch	**David**	Elmadam	Nahum
Enos	Nachor	Nathan	Cosam	Amos
Cainan	Thara	Mattatha	Addi	Mattathias
Mahalaleleel	**Abraham**	Menna	Melchi	Joseph
Jared	**Isaac**	Melea	Neri	Jannai
Enoch	**Jacob**	Eliakim	**Shealtiel**	Melchi
Methuselah	**Judah**	Jonam	**Zerubbabel**	Levi
Lamech	**Perez**	Joseph	Rhesa	Matthat
Noah	**Hezron**	Judah	Joanan	Heli
Shem	**Ram**	Simeon	Joda	**Joseph**
Arphaxad	**Aminadab**	Levi	Josech	**Jesus**
Cainan	**Nahshon**	Matthat	Semein	
Sala	**Salmon**	Jorim	Mattathias	
Heber	**Boaz**	Eliezer	Maath	

Mark Strauss identifies four basic interpretive options for explaining the differences between the two genealogies. *The first proposal is that the two genealogies cannot be reconciled.* The Roman Emperor Julian (AD 331–363), known as "the Apostate," raised this objection against the Gospels (*Against the Galileans* 1). Modern historical critics claim that one or both lists of names were fictions invented by the Gospel writers to strengthen Jesus's credentials as the Davidic Messiah. But as Strauss observes, this skeptical position tends to overlook other references to Jesus's Davidic lineage elsewhere in the NT (see Mark 10:47–48; John 7:42; Rom 1:3; 2 Tim 2:8; Heb 7:14; Rev 5:5; 22:16). The genealogies were not needed to establish Jesus as a descendant of David when it appears that this was common knowledge during his lifetime.

A second possibility is that Joseph had two fathers: a biological father and an adoptive father. The ancient practice of levirate marriage (from a Latin word meaning "brother-in-law") would ensure that a man would marry his brother's widow in the event of her husband's death (Deut 25:5–10). This was an important social safety net in a patriarchal society where women depended on their husbands and sons for their very livelihood and existence. If there were one or more levirate marriages in the lineage of Joseph, that would account for the differences between Matthew and Luke (see Augustine, *Reply to Faustus the Manichaean* 3.2–5).

The third option is that both genealogies belong to Joseph but in different ways. One genealogy (Luke) lists Joseph's physical ancestors. The other (Matthew) presents a series of royal successions, like a list of US presidents in chronological order. On this view, these are all distant relatives of Joseph because they are in the family tree of David, but not all of them are in his direct lineage.

The final option is the claim that one genealogy belongs to Mary and the other belongs to Joseph. Though some throughout church history have claimed Luke's genealogy to be Joseph's and Matthew's to be Mary's, the most common proposal is that Luke includes Mary's physical genealogy whereas Matthew's lists Joseph's. Luke may be suggesting this when he writes "Jesus . . . was thought to be the son of Joseph" (Luke 3:23).

But this common proposal is not without its difficulties. Joseph, not Mary, is at the head of Luke's list. Elsewhere in the Gospel, Luke describes Mary as a "virgin engaged to a man named Joseph, of the house of David" (Luke 1:27; 2:4). The text never explicitly also calls Mary a "daughter of David." However, the two names listed for Joseph's father—Jacob in Matt 1:16 and Heli in Luke 3:23—may be evidence for this traditional view. The Greek text does not specify that Heli is Joseph's father. It is possible that Heli is his father-in-law. Extrabiblical tradition gives Mary's father two names that resemble "Heli": Eli and Joachim (a Hebrew variation of Eliakim).

There are also good contextual reasons for considering this traditional position. After all, Luke recounts Mary's side of the story, and Matthew provides Joseph's story. If Luke's genealogy is Mary's genealogy, then Jesus did physically descend from David on his mother's side. Many have argued that Jesus could not physically come from Solomon's line because of the judgment pronounced on the descendants of Jehoiakim (Jer 36:30) and Jehoiachin (Jer 22:24–30). Both kings were told that none of their descendants would sit on the throne of David. If Matthew and Luke represent two lines from David that lead to Joseph and Mary, then Jesus can be the rightful heir to David's throne (via Joseph's line) and still be the virgin-born physical descendant of David through Mary's line (see Rom 1:3; *Ascension of Isaiah* 11.2). One Syriac manuscript for Luke 2:5 suggests that Joseph and Mary both belonged to the house of David.

Matthew emphasizes a royal line whereas Luke does not. This fits with Matthew's emphasis on Jesus as the Messianic King. Luke's genealogy is traced back to Adam, which means that Jesus belongs not only to the sons of Abraham but also to the whole world. This fits well with his emphasis on God's inclusion of the Gentiles in his plan for salvation. Matthew puts his genealogy at the beginning of his Gospel because he wants his readers to see that Jesus provides us with a "new genesis," a new beginning. Luke places his genealogy after God the Father declares Jesus to be his "beloved Son" (Luke 3:22) because Jesus is the "son of God" in his list (Luke 3:38).

Matthew and Luke may have theological reasons for including the different genealogies they use, but the differences between these family trees by no means imply a genuine contradiction, nor do they give us any reason not to trust the authority of Scripture in these matters.

See Mark L. Strauss, *Four Portraits, One Jesus*, 2nd ed. (Grand Rapids: Zondervan, 2020), 501–3; Richard A. Shenk, *The Virgin Birth of Christ* (Milton Keynes, UK: Paternoster, 2016), 95–115; Machen, *The Virgin Birth of Christ*, 203–9; Craig L. Blomberg, *The Historical Reliability of the New Testament* (Nashville: B&H Academic, 2016), 57–59; Ben Witherington III, "Birth of Jesus," in *Dictionary of Jesus and the Gospels*, ed. Joel B. Green, Scot McKnight, and I. Howard Marshall (Downers Grove: InterVarsity, 1992), 65–66.

3

The Son Who Chose
His Own Parents

Matthew 1:2–16

Behold the strange and wonderful birth of Christ. It came through a
line that included sinners, adulterers, and Gentiles. But such a birth
does not soil the honor of Christ. Rather, it commends his mercy.

—ANONYMOUS, 6TH CENTURY[1]

M y son and I recently embarked on a weekend road trip with my dad
to learn a little about our family history. On one leg of the journey
through north central Mississippi, we traveled to an overgrown cemetery
deep within the woods where many of my ancestors were buried.

---

[1] *Incomplete Commentary on Matthew (Opus imperfectum)*, Homily 1, quoted
in *Matthew*, Ancient Christian Commentary on Scripture, NT vol. 1a, ed.
Manlio Simonetti (Downers Grove: InterVarsity, 2001), 13.

The faded, mildew-covered headstones dating back to the early 1800s told a lot of stories about my family. Some were farmers. Some were circuit-riding preachers. One died a young man in the American Civil War. Another was a failed US presidential candidate. We also saw things that were difficult to process: plots that belonged to slaveholders and their slaves. The wooded area around the cemetery also concealed an unmarked grave for a wounded Union officer who was murdered on the front porch of an ancestor's home.

That whole experience gave me both a greater appreciation for my roots and a sense of grief for the sins of my fathers. Discovering one's roots is an incredibly important task, even if what we uncover is sometimes painful to learn. Our family histories tell us a lot about where we have come from and where we could go. We are all sons and daughters of Adam, born into families that are dysfunctional to varying degrees. For better or worse, we are all shaped by those who went before us. We do not choose the time and place where we are born. We do not pick the people with whom we share a name and a family history.

Only one person in history was an exception to this rule. The virgin-born king was the only individual in human history who chose the family into which he was born. God the Son willingly took on true humanity in a real family with its share of problems.

With his genealogy of Jesus, Matthew defends Jesus's royal pedigree as a descendant of David and demonstrates God's faithfulness to the covenants he made with Abraham and David. But the Evangelist also tells a story about the redemptive way God works in the lives of broken and sinful people. As Herbert McCabe once observed, the Messiah "belonged to a family of murderers, cheats, cowards, adulterers, and liars—he belonged to *us* and came to help *us*, no wonder he came to a bad end, and gave *us* some hope."[2]

---

[2] Herbert McCabe, *God Matters* (London: Continuum, 2005), 249.

God Redeems Sinful People

Some of the kings in Jesus's royal ancestry were faithful men of God, but most of them were idolaters and compromisers whose reigns ended in disaster. The books of Kings and Chronicles detail the long, sordid history of these rulers. Those in David's line who were faithful to the Lord had long, successful reigns, but those who disobeyed the Lord or who pursued other gods usually had shorter reigns that ended poorly. God kept his promise to David, despite the wickedness of many of his descendants. Matthew's genealogy is a helpful reminder of God's promise: "I will humble David's descendants, because of their unfaithfulness, but not forever" (1 Kgs 11:39).

Solomon once claimed the title of the wisest man on the earth (1 Kgs 4:29–31), but a series of foolish decisions brought his reign to a tragic end. He sold his own people into slavery. He burdened his subjects with such a heavy yoke that they were relieved when he died (1 Kgs 9:15–23). Worst of all, this once wise man acquired hundreds of pagan wives and built altars to their gods. The warnings he gave his own sons about following godless and wayward women (Prov 7:6–26) seemed lost on him at the end of his reign (1 Kings 11). "Unlike his father David," Solomon "did not remain loyal to the LORD" (1 Kgs 11:6). Just as God had foretold through the prophet Nathan, David's son would invite the discipline of the Lord and the "rod of men and blows from mortals" (2 Sam 7:14):

> Since you have done this and did not keep my covenant and my statutes, which I commanded you, I will tear the kingdom away from you and give it to your servant. However, I will not do it during your lifetime for the sake of your father David; I will tear it out of your son's hand. Yet I will not tear the entire kingdom away from him. I will give one tribe to your son for the sake of my servant David and for the sake of Jerusalem that I chose. (1 Kgs 11:11–13)

The discipline God promised came through Solomon's opponents, both foreign (1 Kgs 11:14–25) and domestic (1 Kgs 11:26–
40). After Solomon's death, the once united monarchy of Israel's
twelve tribes was divided in two. The foolish and prideful actions
of Rehoboam, Solomon's son, led to the division of Israel into two
kingdoms: Judah and Israel (1 Kgs 12:1–24; 2 Chronicles 10–12).
Rehoboam would rule the southern kingdom composed of the tribes
of Judah and Benjamin (1 Kgs 14:21–31). The idolater Jeroboam,
once a trusted advisor to Solomon, became king over the newly established northern kingdom of Israel composed of the other ten tribes
(1 Kgs 12:25–33; 14:1–20).

The authors of 1–2 Kings and 1–2 Chronicles assessed the kings
of Israel on a few basic criteria: (1) Did the king serve the Lord alone?
(2) Did the king endorse, eradicate, or ignore idolatry? (3) Was the king
faithful to the covenant? Every single king in the 209-year history of the
northern kingdom of Israel failed all these tests. Only eight out of twenty
kings of Judah from whom Jesus descended were considered "good kings"
by these criteria.

This motley crew of Davidic kings in Judah ended with Jeconiah
(also known as Jehoiachin). We do not know much about Jeconiah's short
three-month reign as the king of Judah, but "he did what was evil in the
LORD's sight just as his father had done" (2 Kgs 24:9; see also 2 Chr 36:9).
His father Jehoiakim—whom Matthew struck entirely from his genealogy of Jesus—was a wicked man who brought Babylon's wrath down on
Judah (Jer 36:29–31). Though Jeconiah only reigned three months and
ten days as Judah's king, it appeared to many that he would be the last
king to sit on David's throne. Through the prophet Jeremiah, God cursed
Jeconiah for his unfaithfulness:

> Record this man as childless,
> a man who will not be successful in his lifetime.
> None of his descendants will succeed
> in sitting on the throne of David
> or ruling again in Judah. (Jer 22:30)

Although none of Jeconiah's immediate descendants ruled on the throne again, God continued to show mercy on this line. His grandson Zerubbabel was instrumental in rebuilding the temple after Cyrus allowed Jews to return to Jerusalem from the exile (Ezra 3:2–5:1). Zerubbabel faithfully served God and the people as governor of Judah (Haggai 1–2; Zechariah 4).

Even after David was long gone, the people of God still placed their hopes on God fulfilling this promise to him. As God expounded on this promise through the prophet Jeremiah,

> "Look, the days are coming"—this is the LORD's declaration—
> "when I will raise up a Righteous Branch for David.
> He will reign wisely as king
> and administer justice and righteousness in the land.
> In his days Judah will be saved,
> and Israel will dwell securely.
> This is the name he will be called:
> The LORD Is Our Righteousness. (Jer 23:5–6)

The title "Righteous Branch for David" contrasts the coming king with many of David's descendants who did not seek the Lord or his justice. This coming Davidic king will rule with perfect wisdom and righteousness.

Like other covenants God made with the people of Israel, he placed expectations on David and his descendants. He specifically stated that if the sons of David were faithful to the covenant, they would continue to rule forever. If they were not faithful to the Lord, he would remove the throne from them.

> The LORD swore an oath to David,
> a promise he will not abandon:
> "I will set one of your offspring
> on your throne.
> If your sons keep my covenant
> and my decrees that I will teach them,
> their sons will also sit on your throne forever." (Ps 132:11–12)

Ultimately God judged the house of David and the nation of Judah, but he never forgot the promise he made to David himself. As Matthew proves, God ultimately kept his promise to David through Jesus. Through Christ God redeemed a family name that had been shamed by its sin and rebellion and made it the name of an eternal kingdom.

Women in the Ancestry of Jesus

Ancient Jews in a patriarchal society did not always look favorably on women. There is an old rabbinic prayer that states, "Blessed is the God who has not made me a Gentile, who has not made me a peasant, who has not made me a woman." In the mind of whoever wrote this prayer, Gentiles, peasants, and women are not important to God.

With this genealogy, Matthew shows that this ancient belief could not be further from the truth. In addition to Mary, four other women are listed in Matthew's genealogy of Jesus: Tamar, Rahab, Ruth, and Bathsheba. These women either came from the margins of Jewish society or were total outsiders. Some of them were peasants who had nothing to their names when God intervened. Some of these women would have been cast aside as unclean sinners. Although many in Israel would have gazed at these women with reproach, they had an important role in God's redemptive plan for the world. These Gentile women became savior figures through whom the Messiah would come into the world.[3]

Tamar: God Cares for the Neglected

The scandalous story of Judah and Tamar in Genesis 38 interrupts the Joseph story in Genesis (Genesis 37, 39–50). Although it may feel like a sidenote in the book of Genesis, this story has ripple effects throughout redemptive history. Judah was the son of Jacob who spared Joseph's life by

---

[3] Bruno, Compton, and McFadden, *Biblical Theology According to the Apostles*, 18–22 (see chap. 2, n. 2).

selling him into slavery (Gen 37:26–27) and who later pled with Joseph to release Benjamin for his father's sake (Gen 44:18–34).

In the sidebar of Genesis 38, we discover Judah had three sons: Er, Onan, and Shelah. Judah arranged a marriage between his son Er and a woman named Tamar. The text says nothing about Tamar's nationality, but Judah had brought his family into a Canaanite territory and taken for himself a Canaanite wife (Gen 38:1–2). Tamar very well may have been a Canaanite too.[4] God put Er to death because of his wickedness, but he left his wife Tamar with no children to provide for her in her old age. Without a husband or a male son, women in patriarchal societies had no financial security for the future.

The law of Moses would later prescribe a practice called levirate marriage (from a Latin word meaning "brother-in-law") to help women like Tamar in circumstances like this one (Deut 25:5–10). If a man died and left his wife a childless widow with no inheritance, his brother was obligated to marry her and give her a son who would secure the portion of the inheritance owed to the dead man's family. Judah told Onan, his second-born, to sleep with Tamar and give her a child, but Onan "released his semen on the ground so that he would not produce offspring for his brother" (Gen 38:9). In other words, Onan practiced an ancient form of birth control so he would not have to share his inheritance with the wife and the legal "son" of his dead brother. Angered by this injustice, God struck Onan dead as well.

Judah had a third son, a boy named Shelah, but he hid him from Tamar because he was afraid God would strike another one of his sons dead if he let Tamar marry him. When Tamar saw that neither Judah nor his son Shelah would fulfill their legal obligations to her, she devised a plan to ensure she would have a son and a future. Knowing Judah's

---

[4] See also *Jubilees* 41:1; Richard Bauckham, "Tamar's Ancestry and Rahab's Marriage: Two Problems in the Matthean Genealogy," *NovT* 37, no. 4 (1995): 314–20.

routine, she disguised herself as a cult prostitute but covered her face so Judah would not recognize her.

As expected, Judah propositioned Tamar when he saw her by the roadside. Tamar demanded a young goat for payment but, knowing Judah did not have one with him, she asked for his staff and signet ring as collateral. Tamar's plan worked, and she conceived two sons—including Jesus's forefather Perez. Judah came by later with a goat in tow, but the "prostitute" had absconded with his signet ring and staff.

When Judah later heard that his daughter-in-law had dressed like a prostitute and become pregnant, he was incensed and decided to try her for adultery and have her burned to death. At her trial, all Tamar had to do was flash the signet ring and staff. Judah suddenly knew his sin was exposed for everyone to see: "She is more in the right than I, since I did not give her to my son Shelah" (Gen 38:26). Though we may think of Tamar's action as sinful or underhanded, the narrator of the story vindicates her for her righteous action (Gen 38:27–30). In the midst of scandal, God had seen Tamar's great need and provided for her.

Rahab: God Sees Those Who Fear Him

If anyone had a reason to be excluded from the genealogy of the Messiah, it was Rahab. She was a woman, a Canaanite (Gentile), and a "prostitute." Even with these three strikes against her, Rahab is remembered for her bravery and faith (Heb 11:31; Jas 2:25). She hid two of Joshua's spies from the king of Jericho on her roof. Her reasoning was simple: she had heard what the God of Israel had done to the Egyptians and wanted to be spared from his coming judgment on the Canaanites (Josh 2:8–13).

Rahab knew that "the LORD . . . is God in heaven above and on earth below" and entrusted herself to him for safety and deliverance in a day of judgment (Josh 2:11). Just as God promised, Rahab and her family were spared when the Israelites invaded Jericho. She was counted among Israel when the book of Joshua was composed (Josh 6:22–25).

Matthew's inclusion of faithful women like Tamar and Rahab may be setting the table for what is to come in Jesus's ministry to women of ill repute. Throughout his ministry, religious leaders critiqued Jesus for eating with tax collectors and prostitutes (Matt 9:11). But Jesus asserted that "tax collectors and the prostitutes are entering the kingdom of God ahead of you" because the tax collectors and prostitutes repented and believed when these religious leaders had not (Matt 21:31–32).

Ruth: God Rewards the Faithful

Ruth is one of the most prominent figures in the OT. Along with Esther, she is one of two women in the Bible to have a book focused entirely on her life. After the death of her husband, the Moabite Ruth could have returned to her homeland and served their gods, as her sister-in-law Orpah did (Ruth 1:14–15). But Ruth modeled faithfulness to Naomi and her God by staying with her mother-in-law when she returned to Judah. In the little town of Bethlehem, these widows depended completely on the welfare of others for their survival. Ruth went to the fields and collected fallen grain from another man's harvest, as allowed by the law (Ruth 2:2; see also Lev 19:9–10).

In the field, Ruth met Boaz, Naomi's "family redeemer" (Ruth 2:20). Sometime later, Ruth lay at the feet of Boaz on the threshing floor and asked him to "spread the corner of [his] garment over [her]" (Ruth 3:8–9 NIV). Ruth essentially asked Boaz to fulfill his legal requirement as a "family redeemer" to Naomi by marrying her daughter-in-law. The "family redeemer" helped relatives get out of debts they could not pay (Lev 25:47–49). Seeing the care Ruth had for her mother-in-law, Boaz calls Ruth "a woman of noble character" (Ruth 3:11; see also Prov 31:10).[5]

---

[5] Notably, Ruth is the last book in the original order of the Hebrew Bible. It immediately follows Prov 31:10–31, which describes the "woman of noble character."

When Boaz marries Ruth and redeems Naomi's debts, the people of Bethlehem bless Ruth and prophetically speak of what God will do with this family line:

> We are witnesses. May the LORD make the woman who is entering your house like Rachel and Leah, who together built the house of Israel. May you be powerful in Ephrathah and your name well known in Bethlehem. May your house become like the house of Perez, the son Tamar bore to Judah, because of the offspring the LORD will give you by this young woman. (Ruth 4:11–12)

The book of Ruth concludes with a genealogy that traces the lineage of David through his great-grandfather Boaz to Perez, the son of Tamar (Ruth 4:18–22).

Bathsheba: God Rescues Us from Shame

Matthew does not call Bathsheba by name, but he does note that Solomon was fathered by "Uriah's wife" (Matt 1:6b).[6] This unusual description is not meant to belittle Bathsheba but to highlight the egregious sin of David, who slept with Uriah's wife, then had this faithful man murdered when she conceived the king's child (2 Sam 11:1–24). Bathsheba had to grieve the loss of her husband (2 Sam 11:26–27) and then her first-born son with David (2 Sam 12:15–24). But God still acted mercifully to her by keeping his covenant with David and placing her son on David's throne (1 Kgs 1:28–31).

---

[6] See Richard Bauckham, *Gospel Women: Studies of the Named Women in the Gospels* (Grand Rapids: Eerdmans, 2002), 22. Bathsheba may or may not have been an Israelite. The possible family connection between her father Eliam (2 Sam 11:3; 1 Chr 3:5) and Ahithophel (2 Sam 23:34) may put her in an Israelite lineage. On the other hand, she may have been a Hittite like her husband.

Controversy surrounded every woman on this list. One woman in the line of Jesus was impregnated by disguising herself as a prostitute and sleeping with her father-in-law. Another was a Gentile prostitute who hid spies on her roof. Another was a Moabite woman who lay at the "feet" of her family redeemer. Another would have been counted as an adulteress under the law of Moses (see Lev 20:10).

Yet all these stories of God's redemption in salvation history culminated in the greatest scandal of all: a virgin who conceived a child by the Holy Spirit. As NT scholars observe, "The inclusion of four women besides Mary, all of whose lives were characterized by the appearance or reality of scandal, may be designed to show that the appearance of scandal attached to the virgin birth did not necessarily disprove its authenticity, since God in previous salvation history had repeatedly worked through apparent or actual scandal."[7]

"He Did Them a Favor by Being Their Son"

The virginal conception of Jesus is made much more impressive when one considers the family line into which he was born. In the words of one anonymous sixth-century preacher,

> This is the miracle: He who adopted and begot fathers was born from their sons! They were made his fathers whose son he was not. He did them a favor by being their son. They, however, offered him nothing by being his forefathers. Among men, fathers adopt whomever they wish to be their sons. This son, however, adopted fathers whom he chose for himself. Among men, sons receive the honor of birth from their fathers. But in Christ's case, the fathers received honor from the son.[8]

---

[7] Andreas Köstenberger, L. Scott Kellum, and Charles L. Quarles, *The Cradle, the Cross, and the Crown* (Nashville: B&H Academic, 2009), 196.

[8] *Incomplete Commentary on Matthew* (*Opus imperfectum*), Homily 1.

The son who chose fathers and mothers for himself is elsewhere described as "the Root and descendant of David" (Rev 22:16). As the "root" and "descendant" of his family line, Jesus is both the heir of David's throne and its very source. He is the beginning and the end of his own family line. Only a virgin-born king could choose his own ancestors and establish their thrones. Only a merciful God would choose this lot to be the family through whom he saved the world.

God's commitment to using imperfect people to accomplish his sovereign purpose is a reminder of the grace he still extends to sinners like us. He did not forget or cancel these sinful people; he redeemed them and gave them a place in salvation history. And he providentially brought salvation from unexpected places—like Gentile women or virgin wombs. And as the nativity stories of Matthew and Luke reveal, none of the gracious plans he has for us in Christ can ever be thwarted.

4

Forerunner to the Virgin-Born King

Luke 1:5–25, 57–80

See, I am sending my messenger ahead of you;
he will prepare your way.
A voice of one crying out in the wilderness:
Prepare the way for the Lord;
make his paths straight!

—MARK 1:2–3[1]

The Gospel of Luke begins with a story about a visit from the angel Gabriel, who announced that a long-awaited baby would finally be born through a miraculous conception. But that baby was not Jesus. Some readers may be confused by Luke's choice to begin his version of the

---

[1] See also Mal 3:1; Isa 40:3; Luke 7:27.

Christmas story by talking about the conception and birth of John the Baptist. Why does the Evangelist not skip ahead to the birth of Jesus— the main character of the gospel story? John's story is too important to gloss over, and its placement at the beginning of Luke's Gospel serves several important purposes.

First, John was an important figure in first-century Judea. John's fame spread far beyond what the NT records about him. The first-century Jewish historian Flavius Josephus (not a Christian source) believed that God brought judgment on the reign of Herod Antipas for putting John to death.[2] In the opening decades of the first century, John's disciples spread far and wide across the Roman world (see Acts 19:1–7).

Second, John spoke for God in a time of national crisis. Luke establishes this context of crisis in the opening statement of his narrative: "In the days of King Herod of Judea, there was a priest of Abijah's division named Zechariah" (Luke 1:5). John the Baptist was a Jewish prophet born into the first generation of Roman occupation under Herod the Great. John prophetically spoke against Herod's son Antipas, which ultimately cost him his life (Luke 3:19–20; 9:9).

Third, all four Gospels begin their accounts of Jesus's adult ministry with descriptions of John as the herald of the Messiah. Through John, God fulfilled the promises the prophets made about a forerunner who would go before the Messiah (Isa 40:3–5; Mal 3:1; 4:5). Because John "warmed up the crowd" for the coming of Christ in his ministry, it was only fitting that the story of the forerunner's miraculous conception would set the stage for the incredible way that the Messiah would enter the world.

Finally, John's infancy story shows that Jesus is superior to the old covenant in every way. Luke's nativity story has two miraculous conceptions, two births, and multiple prophetic announcements. By comparing John and Jesus in this way, Luke communicated that as important as John was in salvation history, Jesus was the ultimate salvation. Luke was probably

---

[2] Josephus, *Ant.* 18.5.2. See also Matt 14:1–12; Mark 6:14–29; Luke 9:9; John 3:24.

with Paul when he made a similar announcement to John's disciples in Ephesus (Acts 19:4).

John	Jesus
John's birth was announced by Gabriel (Luke 1:5–20)	Jesus's birth was announced by Gabriel (Luke 1:26–33)
John was supernaturally conceived when God opened an old woman's womb and enabled her to conceive by Zechariah (Luke 1:21–25)	Jesus was supernaturally conceived in a virgin's womb by the Holy Spirit (Luke 1:34–37)
John was born, circumcised, and named (Luke 1:57–66)	Jesus was born, circumcised, and named (Luke 2:7, 21–24).
Zechariah spoke prophetic words over John at his dedication (Luke 1:67–79).	Simeon spoke prophetic words over Jesus at his dedication (Luke 2:29–32).
John grew strong until the time his public ministry began (Luke 1:80).	Jesus grew strong until the time his public ministry began (Luke 2:40, 52).

Not only do the birth stories of Jesus and John relate to one another; they also call back to similar stories in the OT. Luke continues the story of the Hebrew Bible in Roman-ruled Israel. The people of God may be under a new covenant in Christ, but the same God at work in the lives of Abraham, Samson, and Samuel was still at work in the lives of Jesus and John.

Miraculous Conceptions Under the Old Covenant

Apart from the story of Hannah's conception of Samuel (1 Sam 1:1–27), most of the miraculous conception stories in the OT include an angelic messenger announcing to a childless couple that God is going to cause them to have a baby. These angelic messengers promise that their child will serve an important purpose in God's plan for Israel.

Their message is often accompanied by a sign that reassures the recipients of these messages.

Isaac (Gen 12–21:7)

When God seemed slow to deliver on his promises, Abraham's wife Sarah decided to take matters into her own hands. She arranged for her slave Hagar to be the surrogate mother of Abraham's baby (the old-fashioned way). But when she saw that her eighty-six-year-old husband had made Hagar pregnant, Sarah became jealous and spiteful (Gen 16:4–5; 21:10). Sarah bullied Hagar until the slave woman fled into the wilderness. There Hagar encountered "the angel of the Lord" who told her, "You have conceived and will have a son. You will name him Ishmael, for the Lord has heard your cry of affliction" (Gen 16:11). God protected Hagar and promised her that Ishmael would also become the father of a large nation (Gen 16:10).

God later appeared to Abraham in the company of three angelic visitors. This time Sarah overheard the announcement that she would have a baby within a year's time (Gen 18:10). Sarah initially found the whole idea laughable (Gen 18:12). But God challenged her for her lack of faith: "Why did Sarah laugh, saying, 'Can I really have a baby when I'm old?' Is anything impossible for the Lord? At the appointed time I will come back to you, and in about a year she will have a son" (Gen 18:13–14). In a year's time, the woman who had been barren for nearly a century conceived and gave birth to a son.

This pattern of events was replayed in the stories of Isaac and Rebekah and Jacob and Rachel. Like Sarah, Rebekah and Rachel were "childless" or "barren" (Hb. 'ă-qā-rāh) until the Lord heard their cries and caused them to conceive (Gen 25:21; 29:31). In the patriarchal society of the OT without life insurance policies or 401(k)s, these women depended on sons to provide for them in their old age. As James Hamilton observes, for these barren women, the miracle of a having a child mirrors "the resurrection of a corpse from the dead."[3] Miraculous conceptions and resurrections are a fitting comparison. The giver of all life is sovereign over every aspect of it. The same God who created the biological mechanisms of human reproduction can directly intervene in their processes anytime he pleases.

Samson (Judges 13)

The book of Judges tells the story of what happened in Israel between the conquest of the land and the time of the kings. Judges frames moral decline in pre-monarchial Israel as a recurring cycle of events: idolatry, judgment, repentance, renewal, and apostasy. Whenever Israel cried out to God, he would raise up a judge or military leader to deliver them from their enemies. A short time later, the people would rebel against God and the whole cycle would begin again (Judg 2:11–19). These judges bore some superficial similarity to Moses or Joshua in their roles as Israel's defenders, but the judges were nowhere near the spiritual leaders that Moses and Joshua were. In fact, each judge was worse than the one who came before.

Samson, the last judge in the cycle, was the most tragic figure of them all. He bore little resemblance to the heroic figure often depicted in Bible storybooks. But this morally flawed superman had his own miraculous origin story, complete with an angelic announcement and a supernatural conception. Samson's mother was unable to conceive. But then "the angel of the LORD" tells her that she "will conceive and give birth to a son" (Judg 13:3). She is also told that "the boy will be a Nazirite to God from birth" (Judg 13:5). The Nazirite vow gets its name from the Hebrew word *nazar*, which means "to abstain from" or "to consecrate." The angel

---

[3] James M. Hamilton, Jr., *Typology: Understanding the Bible's Promise-Shaped Patterns—How Old Testament Expectations are Fulfilled in Christ* (Grand Rapids: Zondervan Academic, 2022), 105.

instructed Samson's parents never to allow him to drink wine or beer or eat anything unclean (see Num 6:1–21). After this angelic messenger leaves, Samson's parents realize that the messenger they had been speaking with was God himself.

If the conception of Isaac was about God keeping his promises, the conception of Samson was about the liberation of his people from bondage. But Samson was a poor savior figure. God may have given him superhuman strength, but Samson was a reckless, violent, and sexually promiscuous man who repeatedly broke his vows to the Lord. Samson may have sacrificed his life for Israel, but such sacrifice would have been unnecessary if he had been faithful to his vows to God in the first place (see Judg 16:21–31).

The Birth of the Forerunner (Luke 1:5–25, 57–80)

The story of John the Baptist may be found in the NT side of the canon, but John is best understood as the last of the OT prophets. Jesus himself indicated this when he said, "The Law and the Prophets were until John" (Luke 16:16; cf. Matt 11:13). So, it is only fitting that John's conception and birth fulfills the pattern of miraculous births across the OT (Luke 1:5–25, 39–45, 57–80).

Luke begins his narrative by introducing us to the priest Zechariah and his wife Elizabeth. Luke describes them as "righteous in God's sight" (Luke 1:6). This older couple never had children because Elizabeth was "childless" or "barren" (Luke 1:6–7, 36).[4] Zechariah's priestly division was called up for service to the Temple in Jerusalem. Zechariah was then chosen by lot to burn incense in the Lord's sanctuary. While he was offering incense, the angel Gabriel appeared next to the altar. Though Zechariah was initially overcome with fear (something that happens every time people meet angels in the Gospel of Luke), the angel told him not to be

---

[4] Elizabeth is described as "childless" (*steira*) with the same word used to describe Sarah (Gen 11:30), Rebekah (25:21), and Rachel (29:31) in the LXX.

afraid because God had heard his prayer.[5] Gabriel told Zechariah that his wife, who was "well along in years," would bear him a son whom he would name John, which means "graced by God" (Luke 1:7, 13).

Gabriel, whose name means "God is my strength," is the same angelic messenger who spoke to the prophet Daniel (Daniel 8–10).[6] Several elements of Zechariah's encounter with Gabriel parallel Daniel's experience. First, Daniel and Zechariah received a vision of Gabriel when they were offering sacrifices to the Lord on behalf of Israel (Dan 9:20–21; Luke 1:9–11). Second, Gabriel gave Daniel and Zechariah visions of what was to come (Dan 8:17; Luke 1:22). Third, Daniel and Zechariah were both overcome with fear at the sight of Gabriel (Dan 8:17; Luke 1:11–12). Fourth, Gabriel told Daniel and Zechariah that God had heard their prayers (Dan 9:23; Luke 1:13). Finally, both Daniel and Zechariah were silenced (Dan 10:15; Luke 1:20). In both accounts, Gabriel delivers a message of hope for Israel.[7]

Gabriel promises that John will be a source of joy for many and that he will be great in the sight of the Lord. Like Samson before him, John was instructed to "never drink wine or beer" (Luke 1:15a). But that is where the similarity with the biblical judge ends. Unlike the carnal Samson, John would be "filled with the Holy Spirit while still in his mother's womb" (Luke 1:15b). John would be a prophet who would "turn many of the children of Israel to the Lord their God" (Luke 1:16). He would preach in the "spirit and power of Elijah" (Luke 1:17; see also Mal 4:5–6; Matt 17:11–13). Like Isaiah, John would be the herald of the Messiah (Luke 3:4–6; cf. Isa 40:3–5). Luke emphasizes the old covenant activity of the Holy Spirit in John's life as a precursor to the way

---

[5] See also Luke 1:29–30; 2:9–10; 24:1–5.

[6] Gabriel also played a large role in Jewish literature written between the Old and New Testaments. See *1 Enoch* 9:1–3; 10:9; 20:7; 40:9; 54:6; 71:8–12.

[7] David W. Pao and Eckhard J. Schnabel, "Luke," in *Commentary on the New Testament Use of the Old Testament*, ed. G. K. Beale and D. A. Carson (Grand Rapids: Baker, 2007), 255.

he will write about the new covenant activity of the Spirit in the life of the church in Acts.

Zechariah expressed doubt that an old couple could have a baby (Luke 1:18), much like Sarah when she laughed at the same angelic message (Gen 18:11–13). Gabriel rebuked Zechariah and muted him until the naming of John (Luke 1:20).[8] Elizabeth, by contrast, is portrayed as a woman of deep faith. When she conceives John, she, like Hannah before her, extols the Lord for his provision: "The Lord has done this for me. He has looked with favor in these days to take away my disgrace among the people" (Luke 1:25; see also 1 Sam 2:1–10).[9]

The *Benedictus*: The Song of Zechariah (Luke 1:57–79)

After the birth of John, the friends and extended family of his parents expressed confusion about their decision to name him "John." They presumed he would be named after his father. Zechariah, who still could not speak, wrote "His name is John" on a tablet and the power of speech suddenly returned to him (Luke 1:63–64).

Zechariah, who had not spoken in nearly a year, was suddenly filled with the Holy Spirit and began to praise God and prophesy. His song, known as the *Benedictus* (from the Latin word meaning "blessed"), would later become an important part of Christian liturgy and worship. This song celebrates the faithfulness of God to the ancestors of Israel. The promises

---

[8] Zechariah's unbelief here parallels the instruction of Eccl 5:1–3, where the preacher encourages obedience in the offering of the sacrifice and relative silence before the Lord. "God is in heaven and you are on earth, so let your words be few" (Eccl 5:2).

[9] Compare the wording of Luke 1:20 with 1 Sam 2:30, where Hannah prophesies, "This is the declaration of the Lord, the God of Israel: 'I did say that your family and your forefather's family would walk before me forever. But now,' this is the Lord's declaration, 'no longer! For those who honor me I will honor, but those who despise me will be disgraced.'"

he made long ago to Abraham, David, and the prophets were being fulfilled before the eyes of the old priest. But this song also looks ahead to what God is about to do through the respective ministries of John and Jesus.

Zechariah, who just months before doubted whether God could make his elderly wife pregnant, now stood before a crowd of family members with new evidence of the Spirit's illumination on his heart and mind.[10] As a priest, Zechariah may have been a student of the Scripture before this moment, but he did not fully understand what it meant when he lived in unbelief. But now the Holy Spirit had given him the ability to understand Scripture and prophesy its message with power.

> Blessed is the Lord, the God of Israel,
> because he has visited
> and provided redemption for his people.
> He has raised up a horn of salvation for us
> in the house of his servant David,
> just as he spoke by the mouth
> of his holy prophets in ancient times;
> salvation from our enemies
> and from the hand of those who hate us. (Luke 1:68–71)

Zechariah prophesied about the Messiah before he spoke about John. As the prophets of Israel foretold (Luke 1:70), the Messiah would provide redemption for his people (Luke 1:68), rescue from their enemies (Luke 1:74), and forgiveness of sins (Luke 1:77). Zechariah acknowledged the faithfulness of God in keeping the covenants that he made with David (Luke 1:69–70) and Abraham (Luke 1:72–73). Zechariah's call back to these older covenants laid the groundwork

---

[10] Compare with Luke's account of Peter, who thrice denied even knowing Jesus on the night before his crucifixion (Luke 22:54–62). Weeks later, following the new covenant outpouring of the Holy Spirit, Peter "stood up . . . raised his voice . . . and proclaimed" Christ boldly before thousands (Acts 2:14, 41).

for his description of the new covenant established by the Messiah (Ezek 36:24–27).[11]

Zechariah then turned the attention of his prophecy to John, whom he described as the forerunner of the Messiah anticipated in Mal 3:1 and Isa 40:3.

> And you, child, will be called
> a prophet of the Most High,
> for you will go before the Lord
> to prepare his ways,
> to give his people knowledge of salvation
> through the forgiveness of their sins. (Luke 1:76–77)

John would be a "prophet of the Most High" (Luke 1:76) who prepares the people for the coming of the Messiah. Likewise, John would proclaim a message about salvation, repentance, and forgiveness.

The *Benedictus* closes with one of the most moving descriptions of the Messiah in the NT:

> Because of our God's merciful compassion,
> the dawn from on high will visit us
> to shine on those who live in darkness
> and the shadow of death,
> to guide our feet into the way of peace. (Luke 1:78–79)

Zechariah described the soon-coming Messiah as the "dawn from on high," the "dayspring from on high" (Luke 1:78 KJV), or the "rising sun" (Luke 1:78 NIV) who comes to us because of the great mercy of God. Jesus is the "bright morning star" (Rev 22:16) who brings light to a lost and dying world and the shepherd who accompanies us through the valley of death's shadow. As the Word incarnate, the Messiah illuminates the path before our feet, guiding us to true and lasting peace (Luke 1:79;

---

[11] See John MacArthur, *Luke 1–5*, MacArthur New Testament Commentary 7 (Chicago: Moody, 2009), 113–24.

Ps 119:105). As the messianic forerunner, John's role was "to bear witness of that Light" (John 1:8 KJV).

The Virgin-Born King is Superior to the Old Covenant Prophets

Luke is preparing readers for the advent of Jesus by connecting his story to the miraculous activity of God under the old covenant and John the forerunner. John's conception may have been like Isaac's or Samson's, but he was an entirely different kind of man. Jesus himself acknowledged John's superiority over these OT figures: "I tell you, among those born of women no one is greater than John" (Luke 7:28).

The miraculous conception stories under the old covenant culminate in the new covenant conception of Jesus. Gabriel may have made similar announcements to Zechariah and Mary, but Luke shows us how Jesus is superior to John in every way. John is "great in the sight of the Lord" (Luke 1:15). But Jesus is "great" on his own accord as the Son of the Most High (Luke 1:32). John was "filled with the Holy Spirit while still in his mother's womb" (Luke 1:15), but Jesus was conceived by the Holy Spirit. John prepares the way for the Lord, but Jesus is the Lord who himself ushers in God's kingdom.[12]

As Darrell Bock explains, "In every way, Jesus is superior to John. John is born out of barrenness; Jesus is born of a virgin. John is a great prophet before the Lord; Jesus is great as the promised Davidic ruler. John paves the way; Jesus is the Way."[13] It was fitting that the Son who is superior to the prophets would also have a superior conception. The virgin-born king is superior to the patriarchs, judges, and prophets in every way (see Heb 1:1–3; 3:1–6).

---

[12] Raymond Brown, "Note: Luke's Description of the Virginal Conception," *Theological Studies* 35, no. 2 (1974): 360–62.

[13] Darrell L. Bock, *A Theology of Luke and Acts: God's Promised Program, Realized for All Nations* (Grand Rapids: Zondervan, 2012), 100–101.

5

The Virgin-Born King Announced

Luke 1:26–38

Called . . . to bear in her womb
Infinite weight and lightness; to carry
in hidden, finite inwardness,
nine months of Eternity . . .
—Denise Levertov, "Annunciation"[1]

We have become accustomed to seeing extravagant baby announcements in our social media-saturated age. Happy couples will often take to Facebook and Instagram with sonogram photos. Sometimes they post pictures of their other children wearing "big brother" or "big sister" T-shirts. When my wife and I found out we were pregnant with our

---

[1] Denise Levertov, *A Door in the Hive* (New York: New Directions, 1989), 87.

firstborn, we cobbled together a fake movie trailer to announce our pregnancy to friends and family. Unfortunately, as tired and busy parents of a preschooler, we gave our second-born child no such hullabaloo.

No matter how creative some of these pregnancy announcements may be, they all pale in comparison to the angelic announcement Gabriel gave Mary in Luke 1:26–38, which Christians around the world celebrate as the Annunciation. In this passage, the angel Gabriel announces to the virgin Mary that she will supernaturally conceive a son by the power of the Holy Spirit. Gabriel also declares that her son will be the long-awaited Messiah who will reign forever on David's throne.

Mary Received God's Grace (Luke 1:26–30)

In the sixth month, the angel Gabriel was sent by God to a town in Galilee called Nazareth, to a virgin engaged to a man named Joseph, of the house of David. The virgin's name was Mary. And the angel came to her and said, "Greetings, favored woman! The Lord is with you." But she was deeply troubled by this statement, wondering what kind of greeting this could be. Then the angel told her, "Do not be afraid, Mary, for you have found favor with God." (Luke 1:26–30)

First-century Nazareth never would have made its way onto a list of the top-ten most desirable places to live in ancient Israel. It was a small farming village in Galilee, far removed from the hustle and bustle of Jerusalem. Ninety miles north of Jerusalem, Nazareth was culturally, religiously, and politically isolated from the capital city. Because it was north of Samaria, it was also more ethnically diverse, a region inhabited by Gentiles and Jewish descendants.[2]

---

[2] See P. Schreiner, *Matthew*, 81–82 (see chap. 2, n. 14).

Many Jews outside of Nazareth looked down on its residents for having "an unpolished dialect, a lack of culture, and . . . moral laxity."[3] Nathanael later expressed this sentiment when he asked, "Can anything good come out of Nazareth?" (John 1:46). That God chose this reviled little village to be his Son's hometown further underscores the humility of the Suffering Servant described in Isaiah 53:

> He grew up before him like a young plant
> and like a root out of dry ground.
> He didn't have an impressive form
> or majesty that we should look at him. . . .
> He was like someone people turned away from;
> he was despised, and we didn't value him. (Isa 53:2–3)

Gabriel, the same angel who appeared to the prophet Daniel and Zechariah the priest, came from the presence of God to deliver a message to Mary. Mary (or Miriam) was a common woman with a common name.[4] She was betrothed to Joseph, a carpenter who had David's royal blood running through his veins. But she was also a "virgin" who had not yet consummated a sexual relationship with her betrothed husband (Luke 1:27, 34).

Although we do not know with certainty how old Mary would have been here, Jewish tradition recommended marriage for boys between the ages of fourteen and eighteen and marriage for girls immediately upon

---

[3] Jerry W. Batson, "Nazareth, Nazarene," in *Holman Illustrated Bible Dictionary*, ed. Chad Brand, Charles Draper, and Archie England (Nashville: Holman Bible, 2003), 1177–78.

[4] Several women in the New Testament shared Mary's name: Mary Magdalene (Luke 8:2); Mary of Bethany (Luke 10:38–42; John 11:1–43); the wife of Clopas (John 19:25); the mother of James the younger and Joses (Mark 15:40; Luke 24:10); the "other Mary" (Matt 27:61; 28:1); the mother of John Mark (Acts 12:12); and a woman in the Roman church (Rom 16:6). It has been the most common female name in the world ever since.

puberty.[5] Mary likely would have been a young teenager at the time of Gabriel's announcement. The pairing of Joseph and Mary may have been chosen by their parents or leaders in the community. It is also possible that Joseph initiated the arrangement and sought approval from Mary's father. The Bible has examples of both types of arranged marriages (see Genesis 24; 29:1–30).

Unsurprisingly, the angel's greeting "deeply troubled" Mary (Luke 1:29). Her response fits the biblical pattern. Abraham fell facedown before the angel of the Lord (Gen 17:3; 18:2–3). The father of Samson exclaimed, "We're certainly going to die . . . because we have seen God!" (Judg 13:22). Daniel was "terrified and fell facedown" at the sight of Gabriel (Dan 8:17). Zechariah was "terrified and overcome with fear" at the same sight (Luke 1:12).

But Gabriel met Mary with words of peace and assurance. Do not miss the force of the angelic exclamation in his greeting: "Greetings, favored woman!" (Luke 1:28). The title "favored woman," or "favored one" (ESV), indicates that she had been favored by someone else.[6] The Latin Vulgate used by many Roman Catholics places the emphasis on Mary's grace when it translates verse 28 as "Hail [Mary], *full of grace*, the Lord is with thee: blessed art thou among women" (Luke 1:28 DRA). But the Greek text stresses God's grace in Mary's life. By faith, Mary received God's grace and special favor; she was not herself the source of grace or merit (Luke 1:30).[7]

---

[5] Victor P. Hamilton, "Marriage (Old Testament and Ancient Near East)," in *The Anchor Yale Bible Dictionary*, ed. David Noel Freedman (New Haven: Yale University Press, 1992), 4:563.

[6] The perfect middle participle here comes from a verb that means "to show grace, bestow favor." *NIDNTTE* 4:653, s.v. "χαριτόω."

[7] *NIDNTTE* 4:656–57, s.v. "χαριτόω."

He Will Reign Forever (Luke 1:31–33)

Now listen: You will conceive and give birth to a son, and you will name him Jesus. He will be great and will be called the Son of the Most High, and the Lord God will give him the throne of his father David. He will reign over the house of Jacob forever, and his kingdom will have no end. (Luke 1:31–33)

The angel told Mary she would conceive and name her son "Jesus." "Jesus," or "Joshua," which means "Yahweh is salvation" or "the Lord saves," would have been an extremely common name in first-century Judaism, much like "Josh" or "Joshua" is today.[8] But its familiarity did not take away from its great significance in the biblical story. Joseph received the same instruction to name the baby "Jesus" in Matt 1:21, where the angelic visitor explicitly explained the meaning of the name: "He will save his people from their sins."

Gabriel also told Mary that Jesus will be "great"—greater than the prophets, greater than David, and greater than John. The term Luke uses for "great" (*megas*) here is only used in the Greek translation of the OT to describe God himself.[9] The title "Son of the Most High" was "simply another way of saying 'Son of God.'"[10] Others had been called "sons of God" before: angels (Gen 6:2–4; Job 1:6; 2:1; 38:7), the people of Israel (Deut 14:1; Hos 1:10), and kings (Ps 2:6–9). No one, however, had ever

---

[8] Jesus would be *Yeshua* in Hebrew or *Iēsous* in Greek. The New Testament lists two other Jesuses: Joshua, son of Eliezer (Luke 3:29) and "Jesus who is called Justus" (Col 4:11).

[9] See Pss 48:1 [47:2 LXX]; 76:1 [75:2 LXX]; 86:10 [85:10 LXX]; 135:5 [134:5 LXX]. See also Bock, *Luke*, 1:113 (see chap. 2, n. 12).

[10] Bock, 1:113. Bock identifies several places in the OT, apocryphal, and Qumran literature where the title "Most High" refers to God: Gen 14:18–20, 22; Num 24:16; Ps 7:17; Dan 4:24; *1 Enoch* 9:3; Testament of Levi 16:3; Qumran 4Q246.

been declared the Son of God in the same way Christ would be at his baptism just a few chapters later:

> When all the people were baptized, Jesus also was baptized. As he was praying, heaven opened, and the Holy Spirit descended on him in a physical appearance like a dove. And a voice came from heaven: "You are my beloved Son; with you I am well-pleased." (Luke 3:21–22)

Mary did not know what it would mean to have God for a son, but she did share in the common Jewish hope for a Messiah who would sit on David's throne. The promise made to David in 2 Sam 7:12–16 would finally be fulfilled. But the ruler Gabriel promised was not just another Jewish monarch in a long line of failures. Jesus would not be another earthly king who would offer some temporary deliverance from Israel's foreign occupants. This virgin-born king would be the eternal monarch of an everlasting kingdom. This message closely parallels Daniel's prophecy concerning the divine Son of Man:

> He was given dominion
> and glory and a kingdom,
> so that those of every people,
> nation, and language
> should serve him.
> His dominion is an everlasting dominion
> that will not pass away,
> and his kingdom is one
> that will not be destroyed. (Dan 7:14; see also Isa 9:6–7)[11]

Gabriel's announcement relays a tension seen across Scripture. As the Second Person of the Trinity, Christ has eternally existed as God the Son. But when he became a human being, Christ was given the title of being the Son of God and the heir of David's throne. Christ is the eternal,

---

[11] See also Matt 24:30; 26:64; Mark 14:62.

preexistent Son who became the royal Son of David's line in time (Ps 2:7; cf. Heb 1:5).[12]

The Spirit Overshadowed Mary (Luke 1:34–37)

Mary asked the angel, "How can this be, since I have not had sexual relations with a man?" The angel replied to her, "The Holy Spirit will come upon you, and the power of the Most High will overshadow you. Therefore, the holy one to be born will be called the Son of God. And consider your relative Elizabeth—even she has conceived a son in her old age, and this is the sixth month for her who was called childless. For nothing will be impossible with God." (Luke 1:34–37)

When Gabriel announced that Mary would conceive, she asked, "How can this be, since I have not had sexual relations with a man?" Mary may have been an innocent, young Jewish girl, but she was no dolt. Ancient peoples may not have known the intricacies of modern embryonic science, but they knew how babies were made. Mary knew she had not yet consummated her marriage to Joseph. She also knew she had not been sexually active or raped (as some later critics of Christianity would contend).

At first glance, Mary's question, "How can this be?" sounds a lot like Zechariah's, who asked, "How can I know this?" (Luke 1:18). But a closer examination reveals a difference in the way the question was asked and the way the question was received. When Zechariah asked his question, which was about how he could really know that Elizabeth would conceive, Gabriel chided him for his unbelief. When Mary asked her question, which was about how this event would take place, the angel explained how God would cause her to conceive. Zechariah expressed doubt, but Mary expressed holy curiosity.

---

[12] For a helpful exegetical and theological exploration of this tension in the book of Hebrews, see R. B. Jamieson, *The Paradox of Sonship: Christology in the Epistle to the Hebrews* (Downers Grove: IVP Academic, 2021).

Gabriel answered Mary with the promise that the Holy Spirit would cause her to conceive and that the "power of the Most High" would "overshadow" her. Most occurrences of this verb translated "covered" or "overshadowed" (*episkiazō*) throughout Scripture indicate God's power and presence. The Greek translation of the Old Testament uses this verb to describe how the cloud "overshadowed" the tabernacle and filled it with God's glorious presence (Exod 40:34). The Psalter uses the term to describe God's overshadowing presence in our lives (Pss 91:4; 140:7).[13] In the transfiguration of Jesus, a cloud signifying the presence of God "overshadowed" the disciples (Luke 9:34).

Luke does not detail the mechanics of how the Spirit caused Mary to conceive. To do so would rob dignity and sanctity from the event. But this much is clear: The Spirit's presence caused her to conceive.[14] From the very beginning of the biblical story, the Holy Spirit was depicted as an important agent of God's creative power. At creation, the "Spirit of God" cast his shadow over the creation of the world when he "was hovering over the surface of the waters" (Gen 1:2). The same Spirit was at work when "the LORD God formed the man out of the dust from the ground and breathed the breath of life into his nostrils, and the man became a living being" (Gen 2:7). Here in Nazareth, the same life-giving Spirit involved in the creation of the world and the creation of man would create life within a virgin's womb. Because God the Holy Spirit caused Mary to become pregnant, the child produced in this conception would be called "the holy one" and "the Son of God."

To support this prophetic claim, Gabriel cites Elizabeth's pregnancy as evidence of God's power. If God can cause an old woman to conceive, he certainly can bring life to a virgin womb. Gabriel's response to Mary's question also parallels angelic messages associated with miraculous conceptions in the OT:

---

[13] I. Howard Marshall, *The Gospel of Luke*, NIGNT (Grand Rapids: Eerdmans, 1978), 70–71.

[14] Rowe, *Early Narrative Christology*, 39 (see introduction, n. 9).

"'Is anything impossible for the LORD? At the appointed time I will come back to you, and in about a year she will have a son'" (Gen 18:14).

"The angel replied to her, 'The Holy Spirit will come upon you, and the power of the Most High will overshadow you. . . . Consider your relative Elizabeth—even she has conceived a son in her old age . . . For nothing will be impossible with God'" (Luke 1:35a, 36a, 37).[15]

"The angel of the LORD appeared to the woman and said to her, 'Although you are unable to conceive and have no children, you will conceive and give birth to a son'. . . . He said to me, 'You will conceive and give birth to a son'" (Judg 13:3, 7; cf. Gen 16:11).

"The angel came to her. . . . Then the angel told her, 'Do not be afraid, Mary, for you have found favor with God. Now listen: You will conceive and give birth to a son, and you will name him Jesus'" (Luke 1:28, 30–31).[16]

But unlike Elizabeth, Sarah, and the mother of Samson, Mary's pregnancy did not come through the natural means of procreation. Under the old covenant, God merely catalyzed the natural mechanisms of natural sexual reproduction by opening the wombs of older or barren women. However, this young, betrothed woman had never attempted to procreate. The conception of Jesus is no mere enhancement of the normal means of procreation, no divine fertility treatment. This conception by the Holy

---

[15] Early NT manuscripts favor the reading "no message from God will ever fail" (א B D W). See Philip Wesley Comfort, *A Commentary on the Manuscripts and Text of the New Testament* (Grand Rapids: Kregel Academic, 2015), 207–8. Even if the reading "nothing will be impossible" is the later reading, the literary parallels between the stories still hold.

[16] Luke 1:31 (καὶ ἰδοὺ συλλήμψῃ ἐν γαστρὶ καὶ τέξῃ υἱόν) amalgamates the LXX phrasing from Judg 13:3 (καὶ συλλήμψῃ υἱόν) and Judg 13:5 (ἐν γαστρὶ ἕξεις καὶ τέξῃ υἱόν).

Spirit was a direct act of divine creative activity by which God "prepared a body" for Christ (Heb 10:5).

Answering Objections: The Virginal Conception Was Only a Metaphor

Some have suggested that the phrase "the Holy Spirit will come upon you" should be interpreted figuratively, not literally. In a recent book on the virginal conception, Andrew T. Lincoln argued that Luke presents Jesus as both the divine son conceived by the Holy Spirit and a literal, biological son of David (with Joseph as his father). Lincoln cites a sermon from Acts that speaks of Jesus being born of the "seed" or "sperm" (*spermatos*) of David (Acts 13:23).

For Lincoln, the idea of a "virgin birth" needs total redefinition. Lincoln reimagines the Holy Spirit's role in Jesus's conception in a new way that he believes corresponds to OT texts. Lincoln notes that ancient Jews believed it took three to tango: babies were made with a man, a woman, and the direct hand of God. Lincoln has texts like Gen 4:1 in mind, which reads, "The man was intimate with his wife Eve, and she conceived and gave birth to Cain. She said, 'I have had a male child with the LORD's help'" (see also Gen 30:22–23; Job 10:8–12; 31:15; Pss 100:3; 139:13–16; Jer 1:5). Lincoln interprets Luke 1:34–35 in the same way.

Lincoln also insists that this passage must be read in dialogue with other texts that seem to confirm that Jesus is the physical descendant of David. He proposes that Luke's description of the virginal conception is best understood as an intentional paradox: Jesus was conceived by God's help in the virgin's womb and fathered by Joseph. Lincoln claims there is precedent for this in Greco-Roman biographies that paint figures like Alexander the Great as both the son of Philip II and the son of Apollo. Passages that refer to Joseph as Jesus's father (Luke 4:22; John 6:42) must be read literally and biologically, and biblical language about the Holy Spirit coming on Mary is reduced to a metaphor for God's unique presence in the incarnation.

Lincoln's efforts to maintain biblical and creedal authority while denying the virginal conception miscarry on delivery. Lincoln must explain away clear indicators of a virginal conception in Luke's narrative. Why would Mary ask a question like "How can this be?" if the angel was only intending to communicate that she would conceive a child later, after Mary had consummated her relationship with Joseph? Why would Luke go to such great lengths to compare Jesus and John's conceptions if John's conception was so unusual, and Jesus's was so normal?

Furthermore, to make his proposal work, Lincoln must entirely dismiss Matthew's account about Joseph's plan to divorce Mary for adultery. Joseph could not be the biological father of Jesus if Mary was pregnant "before they came together" (Matt 1:18).

See Andrew T. Lincoln, *Born of a Virgin? Reconceiving Jesus in the Bible, Tradition, and Theology* (Grand Rapids: Eerdmans, 2013), 99–124; Friedrich Schleiermacher, *The Christian Faith* §98.2; Joseph A. Fitzmyer, "The Virginal Conception of Jesus in the New Testament," *Theological Studies* 34, no. 4 (1973): 542–74; Oliver D. Crisp, *Analyzing Doctrine: Toward a Systematic Theology* (Waco, TX: Baylor University Press, 2019), 157–78.

The Response of a Servant (Luke 1:38)

"See, I am the Lord's servant," said Mary. "May it happen to me as you have said." Then the angel left her. (Luke 1:38)

Mary knew full well the potential consequences of her pregnancy. She could have lost her betrothed husband Joseph, who would have known that he was not the father of the baby she was carrying. She could have been shamed as a harlot and tried as an adulteress according to the law of Moses (Lev 20:10; Num 5:11–31). Yet Mary did not offer excuses or protest the angelic announcement. Instead, she modeled complete surrender to God's service. Like Jesus, she could say, "Not my will, but yours, be done" (Luke 22:42).

Mary's obedience mirrored the radical obedience of Abraham who was asked to sacrifice his long-awaited son (Gen 22:1–19).[17] Just as Abraham was about to strike Isaac on the altar, "the angel of the LORD," presumably God himself, stopped him and declared, "All the nations of the earth will be blessed by your offspring because you have obeyed my command" (Gen 22:18). This promise did not reach its total fulfillment until the moment Mary was standing before Gabriel and consented to carry God's Son—the true seed of Abraham who blesses the nations—in her womb. But whereas God provided a lamb for the burnt offering in the place of Abraham's son (Gen 22:8), Mary's son would become the burnt offering in her place and ours.

Answering Objections: God Violated Mary

In recent years, critics of Christianity have accused God of impregnating Mary without her consent. They allege that God himself used his position of ultimate authority to force an unwanted pregnancy on Mary—that God "raped" Mary. This rhetoric is irreverent and blasphemous—a heresy unique to our post-sexual-revolution world. Along these same lines, liberal theologians like the late John Shelby Spong (1931–2021) have argued that the Christian doctrine of the virgin birth suppresses women and can be used to justify sexual harassment and assault.

The mere suggestion that God violated Mary in such an evil manner is vile and offensive. However, those making this accusation do not really believe Mary conceived a child by divine rape or any

---

[17] See Hans Urs von Balthasar and Joseph Ratzinger, *Mary: The Church at the Source*, trans. Adrian Walker (San Francisco: Ignatius, 2005), 104–5.

other kind of supernatural conception. They are basically atheists making a thinly veiled argument that the Christian faith is morally repugnant and internally inconsistent. Atheists and agnostics use similar lines of reasoning when they accuse God of moral evil for commanding the Canaanite conquest.

No plain, charitable reading of this passage would lead the reader to conclude that God impregnated Mary in a sexual or nonconsensual manner.

First, God's law strictly prohibited this kind of sexual abuse. Rape was a capital offense morally equivalent to attacking and murdering one's neighbor (Deut 22:25–29). God is the defender of and shelter for the abused and oppressed, not a perpetrator or abuser (Pss 9:9; 72:4; 82:3).

Second, the conception of Jesus described in the Gospels is non-sexual in nature. Unlike the stories of pagan mythology that involve gods like Apollo, Zeus, and Poseidon coming to the earth and sleeping with mortal women, the virginal conception of Jesus involved no sexual contact between God and Mary, let alone nonconsensual sexual contact. Mary asked Gabriel how it was possible for her to conceive if she had not had sexual relations with a man, and the angel told her that the seemingly impossible is completely within God's power. The Creator of the laws of nature is in no way subservient to them.

Finally, Mary gave the angel announcing this news a clear statement of informed consent. Mary had not yet conceived Jesus when the angel came to her (Luke 1:31, 35). But her reply was one of faithful obedience to God: "See, I am the Lord's servant. . . . May it happen to me as you have said" (Luke 1:38). Mary did not begrudgingly accept this offer or merely grant God permission. The phrase "may it happen to me" (*genoito moi*) denotes a willingness and an eagerness on the part of Mary to serve the Lord in this way. Mary saw herself as a servant of the Lord who found fulfillment in her obedience to him (Luke 1:48; cf. 1 Sam 1:11; Ps 86:16b).

See Blake Hereth, "Mary, Did You Consent?" *Religious Studies* 58, no. 4 (2022): 677–700; John Shelby Spong, *Born of a Woman: A Bishop Rethinks the Birth of Jesus* (New York: Harper Collins, 1992), 201–24; Karen Swallow Prior, "'Let It Be': Mary's Radical Declaration of Consent," *The Atlantic*, December 24, 2012, https://www.theatlantic.com/sexes/archive/2012/12/let-it-be-marys-radical-declaration-of-consent/266616/.

6

My Soul Magnifies the Lord

Luke 1:39–56

The tender Mother of Christ . . . teaches us, with her words and by
the example of her experience, how to know, love, and praise God.

–Martin Luther[1]

Some years ago, my wife and I bought our son a telescope for Christmas. To be honest, this gift was probably as much for me as it was for him. I love gazing into the night sky, especially on cold winter nights miles away from the lights of the city.

Stars are colossal objects. Over a million of our worlds could fit within the very average-sized sun at the center of our own solar system. Supergiant stars like Antares are 700 times larger than our sun. Yet even when we look at a star as large as Betelgeuse—it would take over

---

[1] Martin Luther, "The Magnificat," trans. A. T. W. Steinhaeuser, in *LW* 21:301; *WA* 7:548–49.

half-a-quadrillion planet Earths to fill it—it looks small, reddish, and faint to the naked eye.

How could something so large look so small to us? The distance between our planet and these stars gives the appearance or perspective that these massive objects are "little stars." The farther away a star is, the darker it appears to our eyes because less of its light can reach us. Telescopes magnify the stars for us by capturing more light than our naked eyes are capable of perceiving. With their mirrors and lenses, telescopes amplify these distant objects for us. When we magnify the stars, we do not add anything to their actual size. We make our perception and appreciation of them larger.

God, too, is far greater than our finite hearts and minds can possibly imagine. Yet our creatureliness and sin-affected minds sometimes leave us with the false impression that he is small or far removed from us. To change this perception, we magnify God in worship and praise. We "make God great" in our hearts and minds.

Human praise does not magnify God because he is small and needs our praises to be made larger. In our praise, we can do nothing to add to the glory or the splendor of his being. However, when we magnify the Lord, our hearts mirror his greatness. The little mirrors of our hearts, like those Newtonian reflectors in telescopes, cannot do justice to the size and beauty of God's radiance. Yet when we magnify the Lord, we can see his works more clearly. We more fully appreciate who he is and what he has for us.

The mother of our Lord modeled this kind of God-magnifying activity for us in the song of praise recorded in Luke 1:46–55. This song, commonly known as the *Magnificat* (from the Latin word meaning "magnifies"), draws richly from the praise tradition of the OT. Mary's praise embodies the Christian life as a whole—one with heart, mind, and hands wholly devoted to God.

Mary here focused her praise on the way God fulfilled his promises to Israel and the way he had shown mercy to the humble and afflicted. She praised God for his attributes and his works. She also yearned for the coming of God's future kingdom, a time when those who belong to God and his Messiah will reign with him.

The Visitation (Luke 1:39–45, 56)

In those days Mary set out and hurried to a town in the hill country of Judah where she entered Zechariah's house and greeted Elizabeth. . . . And Mary stayed with her about three months; then she returned to her home. (Luke 1:39–40, 56)

The context of Mary's *Magnificat* is her stay in Elizabeth's home (also known as "the Visitation"). Luke tells us that Mary "hurried" to a town in the Judean countryside where her relative Elizabeth lived. Mary stayed there about three months before returning to Nazareth.[2] So why did she make this trip in the first place? Some have suggested that Mary used Zechariah and Elizabeth's house as a home for unwed mothers—a place where she could have escaped the judgmental eyes of her fellow Nazarenes. But the more likely explanation is that Mary made haste to Elizabeth's house to see for herself what Gabriel had told her about her relative's extraordinary pregnancy.

Mary wanted to see the woman who had long been called "childless" and who had "conceived a son in her old age" (Luke 1:36). Mary wanted to see for herself that "nothing will be impossible with God" (Luke 1:37). Upon her arrival, these women spent a remarkable season together reflecting on the things God had done for them.

When Elizabeth heard Mary's greeting, the baby leaped inside her, and Elizabeth was filled with the Holy Spirit. Then she exclaimed with a loud cry, "Blessed are you among women, and your child will be blessed! How could this happen to me, that the

---

[2] Nicholas Perrin suggests a parallel to Moses's mother Jochebed, who hid Moses for three months prior to putting him in the Nile (Exod 2:2). See Nicholas Perrin, *Luke*, TNTC (Downers Grove: IVP Academic, 2022), 39.

mother of my Lord should come to me? For you see, when the
sound of your greeting reached my ears, the baby leaped for joy
inside me. Blessed is she who has believed that the Lord would
fulfill what he has spoken to her!" (Luke 1:41–45)

When she came within hearing distance of Mary's greeting,
Elizabeth was filled with the Holy Spirit (Luke 1:41) and began speaking prophetically—much like Zechariah did after John's birth. The work
of the Spirit in John's family foreshadowed the Spirit's new covenant
activity in the early church when God's Spirit was poured out and "both
men and women" began to "prophesy" (Acts 2:18).

By the Spirit, Elizabeth offered a threefold blessing: She counted
Mary blessed among women (Luke 1:42a); she blessed Jesus (Luke
1:42b); and she blessed Mary again for her trust in God's word (Luke
1:45). This "blessing" or "beatitude" is not praise directed at Mary herself,
but an expression of Elizabeth's "confidence that God will bring to pass
everything he revealed."[3]

Elizabeth identified the unborn Christ as "my Lord" (Luke 1:43)—
something she would have only known through the Spirit's illumination.
As C. Kavin Rowe shows, this designation is ripe with theological connotations.[4] First, this phrase means Christ has finally arrived in person in
the narrative. He is no longer just a promised Savior; he is now a present
Savior—even if Mary still carries him in her womb. Second, Christ is
Lord from the moment of conception. She doesn't say, "The mother of
the child who *will be* my Lord." Third, calling Christ "Lord" in this immediate context is Luke's way of identifying Jesus with the God of Israel
(see Luke 1:38, 45–46). Finally, Elizabeth's blessing presumes a trinitarian
framework. Full of God's Holy Spirit, Elizabeth blesses God the Father
for keeping his word to Mary through the conception of his Son.

---

[3] Bock, *Luke 1:1–9:50*, vol. 1, 138 (see chap. 2, n. 12).
[4] Rowe, *Early Narrative Christology*, 42–47 (see introduction, n. 9).

The Magnificat (Luke 1:46–55)

Elizabeth's words of blessing sparked Mary's hymn of praise known as the *Magnificat*. Mary may have "sung" this song extemporaneously, in the same way Elizabeth spoke prophetically by the Spirit in her greeting. But it is also possible that Mary composed this hymn over her three-month stay with Elizabeth as she reflected on her relative's blessing toward her. When and how Mary came to speak this song are less important than her godly disposition and the contents of her message.

Mary's song of praise shows intimate familiarity with Israel's Scriptures. Whether she was literate enough to read the Scriptures for herself or she learned them by her presence in the local synagogue, the mother of Jesus lived and breathed in the Word of God. But this is not rote memorization on Mary's part. She had internalized Scripture in such a way that it overflowed from her heart when she responded to God in praise. Under the inspiration of the Spirit, she returned praise back to God with his own words.

Mary's song most closely resembles the triumphant prayer of Hannah recorded in 1 Sam 2:1–10. Hannah's song of praise followed her own miraculous conception of Samuel. Although Mary's prayer is not a line-for-line duplication of Hannah's prayer, there are close thematic similarities:

"My heart rejoices in the LORD; my horn is lifted up by the LORD. . . . I rejoice in your salvation" (1 Sam 2:1).	"My soul magnifies the Lord, and my spirit rejoices in God my Savior" (Luke 1:46–47).
"LORD of Armies, if you will take notice of your servant's affliction, remember and not forget me, and give your servant a son" (1 Sam 1:11).	"[God] has looked with favor on the humble condition of his servant" (Luke 1:48).
"There is no one holy like the LORD. There is no one besides you!" (1 Sam 2:2)	"The Mighty One has done great things for me, and his name is holy" (Luke 1:49).

"The bows of the warriors are broken, but the feeble are clothed with strength" (1 Sam 2:4).

"He has toppled the mighty from their thrones and exalted the lowly" (Luke 1:52).

"Those who are full hire themselves out for food, but those who are starving hunger no more. The woman who is childless gives birth to seven, but the woman with many sons pines away" (1 Sam 2:5).

"He has satisfied the hungry with good things" (Luke 1:53).

"The LORD brings poverty and gives wealth; he humbles and he exalts" (1 Sam 2:7).

"Because he has looked with favor on the humble condition of his servant. . . . He has . . . sent the rich away empty" (Luke 1:48, 53).

Mary's song is not a carbon copy of Hannah's. Her language also reflects the Psalter when she states that God's "name is holy" (Luke 1:49; Ps 111:9) and that his "mercy is from generation to generation on those who fear him" (Luke 1:50; cf. Ps 103:17).

The Humble Condition of His Servant (Luke 1:46–50)

My soul magnifies the Lord,
and my spirit rejoices in God my Savior,
because he has looked with favor
on the humble condition of his servant.
Surely, from now on all generations
will call me blessed,
because the Mighty One
has done great things for me,
and his name is holy.
His mercy is from generation to generation
on those who fear him. (Luke 1:48–50)

Mary praises God with her whole being. When Mary said "my soul magnifies" and "my spirit rejoices," she was not speaking of different parts of human nature (as in a "trichotomy" of body, soul, and spirit). Instead, her hymn uses a technique common to Hebrew poetry called *parallelism* that elegantly expresses the same idea in two sequential but different expressions. In other words, Mary's "soul" and "spirit" are two different ways of describing the same thing: She magnifies God with her whole person, from the deepest recesses of her being. As Amy Peeler put it, "Mary with her mind, emotions, body—entire living self—rejoices to magnify God."[5]

Mary recognizes her Savior. Despite extrabiblical claims that Mary was born without sin, she here stresses her need for God's grace and mercy. We have no biblical reason to believe that Rom 3:23 does not apply to her. She is included in that group of "all [who] have sinned and [who] fall short of the glory of God." Like the rest of fallen humanity, Mary needed what God provided for us on the cross of Christ. At that moment in time, Mary probably did not know all her salvation would entail and what her son would do to accomplish it. But she did know the simple truth that she needed a Savior.

Mary praises God for the favor he has extended to her. Mary's response was similar to Elizabeth's: "How could this happen to me, that the mother of my Lord should come to me?" (Luke 1:43). Luke emphasizes the humility of these women who obeyed God without question (unlike Zechariah). Mary displayed no hubris or pride in God choosing her for this sacred duty. Instead, she declared that God "has looked with favor on the humble condition of his servant" (1:48). She identifies herself as a "servant" or "slave," stressing her inferiority to God and her humble station in life as a young virgin from Nazareth.

Mary's words resonate with the psalmist's: "Though the LORD is exalted, he takes note of the humble" (Ps 138:6). God saw her and

---

[5] Amy Peeler, *Women and the Gender of God* (Grand Rapids: Eerdmans, 2022), 214.

ensured she would be seen from generation to generation. Despite her lowly station, God had chosen her to be the mother of the incarnate Lord. Mary's proclamation here was her way of saying "God has chosen to bless me" despite not being worthy of such an honor. As Luther explained, "She does not say, '*My* soul doth magnify itself,' or 'exalt *me*.' She does not desire herself to be esteemed; she magnifies God alone and gives all glory to Him."[6]

Mary knows that future generations will continue to recognize her blessing. In her recognition that future generations will call her blessed, Mary did not endorse prayer or devotion to herself.[7] Instead, she was like Leah who conceived and gave birth to Asher: "I am happy that the women call me happy" or "blessed" (Gen 30:13). Mary was like the woman of noble character whose "children rise up and call her blessed" (Prov 31:28). The endurance of Mary's blessing is tied to Gabriel's promise that her son would rule on David's throne forever, that "his kingdom will have no end" (Luke 1:33).

Mary's blessing had nothing to do with her own virtue, goodness, or righteous acts. She extols God on the basis of his deeds: "He has done great things for me." But she also praises God for his unchanging attributes. He is the "Mighty One," the almighty warrior whose power knows no limits. "His name is holy," meaning he is set apart and wholly distinct from the gods of neighboring nations. He extends mercy and compassion to all those who fear him.[8]

The World Turned Upside Down (Luke 1:51–53)

He has done a mighty deed with his arm;
he has scattered the proud

---

[6] Luther, "The Magnificat," *LW* 21:308.

[7] Jesus himself appears to discourage devotion to Mary in Luke 11:27–28. When a woman from the crowd yells out, "Blessed is the womb that bore you and the one who nursed you!" He replied, "Rather, blessed are those who hear the word of God and keep it."

[8] See also Matt 5:7. "Blessed are the merciful, for they will be shown mercy."

because of the thoughts of their hearts;
he has toppled the mighty from their thrones
and exalted the lowly.
He has satisfied the hungry with good things
and sent the rich away empty. (Luke 1:51–53)

Mary here reflects on the providential working of God in human history.
God ensured the birth of his Son "with his arm" (see also Pss 89:13; 136:12;
Isa 51:5, 9; 52:10). God rescued the Hebrews from bondage in Egypt
"by a strong hand and an outstretched arm" (Deut 4:34; see also Exod
6:6; Deut 5:15; 7:19). But the same strong "arm" would work a different
kind of redemption in the son of Mary. The stage for the gospel message
was set by some of the most significant geopolitical events in human history. The news of the death, burial, and resurrection of Jesus would never
have travelled as far and as wide across the ancient world without the
rise of the Roman Empire just prior to Jesus's birth. The destruction of
Jerusalem seventy years after Jesus's birth would create a marked change in
the Jewish way of life that was for so long centered around temple worship.

Mary anticipates the future reversal of fortunes in God's eternal kingdom.
The kingdom of men is built on power, wealth, and influence. Evil men
clamor for such things because that is how they seek to control the world
around them. But God has "toppled the mighty from their thrones" and
"exalted the lowly." Mary here anticipates teaching from Jesus's Sermon
on the Mount:

Blessed are the poor in spirit,
for the kingdom of heaven is theirs. . . .
Blessed are the humble,
for they will inherit the earth.
Blessed are those who are persecuted because of righteousness,
for the kingdom of heaven is theirs. (Matt 5:3, 5, 10)[9]

---

[9] A. T. Robertson discerned the same theme in the letter of James (Jas
4:1–10), suggesting that James himself may have been influenced by the

The nineteenth-century Anglican theologian H. P. Liddon put the reversal of Mary's station and fortune in more concrete historical terms:

> Compare Mary . . . with some of the great ladies who were nearly or exactly her contemporaries. While Mary was fetching water day by day from the well of Nazareth, or gathering wood and wild fruits on the hill above the village, these stately dames, surrounded by a crowd of slaves, swept proudly through the halls of the Caesars. But, if we except a professed student of history here or there, what do men know about them now? What do you know of Livia, who parted from an honourable husband that she might be the wife of Augustus; or of Julia, the ill-used daughter of Augustus and wife of Tiberius; or of Octavia, the sister of Augustus, whom Antony divorced that he might wed Cleopatra; or of Antonia, the high-minded daughter of Octavia, who lived, they say, to be poisoned by her grandson Caligula. . . . The names of these ladies were once as familiar to the vast population of the Empire as are those of the members of our own royal family to ourselves. . . . Now they are, for all practical purposes, forgotten; while the lowly maiden who was living unknown in a remote province of the vast Empire that was ruled by their nearest relatives, is at this hour more borne in mind by civilized men than any other member of her sex who ever lived.[10]

The Unfailing Mercy of God (Luke 1:54–55)

He has helped his servant Israel,
remembering his mercy
to Abraham and his descendants forever,
just as he spoke to our ancestors. (Luke 1:54–55)

Magnificat. See A. T. Robertson, *Studies in the Epistle of James*, rev. ed., ed. Heber F. Peacock (Nashville: Broadman, 1959).

[10] H. P. Liddon, *The Magnificat: Sermons in St. Paul's*, 2nd ed. (London: Rivington's), 38–40.

Mary remembers God's faithfulness to the covenants. Matthew's nativity story begins with the promise made to Abraham, as Matthew calls Jesus the "son of Abraham" in the first verse of his Gospel. Zechariah and Elizabeth's story clearly echoes Abraham and Sarah's story, but this is the first time Luke mentions Abraham by name in the Gospel. But the words of a teenage girl from Nazareth highlight the importance of the Abrahamic covenant for God's people. This promise is at the heart of their shared national identity. Most Jewish boys and girls in first-century Israel still hung their hopes on the promises made to the patriarchs. But on the other side of Pentecost, Luke knows that this promise would also have significant implications for Gentiles who are co-heirs of this promise.

When We Are More Blessed Than Mary

We belong to the future generations Mary prophesied would rise up and call her blessed. Mary was blessed, as Jonathan Edwards (1703–1758) remarked, because God made her "the mother of Jesus Christ, the Son of God, the Creator of the world, and the Savior of sinners and the Judge of angels and men."[11] She carried, delivered, and nursed "a Child who was the Son of the highest, who was the great and eternal and infinitely beloved Son of God, the Creator and mighty Governor of heaven and earth and the great Savior of mankind."[12] No wonder Mary magnified the Lord!

But as blessed as Mary must have been to be the woman who bore God in her body, Jesus said that her blessing paled in comparison to the blessing of those "who hear the word of God and keep it" (Luke 11:27–28). To hear the word of God, Edwards explained, was to "hear" it

---

[11] Jonathan Edwards, "To Be More Blessed Than Mary," in *Come, Thou Long-Expected Jesus: Experiencing the Peace and Promise of Christmas*, ed. Nancy Guthrie (Wheaton, IL: Crossway, 2008), 56.

[12] Edwards, "To Be More Blessed Than Mary," 57.

inwardly and spiritually by the illuminating work of the Holy Spirit. To "obey" the word is to observe the word of God and persevere in it.[13]

New covenant believers who have the permanent indwelling of God's Spirit have a greater blessing than Moses did when he saw the backside of God's glory or Mary did when she carried God in her body for nine months (see John 20:29). As Edwards extolled this blessing, "Tis more blessed to have Christ in the heart than in the womb. Tis more blessed to have Christ in the arms of faith and love than in the arms or at the breast as the virgin Mary had."[14]

If Mary had a great reason to magnify the Lord and sing of his greatness, how much more do we who have the indwelling of God's Spirit when he indwells our spiritual natures? For this gracious mystery, the people of God should say in unison, "O magnify the Lord with me, and let us exalt his name together" (Ps 34:3 KJV).

---

[13] Edwards, 57–58.
[14] Edwards, 59.

7

The Virgin-Born Savior

Matthew 1:18–21, 24–25

Jesus . . . freed the sons of God from their sins and in the
same manner from all evil. For the command from the
angel was that Mary's husband, Joseph, name him Jesus,
who said, 'He will save his people from their sins.'
—PETER MARTYR VERMIGLI (1499–1562)[1]

In the first scene of Matthew's nativity story, Joseph discovered that
Mary, the woman to whom he was betrothed, was pregnant—allegedly
"from the Holy Spirit" (Matt 1:18). Joseph probably made this discovery after her three-month stay with Elizabeth (Luke 1:56). It is unclear
whether Mary told Joseph she was pregnant or her pregnancy was far
enough along that she was beginning to show. Either way, Joseph knew

---

[1] Peter Martyr Vermigli, *Loci communes* (1576), 423, quoted in *Matthew*,
Reformation Commentary on Scripture, NT vol. 1, ed. Jason K. Lee and William
M. Marsh (Downers Grove: IVP Academic, 2021), 14.

Mary was pregnant and that he was not the father. The carpenter initially planned to divorce Mary, but God intervened and told Joseph that the child she was carrying was the long-awaited Savior.

The Evangelist depicts Joseph as a righteous and caring man, a faithful son of David from the tribe of Judah. Joseph wanted to do what was right by God's word but also wanted to ensure that no harm came to the woman he loved. In his gracious providence, God chose a man to raise his Son who would model for him faithfulness, righteousness, and obedience.

Joseph, Did You Know?

The birth of Jesus Christ came about this way: After his mother Mary had been engaged to Joseph, it was discovered before they came together that she was pregnant from the Holy Spirit. So her husband, Joseph, being a righteous man, and not wanting to disgrace her publicly, decided to divorce her secretly. (Matt 1:18–19)

Many biblical scholars and theologians who deny the virginal conception often presume that Joseph was the biological father of Jesus.[2] But Matthew is emphatic here that Joseph discovered this pregnancy "before they came together" (Matt 1:18)—before they consummated their marriage with a sexual relationship. One cannot take the whole witness of Scripture seriously and claim Joseph—or any other human man—as the father of Jesus.

Matthew does not tell us what details Joseph knew and when he knew them. Joseph knew that Mary was pregnant and that he was not the father. But did Joseph know that Mary's baby was from the Holy Spirit

---

[2] See Geoffrey Parrinder, *Son of Joseph: The Parentage of Jesus* (Edinburgh: T&T Clark, 1992); Kyle Roberts, *A Complicated Pregnancy: Whether Mary Was a Virgin and Why It Matters* (Minneapolis: Fortress, 2017), 137–57; Lincoln, *Born of a Virgin?*, 115–24 (see chap. 5, n. for "Answering Objections: The Virginal Conception").

right away? Some have argued that Joseph believed the child to be from the Holy Spirit and did not want to proceed with the marriage because he did not feel worthy of this woman so highly favored by God. Thomas Aquinas held this view: "Joseph was minded to put away the Blessed Virgin not as suspected of fornication, but because in reverence for her sanctity, he feared to cohabit with her."[3]

But this view makes little sense considering Joseph's decision to divorce Mary. Divorce might very well have ruined Mary's reputation because very few people would find it easy to believe that she had conceived this child by the Holy Spirit. The more natural reading of the text is that Joseph initially suspected Mary of committing fornication or adultery. As Augustine of Hippo (AD 354–430) explained, "Joseph knew two things. He knew that Mary's pregnancy was beginning to show. He also knew that he wasn't the one who put her in the family way. The only possible conclusion? She was an adulteress."[4] His decision to divorce Mary was a natural response to the belief that she was carrying another man's baby.

Even if Mary had gotten pregnant by another man, how would this alleged indecency constitute adultery if Mary and Joseph were not yet married? Contemporary English translations may state that Mary was "engaged" to Joseph, but it is important not to read contemporary courtship practices back into the text. "Betrothal" (from a Hebrew word meaning "consent") was different from modern engagements. It was a binding arrangement between the families of the bride and the groom that was formally entered into in the presence of witnesses (see Mal 2:14).

Even though they did not yet live together, the betrothed bride and groom were legally husband and wife (hence the reason Joseph is

---

[3] Thomas Aquinas, *Summa Theologica* IIIa Suppl. q. 62, a. 3; see also John McHugh, *The Mother of Jesus in the New Testament* (New York: Doubleday, 1975), 164–72.

[4] Augustine, Sermon 1.9 [51.9], quoted in Augustine of Hippo, *Sermons to the People*, trans. and ed. William Griffin (New York: Doubleday, 2002), 18; see also Augustine, Sermon 32.10; cf. Augustine, *Enchiridion* 37.

already called Mary's "husband" in Matt 1:19). Couples usually married a year after the betrothal in a public ceremony in which the groom took his bride to come and live in his family home. Following this marriage ceremony, a husband and wife would consummate their marriage with sexual relations.[5]

If a woman betrayed the bonds of her betrothal, even before the wedding ceremony, she would be legally considered an adulteress. If Joseph had suspected Mary of adultery, he would have been within his legal rights to make a public example of her, to have her tried publicly. The law of Moses established death as the maximum penalty for a betrothed woman who commits adultery:

> If there is a young woman who is a virgin engaged [betrothed] to a man, and another man encounters her in the city and sleeps with her, take the two of them out to the gate of that city and stone them to death—the young woman because she did not cry out in the city and the man because he has violated his neighbor's fiancée. You must purge the evil from you. (Deut 22:23–24; cf. Lev 20:10)[6]

Joseph also could have requested an adultery trial like the one described in Numbers 5. In this trial, the woman suspected of adultery had to drink a concoction of bitter water. If the woman had committed adultery, God would have supernaturally used the bitter water to shrivel her womb (Num 5:21–22). We have no biblical record of this ritual ever being practiced.[7]

---

[5] These types of marriage ceremonies are depicted in Matt 25:1–13; John 2:1–12; 3:29.

[6] See also John 8:3–11. The law also makes provisions for women who are raped, in which case the rapist or sexual abuser is held liable for the crime, not the woman (Deut 22:25–27).

[7] The apocryphal *First Gospel of James* (*Protoevangelium of James*) fabricates an account where Mary drinks the bitter water at the order of a priest (see *Prot. Jas* 16).

Because betrothal was a binding arrangement between the families of the bride and groom, it could only be dissolved by death or divorce. Joseph, being a "righteous man," had an obligation to uphold the law. But out of apparent concern and compassion for Mary, he opted to "divorce her secretly" (Matt 1:19). Joseph loved Mary too much to see her publicly humiliated, or worse, physically punished. But a completely secret divorce would have been impossible in this Jewish culture. Two witnesses were required for a divorce to be ratified.

So the "quiet" divorce described by Matthew probably means that Joseph requested a divorce on less serious grounds than adultery.[8] It would be like requesting a divorce today on the grounds of irreconcilable differences rather than on the charge of domestic violence, which could also bring criminal penalties to the accused. A "quiet" divorce was as close to an uncontested divorce as one could find in the world of first-century Judaism.

Answering Objections: Jesus Was Illegitimate

Later critics of Christianity spread the rumor that Jesus was a *mamzer*—an illegitimate son. As the children of illicit relationships, mixed marriages, and prostitutes, mamzers were viewed as second-class citizens in Israel. According to the law of Moses, "No one of illegitimate birth may enter the LORD's assembly; none of his descendants, even to the tenth generation, may enter the LORD's assembly" (Deut 23:2). The Pharisees and scribes may have been insinuating that Jesus was a mamzer when they told Jesus "We weren't born of sexual immorality" (John 8:41, emphasis added; see also *Acts of Pilate* 2:3).

---

[8] Brown, *Birth of the Messiah*, 128 (see chap. 1, n. 6); cf. Carson, "Matthew," 211 (see chap. 2, n. 11); Angelo Tosato, "Joseph, Being Just a Man (Matt 1:19)," *Catholic Biblical Quarterly* 41, no. 4 (1979): 547–51. Brown suggests that this would be a more "lenient" divorce like those allowed by Hillel. Jesus seemed to oppose Hillel's interpretation of divorce law in Matt 19:1–11; cf. 5:27–32.

But the accusation of Mary's infidelity was more explicit in the writings of a late second-century pagan philosopher named Celsus, who accused Mary of having an affair with a Roman soldier named Panthera (see Origen, *Against Celsus* 1.28, 32, 39, 69). Without calling Jesus by name, a later medieval Jewish text called the *Toledot Yeshu* ("Generations of Jesus") described the bastard son of Miriam and Panthera as a powerful magician who had learned magic from his childhood in Egypt.

In the 1980s, the feminist biblical scholar Jane Schaberg proposed a modified version of this illegitimacy thesis. Schaberg denied the virginal conception but also rejected the common critical claim that Joseph was Jesus's biological father. She proposed the theory that Mary likely conceived Jesus by sexual assault. Schaberg suggests that Matthew and Luke knew this but could not speak openly about it because of sexual politics in their patriarchal setting. Mary, as an oppressed victim, longed for God to liberate her and free her from the shame of her sexual abuse.

Although it is possible that rumors circulated about Jesus's illegitimacy in his own lifetime—especially if one were to read John 8:41 as a slight toward Jesus—these rumors would have had nothing to do with Mary having an illicit affair with or being raped by a Roman soldier. The earliest sources for this rumor postdate the biblical nativity stories by more than a century. Both Jewish and pagan sources of this rumor had an axe to grind with Christian beliefs, including the notion of a virginal conception. Even the officer's reported name "Panthera" was probably an intentional parody of the word used in the NT for "virgin" (*parthenos*).

See Bruce Chilton, *Rabbi Jesus: An Intimate Biography* (New York: Doubleday, 2000), 3–22; Jane Schaberg, *The Illegitimacy of Jesus: A Feminist Theological Interpretation of the Infancy Narratives* (New York: Harper & Row, 1987); Charles L. Quarles, "Jesus as *Mamzer*: A Response to Bruce Chilton's Reconstruction of the Circumstances Surrounding Jesus' Birth in *Rabbi Jesus*," *Bulletin for Biblical Research* 14, no. 2 (2004): 243–55; Sarit Kattan Gribetz, "Toledot Yeshu," in *Early New Testament Apocrypha*, Ancient Literature for New Testament Studies, vol. 9, ed. J. Christopher Edwards (Grand Rapids: Zondervan, 2022), 154–74.

Joseph Did as the Lord Commanded Him (Matt 1:20–21, 24–25)

But after he had considered these things, an angel of the Lord appeared to him in a dream, saying, "Joseph, son of David, don't be afraid to take Mary as your wife, because what has been conceived in her is from the Holy Spirit. She will give birth to a son, and you are to name him Jesus, because he will save his people from their sins." . . . When Joseph woke up, he did as the Lord's angel had commanded him. He married her but did not have sexual relations with her until she gave birth to a son. And he named him Jesus. (Matt 1:20–21, 24–25)

While Joseph was giving divorce serious consideration, an angel of the Lord came to him in a dream. Though it was never an ordinary form of communication, God had used dreams and visions to reveal his will in the past (Gen 28:12; 37:5–9; Dan 2:19). The way God spoke to Joseph, the husband of Mary, clearly echoed the way God had spoken to Joseph, the son of Jacob (Gen 37:9, 19; 40; 41:1–36). The husband of Mary, like his patriarchal namesake, received messages from God in his dreams. Unlike the dreams of Joseph the patriarch, these dreams needed no additional interpretation or explanation.[9] The angel told Joseph not to

---

[9] Matthew references dreams with messages on one other occasion outside of his nativity story. When Pilate was about to offer judgment on Jesus, his wife sent a message to him saying, "Have nothing to do with that righteous man, for today I've suffered terribly in a dream [Gk. *onar*] because of him" (Matt 27:19).

be afraid to take Mary home as his wife. His instruction mirrored what Gabriel told Mary in Luke 1:28-38:

"Don't be afraid to take Mary as your wife, because what has been conceived in her is from the Holy Spirit. She will give birth to a son, and you are to name him Jesus, because he will save his people from their sins" (Matt 1:20b-21).

"Do not be afraid, Mary, for you have found favor with God. Now listen: You will conceive and give birth to a son, and you will name him Jesus. . . . The Holy Spirit will come upon you, and the power of the Most High will overshadow you" (Luke 1:30-31, 35).

The Lord's messenger brought good news to this righteous man: Mary never violated the bonds of their betrothal. Instead of following through with the divorce, Joseph could take this angelic message as an assurance of Mary's innocence. She had, in fact, conceived a son through the power of the Holy Spirit.[10]

The command for Joseph to name Jesus was essentially a command to adopt Jesus as his own son.[11] Throughout his life, Jesus would be known as "Joseph's son" (Luke 4:22; cf. John 1:45; 6:42) or the "carpenter's son" (Matt 13:55). Joseph gave legitimacy to Jesus—protected him from being a mamzer in the eyes of Israel—by taking Mary as his wife. But because Joseph understood the significance of the sign of the virginal conception, he did not consummate his marriage with Mary until after Jesus was born.[12]

Joseph was not Jesus's biological father, but he was the man God chose to raise his Son. In this sense, he was favored by God much like

---

[10] See Malcolm B. Yarnell III, *Who is the Holy Spirit? Biblical Insights into His Divine Person* (Nashville: B&H Academic, 2019), 56–57. The aorist passive participle *gennēthen* emphasizes the passive role played by Mary and Jesus in this conception. The Spirit is the initiator and completer of this work.

[11] Fathers played a key role in naming their own sons (see Luke 1:62–63).

[12] A. T. Robertson, *The Mother of Jesus: Her Problems and Her Glory* (New York: George H. Doran, 1925), 24–25.

Mary. The reasons for God's choice are clear: Joseph was faithful to the law of Moses and cared very deeply for those whom he loved. Like his patriarchal namesake, Joseph was a protective figure who modeled obedience, personal integrity, and mercy.

The Virgin-Born King Will Save His People from Their Sins

Through the angel's message, Matthew finally reveals the reason the Christ was coming into the world. He would be called "Jesus," which means "the LORD is salvation," because "he will save his people from their sins" (Matt 1:21). At first glance, the angel's statement sounds a lot like Ps 130:8, which states that the Lord "will redeem Israel from all its iniquities" (see also Zeph 3:15; Ezek 36:29). It also has echoes of the message from Judges 13, where the angel tells Samson's mother that she will "conceive and give birth to a son" and that "he will begin to save Israel" (Judg 13:5).[13]

But notice that the angel did not tell Joseph that this child would "save Israel." Rather, this son "will save his people."[14] The promises made to Israel through Abraham and David were part of Christ's messianic agenda, but the mission was always bigger than Israel. God always intended to make Israel a "light for the nations, to be [his] salvation to the ends of the earth" (Isa 49:6). Christ came with a universal saving purpose. By his blood, he would create a new people—"his people"—"from every tribe and language and people and nation" to be a "kingdom and priests to our God" (Rev 5:9, 10).

Observe that Jesus did not come just to save us from the consequences of our sins or from God's judgment on sin—though he did all that too.

---

[13] Charles L. Quarles, *A Theology of Matthew: Jesus Revealed as Deliverer, King, and Incarnate Creator*, Explorations in Biblical Theology (Phillipsburg, NJ: P&R, 2013), 56.

[14] Bede, *Expositio in Lucae Evangelium* 1.31.

He also came to save us from sin itself. As Charles Quarles points out, "sins" are personified here as "cruel masters who enslave mankind and force it into a harsh bondage."[15] The Savior, like Moses, would lead his people out of bondage—not to another nation, but to the dark forces at work within our own lives. Jesus would become Israel's Savior—but not the conquering warrior so many of his contemporaries anticipated. His enemy was much larger than a foreign occupant. Jesus was going to save his people from the power and curse of sin, Satan and his demonic powers, and death itself.

---

[15] Quarles, *A Theology of Matthew*, 49.

8

The Virgin-Born King Is God with Us

Matthew 1:22–23; Isaiah 7:14

Now all this took place to fulfill what was spoken by the
Lord through the prophet: **See, the virgin will become
pregnant and give birth to a son, and they will name
him Immanuel,** which is translated 'God is with us.'

–Matthew 1:22–23

One of the central themes of the Gospel of Matthew—if not the central theme—is that Jesus fulfilled Israel's Scriptures.[1] To provide proof of this, Matthew quotes more OT Scripture than any other NT book. Whereas Luke's nativity story continues the OT by employing

---

[1] See R. T. France, *Matthew: Evangelist and Teacher* (Exeter, UK: Paternoster, 1989), 166–205.

its storytelling features, Matthew extensively quotes from the OT in his nativity story. Each of the five scenes in Matthew's nativity story features a quotation from or an allusion to an OT text that the author believes Jesus has fulfilled.

Each OT quotation is introduced like this: "Now all this took place to fulfill what was spoken by the Lord through the prophet" (Matt 1:22). "This is what was written by the prophet" (Matt 2:5). "So that what was spoken by the Lord through the prophet might be fulfilled" (Matt 2:15). "What was spoken through Jeremiah the prophet was fulfilled" (Matt 2:17). "To fulfill what was spoken through the prophets" (Matt 2:23). Matthew uses a very similar formula throughout his whole Gospel.[2] Matthew uses the word "fulfill" (*pléroó*) to indicate that Jesus is the one who ultimately completes God's prophetic word.[3]

Scene	Text	Prophetic Fulfillment	Description
Prologue	Matt 1:1-17	Draws from the entire OT	Matthew's list of Jesus's ancestors that establishes Jesus as the Messiah, the son of David, and the son of Abraham
Scene 1	Matt 1:18–25	Isa 7:14	The discovery of Mary's pregnancy; Joseph's first dream

---

[2] See also Matt 3:3; 4:14; 8:17; 11:10; 12:17; 13:14, 35; 15:7; 21:4; 26:31; 27:9. This formula conforms to a similar pattern seen in 1 Kgs 2:27; 8:15; 2 Chr 6:4; 36:21–22; Ezra 1:1. See Robert H. Gundry, *Matthew: A Commentary on His Literary and Theological Art* (Grand Rapids: Eerdmans, 1982), 24; Quarles, *Theology of Matthew*, 28–29 (see chap. 7, n. 13).

[3] This chart was adapted from Brown, *The Birth of the Messiah*, 51 (see chap.1, n. 6).

Scene 2	Matt 2:1–12	Mic 5:2	Wise men from the east visit Herod in Jerusalem, Jesus in Bethlehem
Scene 3	Matt 2:13–15	Hos 11:1	Joseph's second dream; the flight to Egypt
Scene 4	Matt 2:16–18	Jer 31:15	Herod massacres innocent children in Bethlehem
Scene 5	Matt 2:19–23	Unknown (Isa 11:1? Judg 13:5, 7?)	Joseph's third dream; the return to Nazareth

In the first scene of Matthew's nativity story (Matt 1:18–25), Joseph discovered that his future wife had conceived a son by the Holy Spirit and that this child was the long-awaited Savior of Israel. Matthew interpreted this event as a fulfillment of the prophecy recorded in Isa 7:14. Since the second century, critics and skeptics have challenged Matthew's interpretation of this text.[4] They claim that Matthew misunderstood Isaiah's intention here, or worse, deliberately made up this elaborate story about a pregnant virgin and a carpenter just to show how Jesus fulfilled prophecy.[5] Other scholars make the softer claim that Matthew 1–2 is not history but *midrash*—a type of ancient Jewish commentary on Scripture.[6]

But nothing from the original context of Isa 7:14 or its later interpretations would suggest that first-century Jews were sitting around waiting on a virgin to conceive the Messiah through supernatural

---

[4] See Justin Martyr, *Dialogue with Trypho*, 66–67.

[5] See Adolf von Harnack, *History of Dogma*, vol. 1, trans. Neil Buchanan (New York, 1905), 100n1.

[6] See Alfred Loisy, *Les évangiles synoptiques* (Ceffonds: Chez l'Auteur, 1907); M. D. Goulder, *Midrash and Lection in Matthew* (Eugene, OR: Wipf and Stock, 2004); Gundry, *Matthew*. See also Charles L. Quarles, "Midrash as Creative Historiography: Portrait of a Misnomer," *JETS* 39, no. 3 (1996): 457–64. As Quarles has demonstrated, the term *midrash* is widely misused when applied to texts like Matthew 1–2.

means. If early Christians had invented the story of the virginal conception to prove that Jesus fulfilled Isa 7:14, why did Luke not mention this prophecy in his account of Jesus's virginal conception? Why would Matthew feel obligated to invent such a wild story to fulfill a relatively obscure 800-year-old prophecy given to one of Judah's worst kings? There seems to be a simpler explanation for the Evangelist's quotation of this verse: Matthew did not invent a far-fetched story; instead, he began with an extraordinary event in recent history—the miraculous way Jesus entered the world—and then interpreted this event through the lens of biblical prophecy.

For Matthew, Christ's fulfillment of Isa 7:14 goes beyond the unusual way he was conceived. Christ "completes" this prophecy by becoming for us a new way to experience God's presence in creation. In Christ, God entered the world he created, and Christ forever communicates his presence to us as the risen Lord seated at the right hand of God.

Isaiah 7:14 in Context

Eight centuries before Jesus was born, the prophet Isaiah was God's spokesman to four kings in the southern kingdom of Judah, but Ahaz's fate was central to Isaiah's Immanuel prophecy. According to the historical books of the OT,

> Ahaz . . . did not do what was right in the LORD's sight like his ancestor David, for he walked in the ways of the kings of Israel and made cast images of the Baals. He burned incense in Ben Hinnom Valley and burned his children in the fire, imitating the detestable practices of the nations the LORD had dispossessed before the Israelites.[7] He sacrificed and burned incense on the high places, on the hills, and under every green tree. So the LORD his God handed Ahaz over to the king of Aram. He attacked

---

[7] See Lev 20:1–5; Deut 12:31; 2 Kgs 21:6; Ps 106:37–38.

him and took many captives to Damascus. (2 Chr 28:1–5; see also 2 Kgs 16:2–4)

Ahaz may have been a physical descendant of David, but he was an idol-worshipping, child-murdering pagan who defiantly chose the gods of neighboring nations over David's God. The great irony of Ahaz's story is that God ultimately used the foreign enemies whose gods Ahaz served to cause his downfall.

The most important decision in the life of Ahaz is described in Isaiah 7. Fear and paranoia gripped the people of Judah when they discovered that the kings of Aram (Syria) and Israel (Ephraim) were conspiring together against Jerusalem. Aram and Israel had already taken captive or killed many of Judah's brave warriors "because they had abandoned the Lord God of their ancestors" (2 Chr 28:5–6). Ahaz worried that Aram and Israel wanted to depose him and install a king of their own choosing over Judah (Isa 7:6), so he thought about going to Tiglath-pileser, the king of Assyria, to beg for help in dealing with his enemies.[8]

God sent Isaiah to Ahaz with a simple message: "Calm down and be quiet. Don't be afraid or cowardly because of these two smoldering sticks" (Isa 7:4). In other words, the kings of Aram and Israel are like candle wicks that are about be snuffed out. Their threats are empty because the assault they are planning against Judah "will not happen; it will not occur" (Isa 7:7b). However, Isaiah warns, "If you do not stand firm in your faith, then you will not stand at all" (Isa 7:9b). If Ahaz would trust God, he would be fine. But were he to act impulsively and disobey God, there would be serious consequences. Isaiah warned that the threat from Aram and Israel paled in comparison to the threat from mighty Assyria.

The historical books of the OT fill in the rest of the story for us. When the kings of Aram and Israel besieged Judah, Ahaz did seek the help of Tiglath-pileser after all (2 Chr 28:16). Ahaz groveled, "I am your servant and your son. March up and save me from the grasp of the

---

[8] History remembers these events as the Syro-Ephraimite War (736–732 BC).

king of Aram and of the king of Israel, who are rising up against me" (2 Kgs 16:7). Ahaz stole silver and gold from God's temple to give to Tiglath-pileser as bribe money.

As requested, the Assyrian king marched into Damascus and killed Rezin, the king of Aram. But when Ahaz traveled to Damascus to thank Tiglath-pileser, he discovered that the Assyrian king had no intention of helping Judah (2 Chr 28:21). In a panic, Ahaz turned to "the gods of Damascus which had defeated him" (2 Chr 28:23). Ahaz stole what was left from the Lord's temple to build new altars to the pagan gods of Damascus.

But before all this took place, Isaiah told Ahaz to ask for a sign from God—something that was usually frowned on in Israel (see Deut 6:16; Matt 4:7). Putting on the airs of piety, Ahaz responded, "I will not ask. I will not test the LORD" (Isa 7:12). Isaiah had no patience for Ahaz's phony adherence to the law of Moses, nor did God. If you will not ask God for a sign, Isaiah retorted, "The LORD himself will give you a sign" (Isa 7:14a).

When Isaiah told Ahaz to ask for a sign, he used the singular pronoun "you" (Isa 7:10–11), meaning he was talking directly to the king. But when Isaiah told Ahaz that the Lord would provide a "sign," he used the plural pronoun "you" (Isa 7:14a). This meant that the sign was not just for Ahaz, but for the whole nation. Isaiah then explained the sign to Ahaz:

> See, the virgin will conceive, have a son, and name him Immanuel. By the time he learns to reject what is bad and choose what is good, he will be eating curds and honey. For before the boy knows to reject what is bad and choose what is good, the land of the two kings you dread will be abandoned. The LORD will bring on you, your people, and your father's house such a time as has never been since Ephraim separated from Judah: He will bring the king of Assyria. (Isa 7:14b–17)

God had promised a man who sacrificed his own babies to other gods that a baby would be the ultimate sign of his people's redemption.

Interpreters have long debated the precise nature of the "sign." Non-Christian interpreters reject the notion that Christ fulfilled this prophecy. Some Christian interpreters have argued that there was no immediate fulfillment in Isaiah's day—that this promise was only fulfilled when Jesus was born. But other Christian interpreters argue that this prophecy had both an immediate fulfillment in Ahaz's day and a later, more complete fulfillment in the person of Christ. Either way, Christ ultimately fulfilled this promise.

How Did Jesus Fulfill Isaiah 7:14?

How did Matthew make the leap from this eighth-century sign made to Ahaz to a story about his master's birth? As someone radically changed by Jesus, Matthew understood a key principle for interpreting Scripture that many critics and scholars cannot seem to grasp (or do not want to grasp): All Scripture is a witness to Christ.[9] The same Holy Spirit who inspired Isaiah to record this prophecy is the same Holy Spirit who inspired Matthew to write about its fulfillment. Only interpreters with an anti-supernatural bias discount the possibility that the birth of Jesus could fulfill the words of Isaiah eight centuries later.

The key question for Christian interpreters is not whether texts like Isa 7:14 are fulfilled in Jesus, but how. Martyr, Irenaeus, and Origen interpreted this prophecy as exclusively a future prediction of the Messiah's coming—a sign that Ahaz never lived to see.[10] Some who support the *singular fulfillment* view insist that it is more consistent with the supernatural

---

[9] Craig Carter makes a similar observation about some critical approaches to Isaiah 53. See Craig A. Carter, *Interpreting Scripture with the Great Tradition: Recovering the Genius of Premodern Exegesis* (Grand Rapids: Baker, 2018), 229. Carter asks, "Does the non-Christian scholar not *know* Isaiah 53 is about Christ? Or does that person not *want to know* Isaiah 53 is about Christ?"

[10] Justin Martyr wrote, "Things which were incredible and seemed impossible with men, these God predicted by the Spirit of prophecy as about to come to pass, in order that, when they came to pass, there might be no unbelief, but faith, because of their prediction" (*First Apology* 33). See also Irenaeus, *Against Heresies* 21.4; Origen, *Against Celsus* 1.34–35.

worldview of the Bible.[11] Other interpreters have argued that prophecies quoted throughout Matthew's Gospel have *multiple fulfillments*—partial fulfillments in their immediate context and a more complete fulfillment later on in the life of Christ.

If this prophecy had an original eighth-century fulfillment, then it seems that the emphasis of the original prophecy was not about the nature of the conception but about God's timing in bringing deliverance (No other virgins in the eighth century BC miraculously conceived). When Isaiah gave this prophecy, a virginal woman was not married or sexually active. But one day she would get married and have a baby the natural way. Before that baby was old enough to know the difference between good and evil, the enemies of Judah would be no more. Because Ahaz did not trust the Lord to handle Israel and Syria, Judah would become a slave to Assyria. The "sign" offered to Ahaz was a description of how long all this would take to unfold.

What eighth-century child did the prophet have in mind? A few options have been offered. First, the "child" may have been a simple figure of speech for God's timeline. According to this view, no actual child was necessary for the sign. Ahaz was just given a timeline of how long it would take to carry out God's plan in Judah. However long it would take for a virgin to marry, conceive, and give birth is how long it would take for Judah's enemies to falter.

Second, the child may refer to Hezekiah, the son of Ahaz. In this case, the "virgin" would have been Ahaz's wife. But this is unlikely considering Hezekiah was probably born before Ahaz began his reign.[12]

Third, the immediate context of this passage might suggest that the child who immediately fulfilled this prophecy was the son of Isaiah described in the next chapter:

---

[11] Robert Gromacki, *The Virgin Birth: A Biblical Study of the Deity of Christ*, 2d ed. (Grand Rapids: Kregel, 2002), 167–77.

[12] Ahaz only ruled for sixteen years before his death (2 Chr 28:1).

I was then intimate with the prophetess, and she conceived and gave birth to a son. The LORD said to me, "Name him Maher-shalal-hash-baz, for before the boy knows how to call 'Father,' or 'Mother,' the wealth of Damascus and the spoils of Samaria will be carried off to the king of Assyria." (Isa 8:3–4)

If Maher-shalal-hash-baz was the original child described in Isa 7:14, the prophet's wife may have been a virgin when Isaiah prophesied, but she later conceived this child by natural means with the prophet. They named their child Maher-shalal-hash-baz, which means, "Rush to the spoil, hurry to the plunder!" This baby's unfortunate name would remind Judah that Assyria would crush the enemies of Judah and then plunder their riches, all before the baby was able to say "Da-da" or "Ma-ma." Maher-shalal-hash-baz may have been nicknamed "Immanuel" to remind them of God's presence in a time of judgment.

If there was a partial fulfillment in Isaiah's day, the specific identity of this child is less important than the message itself: God is Immanuel. He offers his comforting presence to his people in times of trouble (see Joel 2:27; Zech 2:10–11). They can trust in his timing and ability to handle their circumstances.

Isaiah 9 looks ahead to another child who was neither the son of Ahaz nor Maher-shalal-hash-baz. "In the future," Isaiah foretold, God "will bring honor to the way of the sea, to the land east of the Jordan, and to Galilee of the nations" (Isa 9:1). Of this future child the prophet wrote,

For a child will be born for us,
a son will be given to us,
and the government will be on his shoulders.
He will be named
Wonderful Counselor, Mighty God,
Eternal Father, Prince of Peace.
The dominion will be vast,
and its prosperity will never end.
He will reign on the throne of David

and over his kingdom,

to establish and sustain it

with justice and righteousness from now on and forever.

The zeal of the LORD of Armies will accomplish this. (Isa 9:6–7)

No eighth-century child fulfilled this particular promise. This "future" son (Isa 9:1) would be called "Wonderful Counselor, Mighty God, Eternal Father, Prince of Peace" (Isa 9:6). Unlike Hezekiah or Isaiah's son, this future son would reign forever on the throne of David (Isa 9:7).

"Virgin" or "Young Woman"?

Much of the debate over Isa 7:14 surrounds the Hebrew word translated as "virgin" (Hb. *almah*), which can also mean "young woman" or "young maiden." Will a virgin or a young maiden conceive? Some may suggest that if Isaiah wanted to stress her virginity, he could have used the word *betulah*, which describes a woman who has never had sex.[13] But even if Isaiah meant *almah* to describe a young woman of marriable age, she most probably would have been a sexually inexperienced virgin when the prophecy was given.

The Greek translation of Isaiah uses *parthenos*, a word that clearly describes a virginal woman who has never had sex. Even if the original eight-century fulfillment only described a woman who was of virginal age, Matthew clearly intends to use this term to express Mary's sexual purity at the time she conceived Jesus.

The Interpretive Key: Two Types of Prophetic Fulfillments in Matthew

As James Hamilton explains, the word *fulfill* has two basic senses in Matthew's Gospel: *predictive fulfillment* and *typological fulfillment*.[14]

---

[13] This word appears in Gen 24:16; Exod 22:16–17; Lev 21:3, 14; Deut 22:19, 23, 28; Judg 19:24; 21:12; 2 Sam 13:2, 18; Esth 2:2–3, 19; Pss 45:14; 78:63.

[14] See James M. Hamilton, Jr. "'The Virgin Will Conceive': Typological Fulfillment in Matthew 1:18–23," in *Built Upon the Rock: Studies in the Gospel of*

Predictive fulfillment is the idea that a prophecy predicts a future event, like the specific location where the Messiah would be born in Mic 5:2. But this type of prophecy is far less common in the OT. Both types of fulfillment presume a divinely intended authorial intent in OT texts that Christ completes. NT writers do not use these texts however they please.[15]

Typological fulfillment speaks of the way God uses repeated patterns or types throuhout Scripture to express layers of meaning or significance. Whenever an OT author looks back at something that God did for Israel in the past and anticipates God doing something similar in the future, this is a typological promise. These repeated patterns or types intensify throughout Scripture and culminate in Jesus. Adam, Moses, and David all patterned who Jesus would be for his people. Their lives were not predictions of Jesus's life but imperfect types of who he would be in his incarnation. Jesus is the new head of the human race (the last Adam), the perfect lawgiver (a new and better Moses), and the eternal king of Israel who sits on David's throne.

If Isaiah only had one fulfillment in mind in 7:14, then we may count this prophecy as a predictive fulfillment. In this case, the prophet only spoke futuristically about Mary's virginal conception. But if this prophecy had multiple fulfillments—an event in the eighth century BC and the incarnation event in the first century AD—then we may regard Jesus's fulfillment of this text as typological. In this case, whatever prophetic fulfillment was experienced by the people of Judah in the eighth century was later surpassed by Christ. Matthew has seen an incomplete pattern in Isa 7:14 that Jesus more perfectly fulfills.[16]

Matthew, ed. Daniel M. Gurtner and John Nolland (Grand Rapids: Eerdmans, 2008), 232–34.

[15] Compare with the "vehicular view" of prophetic fulfillment described in C. F. D. Moule, *The Origin of Christology* (New York: Cambridge University Press, 1977), 127–34.

[16] Hamilton, "'The Virgin Will Conceive,'" 242–46.

- Eighth-century Judah faced threats from Aram and Israel in the original context of the prophecy. In Matthew's context, the Roman Empire recently began its occupation of Judea.
- Ahaz faced the threat of temporary enemies in Aram and Israel. The virgin-born king in Matthew conquers much more significant enemies: sin, death, and Satan.
- The sign provided for Ahaz was ordinary—and only for one generation. But the sign of Immanuel in Matthew was miraculous and for all generations.
- In Ahaz's context, the sign could have involved a virginal maiden getting married and then conceiving a child by natural means. But in Matthew's context, the sign involved a virginal maiden conceiving by supernatural means and then getting married.
- Nothing extraordinary could be said about the eighth-century child, but the child born to Mary is the eternal heir to David's throne.
- The child in Ahaz's context may have been called "Immanuel" in a symbolic way to remind the people of Judah of God's presence in a time of foreign oppression. The child born to the virgin Mary was called "Immanuel" because he was literally God present to his people in bodily form.
- The child born in Ahaz's time would have reminded Judah of God's deliverance from foreign enemies. The child born to Mary would rescue his people from sin, death, and the powers of evil in the world.

If Matthew had this kind of typological fulfillment for Isa 7:14 in mind, then we could see how the sign given in Isaiah's day served one purpose and how the sign of the virginal conception served a larger and more significant purpose as the ultimate fulfillment of this prophecy. As Ray Ortlund, Jr. explains, Matthew "saw in Isaiah's prophecy of the Immanuel sign-child a picture of our ultimate salvation. We face a coalition of hostile powers far worse than Syria or Ephraim of old. We face the alliance of sin and death, they never go away, and we are no match for them. But at this ultimate level the baby Jesus fulfills the truest meaning of Immanuel, 'God with us.'"[17]

Christians may disagree about whether texts like Isa 7:14 had one fulfillment or two, but whether we hold to singular or multiple fulfillments, we must deny the idea that Matthew misunderstood or misused Isaiah's prophecy. The divine inspiration of Scripture leaves room for the possibility of meaning not fully known or understood by the human author—what we call *sensus plenior* or the "fuller sense" of Scripture (see 2 Pet 1:20–21). Even if Isaiah did not fully expect a future virgin to give birth to the Messiah, the divine author who inspired Isaiah to prophesy always did. The virginal conception of Christ was always going to be the supreme fulfillment of this promise.

The Ever-Present Messiah

Ahaz may have described himself as a worshipper of the God of Israel, but his actions exhibited a practical atheism, or at least he was only devoted to whatever god he thought would help him out in the moment. Ahaz did not really believe God was present with Judah or that he was capable of handling Judah's enemies. God communicated his presence to his people in various ways throughout the history of Israel and Judah, but he never revealed himself more clearly than he did in the incarnation of his Son (Heb 1:1–3). In the virgin-born Immanuel, God was bodily present among us.

God is eternally present to all creation as the cause and source of its existence. Without his sustaining presence, the world would cease to exist. But in the incarnation of Christ, God was present in creation in a new way. He was among us, taking on the essence of created humanity. "For the entire fullness of God's nature dwells bodily in Christ" (Col 2:9).

---

[17] Raymond C. Ortlund, Jr., *Isaiah: God Saves Sinners*, Preaching the Word (Wheaton, IL: Crossway, 2005), 91.

Because God the Father and God the Holy Spirit dwell in Christ and Christ dwells in our humanity, the triune God now dwells with us in the same manner.[18]

Christians sometimes get the mistaken idea that Christ was "God with us" during his earthly ministry but is now "God absent from us" since he ascended to the Father. In one sense, Jesus did "go away" from us (John 16:5, 7). We also expect him to come again in the same way he left (Acts 1:9–11). But as Matthew is quick to remind his readers, Christ is still God with us, even if he is bodily seated at the right hand of God. Though we could identify others, Matthew provides two concrete examples of Jesus's continuing presence with us as Immanuel.[19]

First, Christ is "God with us" in his rule over the church. In Matt 18:15–20, Jesus outlines a three-step process to deal with church discipline. The church has authority on earth to make spiritual judgments like this because, as Jesus says, "where two or three are gathered together in my name, I am there among them" (Matt 18:20). We have *deputized authority* that is given to us by the One who is really in charge of the church. When NT authors called Christ "the head of the body, the church" (Col 1:18; cf. Eph 1:22; 5:23), they did not mean he was a divine figurehead or the church's heavenly mascot, rooting for us from above. As Lord of the church, Immanuel walks among the churches and holds them in his right hand (Rev 1:12–13, 16, 20).

Second, Immanuel is present with us as we carry out the Great Commission that he has given us. Christ told us to make disciples of all nations, baptizing them in the name of our triune God, and teaching them to obey the new commandments he gave us (Matt 28:19). Parallel to what Jesus said in Matthew 18, we fulfill this mission with his divine authority behind us

---

[18] Christian theologians call the mutual indwelling of the persons of the Trinity *perichoresis*.

[19] The major work that explores this theme in the Gospel of Matthew is David D. Kupp, *Matthew's Emmanuel: Divine Presence and God's People in the First Gospel*, Society for New Testament Studies Monograph Series, 90 (New York: Cambridge University Press, 1997).

(Matt 28:18). But Jesus also promised, "I am with you always, to the end of the age" (Matt 28:20). Through the spiritual gifts bestowed on us by the Father, Son, and Holy Spirit (see 1 Cor 12:4–6), Jesus empowers us to fulfill this unfinished task.[20]

When Jesus promises he will be with us always, he is not speaking figuratively, as Paul did when he told churches he was with them "in spirit" (1 Cor 5:3–4; Col 2:5). Because God the Son possesses all the attributes of deity, including divine immanence and omnipresence, Jesus is literally present among us, even now. Though he is always present to us, we are never more aware of his presence than when we are living in Spirit-filled obedience to him. God may feel distant in times of despair or disobedience, but we know he is always present to us in Christ.

Key Theological Concept: Jesus Never Left Heaven

How exactly does that work? How can Christ be bodily on his throne in heaven and literally present to us now? We must answer this the same way we would answer the question "How could Jesus have been a baby in a manger in Bethlehem and still be the eternal God who holds the universe together?"

One answer we must reject is the "kenotic Christology" held by many nineteenth-century theologians. (This teaching gets its name from the Greek word *kenoó*, used in Phil 2:7 to describe Christ's self-emptying). According to those who advocate for this position, Christ essentially emptied himself of divine attributes like omnipresence and omniscience in the incarnation. He effectively ceased being God in the time he walked the earth. Those who hold this view fundamentally misunderstand Paul's argument in Phil 2:5–11. Yes, Christ modeled perfect humility for us when he "emptied himself by assuming the form of a servant" (Phil 2:7),

---

[20] A third possible allusion to Immanuel's presence in the church may be in Christ's description of the Lord's Supper: "Take and eat it; this is my body" (Matt 26:26).

but Christ never ceased being God, nor did he empty himself of his divine attributes. As the unchanging, immutable God of the universe, "Jesus Christ is the same yesterday, today, and forever" (Heb 13:8). When he assumed the form of a servant, the divine nature did not change or cease to exist. Rather, God the Son added to himself a true human nature with its inherent limitations.

The church fathers acknowledged the limitations of Christ's human nature but also observed how these limitations did not exhaust who he was as God the Son. As Athanasius of Alexandria (c. AD 295–373) remarked, the Word took on flesh but was not fully contained by this nature, nor "was the universe left void of his activity and providence."[21] Even while he lay in a manger or walked along the sea of Galilee, Christ remained "before all things" and held "all things . . . together" (Col 1:17).

In his human nature, God the Son experienced limitations: fatigue, limited knowledge, hunger, thirst, pain, etc. But in his divine nature, the Son was still "outside" the human body with full retention of his divine attributes. As human persons, we are completely bound to our corporeal bodies and limited by their capabilities,

> but such was not the case for the Word of God in the human being; for he was not bound to the body, but rather was himself wielding it, so that he was both in it and in everything, and was outside everything, and at rest in the Father alone. And the most wonderful thing was that he both sojourned as a human being, and as the Word begot life in everything, and as Son was with the Father.[22]

Scripture frequently speaks of the incarnation as Christ coming down from heaven (see John 3:13, 31; 6:38, 41, 51; Eph 4:10). The church fathers taught that Christ "for us men, and for our salvation, came

---

[21] Athanasius, *On the Incarnation* 17; cf. Robert Letham, *Systematic Theology* (Wheaton, IL: Crossway, 2019), 110.

[22] Athanasius, *On the Incarnation* 17.

down from heaven, and was incarnate by the Holy Spirit and of the virgin Mary, and was made man."[23] This "coming down" is a word picture, a metaphor. When we say, "He came down from heaven," we do not mean that Jesus literally rode a cloud down from heaven in the same manner he will when he returns (see Acts 1:11). Instead, we are simply speaking of his heavenly origin as God the Son.

We must recognize another important facet of this descent metaphor: although the Son came down from heaven, he did not leave heaven. Calvin unpacked this idea:

> For even if the Word in his immeasurable essence united with the nature of man into one person, we do not imagine that he was confined therein. Here is something marvelous: the Son of God descended from heaven in such a way that, without leaving heaven, he willed to be borne in the virgin's womb, to go about the earth, and to hang upon the cross; yet he continuously filled the world even as he had done from the beginning![24]

God the Son was united to a true human nature in time and space, but that human nature could not fully contain or enclose his divine nature. Christ was incarnate in Mary's womb and simultaneously present to all creation.[25] Even as a man, Christ Jesus was all-powerful and present everywhere, but in his divine nature, not his human nature.[26] As Stephen Duby describes this mystery, "The 'whole Christ,' who is God and man, is present everywhere even if the 'whole of Christ' is not so."[27]

---

[23] The Niceno-Constantinopolitan Creed (AD 381).

[24] John Calvin, *Institutes of the Christian Religion*, ed. John T. McNeill, trans. Ford Lewis Battles (Philadelphia: Westminster Press, 1960), 1:481 [2.13.4].

[25] The Lutheran opponents of this teaching called it the "Calvinistic beyond" (*extra calvinisticum*). Though this doctrine is often associated with Calvin, it predates him by over a millennium. I prefer the term "the *extra-corporeal Christ*."

[26] Steven J. Duby, *Jesus and the God of Classical Theism: Biblical Christology in Light of the Doctrine of God* (Grand Rapids: Baker Academic, 2022), 178–79.

[27] Duby, 190.

If Christ could be present in heaven in his divine nature and present to us on earth in his human nature during his earthly ministry, then Christ can be present in heaven in his human nature and present to us in his divine nature after the ascension. He has not abandoned us, nor has he left us as orphans. Christ was, is, and ever will be "God with us," the ever-present, virgin-born king.

9

In the Fullness of Time

Luke 2:1–7

But when the fullness of time had come, God sent forth his Son.
–Galatians 4:4a (ESV)

According to classical Christian theology, God exists outside of space and time. After all, he created time and space! Consequently, God does not experience the passing of time the way we creatures do.[1] As C. S. Lewis once illustrated this idea, God is like the author of a book who exists outside of the imaginary timeline the characters of his story experience.[2]

The NT doesn't speculate about God's relationship to time, but it does tell the story of how this eternal God entered time. "In the fullness

---

[1] The fifth-century Christian philosopher Boethius famously defined God's eternity as his "possession of life, a possession simultaneously entire and perfect, which has no end." See Boethius, *Consolation of Philosophy* 5.6.

[2] C. S. Lewis, *Mere Christianity* (New York: HarperCollins, 2001), 166–70.

of time," the moment God had been directing all human history toward, "God sent forth his Son, born of a woman, born under the law" (Gal 4:4 ESV). The eternal Son was born of a virgin in a real place and time at an unusually important moment in world history. But Christ did more than enter the timeline. He gave time itself new meaning and significance.

As a historian, Luke strives to situate his story of Jesus's birth in the social, political, and cultural context in which it unfolded. Luke locates God the Son in a well-attested moment in world history. But Luke also gives us a window into the physical space where the infant Savior was laid in a feeding trough. The timeless, unbound God lay in a manger in a real place and a real time to set the stage for his revealing and redemptive activity.

God in Real Time (Luke 2:1–5)

> In those days a decree went out from Caesar Augustus that the whole empire should be registered. This first registration took place while Quirinius was governing Syria. So everyone went to be registered, each to his own town. Joseph also went up from the town of Nazareth in Galilee, to Judea, to the city of David, which is called Bethlehem, because he was of the house and family line of David, to be registered along with Mary, who was engaged to him and was pregnant. (Luke 2:1–5)

The most significant geopolitical events in ancient history set the stage for the Christmas story in Bethlehem. Five decades before the birth of Jesus, the Roman General Julius Caesar crossed the Rubicon and sparked a civil war that spelled the end of democracy in the old Roman Republic. In a last-ditch effort to save the Republic and their own political futures, members of the senate assassinated Julius Caesar on March 15, 44 BC. His great-nephew and heir Octavian claimed the title of the first emperor of Rome in 31 BC after his army trounced the army of his rivals Mark Antony and Cleopatra.

The two-hundred-year period of peace and prosperity that Octavian brought to the Roman Empire came to be known as the *pax Romana* ("peace of Rome") and earned him the title of "Augustus" (from a Latin word meaning "venerable" or "majestic"). Luke's passing reference to the first Roman emperor as a mere background character tinges with subtle irony. Emperor Augustus may have brought a brand of "peace" to the inhabited world through imperial force, but the true Prince of Peace (Isa 9:6) entered the world unnoticed in a remote outpost of the Roman Empire.[3]

In Luke 2:1, the Evangelist uses a phrase that literally means "the whole world." Roman citizens saw the empire as the "whole world"—or at least the only parts on the globe that really mattered. In the eyes of Roman authorities, the lands they conquered technically became properties of Rome and its citizens. The emperor taxed the natives of the lands he conquered to ensure that they paid the money that he felt was owed him for the "peace" he helped create. To ensure every imperial subject was accounted for, and more importantly, properly taxed, the emperor required counts of all the provinces throughout the empire.

For whatever reason, the census in Judea brought families like Joseph's back to their ancestral home, maybe out of custom or perhaps because individuals like Joseph were listed on the title deeds of their ancestral properties. There, in Bethlehem, the family from Nazareth would witness the fulfillment of a centuries-old prophecy that the Messiah from David's line would be born in his city (Mic 5:2). Bethlehem was called "the city of David" (Luke 2:4) because it was the king's ancestral home (see Ruth 4:11; 1 Sam 16:18; 17:12, 15). Luke seems to suggest that God was moving the shapers of world history around like pawns on a chessboard—small and inconsequential pieces used to achieve a greater goal.

---

[3] Bock, *Luke 1:1–9:50*, 202–3 (see chap. 2, n. 12).

Answering Objections: Luke Invented the Census

Luke states that a Roman census ordered by Augustus (Octavian) brought Joseph and Mary to Bethlehem (Luke 2:1–5). But since the nineteenth century, critical scholars have raised five key objections to this account of the Roman census.

1. There is no record of any empire-wide census during the reign of Caesar Augustus.
2. No such imperial census would have required Joseph and Mary to travel back to Bethlehem.
3. A Roman census would not have been carried out during the reign of Herod the Great because Palestine was not officially a Roman province at this time.
4. The first-century Jewish historian Josephus does not mention a census under Herod and describes the census of Quirinius in AD 6 or 7 as something new and unprecedented.
5. Quirinius was never governor during the lifetime of Herod the Great.

Many of these objections (1–4) rely on the erroneous assumption that we possess an exhaustive record of everything that went on in the ancient world. We do, however, have a wide array of records that are consistent with Luke's description here.

Octavian earned a reputation as an efficient government administrator. We know he ordered several censuses across the empire for the purpose of taking count of those under his rule and assessing their taxes. But take note: In and around the first century, an empire-wide census would not take place overnight. The censuses were completed in several phases. In the first phase, a detailed registry of all people and property was created. According to Ethelbert Stauffer, this was the phase Luke mentions in the nativity story. In the second phase, taxes were assessed when the "bill" came due. This second phase explains the "unprecedented" element of census taking described by Josephus (*Ant.* 17.3).

Depending on the region, some censuses could take years to complete. Censuses also tended to adapt to the needs of a region. When Egypt came under Roman occupation, it already had an efficient system of assessment and taxation that the Romans adopted. When Rome entered Gaul, Augustus made war with those regional leaders who opposed his taxation practices. It is not hard to imagine a distinct process in Israel where men were required to report to the ancestral homes associated with their tribe, especially if someone like Joseph had ancestral property in Bethlehem.

During the reign of Augustus, Palestine was not a true independent state. Herod, a client-king installed by Rome, may have imposed an imperial census on his region to please his master, the emperor. Herod had done equally extravagant things before: He named cities after Augustus and even built a white marble temple in his honor (the Augusteum). In return, Caesar looked the other way when Herod was accused of tyranny toward his people (*Ant.* 15.10.3). But historians also note that the relationship between Herod and Augustus went south in 8 BC, when Herod was essentially demoted in rank. Given this demotion, Palestine could have been required to perform the same kind of census all other Roman subjects were forced to participate in.

The most problematic issue with Luke's timeline comes with the statement in Luke 2:2 that speaks of the "first registration" under Quirinius (objection 5). Quirinius instituted a controversial census in AD 6 or 7—when Jesus was almost a teenager. The taxes levied against the Jews in this census sparked a revolt (*Ant.* 18.1.1). We also have no records of Quirinius as governor of Syria during the lifetime of Herod. Biblical scholars have offered multiple solutions to this problem:

1. Josephus was mistaken about the years when Quirinius came to power.
2. Quirinius gave one census as a government official in the decade prior to becoming governor and a second census when he became governor.
3. Quirinius had two nonconsecutive terms as governor of Syria.

But the simplest solution may be grammatical:

4. The adjective *prōtē* often translated as "first" may also be translated as "before."

Biblical scholar N. T. Wright believes this to be the most natural reading of the text: "This census took place *before the time when* Quirinius was governor of Syria" (Wright, *Who Was Jesus?*, 115). If Wright's translation is correct, all Luke is doing is telling us that this census in Judea predated the more infamous one Quirinius conducted nearly a decade later.

Luke desired to investigate the tradition handed over to him and to write an accurate and orderly sequence of what transpired in the life of Jesus (Luke 1:1–4). The idea that he would fabricate a tax assessment to advance his narrative seems wholly inconsistent with the skill he demonstrates as a historian elsewhere throughout the Gospel and in Acts.

The five objections are laid out in David F. Strauss, *Das Leben Jesu*, vol 1., ch. 4, §32; and Emil Schürer, *The History of the Jewish People in the Age of Jesus Christ*, rev. ed., ed. Geza Vermes, Fergus Millar, and Matthew Black (New York: T&T Clark, 2014), 399–427. For detailed responses to each of Strauss and Schürer's objections, see Ethelbert Stauffer, *Jesus and His Story*, trans. Richard and Clara Winston (New York: Knopf, 1974), 21–32; Bock, *Luke 1:1–9:50*, 903–9 (see chap. 2, n. 12); Marshall, *The Gospel of Luke*, NIGNT, 99–104 (see chap. 4, n. 13); Wayne Brindle, "The Census and Quirinius: Luke 2:2," *JETS* 27, no. 1 (1984): 43–52; N. T. Wright, *Who Was Jesus?* (Grand Rapids: Eerdmans, 2014): 88–119.

God in Physical Space (Luke 2:6–7)

While they were there, the time came for her to give birth. Then she gave birth to her firstborn son, and she wrapped him tightly in cloth and laid him in a manger, because there was no guest room available for them. (Luke 2:6–7)

According to one popular retelling of the first Noël, Mary and Joseph rode into Bethlehem on a donkey late one evening looking for a place to stay. Joseph took Mary, who was already in labor, to a local inn, but the "no vacancy" sign was flashing. In this version of the story, the inn was apparently overbooked because of all the people who were in town for the census. Recognizing their need for shelter, a kindly innkeeper walked the couple over to a nearby stable where Mary gave birth to Jesus, surrounded by livestock. This story of the crowded inn and the kindly innkeeper is one way Bible readers try to make sense of the more bare-bones statement in Luke 2:7: Jesus was "laid in a manger" because, as many translations of the Bible render this verse, "there was no room for them in the inn."

Another tradition takes this version of the Christmas story one step further. Because there was no room in the inn, Mary and Joseph found a nearby grotto or cave by which they could take shelter. This version of the story became very popular in the second century when other non-canonical "gospels" placed Mary and Joseph in a cave at the time of Jesus's birth. By the fourth century, Emperor Constantine built a basilica around such a grotto that was rumored to be the birthplace of Jesus. Over the centuries that basilica grew into the Church of the Nativity that stands in Bethlehem today. But these familiar accounts are shaped more by extra-biblical tradition than what is described in Luke 2:7.[4]

---

[4] Many of these narrative features like the late-night arrival and labor pains come from the apocryphal book *The First Gospel of James* (or *The Protoevangelium of James*). The well-attested cave tradition appears in Justin Martyr, *Dialogue*

What does Luke 2:6–7 say about the time and place of Jesus's birth? Perhaps to the surprise of many readers, Luke says nothing about Mary and Joseph arriving in Bethlehem on the night Jesus was born, only that Jesus was born "while they were there." Joseph and Mary may have travelled to Bethlehem weeks or months before Jesus was born, which would make more sense than Mary traveling the long road from Nazareth in the very late stages of her pregnancy. Luke does not specifically claim that Jesus was born at night (though we might infer that from the angelic birth announcement given to the shepherds at night).

What about the crowded inn and the kindly inkeeper? The Bible does not mention an innkeeper and very likely does not describe a crowded inn—at least in the original language. Many contemporary Bible translations render Luke 2:7 this way: Jesus was "laid in a manger, because there was no guest room for them." Luke did not use the word for a commercial "inn" (*pandocheion*) that he used in the parable of the Good Samaritan (Luke 10:34). Instead, Luke uses the same word (*kataluma*) used to describe the "upper room" where Jesus shared the Passover meal with the disciples in Luke 22:12.[5] The *kataluma* was not a motel room; it was the guest room built onto a family home. Because there was no space for the holy family in the guest room, Jesus was probably born in the main part of a family home, not a separate barn or stable.

Typical homes in ancient Palestine had a "family room" and a sunken "animal room" or "stable" that shared the same open floorplan. The "family

---

with *Trypho*, 74; Paulinus of Nola, *Epistles* 31.3; *Prot. Jas* 18–21; Origen, *Against Celsus*, 1:15; Jerome, *Letter* 58 to Paulinus 3. The tradition of the donkey first appears in *Pseudo-Matthew* 14. Though many in Bethlehem today would like to point to a cave where Jesus was born, I personally prefer the idea that Jesus was born in an ordinary house that was eventually consumed by the time and the elements. Providential history seems to indicate that God has no use for permanent relics—even the Ark of the Covenant—that could be worshipped or treasured in his place.

  [5] Kenneth E. Bailey, *Jesus Through Middle Eastern Eyes: Cultural Studies in the Gospels* (Downers Grove: IVP Academic, 2008), 32–33; Witherington, "Birth of Jesus," 69 (see chap. 2, n. for "Answering Objections: The Genealogies").

room" would be elevated a few steps higher than the "animal room"—like rooms in a modern split-level house—but often the only physical object dividing these two spaces would have been a stone-cut manger or stall. Many families ate, cooked, played, and slept in the same large open space where their animals were kept. The stable was rarely if ever a separate building from the house. Think of it as a sunken "animal garage" that flowed into the floorplan of the home. In a one-story house, either the manger or a timber wall separated the family room from the animals. In a two-story house, the animal room was directly beneath the family room.

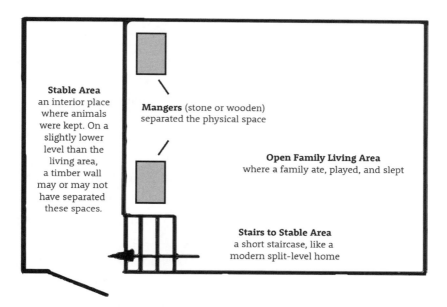

Figure 9.1 A typical village home in Palestine, viewed from above[6]

As one might imagine, the smell that permeated a split-level home that was open to the stable was probably less than desirable by modern standards. But in the same way that animal lovers today think nothing of their pets sleeping in their beds, these ancient families thought nothing

---

[6] Adapted from the figure in Bailey, *Jesus Through Middle Eastern Eyes*, 29.

of farm animals like a donkey, a cow, and some sheep sleeping in their "indoor stable" space. When the animals were inside the house, people didn't have to worry about thieves stealing them. And in winter months, these animals provided extra heat within the home.[7]

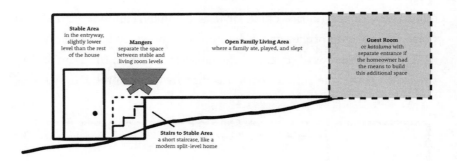

**Figure 9.2 A village house with a guest room
in Palestine, viewed from the side[8]**

The Bible depicts several houses like this. The presence of an animal room in the house explains why Jephthah would have made the foolish vow described in Judg 11:29–40 to sacrifice as a burnt offering "whatever comes out of the door of my house to meet me when I return in triumph from the Ammonites" (11:31 NIV). When he made this hasty vow, Jephthah was expecting one of the animals who lived in the house to come out, not a human being—and certainly not his only daughter. In 1 Sam 28:24, the medium at Endor takes the "fattened calf in the house" (NASB) and slaughters it. When Elijah stayed with the widow and her son, he probably stayed in the guest room upstairs that was adjacent to the family room (see 1 Kgs 17:19). The open floor plan of these homes

---

    [7] Bailey, *Jesus Through Middle Eastern Eyes*, 28–29; Sandra L. Richter, *The Epic of Eden: A Christian Entry into the Old Testament* (Downers Grove: IVP Academic, 2008), 37–38.

    [8] Adapted from the figure in Bailey, *Jesus Through Middle Eastern Eyes*, 29.

also explains why Jesus talks about a single lamp giving light to everyone in the house (Matt 5:14–15).[9]

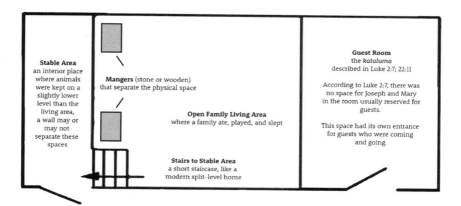

Figure 9.3 A village home with a guest room (*kataluma*), viewed from above[10]

Joseph probably took Mary to the home of a relative or friend in Bethlehem, but because another family occupied the *kataluma* or guest room, they had to stay in the larger space shared with the animals. Instead of the private, solitary space often depicted in traditional manger scenes, Mary probably gave birth to Jesus in cramped quarters with the family living in the main room and unpleasantly fragrant livestock. These cramped and unsterile quarters were no place for any baby to be born, let alone the eternal heir to David's throne.

Jesus was then "wrapped . . . tightly in cloth" or in "swaddling clothes," something practiced by mothers in the ancient world and today (see Ezek 16:4). This tight wrap—which my wife and I lovingly referred to as the "baby burrito" with our own children—helps newborns sleep better by restraining the startle reflexes in their arms that can wake them up mid-sleep. The arms of the Lord were tightly wrapped to help him sleep.

---

[9] Bailey, *Jesus Through Middle Eastern Eyes*, 28, 30.
[10] Adapted from the figure in Bailey, 33.

After all the excitement of angelic announcements, miraculous conceptions, and fulfilled prophecies, the birth of Jesus in a crowded house is, as Thomas Weinandy observed, "almost anti-climactic." Mary may have conceived Jesus in a supernatural way, but she delivered Jesus naturally, and as far as we know, without complication. Everything about Jesus's birth was human and ordinary. Weinandy adds,

> The doctrinal significance of Luke's account of Jesus's birth lies in its simplicity and brevity—nothing extraordinary or miraculous happened because that is the point of the Incarnation. What is extraordinary is that the Son of God was born into our world as a Jewish child of the house and lineage of David in the small town of Bethlehem and wrapped, like all newborns, in swaddling cloths, and because there was no room in the inn, his mother laid him in an animal's feeding box. That is what is doctrinally significant.[11]

The Providential Care of the God of Space and Time

Pagan mythologies tell stories about their gods in abstract ways, removed from the happenings of human history. But the Bible tells a different kind of story about a different kind of God. As Paul described this God to pagan philosophers,

> The God who made the world and everything in it—he is Lord of heaven and earth—does not live in shrines made by hands. Neither is he served by human hands, as though he needed anything, since he himself gives everyone life and breath and all things. From one man he has made every nationality to live over the whole earth and has determined their appointed times and the boundaries of where they live. He did this so that they

---

[11] Thomas C. Weinandy, *Jesus Becoming Jesus: A Theological Interpretation of the Synoptic Gospels* (Washington, DC: Catholic University of America Press, 2018), 1:36.

might seek God, and perhaps they might reach out and find him, though he is not far from each one of us. (Acts 17:24–27)

This God cannot be enclosed in physical space like temples or shrines because he is Lord over all creation. This God cannot be contained in time but reigns over all human history, determining where every individual and nationality will live and when. He orders all things—the rise of emperors, the appointments of kings, and the fall of nations—toward his magnificent ends and purposes. This God orchestrates all things so that he may be perceived and known by creatures. In another stage of human history, God allowed human beings to wander aimlessly in their ignorance. But at the opportune time, God made himself known through "the man he has appointed"—the same man he raised from the dead (Acts 17:31).

As Luke-Acts makes clear, God called Israel and allowed the Roman Empire to form when and how it did to achieve his saving purposes in the world. God providentially crafted the geopolitical conditions that set the stage for the incarnation of the Son in Bethlehem. He also allowed an empire to create a kind of "peace" between foreign lands so that good news of Jesus could spread easily across the inhabited world.

But the greater miracle may not be a timeless and spaceless God in time and space: It was the way this God presented himself as a servant. The God who cannot be contained in shrines or temples made by human hands chose to live in a manger. Surely this "God chose the weak things of the world to shame the strong" (1 Cor 1:27 NIV). If the cross was a sign of foolishness and weakness, so too was the bed chosen for a virgin-born king.

Of this paradox, Fleming Rutledge marveled, "It never ceases to stagger the imagination: the utter audacity of the Advent proclamation that the baby in the manger is the reigning Messiah, that the crucified Jesus will come again in glory to judge the living and the dead, that the one who is to be delivered up is the one who will dispose of all earthly power and authority with imperial ease, being King of kings and Lord of lords."[12]

---

[12] Fleming Rutledge, *Advent* (Grand Rapids: Eerdmans, 2018), 356.

10

The First Witnesses to the Virgin-Born King

Luke 2:8–17

Come to Bethlehem and see
Him whose birth the angels sing,
Come, adore on bended knee,
Christ the Lord, the newborn King.

—JAMES CHADWICK (1813–1882)

Shepherds had one of the dirtiest jobs in ancient Israel. Not only would their smells assault the senses; their reputations were equally repugnant. The elites of ancient Israel's ruling class looked down on the whole occupation of sheep farming. They viewed shepherds as scoundrels and lowlifes who unlawfully grazed on other people's property for dishonest gain.[1]

---

[1] Brown, *Birth of the Messiah*, 420 (see chap. 1, n. 6); b. *Sanhedrin* 25b.

Israel's God, on the other hand, had a special fondness for the sheep farmer. Throughout the biblical story, he often called men from this line of work to deliver his message and to lead his people.

- Abel was a "shepherd of flocks" whose offering pleased the Lord (Gen 4:2, 4).
- God called Abraham out of Haran and blessed him with great wealth in livestock and sheep herds (Gen 12:16).
- When Jacob appeared before the Pharaoh, he professed his family business and the business of his ancestors to be sheep herding. The narrator adds that "all shepherds are detestable to Egyptians" (Gen 46:34).
- Moses was tending his father-in-law's sheep when "the angel of the Lord appeared to him in a flame of fire within a bush" (Exod 3:2). God would use this shepherd to redeem his people from bondage in Egypt.
- David was keeping watch over the flock in the fields around Bethlehem when the prophet Samuel called him in to anoint him as the next king over Israel (1 Sam 16:11–12).
- The eighth-century prophet Amos was a sheep breeder from a little village about ten miles south of Jerusalem when God called him to be his spokesman before the pagan kings of Israel (Amos 1:1–2).

For his faithful care and leadership over his people, God was also known as the Shepherd (Gen 48:15; 49:24; Psalms 23; 80:1; Isa 40:11). Jesus professed to be the "good shepherd" who lays his life down for the sheep (John 10:14–15). Peter referred to Jesus as "the Shepherd and Overseer of your souls" (1 Pet 2:25) and the "chief Shepherd" (1 Pet 5:4; see also Heb 13:20). Because they were called to reflect the shepherding care of the Great Shepherd, church elders were also called "shepherds" (*poimén*) or "pastors" (from the Latin translation of the same Greek word).

Shepherding imagery also pervaded Micah's prophecy about the Messiah who would be born in Bethlehem:

Bethlehem Ephrathah,
    you are small among the clans of Judah;
one will come from you
    to be ruler over Israel for me.
His origin is from antiquity,
    from ancient times. . . .
He will stand and shepherd them
    in the strength of the LORD,
    in the majestic name of the LORD his God.
They will live securely,
    for then his greatness will extend
    to the ends of the earth. (Mic 5:2, 4; cf. 4:6–8)

Micah prophesied that a shepherd-like Messiah from eternity past would be born in Bethlehem. In God's name and by his strength, this man would shepherd Israel and keep them secure. His name and greatness would be known to "the ends of the earth" (see also Acts 1:8).

Ezekiel also envisaged the Lord's Messiah as a shepherd: "I will establish over them one shepherd, my servant David, and he will shepherd them. He will tend them himself and will be their shepherd. I, the LORD, will be their God, and my servant David will be a prince among them. I, the LORD, have spoken" (Ezek 34:23–24).

Against this prophetic backdrop, Luke introduces us to the shepherds of Bethlehem invited by the angels to witness the newborn king. The shepherds again remind us of the humble circumstances of Jesus's birth. These men belong to a lower station than the gold-bearing royal emissaries who visit the baby Jesus in Matthew 2. The only gifts these shepherds could afford to bring were their celebration and praise. These shepherds also come away with a special calling: to be the first people to bear witness to the virgin-born king.

The Shepherds Witnessed the Glory of God

In the same region, shepherds were staying out in the fields and keeping watch at night over their flock. Then an angel of the Lord stood before them, and the glory of the Lord shone around them, and they were terrified. But the angel said to them, "Don't be afraid, for look, I proclaim to you good news of great joy that will be for all the people: Today in the city of David a Savior was born for you, who is the Messiah, the Lord. This will be the sign for you: You will find a baby wrapped tightly in cloth and lying in a manger." (Luke 2:8–12)

Many have used Luke's chronicle of the shepherds out in the fields at night to argue that Jesus was born in the spring or summer months, not December.[2] But if these shepherds in close proximity to Jerusalem were guarding sheep that would be used for the Passover sacrifices, then the winter months cannot be completely ruled out either.[3] Because we are agnostic about when Jesus was born, the traditional date of December 25 is as good a time as any to celebrate this blessed event.

---

[2] Adam Clarke, *The New Testament*, vol. 1, Matthew–Acts (New York, 1855) 370. Clarke speculated that Jesus's birth must have been sometime between spring when Jewish shepherds sent their flocks out to pasture and the beginning of the rainy season in October when they brought their sheep home. Other factors, such as the time of the year when Zechariah's priestly division was called up, have also been used to calculate a summer birth for Jesus. See John Thorley, "When Was Jesus Born?" *Greece & Rome* 28, no. 1 (1981): 81–89.

[3] Leon Morris, *Luke*, TNTC, rev. ed. (Downers Grove: InterVarsity, 1988), 93. The third-century theologian Hippolytus of Rome is often credited as the source of the traditional date. See Thomas C. Schmidt, "Calculating December 25 as the Birth of Jesus in Hippolytus' *Canon* and *Chronicon*," *Vigiliae Christianae* 69, no. 5 (2015): 542–63; Paul Bradshaw, "The Dating of Christmas: The Early Church," in *The Oxford Handbook of Christmas*, ed. Timothy Larsen (Oxford: Oxford University Press, 2020), 3–14; Witherington, "Birth of Jesus," 69 (see chap. 2, n. for "Answering Objections: The Genealogies").

More importantly, this evening setting provides a stark contrast between the radiant glory of God and the darkness of the night sky. Otherworldly angels made their presence known to these shepherds, and like every other angelic encounter recorded in Luke's Gospel, these men were terrified. The Greek phrase here is literally rendered "they were frightened with fear" (*ephobēthēsan phobon*). Also like every other angelic encounter in this book, the angelic messenger brought words of assurance and peace, telling hearers not to be afraid.

The "glory of the Lord" that shone around the shepherds (Luke 2:9a) calls to mind the "Shekinah glory" of God that appeared to Israel.[4] When Moses asked to see God's glory, God hid him in the cleft of the rock so he could watch the Lord pass by from behind (Exod 33:18–23). Ezekiel's awe-inspiring vision of the glory of the Lord bears a striking resemblance to the shepherds:

> The appearance of the brilliant light all around was like that of a rainbow in a cloud on a rainy day. This was the appearance of the likeness of the LORD's glory. When I saw it, I fell facedown and heard a voice speaking. (Ezek 1:28)

The angel's message was even more important than the glorious means by which it was pronounced: "I proclaim to you good news of great joy that will be for all the people." The verb translated "to proclaim good news" is an early form of the verb "evangelize," or "to proclaim the gospel."[5] In its pre-Christian usage, the word for "gospel" or "good tidings" (*euangelion*) often carried political connotations. Sometimes "good tidings" would be used to describe a military conquest over a foreign

---

[4] Bock, *Luke 1:1–9:50*, 214 (see chap. 2, n. 12). The word "Shekinah" does not appear in the Hebrew Bible. This theological term that describes beatific visions in the Old Testament only developed in later rabbinical writings.

[5] Bock, 210. Bock notes that this verb *euangelizomai* is common to the writings of Luke and Paul but is sparce elsewhere across the NT. The shared language between Luke and Paul may provide further evidence of the traditional authorship of Luke.

enemy. Other times it would be used to speak of a new ruler rising to power. One well-known inscription from 9 BC announced the "beginning of the gospel for the world" that came through the "god" and "savior" Caesar Augustus.[6]

Up to this point in Luke's nativity story, all the "good news" centered around Israel's deliverance and the promises God made to David and Abraham. But here, in this angelic announcement, the gospel message is good news "for all the people"—Jew and Gentile alike. This gospel is, as Paul later wrote, "the power of God for salvation to everyone who believes, first to the Jew, and also to the Greek" (Rom 1:16).

What is this good news proclaimed by the angel? "Today in the city of David a Savior was born for you, who is the Messiah, the Lord" (Luke 2:11). The threefold description of Jesus as "Savior," "Messiah," and "Lord" never again appears in the New Testament. The angel calls Jesus "a Savior," which literally describes someone who delivers a person from peril or danger. Through Christ, God "has rescued us from the domain of darkness and transferred us into the kingdom of the Son he loves. In him we have redemption, the forgiveness of sins" (Col 1:13–14). The angel further describes this Savior as "the Messiah," or the "anointed one" who fulfills the promises made long ago to Israel.

Finally, the angel reveals Christ as "the Lord," suggesting the true divinity of the child who was born in Bethlehem. In the previous chapter, Luke used this title to refer broadly to the work of Yahweh in Israel: "the commands and requirements of the Lord" (Luke 1:6); "the sanctuary of the Lord" (Luke 1:9); "the Lord their God" (Luke 1:16); and "the Lord God" (Luke 1:32). Those designations properly refer to the entire

---

[6] See the Priene Calendar Inscription (*IT* 14). Craig A. Evans, "Mark's Incipit and the Priene Calendar Inscription: From Jewish Gospel to Greco-Roman Gospel," *Journal of Greco-Roman Christianity and Judaism* 1 (2000): 67–81. Compare this edict with the opening statement of Mark's Gospel: "The beginning of the gospel of Jesus Christ, the Son of God" (Mark 1:1).

Godhead. But Elizabeth and the angels here appropriate the term to refer specifically to Christ (Luke 1:43; 2:11).

The angels tell the shepherds to look for the "sign"—a manifestation or revelation from God. Other angelic messages in Luke were accompanied by supernatural signs. The supernatural muting of Zechariah provided evidence for Elizabeth's conception. When Gabriel told Mary she would conceive, Elizabeth's pregnancy past childbearing years provided the necessary proof of God's great power. But when these angels told the shepherds what had transpired in Bethlehem, the "sign" given was, by comparison, mundane and ordinary. The shepherds were told that they would find the Savior, the long-awaited Messiah, and the Lord of the universe, wrapped up like any other newborn baby and lying in a manger.

Yet even this "ordinary" sign was a greater manifestation of God's glory than any other angelic spectacle they witnessed that night. For the "entire fullness of God's nature" dwelt bodily in that babe in the manger (Col 2:9). True knowledge of the glory of God can only be found in the face of Christ (2 Cor 4:6). Christ himself is the sign: the image of the invisible God (Col 1:15), the Word made flesh (John 1:14), and "the radiance of God's glory and the exact expression of his nature" (Heb 1:3).

The Shepherds Witnessed the Praise of Heaven

Suddenly there was a multitude of the heavenly host with the angel, praising God and saying:

> Glory to God in the highest heaven,
> and peace on earth to people he favors! (Luke 2:13–14)

The individual angel speaking to the shepherds was unexpectedly accompanied by the heavenly host who surround God's throne. The word translated here as "suddenly" (*exaiphnés*) always accompanies unexpected supernatural activity in the New Testament: the sudden return of Christ (Mark 13:36), unexpected demonic oppression (Luke 9:39), and the sudden appearance of heavenly light on the road to Damascus (Acts 9:3; 22:6).[7] Here, the curtain of heaven is suddenly pulled back, and these ordinary shepherds catch a glimpse of the army of angels who continually serve and praise God around the throne (Pss 103:19–21; 148:2; Isa 6:1–5). Jacob the shepherd dreamt something similar when he was sleeping under the night sky at Bethel: "A stairway was set on the ground with its top reaching the sky, and God's angels were going up and down on it" (Gen 28:12). But the heavenly vision in Luke's Gospel is even more remarkable because multiple shepherds saw it while they were wide awake.

The heavenly chorus praised God with the third "song" recorded in Luke's nativity story. The angels give "glory to God in the highest heaven" (the song we know by the Latin title *Gloria in excelsis Deo*) because he has brought peace to those who are below on earth. But God's "peace" or "good will" is not directed toward all men, as some older translations might suggest. The "peace" God offered was different from the imperial "peace" enforced by the sword of Rome in the *Pax Romana*.[8] The angels do not proclaim the universalism or utopian peace of popular Christmas music. Instead, the heavenly host declare that God's peace is for "people of his good pleasure" (*anthrōpois eudokias*)—a common term in ancient Judaism for God's elect.[9] The peace promised is not peace between men but peace between God and men.

Whereas the gospel is good news "for all the people" (Luke 2:10), God's peace exclusively belongs to those whom "he favors" (Luke 2:14). In other words, the gospel call may be universal, but only those whom he chooses are its beneficiaries. Those whom God favors now were once his enemies but were "reconciled to God through the death of his Son"

---

[7] Bock, *Luke 1:1–9:50*, 219.

[8] Grant R. Osborne, *Luke: Verse by Verse* (Bellingham, WA: Lexham Press, 2018), 76.

[9] Bock, *Luke 1:1–9:50*, 220.

(Rom 5:10; see also 2 Cor 5:19). Because "we have been justified by faith, we have peace with God through our Lord Jesus Christ" (Rom 5:1). We "who were far away have been brought near by the blood of Christ. For he is our peace" (Eph 2:13b–14a). Christ is the peace of all who entrust their lives to him in faith.

The Shepherds Witnessed the Incarnate Word

When the angels had left them and returned to heaven, the shepherds said to one another, "Let's go straight to Bethlehem and see what has happened, which the Lord has made known to us." They hurried off and found both Mary and Joseph, and the baby who was lying in the manger. After seeing them, they reported the message they were told about this child, and all who heard it were amazed at what the shepherds said to them. But Mary was treasuring up all these things in her heart and meditating on them. The shepherds returned, glorifying and praising God for all the things they had seen and heard, which were just as they had been told. (Luke 2:15–20)

Andreas Köstenberger and Alexander Stewart contrast God's arrival in Bethlehem with his frightful appearance on Mt. Sinai. There God appeared in "a blazing fire . . . darkness, gloom, and storm, to the blast of a trumpet, and the sound of words. Those who heard it begged that not another word be spoken to them" (Heb 12:18–19). But as Köstenberger and Stewart observe, "There was no earthquake, fire, or smoke the night Jesus took his first breath and cried for the first time."[10] Instead of instilling fear, when the shepherds finally witnessed the Word himself, they were overcome with joy, peace, and comfort.

---

[10] Andreas J. Köstenberger and Alexander E. Stewart, *The First Days of Jesus* (Wheaton, IL: Crossway, 2015), 146.

The shepherds could not wait to tell people about Jesus. Their response to this message closely parallels Mary's response to Gabriel: they "hurried off" to witness for themselves the sign the angel told them about (Luke 2:16; see also Luke 1:39). The word Luke uses to say that the shepherds "found" the holy family indicates a search process when they arrived in Bethlehem.[11] Just imagine: the shepherds may have gone from home to home in Bethlehem asking, "Did anyone in this house have a baby today? Do you mind if we look in your manger?"

Those who heard the shepherds' testimony marveled at their message. When the shepherds finally discovered Jesus in the manger, confirming what the angels had foretold, they enthusiastically reported everything the angels had told them. "All who heard it were amazed" (Luke 2:18), meaning we can likely dispel the image of Mary and Joseph delivering a child by themselves in a stable. "All who heard it" may include the people the shepherds met in town when they went looking for the baby, or "all who heard" may refer to the people who were staying in the house where Jesus was born. Whoever heard it responded the same way Peter did when he saw the empty tomb: with amazement (Luke 24:12).

Luke comments that Mary "was treasuring up all these things in her heart and meditating on them" (Luke 2:19). The aspect of these Greek verbs indicated that Mary continued to ponder and think about these things long after the shepherds were gone. Luke makes a similar comment in 2:51: "his mother kept all these things in her heart." The truths about Jesus's identity stirred her affections and left a lasting impression on her memory. Perhaps these are the clues Luke leaves behind to point us back to the source of these eyewitness accounts.

The good news came from unexpected places. The first men to hear the "good news" or "gospel" from the angels were not experts in the law of Moses or those deemed faithful and credible Jewish citizens. Rabbinical law deemed shepherds to be lowlifes and unreliable witnesses whose

---

[11] The aorist *aneuran* ("found") come from *aneuriskó*, which means "to seek out" or "to discover."

testimony could not be admitted in court.[12] Courts likewise refused to let "the testimony of women be admitted, on account of the levity and boldness of their sex."[13] It was fitting, then, that the first recorded witnesses to Jesus's birth would have been met with the same kind of skepticism as the women who were the first witnesses to his resurrection (see Luke 24:11).

Unbelievers still balk at the words of simple people of God who profess deep truths. We can never be educated enough, wealthy enough, winsome enough, or powerful enough to convince everyone of the truthfulness of the gospel. But we can be like these shepherds who heard the gospel, experienced Jesus for themselves, and told everyone they could about him. If we truly are excited about what God did by taking on true humanity like ours, then we should be like these shepherds, eager to proclaim good news to anyone who will hear it. Those who respond to the Spirit's call and believe will be amazed and learn to treasure the good news of Jesus for themselves.

---

[12] b. *Sanhedrin* 25b.

[13] b. 25b; see also Josephus, *Ant.* 4.8.15.

11

Born Under the Law

Luke 2:21–24

Christ has perfectly fulfilled the law, so that all those who believe in
him might be redeemed from this heavy yoke of the law and that the
law might henceforth have no power to curse or condemn them.

–MARTIN BUCER[1]

For many years in my early Christian life, I made a New Year's resolu-
tion to read the Bible from Genesis to Revelation in a year's time.
And almost every year, I fell miserably short of my desired goal. Things
always started out well enough. Reading a few chapters every day, I
blazed right through the action-packed stories in Genesis and the opening chapters of Exodus. But I began to slow down somewhere around

---

[1] Martin Bucer, *An Ecclesiastical Exposition upon Saint Luke* 2.3, quoted in
Luke, Reformation Commentary on Scripture, NT, ed. Beth Kreitzer (Downers
Grove: InterVarsity, 2015), 3:58.

the discussions about priestly garments and tabernacle dimensions in the second half of Exodus.

But by mid-February, my noble efforts to read the Bible from cover to cover hit the brick wall that is the book of Leviticus. As a young Christian, I was perplexed by this book that had so many strange rules about animal sacrifices, grain offerings, blood-spattering priests, and unclean food. Yet even more experienced believers tend to tune out OT law. We tell ourselves, "We're not under the law anymore. This section of Scripture just isn't relevant to my life." The law of Moses can certainly bewilder and even bore those who do not understand its significance in the larger story of Scripture.

Remember what the risen Lord did for our comparably confused brothers on the road to Emmaus: "Beginning with Moses . . . he interpreted for them the things concerning himself in all the Scriptures" (Luke 24:27). Jesus started with the five books of Moses—including Leviticus—and explained to them all the ways he fulfilled them. That same evening when he was in the company of the other disciples, he said, "Everything written about me in the Law of Moses . . . must be fulfilled" (Luke 24:44). The crucial key to grasp is that Jesus fulfilled all of Scripture—even those strange OT laws we do not fully understand.

Luke scattered breadcrumbs all across his Gospel that lead us back to Emmaus, connecting the seemingly insignificant details of Jesus's life with the whole biblical story. In Luke 2:21–24, the Evangelist briefly mentions three rituals Jesus's parents partook in when he was a newborn baby: circumcision, purification, and the dedication of the firstborn male. Luke draws attention to the obedience of Jesus's parents and the need "to perform for him what was customary under the law" (Luke 2:27). These mundane details serve a greater theological purpose. They situate Jesus as a full citizen in the community of Israel. They show how Jesus met the obligations of the law from birth to adulthood.

But more importantly, Luke illustrates what his associate Paul said about Jesus's relationship to the law: "When the time came to completion,

God sent his Son, born of a woman, born under the law, to redeem those under the law, so that we might receive adoption as sons" (Gal 4:4–5). From infancy, the virgin-born king perfectly fulfilled the law so that he might redeem us as God's sons and daughters.

Jesus Met All the Requirements of the Law

> When the eight days were completed for his circumcision, he was named Jesus—the name given by the angel before he was conceived. (Luke 2:21)

Following the birth of Jesus, the holy family likely began an extended stay in Bethlehem. This change of residency would explain why they were in a house in Bethlehem when the magi came to see Jesus later (Matt 2:9–11). Rabbis often performed circumcisions in the homes of the child and his parents. But if Joseph and Mary had not yet established themselves in Bethlehem, it is possible that the infant was taken to a local synagogue for the ritual. It is also likely that Joseph himself had a hand in co-officiating the circumcision.[2]

Why was Jesus circumcised? Since the turn of the twentieth century, most boys born in American hospitals have been circumcised for nonreligious reasons like hygiene or cosmetic appearance. But circumcision played a much different role in ancient Israel. The law of Moses required male children to be circumcised eight days after their birth (Lev 12:3). God had instructed Abraham to circumcise his sons as an enduring "sign of the covenant":

> "As for you, you and your offspring after you throughout their generations are to keep my covenant. This is my covenant between me and you and your offspring after you, which you are to keep: Every one of your males must be circumcised. You must

---

[2] Paul L. Maier, *In the Fullness of Time: A Historian Looks at Christmas, Easter, and the Early Church*, rev. ed. (Grand Rapids: Kregel, 1998), 70.

circumcise the flesh of your foreskin to serve as a sign of the covenant between me and you. Throughout your generations, every male among you is to be circumcised at eight days old. . . . My covenant will be marked in your flesh as a permanent covenant. If any male is not circumcised in the flesh of his foreskin, that man will be cut off from his people; he has broken my covenant" (Gen 17:9–12a, 13b–14)

Every day Jewish men were physically reminded of the promise God made to Abraham by the permanent physical change of circumcision. The "cut" of the blade pictured the act of "cutting" a covenant with God. The cut also reminded Israel that the Israelite man who was not cut by the blade would be "cut off" from his people. For Christ, this physical cut also marked the first time that his blood was spilt to satisfy the law's demands.

Like baptism under the new covenant, the act of circumcision was an outward sign of the old covenant. Circumcision identified the people of God, but it did not make them. Under the new covenant, those who were uncircumcised when they came to faith were not required to be circumcised then (1 Cor 7:18; Gal 2:3; 5:2).

Jesus was circumcised to show that he was a full member of the covenant community of Israel. The "mediator of a new covenant" (Heb 9:15) was sealed with the sign of the old. Through his circumcision and perfect obedience to the point of death, Christ made provision for circumcised Jews and uncircumcised Gentiles alike: "For I say that Christ became a servant of the circumcised on behalf of God's truth, to confirm the promises to the fathers, and so that Gentiles may glorify God for his mercy" (Rom 15:8–9a).

At his circumcision, the child's mother and adoptive father also named him Jesus, just as the angels had instructed them (Matt 1:21; Luke 1:31). This common Jewish name, which means "Yahweh saves," foretold the mission of God the Son incarnate.

Jesus Was Set Apart from the Beginning

And when the days of their purification according to the law of Moses were finished, they brought him up to Jerusalem to present him to the Lord (just as it is written in the law of the Lord, **Every firstborn male will be dedicated to the Lord**) and to offer a sacrifice (according to what is stated in the law of the Lord, **a pair of turtledoves or two young pigeons**). (Luke 2:22–24)

Forty days after the birth of Jesus, the holy family made the six-mile journey from Bethlehem "up to Jerusalem." In the temple, the family would undergo two rituals: the dedication of Jesus and the purification of his mother. Purification rituals like the one described here may seem foreign to twenty-first century Christians, but they played a pivotal role in the belief system of ancient Israelites. Through the purity code in the book of Leviticus, God provided Israel with a helpful way of organizing the world around them.

For Israelites, every person, place, and thing in the world fits into one of two basic categories: something that is *holy* or *common* and something that is *clean* or *unclean* (Lev 10:10). (We do something similar whenever we distinguish between "sacred" and "secular" or when we label people as "lost" or "saved.")

For something to be "holy," it had to be set apart, different, and uncommon. God set Israel apart and commanded them to be a "holy" people because they serve a different kind of God: "You are to be holy to me because I, the LORD, am holy, and I have set you apart from the nations to be mine" (Lev 20:26). The Bible calls several places "holy": Mt. Sinai (Exod 3:5), Mt. Zion (Zeph 3:11), and the promised land Israel inhabited (Zech 2:12). The law identifies several holy things as well: the tabernacle (Exod 40:9), the altar (Exod 29:37), sacrifices (Lev 27:9; Num 18:17), and the temple (Pss 11:4; 138:2; Isa 64:11).

Holy things were "not common" because they were set apart unto the Lord. "Common" things could be "clean" or "unclean." We must resist the temptation to think about "clean" and "unclean" in terms of modern hygiene (though this is my normal thought process as a germaphobe). "Clean" and "unclean" were symbolic ways of ordering behavior and life in ancient Israel. Sometimes God commanded his people not to eat certain foods, not to dress in certain clothes, and not to behave in certain ways because he simply wanted them to be different from their pagan neighbors.

Any number of things could make a "clean" person "unclean": skin disease, touching an unclean object like an animal carcass, eating unclean animals, menstruating, having sex, or giving birth. These natural things were not inherently sinful, but they did make a person ritually "unclean." Israel associated blood, bodily discharges, carcasses, and disease with death. These "unclean" things served as symbolic reminders that death was not part of God's design but part of living in a fallen and broken world.

Certain steps needed to be taken to make a person or a thing clean again so that holy things would not be contaminated. In some cases, the only way to remove the stain of death was by the sacrificial death of another animal. The author of Hebrews tells us why this is important: "According to the law almost everything is purified with blood, and without the shedding of blood there is no forgiveness" (Heb 9:22). The entire sacrificial system of Leviticus was an imperfect copy of the perfect sacrifice that Christ would eventually make on our behalf (Heb 9:23–28).

Mary and the Purification Ritual

The law provided detailed instructions for how postpartum women could be made ritually clean again. When a mother gave birth to male children, she was considered unclean for seven days after childbirth, the same length of time she was considered unclean during her menstrual cycle (Lev 12:2). Their sons were to be circumcised on the eighth day

(Lev 12:3). For the next thirty-three days, she was instructed not to enter the sanctuary or touch anything holy until her purification period was complete. (Think of this time like an ancient, religious version of maternity leave.) For reasons unknown to us, these timetables were doubled in length when daughters were born (Lev 12:5).

At the end of her days of purification (forty days for a male child, eighty for a female), the mother was instructed to bring an animal for sacrifice to the priest at the tent of meeting. When the priest offered the sacrifice, it would ceremonially cleanse her from the discharge of blood she experienced during childbirth. The normal sacrifice to be offered was a year-old lamb for a "burnt offering" and a pigeon or a turtledove for a "sin offering" (Lev 12:6). But if she could not afford a lamb, she could take two turtledoves or two pigeons for the burnt offering and the sin offering (Lev 12:8).

The mother of Jesus needed to follow this purification ritual so she could be made "clean" again. The holy family's participation in this ritual indicates several things.

First, Jesus's parents faithfully observed God's law. Jesus was raised by a couple who, from an early age, instructed him in the law and modeled obedience for him. We can imagine many long walks up and down the streets of Nazareth where, just like Moses commanded, Jesus's parents repeated the words of the law to him and his brothers and sisters (see Deut 6:6–7, 20–25).

Second, Mary's "unclean" status indicates that she delivered a truly human Savior through ordinary childbirth. Though we sometimes call the miraculous way Jesus was conceived the "virgin birth," the Bible gives us no indication that anything miraculous happened in the birth process itself. Many early and medieval Christians were convinced that Jesus could not have been delivered through natural childbirth because a natural delivery would have broken Mary's hymen, the physical evidence of her virginity (see Deut 22:15–17). The second-century pseudo-gospel known as *The First Gospel of James* (c. 150) concocted an elaborate story for how Mary could continue to be a virgin after Jesus was born, including a pain-free

birth (see *Prot. Jas* 19:19–20).[3] But the biblical account of Mary's purification ritual means we can dispense with this later, extrabiblical tradition
that says she had a painless childbirth or that she somehow delivered
Jesus without incurring any changes to her body.

Third, her participation in the "sin offering" indicates that Mary was a
sinner in need of forgiveness. The sin offering and burnt offering made
atonement for the sins committed by the one offering them (Lev 5:7–
10). Scripture never even hints at the idea of an "immaculate conception"—the idea that Mary's parents miraculously conceived a daughter
without the effects of Adam's sin. Just the opposite. Scripture is clear that
"all have sinned and fall short of the glory of God" (Rom 3:23) except for
"the one who did not know sin" (2 Cor 5:21), namely Jesus.

Finally, Mary's offering is evidence of the holy family's poverty. By his
selective quotation of Lev 12:8, Luke implies that Mary and Joseph
offered two pigeons or two turtledoves as a sacrifice because they were
too poor to offer the year-old lamb normally required by the law. Luke
implies the same irony Paul openly celebrates in 2 Cor 8:9: "Though he
was rich, for your sake he became poor, so that by his poverty you might
become rich." The king of heaven who owns "the cattle on a thousand
hills" (Ps 50:10) and "the world and everything in it" (Ps 50:12) came
down to dwell with a family who could not afford the standard sacrifice. Mary and Joseph could not afford a lamb, but the baby in their
arms would be called "the Lamb of God, who takes away the sin of the
world" (John 1:29).

Jesus Dedicated to the Lord

Joseph and Mary presented Jesus to the Lord to fulfill the requirement
of the law that "every firstborn male will be dedicated to the Lord"
(Luke 2:23). The phrase rendered here as "will be dedicated to the Lord"
is more literally translated "will be called holy to the Lord." As God

---

[3] See appendix 2.

commanded Israel, "Consecrate every firstborn male to me, the firstborn from every womb among the Israelites, both man and domestic animal; it is mine" (Exod 13:1).

The original instruction for this ritual appears in the same sequence as the Passover and the Exodus (Exod 11–13:16). During the Passover, God showed that all firstborn sons belong to him—human and livestock, Israelite and Egyptian. In the same way God receives all the firstfruits of our labor because he provides for us (Lev 23:9–14), God wants the firstborn son and animal for himself. Some firstborn sons, like Samuel, were given as a permanent gift to God's service (1 Sam 1:11), but most were redeemed or "bought back" from God with a price that their parents could afford (Exod 13:15; Num 18:14–15).

God gave Israel this practice as an enduring reminder of the time when he struck down all firstborn sons and livestock in Egypt. The act of consecration and sacrifice reminded them that "the LORD brought us out of Egypt by the strength of his hand" (Exod 13:16), but it also looked ahead toward the ultimate sacrifice of the divinely appointed substitute who would be punished for our sin (Isa 53:5–6). In the same way parents paid a financial price to "buy" their firstborn sons back, we who belong to Christ "were bought at a price" (1 Cor 6:20).

When Mary presented her "firstborn son" (Luke 2:7) before the Lord as holy, she declared him to be uncommon and set apart for God. Although all firstborn sons were considered holy to the Lord, this was especially true of the virgin-born son of Mary, who was called "the holy one" and "the Son of God" (Luke 1:35).

Jesus Redeemed Us from the Curse of the Law

Jesus often challenged the way Pharisees and scribes misunderstood or misapplied the law of Moses (Luke 6:1–11; 13:10–17), but Jesus never rejected the law itself (Matt 7:23; 23:28). Jesus wholeheartedly endorsed the law of Moses because he himself was Israel's lawgiver. Jesus did not want to dispense with the law; he wanted to complete it:

Don't think that I came to abolish the Law or the Prophets. I did not come to abolish but to fulfill. For truly I tell you, until heaven and earth pass away, not the smallest letter or one stroke of a letter will pass away from the law until all things are accomplished. (Matt 5:17–18)

Through subjection to the law that began at his birth, Jesus did what no other individual in history ever could: He fulfilled the law by obeying it perfectly. Like every other firstborn male in Israel, he was circumcised and dedicated to the Lord. But unlike everyone else in Israel, he had no sin or guilt that required atonement or offering.

When John said that "the law was given through Moses; grace and truth came through Jesus Christ" (John 1:17), he did not pit Jesus against the law of Moses but contrasted two stages in God's redemptive plan. God revealed our need for a Savior through the law and revealed his grace and truth through the Savior himself. God's law provided wonderful, life-giving instruction, but those who do not do everything written in it are cursed by it (Gal 3:10).

Through his active obedience to the law and his passive obedience unto death, "Christ redeemed us from the curse of the law by becoming a curse for us" (Gal 3:13). On this side of the cross, we can read Leviticus with a clear awareness of God's holiness. Then and only then can we begin to appreciate the great lengths God went to in order to make a holy people for himself.

12

Come Thou Long Expected Jesus

Luke 2:25–38

The LORD is good to those who wait for him,
    to the person who seeks him.
    It is good to wait quietly
    for salvation from the LORD.
                                            —LAMENTATIONS 3:25–26

During Advent season, followers of Jesus reenact the experience of Old Testament saints who eagerly awaited the coming of Israel's Messiah. We know that the Messiah has already visited humanity once before. But on this side of Easter, we wait with the same kind of anticipation "for the blessed hope, the appearing of the glory of our great God and Savior, Jesus Christ" (Titus 2:13). Advent recalls the completed work

159

of God the Son incarnate and looks ahead toward the final consummation of his kingdom in his second coming.

Few people in Scripture exemplify the proper posture of Advent season more than Simeon and Anna. When Jesus's parents brought their son into the temple to fulfill the requirements of the law, they encountered Simeon who blessed them and prophesied over Jesus, and Anna who prophesied to the masses God's redemption of Jerusalem. These interrelated scenes manifest the activity of the Holy Spirit in God's people and point us to several ways in which the virgin-born king fulfills the prophetic expectations of the messianic Servant.

Israel's Strength and Consolation

There was a man in Jerusalem whose name was Simeon. This man was righteous and devout, looking forward to Israel's consolation, and the Holy Spirit was on him. It had been revealed to him by the Holy Spirit that he would not see death before he saw the Lord's Messiah. Guided by the Spirit, he entered the temple. When the parents brought in the child Jesus to perform for him what was customary under the law, Simeon took him up in his arms, praised God, and said,

Now, Master,
you can dismiss your servant in peace,
as you promised.
For my eyes have seen your salvation.
You have prepared it
in the presence of all peoples—
a light for revelation to the Gentiles
and glory to your people Israel.

His father and mother were amazed at what was being said about him. Then Simeon blessed them and told his mother Mary, "Indeed, this child is destined to cause the fall and rise of many in

Israel and to be a sign that will be opposed—and a sword will pierce your own soul—that the thoughts of many hearts may be revealed." (Luke 2:25–35)

Simeon was a faithful man of God nearing the end of his life. Though Luke makes no direct statements about Simeon's age, the prophet's expectation of an imminent death indicates that he was well advanced in years. Simeon was "righteous and devout" with respect to God's law and commandments (Luke 2:25; cf. 1:6).

Simeon eagerly awaited the "consolation" of Israel prophesied by Isaiah. When King Hezekiah was visited by royal representatives from Babylon who flattered him with kind words, the king of Judah made the foolish decision to flaunt Judah's treasure before them. Isaiah warned the king of a future invasion when Babylon would invade, empty the treasuries, and deport most people in Judah to a foreign land. (This invasion eventually took place in 587 BC—nearly 100 years after Hezekiah died.) Essentially saying, "That's the next guy's problem," Hezekiah shrugged off this warning, relieved to hear that none of this would transpire in his own lifetime (see Isaiah 39). But this message of delayed suffering brought little relief to later Jews who would be shipped off and deported to Babylon. God sought to bring comfort and consolation to the people in exile through Isaiah's predictive prophecy:

> "Comfort, comfort my people,"
> says your God.
> "Speak tenderly to Jerusalem,
> and announce to her
> that her time of hard service is over,
> her iniquity has been pardoned,
> and she has received from the LORD's hand
> double for all her sins." (Isa 40:1–2)

God partially fulfilled this promise in 539 BC when Persia—the predicted nation "from the east" (Isa 41:2)—conquered Babylon. As predicted by

Isaiah, the Persian king Cyrus the Great "restored" Israel by allowing the Jews to return to the land and rebuild Jerusalem (Isa 44:24–45:13).

Yet Simeon still clung to the promise of Isaiah 40 when Jesus was born. Though Jews had returned to the land after the Babylonian exile, they still lived under one foreign oppressor after another, Rome being the latest. Consequently, the people of Israel still felt as if they were in a state of exile even if they were still technically living in the land. They longed to be restored to their former glory as an independent nation state like they were in the united monarchy under David.[1] Simeon shared in the hope that Israel's Messiah would eventually bring peace and usher in God's kingdom (see also Luke 2:25; cf. 2:38; 23:51). But following Isaiah's prophecy, Simeon had a larger vision than just the restoration of Israel from exile. He also looked ahead to the eventual inclusion of the Gentiles among the people of God.

The Holy Spirit anointed Simeon. Luke says plainly that "the Holy Spirit was on him" (Luke 2:25). With his account of Simeon and Anna's prophecy, Luke foreshadows the new covenant work of the Spirit prophesied by Joel and fulfilled on the day of Pentecost: "I will pour out my Spirit on . . . men and women and they will prophesy" (Acts 2:17–18; see also Joel 2:28–29). Simeon, like Elizabeth and Zechariah, displayed a remarkable sensitivity to the Holy Spirit. The Spirit revealed a promise to Simeon that he would not see death before he had laid his eyes on the "Lord's Messiah."

The Spirit led Simeon to the temple where he would encounter the family of Jesus. Simeon likely met them when they came in from the temple gates into the court of women—the furthest place Mary could go in the temple complex. This stranger hoisted their six-week-old up in his

---

[1] See N. T. Wright, "Yet the Sun Will Rise Again: Reflections on the Exile and Restoration in Second Temple Judaism, Jesus, Paul, and the Church Today," in *Exile: A Conversation with N. T. Wright*, ed. James M. Scott (Downers Grove: IVP Academic, 2017), 19–81; Wright, *The New Testament and the People of God*, 299–307 (see chap. 2, n. 2).

arms and began to prophesy in the Spirit. With Jesus in his arms, Simeon gave two prophetic oracles about the Messiah's future ministry.

Dear Desire of Every Nation

Simeon's first prophetic oracle (Luke 2:29–32) is the fourth and final song of Luke's nativity story. This canticle, known as the *Nunc dimittis* ("Now Let Go"), received its name from the first two words of the Latin translation of Luke 2:29. Simeon began his prophecy by thanking his "Sovereign Lord" (Luke 2:29 NIV) for allowing him to lay his own eyes on Israel's Messiah—just as the Spirit had promised. But the old man also glorified God for his chance to see the salvation God prepared for all people "in the sight of all nations" (Luke 2:31 NIV). This theme of Gentile redemption permeates the Gospel of Luke and Acts, providing further proof that Luke is himself the author of this nativity story.[2]

Though Simeon does not directly quote from Scripture, his prophecy makes several allusions to the songs of the Lord's Servant from Isaiah 40–55. This Servant of the Lord, whom God himself "formed . . . from the womb," would restore Israel (Isa 49:5). Although the Servant identifies with Israel, his mission is broader than Israel:

"I will also make you a light for the nations,
to be my salvation to the ends of the earth." (Isa 49:6)

Simeon, echoing Isaiah, calls Jesus "a light for revelation to the Gentiles" (Luke 2:32). Elsewhere Isaiah associates the "light" brought to the Gentiles with the birth of the "Prince of Peace" who will eternally rule over David's throne (Isa 9:1–7).

The universal revelation of God's saving purposes is a "glory" and blessing to the people of Israel through whom it was revealed. In other words, Israel is honored to be the nation through whom God reveals himself to the world (see also John 4:22; Rom 9:4–5). By the power of

---

[2] Hays, *Echoes of Scripture in the Gospels*, 200 (see introduction, n. 9).

God's Spirit, the good news of Christ would be preached "in Jerusalem, in all Judea and Samaria, and to the ends of the earth" (Acts 1:8). The good news of the life, death, and resurrection of Israel's Messiah is "the power of God for salvation to everyone who believes, first to the Jew, and also to the Greek" (Rom 1:16).

Joseph and Mary both marveled at this complete stranger who prophesied over their son. Angels had told them that "the Lord God will give him the throne of his father David" (Luke 1:32) and that "he will save his people from their sins" (Matt 1:21). But now to their shock and amazement, they heard for the first time that this child would also bring salvation to the Gentiles. Mary had a similar reaction when the shepherds reported what the angels had told them (Luke 2:19) and after she found Jesus in the temple (Luke 2:51).

Joy of Every Longing Heart

Mary's amazement was met with a second prophecy from Simeon that was directed specifically toward her. This news would be a harder pill to swallow. Simeon told her that "this child is destined to cause the fall and rise of many in Israel and to be a sign that will be opposed" (Luke 2:34). In other words, the child whom he predicted would restore Israel would also be a stumbling block to many in Israel (Isa 8:14; see also Jer 6:21; 1 Cor 1:23; 1 Pet 2:8). Because Jesus "did not come to bring peace, but a sword" (Matt 10:34), families in Israel would be divided over the identity of Jesus (Matt 10:35–39; Luke 12:49–53). The child was destined to reveal the "thoughts of many hearts" (Luke 2:35), meaning that Israel's Messiah would reveal that "not all who are descended from Israel are Israel" (Rom 9:6). Those who truly belonged to the people of God would acknowledge his Messiah.

Simeon also told Mary that "a sword will pierce your own soul" (Luke 2:35), indicating that Jesus's future ministry would cause her great pain and grief. Even the word used for "sword" here (*rhomphaía*) describes a long, double-edged sword that inflicts serious damage on anyone or anything pierced by it.[3] Again, this may be Simeon appealing back to Isaiah 49, where the words of the Servant are compared to a "sharp sword" (Isa 49:2; see also Rev 1:16; 19:21). Simeon indicated that Jesus would bring excruciating pain to his mother's heart.

The strain Jesus's ministry put on his family likely grieved his mother (Mark 3:21; Luke 8:19–20; John 7:3–5). But the greatest grief Mary would endure would be the loss of her son on a Roman cross.[4] Standing before Simeon in the court of the women with her six-week-old son, she probably could not conceive what Simeon's prophecy meant. But did she recall Simeon's prophecy when she stood at the foot of the cross with the beloved disciple and her friends and family?

Born Thy People to Deliver

There was also a prophetess, Anna, a daughter of Phanuel, of the tribe of Asher. She was well along in years, having lived with her husband seven years after her marriage, and was a widow for eighty-four years. She did not leave the temple, serving God night and day with fasting and prayers. At that very moment, she came up and began to thank God and to speak about him to all who were looking forward to the redemption of Jerusalem. (Luke 2:36–38)

Anna was a prophetess who spoke for the Lord. Including Anna, the Bible speaks of seven total prophetesses. Two were false prophetesses: Noadiah (Neh 6:14) and "Jezebel" (Rev 2:20). Four OT prophetesses spoke for God: Moses's sister Miriam (Exod 15:20), Deborah (Judg 4:4–14), Huldah (2 Kgs 22:14–20), and Isaiah's wife (Isa 8:3). Anna earned the reputation of prophetess in the New Testament because she spoke boldly about the redemption of Jerusalem through Christ.

---

[3] Bock, *Luke 1:1–9:50*, 249 (see chap. 2, n. 12).

[4] See Balthasar and Ratzinger, *Mary*, 75–79 (see chap. 5, n. 17); Robertson, *The Mother of Jesus*, 56–61 (see chap. 7, n. 12).

Anna had been widowed for a very long time. How old was Anna? The Greek from Luke 2:37 can be translated two basic ways.[5] On the reading reflected here in the CSB, Anna was married for seven years and then "was a widow eighty-four years," making her over 100 years old. According to another reading reflected in the NIV, she "was a widow until she was eighty-four." Whether she was in her eighties or in her early one-hundreds, Anna never remarried. Instead, she dedicated her life to God's service—fasting and praying day and night in the court of women.

Anna gained a significant reputation for her faithful service to the Lord in the temple. The inclusion of her father's name Phanuel suggests that people in Jerusalem still remembered her at the time of Luke's writing. Anna was also of the tribe of Asher, one of the rebellious tribes of northern Israel. Her presence in the temple reminds the reader of God's assurance to Elijah that a faithful remnant remained in the tribes of Israel who did not bow the knee to Baal (see 1 Kgs 19:18).

Anna prophesied about the "redemption of Jerusalem." Like Simeon, Anna approached the holy family in the court of women and began to prophesy. We have no record of precisely what Anna said, but she gave thanks to God and began to speak about Jesus to those who awaited Jerusalem's redemption. This message of redemption parallels Simeon's hope for Israel's consolation and Zechariah's earlier prophecy that "the God of Israel . . . has visited and provided redemption for his people" (Luke 1:68).

Hope of All the Earth Thou Art

The providential encounters of Jesus's family with two aged prophets from Israel in the temple trace several important themes for understanding Jesus's mission—all of which are predicted by Isaiah. The messages offered by Simeon and Anna echo Isaiah's words about the "Servant of the Lord":

---

[5] John Nolland, *Luke 1–9:20*, WBC 35a (Nashville: Thomas Nelson, 1989), 114–15; Bock, *Luke 1:1–9:50*, 251–52.

Be joyful, rejoice together,
you ruins of Jerusalem!
For the LORD has comforted his people;
he has redeemed Jerusalem.
The LORD has displayed his holy arm
in the sight of all the nations;
all the ends of the earth will see
the salvation of our God. (Isa 52:9–10)

The Servant prophesied about in Isaiah 40–55 brings both comfort to Israel and redemption to Jerusalem, but he also brings salvation to the ends of the earth. As Simeon and Anna rightly discerned, Jesus himself would fulfill Isaiah's prophetic description of the Servant.

First, Christ is the Servant who restores and consoles Israel. Cyrus may have allowed the Jews to return to Jerusalem after a half century in Babylonian captivity, but after centuries in the land with one foreign occupant after another, the people of God still yearned for the freedom from bondage that Isaiah had promised. Yet the true consolation of Israel would come from a place they did not expect. This Servant would suffer on their behalf to make them right with God. For Luke, Christ's mission corresponds to the four songs of the Servant:

- The first song, Isa 42:1–9, depicts the Servant as the one who establishes God's justice in the world. Matthew makes the direct claim that Jesus fulfills this song (Matt 12:18–21). Jesus's adult ministry began with the baptism of Jesus, where God the Father said, "You are my beloved Son; with you I am well-pleased" (Luke 3:22). These words bear a close resemblance to the first words of the servant song: "This is my chosen one; I delight in him" (Isa 42:1).
- The second song, Isa 49:1–13, portrays the Servant as one formed in the womb by God himself (Isa 49:1). Simeon appears to have this song in mind when he proclaims that the Messiah will restore Israel and provide light for the Gentiles (Isa 49:5–6; cf. Luke 2:30–32).

- The third song, Isa 50:4–11, paints the picture of the obedient Servant. Where Israel failed, the Servant was perfectly obedient—even in the face of mockers who beat him and tore his beard (Isa 50:6).
- The final song, Isa 52:13–53:12, painstakingly details the way that the Servant of the Lord will suffer for his people. Luke clearly understands Jesus to be this Servant—the "lamb led to the slaughter" (Isa 53:7–8; Acts 8:30–35; see also 1 Pet 2:21–24).

The servant songs shaped the way Jesus saw his entire earthly ministry: "For even the Son of Man did not come to be served, but to serve, and to give his life as a ransom for many" (Mark 10:45). In Luke's Gospel, an allusion to the first verse of the first song (Isa 42:1) launches Jesus's ministry (Luke 3:22) and a quotation from the last verse of the last song (Isa 53:12) accompanies the end of Jesus's ministry (Luke 22:37).

Second, Christ is the Servant who has brought salvation to the ends of the earth. Simeon identified Jesus as the Servant in Isa 49:6 whose light would reach the Gentiles. This theme resonates all throughout Luke's Gospel and the book of Acts. Paul understood this verse as the mandate God had given him for missions to the Gentiles. As Benjamin Gladd observes, this aspect of Jesus's ministry is crucially important for understanding our own place in the biblical story:

> Today, most Christians, particularly in the West, often struggle with reading the Bible and seeing themselves as participants in its grand story line. Though two thousand years separate us from the New Testament, we must resist the temptation to read the Bible as mere observers. The story of the Bible, spanning Genesis 1–2 to Revelation 21–22, is *our* story. Christ is the true people of God, and all those who unswervingly trust in the Son of Man likewise inherit his identity. There are no second-class citizens in the kingdom.[6]

---

[6] Benjamin L. Gladd, *From the Manger to the Throne: A Theology of Luke* (Wheaton, IL: Crossway, 2022), 97.

Our story matters as much as Israel's. When Simeon held the virgin-born king in his arms, he realized that this baby would make salvation possible for Gentiles like us.

Finally, Christ is the Servant whose suffering brings redemption. Before we used words like "redeem," "ransom," and "redemption" to describe God's salvation, these words had real-world meanings. To "redeem" something meant to take something back into one's legal possession—to buy something back or to pay off a debt. Houses could be redeemed or bought back from their new owners (Lev 25:33). A close family member could help redeem another family member from their debts or their poverty (Lev 25:48; see also Ruth 3:8–13; 4:1–14).

Biblical authors employed this mundane act of buying back what was lost and paying off debt as a central metaphor for God's salvation of Israel. God redeemed or bought Israel back from slavery (Exod 15:13; Deut 7:8; 2 Sam 7:23). When the psalmists cried out to God for help, they used the language of redemption (Pss 25:22; 26:11). God has redeemed or rescued his people from the grave (Pss 49:15; 103:4). God redeems us from his enemies (Pss 106:10; 119:134). But as Sandra Richter explains, the most significant ransom God paid to redeem his people came through his Son:

> Yahweh is presenting himself as the patriarch of the clan who has announced his intent to redeem his lost family members. Not only has he agreed to pay whatever ransom is required, but he has sent the most cherished member of his household to accomplish his intent—his firstborn son. And not only is the firstborn coming to seek and save the lost, but he is coming to share his inheritance with all those who squandered everything they had been given.[7]

The Father redeemed us, "not with perishable things like silver or gold, but with the precious blood of Christ, like that of an unblemished and spotless lamb" (1 Pet 1:18–19).

---

[7] Richter, *The Epic of Eden*, 45 (see chap. 9, n. 7).

Simeon and Anna serve the church as models for men and women of God who lived Spirit-filled lives, who filled themselves with the promises of Scripture, and who trusted in God for consolation and redemption. May we who are on this side of the Lord's first advent learn to live like this as we eagerly await his second.

13

The Virgin-Born King Manifested to the Nations

Matthew 2:1–12

This Birth was
Hard and bitter agony for us, like Death, our death.
We returned to our places, these Kingdoms,
But no longer at ease here, in the old dispensation,
With an alien people clutching their gods.
I should be glad of another death.
–T. S. Eliot, "Journey of the Magi"[1]

Few characters in the nativity story capture the Christian imagination like the "wise men from the east" (Matt 2:1). Though the Bible never counts them, most nativity sets feature three wise men, prominently

---

[1] T. S. Eliot, *Collected Poems 1909–1962* (New York: Harcourt Brace, 1963), 100.

placed beside the shepherds on the night of Jesus's birth. Most of our nativity sets bear the influence of extrabiblical tradition. So, in an act of Protestant rebellion, I like to place the wise men in a different corner of the room from the rest of our nativity set, indicating that the wise men are on the way but not quite there yet.

Though the text of John Henry Hopkins Jr.'s "We Three Kings" (1857) may be shaped more by extrabiblical tradition than the story recorded in Matthew, its chorus is as powerful lyrically as it is musically:

> Star of Wonder, Star of Night
> Star with Royal Beauty bright,
> > Westward leading,
> > Still proceeding,
> Guide us to Thy perfect Light.

As beautiful and radiant as the star that took the wise men to Jesus might have been, it was dull and dim in comparison to the light it revealed—the "true light that gives light to everyone" (John 1:9).

Works of the Christian imagination aside, who are these mysterious figures described in the second chapter of Matthew's Gospel? More importantly, what role do they play in the grand story of Scripture? The magi are the first Gentiles to whom the "light for the nations" is revealed (Isa 49:6; see also Luke 2:32). We call this event the "epiphany" or "manifestation" of Christ to the nations. In this event, Christ was revealed to unbelievers outside of Israel, providing hope that God could rescue anyone from sin and darkness.

Wise Men from the East (Matt 2:1–2)

After Jesus was born in Bethlehem of Judea in the days of King Herod, wise men from the east arrived in Jerusalem, saying, "Where is he who has been born king of the Jews? For we saw his star at its rising and have come to worship him." (Matt 2:1–2)

The tradition about the magi outside of Scripture becomes wildly inventive. Matthew did not say how many magi came looking for Jesus, and ancient writers had a wide range of opinions about their number (One ancient source allegedly claimed that there were fourteen wise men.[2]). The most common theory—and one that is widely reflected in the art and iconography of the church—is that there were three wise men, one corresponding to each gift given to Jesus. Tradition written centuries after the NT gave various names to these magi, the most common set of names being Melchior, Balthasar, and Gaspar.[3]

Although tradition sometimes depicts these wise men as "kings," Matthew gives no such suggestion. Catholic interpreters occasionally linked OT texts about Gentile kings to the wise men in the infancy narratives.[4] Although the wise men were likely not kings, it is quite possible that they served as emissaries from a king.[5] We know that eastern magi did occasionally travel on behalf of kings to pay homage to royalty, as they did to Nero in AD 66.[6]

---

[2] See John Calvin, *Harmony of Matthew, Mark, and Luke*, vol. 1, in *Calvin's Commentaries* 16, trans. and ed. William Pringle (Grand Rapids: Baker, 2009), 129. Calvin claims that this number can be found in the "imperfect Commentary on Matthew [that] bears the name of Chrysostom." He is likely referring to the *Incomplete Commentary on Matthew* (*Opus imperfectum*).

[3] These names first appeared in "A Barbarian's Latin Excerpts" (*Excerpta Latina Barbari*), an eighth-century translation of the sixth-century Greek chronicle.

[4] A sixth-century Syriac book called the *Cave of Treasures* referred to the magi as kings of Saba (Seba), Sheba, and Persia described in Ps 72:10–11. But as John Calvin observed, whoever suggested that Psalm 72 predicted where the wise men would come from would have failed Geography 101. These "ingenious workmen . . . have changed the south and west into the east!" Calvin, *Calvin's Commentaries*, 16/1, 129.

[5] Mark Alan Powell, "The Magi as Kings: An Adventure in Reader-Response Criticism," *Catholic Biblical Quarterly* 62, no. 3 (2000): 459–80.

[6] France, *The Gospel of Matthew*, 64 (see chap. 2, n. 16); Dio Cassius, *Roman History*, bk. 63; Suetonius, *Nero* 13.

Scholar Eric Vanden Eykel alleges that the "wise men from the east" were fictional characters created to serve Matthew's theological agenda.[7] Matthew included this story about the magi because he found theological significance in it, but the inclusion of a meaningful event does not entail wholesale invention. The "wise men" or "magi" (*magoi*) depicted here closely parallel what we know about this ancient Persian religious sect. Their search for the "star" reflects ancient Eastern beliefs in omens and prophetic fulfillment.

The term "magi" comes from an older Persian word (*maguš*) that described a priest or astrologer.[8] According to Matthew, these magi came "from the east," which may refer to the first-century Parthian empire (ancient Persia and modern-day Iran). Other ancient sources argued that the magi were from Arabia.[9] The magi were members of a pagan priestly tribe who would offer sacrifices to the gods, give fortunes, and interpret dreams.[10] In Matthew's nativity story, the magi came to Jerusalem looking for "he who has been born king of the Jews" because they "saw his star at its rising" (Matt 2:2). This detail is consistent with ancient magi religion, which developed the signs of the zodiac still used today in modern astrology.[11]

Many in Matthew's original Jewish audience would have condemned these stargazers as pagan lawbreakers. The Bible repeatedly prohibits astrology and divination (Deut 4:19; 18:9–12; Isa 47:13–14). The Greek translation of the book of Daniel used the term *magoi* to describe the

---

[7] See Eric Vanden Eykel, *The Magi: Who They Were, How They've Been Remembered, and Why They Still Fascinate* (Minneapolis: Fortress, 2022), xviii. Eykel contends that questions about the historical background of the magi are somewhat inconsequential because they are "fictional characters in Matthew's narrative."

[8] Edwin Yamauchi, *Persia and the Bible* (Grand Rapids: Baker, 1997), 467–68; Mary Boyce, *Zoroastrians: Their Religious Beliefs and Practices* (New York: Routledge, 1979), 48.

[9] Justin Martyr, *Dialogue with Trypho* 78.

[10] Jenny Rose, *Zoroastrianism* (New York: I. B. Tauris, 2010), 52.

[11] Yamauchi, *Persia and the Bible*, 474–77.

magicians of the Babylonian court. These astrologers were depicted as wicked men who were enemies of God and his people (Dan 2:2, 10, LXX). In Acts 8:9–23, we meet the Samaritan sorcerer known as Simon Magus. Simon attempted to purchase the gift of the Spirit from the apostles so he could sell more tickets to his magic shows.[12] Given this Jewish and Christian intolerance toward their practices, it seems unlikely that Matthew and the early church would have invented a story that cast such a positive light on magi.[13]

"A Star Will Come from Jacob"

The magi claimed that they came to Israel because they saw "his star at its rising" (Matt 2:2).[14] But why would astrologers from Persia or Arabia associate a star with the birth of the king of the Jews? The first-century Roman historian Suetonius wrote, "There had spread over all the Orient an old and established belief, that it was fated at that time for men coming from Judaea to rule the world."[15] Tacitus recorded a similar "prophecy."[16]

Where did this star come from? Astronomers offer several natural explanations of what this astral phenomenon could have been: (1) a comet, (2) a planetary conjunction where two astronomical objects appear as if they are very close together in the night sky, or (3) a nova resulting from

---

[12] Many early Christian theologians regarded this member of the "magi" to be the granddaddy of all ancient heresy! See Hippolytus, *Refutation of All Heresies* 6.2.

[13] Craig S. Keener, *The Gospel of Matthew: A Socio-Rhetorical Commentary* (Grand Rapids: Eerdmans, 2009), 97–98; France, *The Gospel of Matthew*, 68.

[14] Notably, Matthew does not claim that the star led the magi to Jerusalem, only that it led them to Israel. They arrived in the capital city because it would have been fitting for a Jewish king to be born there, as highlighted in Carson, "Matthew," 231 (see chap. 2, n. 11).

[15] Suetonius, *Vespasian* 4.

[16] Tacitus, *Histories* 5:13.

the explosion of a star.[17] Each one of these explanations is compelling in its own way: Halley's Comet appeared over the sky around 11 BC. Jupiter and Saturn would have been seen together around 7 BC. Chinese astronomers recorded a supernova lasting seventy days around 4 or 5 BC—the timeframe of King Herod's death. But the most likely explanation of this moving star that eventually rests over the house of Jesus is a supernatural light provided by God to guide the magi on their journey.[18]

Early church theologians often linked the star of the magi to Balaam's prophecy in Num 24:17–19: "A star will come from Jacob, and a scepter will arise from Israel."[19] The original "star . . . from Jacob" was David, who fulfilled this prophecy with his successful military campaigns in Moab and Edom (2 Sam 8:2, 14). But this "star . . . from Jacob" came to be a symbol for messianic figures and leaders who sought to overthrow foreign invaders.[20]

NT scholars have also observed several similarities between Balaam and the magi of Matthew's nativity story.[21] First, Balaam was a Gentile holy man whom some ancient Jewish sources refer to as a magi.[22] Second, the Greek translation of Num 23:7 uses the same phrase Matthew employs in 2:1 to describe the magi "from the east."[23] Finally,

---

[17] France, *The Gospel of Matthew*, 68–69. See also Konradin Ferrari-D'Ochchieppo, "The Star of the Magi and Babylonian Astronomy," in *Chronos, Kairos, Christos: Nativity and Chronological Studies Presented to Jack Finegan*, ed. Jerry Vardaman and Edwin M. Yamauchi (Winona Lake, IN: Eisenbrauns, 1989), 41–53; Colin R. Nicholl, *The Great Christ Comet: Revealing the True Star of Bethlehem* (Wheaton, IL: Crossway, 2015).

[18] The third- or fourth-century apocryphal gospel *Revelation of the Magi* goes further, claiming that the star is itself a manifestation of the Son (*Rev. Magi* 4.4). Other interpreters suggest that these stars are angelic beings.

[19] Athanasius, *On the Incarnation* 33; Jerome, *Commentary on Matthew* 1.2.2.

[20] Dennis R. Cole, *Numbers* (Nashville: B&H Academic, 2000), 426.

[21] See France, *The Gospel of Matthew*, 62; Brown, *Birth of the Messiah*, 168 (see chap. 1, n. 6), 182, 190–96.

[22] Philo, *On the Life of Moses* 1.276.

[23] ἀπὸ ἀνατολῶν (Num 23:7, LXX; Matt 2:1). The Hebrew of Num 23:7 reads "from the eastern mountains" (מהררי קדם).

Herod put pressure on the wise men to betray God's people in a way similar to Balak the king of Moab's attempts to get Balaam to curse the Israelites (Numbers 22–24). In the same way Balaam preserved the lives of Moses and the Israelites, the magi helped protect the new Moses named Jesus.[24]

The magi who came to Jerusalem for the birth of Jesus likely traveled in a large caravan, which may have been perceived by Herod as a group of royal emissaries. When they arrived in Jerusalem, they may have expected to find the newborn king of the Jews born in a palace there.[25] They may have expected the child to belong to Herod himself. Whatever the case, Herod likely brought them in before him because they were drawing a lot of unwanted attention in the city.

Deeply Disturbed (Matt 2:3–8)

When King Herod heard this, he was deeply disturbed, and all Jerusalem with him. So he assembled all the chief priests and scribes of the people and asked them where the Messiah would be born.

"In Bethlehem of Judea," they told him, "because this is what was written by the prophet:

And you, Bethlehem, in the land of Judah,
are by no means **least among the rulers of Judah:**
Because out of you will come a ruler
who will shepherd my people Israel."

Then Herod secretly summoned the wise men and asked them the exact time the star appeared. He sent them to Bethlehem and said, "Go and search carefully for the child. When you find him, report back to me so that I too can go and worship him." (Matt 2:3–8)

---

[24] Brown, *Birth of the Messiah*, 193–94.
[25] Keener, *The Gospel of Matthew*, 98.

Despite the power and influence wielded by Herod the Great, few in Israel would have recognized him as the true "king of the Jews." He was neither truly Jewish nor a true king. He was an Idumean with an Edomite father and a Nabatean mother. Herod reigned as a "client king" subordinate to the Roman emperor.

Between 142–37 BC, the Hasmonean dynasty led an independent Jewish state in Israel. But infighting and Roman intervention marked the end of this short-lived experiment. Herod's family gained significant political power, first under Pompey, then under Julius Caesar, and finally, under Mark Antony and Caesar Augustus, who appointed Herod to be the "king of Judea."[26] Though he was not a true sovereign, Herod had great success in building projects and expanding Roman interests throughout the region.

When word got back to Herod that the magi were searching Jerusalem for the one who was born "king of the Jews," he was "deeply disturbed," as was the rest of the city (Matt 2:3). No faithful Jewish monarch would have worried much about the rumor of an astrological sign pointing to a new king because Scripture strongly condemned such divination (see Deut 18:9–14; Isa 47:13). But Herod was no faithful or observant Jewish monarch. He was a narcissistic madman concerned only with his own self-interests, willing to kill even his own children to preserve them.

Herod's superstitious fear of this rumor was completely consistent with the way other Roman rulers responded to astrological predictions of their demise.[27] Although a city full of Jews would have welcomed a truly Jewish king, they also would have been reasonably concerned with how Herod might have reacted to this news. As we learn from Matt 2:16–18 and the records of Josephus, violent retaliation was a favorite pastime of the insecure client-king.

---

[26] Josephus, *Ant.* 14.8.1–14.14.6.
[27] Keener, *The Gospel of Matthew*, 100–101. See Tacitus, *Annals* 14.22. A blazing comet was interpreted as a sign of the end of Nero's reign.

Following the arrival of the magi in Jerusalem, Herod consulted with Jewish religious leaders (likely Pharisees and Sadducees) about where the Messiah was prophesied to be born. Their answer—Bethlehem, the city of David—may have been common knowledge to most Jews (see John 7:41–42), but Herod had little biblical literacy. He also had very little understanding of his Jewish constituency. On another occasion, Herod posted a large golden eagle, a graven image and the symbol of Caesar, on the gates of God's Temple. Herod became suicidal when, to his surprise, a mob of Jewish men took the eagle down and hacked it to pieces.[28]

Matthew takes small liberties in his quotation of Mic 5:2, but these alterations would have reflected a common Jewish understanding of the text. Matthew changes the wording of "Bethlehem Ephrathah" to "Bethlehem, in the land of Judah" to differentiate between the Bethlehem of Judea and the Bethlehem of Galilee (see Josh 19:15).[29] Matthew also adds the phrase "who will shepherd my people Israel" from David's coronation in 2 Sam 5:2 to strengthen the connection between the Messiah and the promise God made to David.[30] The Messiah born in the city of David is a shepherd who will rule Israel from David's throne.

Upon hearing this explanation, Herod secretly requested the presence of the magi and asked them for "the exact time the star appeared" (Matt 2:7). Herod's interest was not in astronomy but in calculating how old this child would have been. He was already formulating a plan to slaughter all the young boys in and around Bethlehem (Matt 2:16) and simply needed an age range for his targets. This cold, calculating killer hid his murderous intentions behind the pretense of piety: "Go and search carefully for

---

[28] Josephus, *Wars of the Jews* 1.33.3–5.

[29] R. T. France, "The Formula-Quotations of Matthew 2 and the Problem of Communication," in *The Right Doctrine from the Wrong Texts? Essays on the Use of the Old Testament in the New*, ed. G. K. Beale (Grand Rapids: Baker, 1994), 124; cf. R. T. France, *The Gospel of Matthew*, 72–73. "Ephrathah," a Hebrew word meaning "fruitful" was a common designation given to the Judean Bethlehem (Gen 35:19; 48:7; Ruth 4:11).

[30] ποιμανεῖς τὸν λαόν μου τὸν Ἰσραήλ (LXX).

the child. When you find him, report back to me so that I too can go and worship him" (Matt 2:8). Nothing in the immediate context suggests that the magi did not believe him when they first heard this instruction.

Pagans Worship the King of Kings

After hearing the king, they went on their way. And there it was—the star they had seen at its rising. It led them until it came and stopped above the place where the child was. When they saw the star, they were overwhelmed with joy. Entering the house, they saw the child with Mary his mother, and falling to their knees, they worshiped him. Then they opened their treasures and presented him with gifts: gold, frankincense, and myrrh. (Matt 2:9–11)

The magi initially went to Jerusalem expecting Israel's king to be born in the capital city, only to discover that Jews long expected their true king to be born in Bethlehem. Sent with the disingenuous blessings of Herod, they resumed their travel toward the city of David. But this time they were not guided by an ordinary astronomical sign. The same star they had seen at its rising now appeared to be moving with them! The star, as if animated by an outside force, "led them until it came and stopped above the place where the child was" (Matt 2:9).

No naturally occurring phenomenon adequately explains what the magi saw here. We can think of this star like a supernatural manifestation akin to those in the OT. In the OT, God manifested himself as a pillar of cloud by day and a pillar of fire by night to guide Israel as they traveled through the wilderness (see Exod 13:21–22; 14:19, 24; 33:9–10; Num 12:5; Deut 31:15). The star came to rest in one place—something reminiscent of the sun and moon standing still over Gibeon (Josh 10:12–13). Whatever God is doing here stirs in the magi a response of exuberant joy. No matter how jaw-dropping this starry sight may have been, its light paled in comparison to the true Light it revealed.

The joyful magi entered "the house" where Jesus was staying—perhaps the same house where Jesus was born and laid in a manger. Maybe Jesus's family had finally moved into the guest room that had been occupied when he was born. Depending on the amount of time that had passed, Jesus's parents could have established a more permanent home elsewhere in Bethlehem.

The magi fell to their knees and "worshipped" (*prosekynēsan*) the child, just as they had expressed a desire to do so in Matt 2:2. The authors of the Gospels frequently associated this verb meaning "to worship" with the physical act of bowing down or prostrating oneself before the person or object worshipped. A form of the same verb appears three verses earlier where Herod insincerely stated, "When you find him, report back to me so that I too can go and worship him" (Matt 2:8).

In the case of the magi, something wonderful and unusual was happening. These men of a higher station—potentially emissaries from an eastern king—were lying prostrate in a humble Jewish home before a small child, revering him as a king unlike any other. More remarkable still, God had called these pagan men from a faraway land to worship at the feet of his Son. What Matthew depicts in this humble, earthly scene mimics the future heavenly scene where "a vast multitude from every nation, tribe, people, and language, which no one could number" stand around the throne and sing praises to God and to the Lamb (Rev 7:9).

The gifts of the magi include a precious metal (gold) and two fragrances (frankincense and myrrh). Throughout the years theologians have attempted to attach a special significance to each gift. According to Irenaeus, the magi gave Jesus gold because he was a king, frankincense because he was God, and myrrh because he was going to die for our sins.[31] However elegant this interpretation may sound, it is difficult to derive from the text itself. These spices and fragrances commonly came together as a package deal in the biblical world (see Song 3:6; 4:6, 14; Rev 18:13).

---

[31] Irenaeus, *Against Heresies* 3.9.1.

The individual gifts are less important than what their gifting conveys. This child born to humble parents is the rightful heir of David's throne and the recipient of gifts that only belong to a king. Jesus, like Solomon before the Queen of Sheba, is the recipient of "gold" and "a great quantity of spices" (1 Kgs 10:10). Matthew may also be expanding on the Immanuel prophecy of Isa 7–9: "Before the boy knows how to call 'Father,' or 'Mother,' the wealth of Damascus and the spoils of Samaria will be carried off to the king of Assyria" (Isa 8:4).[32] But most importantly, Jesus is the light of the Lord that shines on the Gentile nations and draws them to himself.

> Arise, shine, for your light has come,
> and the glory of the LORD shines over you.
> For look, darkness will cover the earth,
> and total darkness the peoples;
> but the LORD will shine over you,
> and his glory will appear over you.
> Nations will come to your light,
> and kings to your shining brightness. . . .
> Caravans of camels will cover your land—
> young camels of Midian and Ephah—
> all of them will come from Sheba.
> They will carry gold and frankincense
> and proclaim the praises of the LORD. (Isa 60:1–3, 6)

Just as Isaiah foretold, gift-bearing Gentiles from another land beheld the glory and light of Israel's God and proclaimed his praises.

Dreams and Visions

And being warned in a dream not to go back to Herod, they returned to their own country by another route. (Matt 2:12)

---

[32] Tertullian, *Against Marcion* 3.13.

The supernatural sign of the star led the magi to the place where Jesus was staying, but now God used another supernatural form of communication to lead them home. The magi may have initially believed Herod when he told them he too desired to worship the newborn king, but God made it clear in this dream that Herod was not to be trusted. Though Matthew makes no direct reference to an angel here, this warning closely resembled those given by the angel to Joseph in the verses that follow.

Although dreams like these are not the normal means of divine revelation, God occasionally uses extraordinary forms of communication to draw men unto himself. I have met with pastors and missionaries from the region of the world where the magi likely came from, and they have told me about the way God still uses dreams and visions to draw Muslims to Christ. These testimonies often involve a dream or a vision of Jesus who directs them to see an individual who will share the gospel with them. Although the sufficiency of Scripture means we need not seek out dreams and visions as an additional source of revelation, we can acknowledge that the same God who called magi to himself in the first century is still active in the world today.

"Every Kind of Magic Was Destroyed"

Many Jews in the biblical world were under the mistaken impression that salvation was exclusively for the Jewish people. But this was never God's intention. Israel was never meant to be a cul-de-sac of God's blessing but the channel through which God's blessing came to the world. This intention was at the heart of the promise made to Abraham: "All the nations will be blessed through you" (Gal 3:8).

The Israelites were recipients of the adoption, the law, the covenants, the promises, and ultimately, the Messiah. Yet God's desire all along was that he would draw all the nations to himself through his work in Israel.

The people walking in darkness
have seen a great light;

a light has dawned
on those living in the land of darkness. (Isa 9:2)

The magi were pagans who practiced a godless religion guided by
the stars. A little over a century after the magi visited Jesus, Ignatius of
Antioch (d. AD 118) wrote this about these unlikely converts:

> A star shone forth in heaven above all the other stars, the light of
> which was inexpressible, while its novelty struck men with aston-
> ishment. And all the rest of the stars, with the sun and moon,
> formed a chorus to this star, and its light was exceedingly great
> above them all. And there was agitation felt as to whence this
> new spectacle came, so unlike to everything else [in the heavens].
> Hence every kind of magic was destroyed, and every bond of wick-
> edness disappeared; ignorance was removed, and the old kingdom
> abolished, God Himself being manifested in human form for the
> renewal of eternal life. And now that took a beginning which had
> been prepared by God. Henceforth all things were in a state of
> tumult, because He meditated the abolition of death.[33]

With no small dose of irony, the God of Israel who condemned astrological practices used a shining star as a sign and a witness that pointed
astrologists to "the morning star" (2 Pet 1:19). Unlike Herod, the insecure
despot who felt threatened by a baby claimant to his phony throne, these
royal emissaries came and knelt before the virgin-born king. In so doing,
they pictured a future event when all kings from every corner of creation
will come and bow before the King of kings and Lord of lords.

---

[33] Ignatius, *Letter to the Ephesians* 19.

14

Out of Egypt I Called My Son

Matthew 2:13–23

And the dragon stood in front of the woman who was about to give
birth, so that when she did give birth it might devour her child.

—REVELATION 12:4B

Every year in the Putman household, my wife Micah and I have a cor-
dial debate about whether *Die Hard* properly counts as a Christmas
movie. Her idea of a Christmas movie usually follows the same made-for-
TV-movie formula: A big-city career girl forced by circumstances beyond
her control must return to her small, snow-laden hometown for the hol-
idays, where she falls head over heels for the most handsome eligible
bachelor/widower in town. On the other hand, my idea of a Christmas
movie involves a barefooted Bruce Willis running across shards of broken
glass while blasting terrorists with an HK94 submachine gun. My wife
may say *Die Hard* does not "feel like a Christmas movie," but nothing

puts me in a more festive mood than watching Hans Gruber fall from Nakatomi Plaza like lightning.

Of course, this silly debate is all in good fun, but it does point to a neglected facet of the biblical nativity stories. The nativity stories recorded in Scripture are not feel-good stories with charming settings or happy, romantic resolutions. The original Christmas story involved a murderous tyrant, a foreboding sense of danger, and a daring escape by night.

More importantly, the suspenseful story of the holy family's flight to Egypt in Matt 2:12–23 revisits the story of Israel in the OT and establishes an important theme in Matthew's Gospel: Jesus is the new and better Moses.

Jesus Reenacts the Exodus

> After they were gone, an angel of the Lord appeared to Joseph in a dream, saying, "Get up! Take the child and his mother, flee to Egypt, and stay there until I tell you. For Herod is about to search for the child to kill him." So he got up, took the child and his mother during the night, and escaped to Egypt. He stayed there until Herod's death, so that what was spoken by the Lord through the prophet might be fulfilled: **Out of Egypt I called my Son.** (Matt 2:13–15)

The angel's first message to Joseph brought assurance and peace—Mary had conceived the Savior by the Holy Spirit. The second message was a dire warning that required immediate obedience. To escape Herod's murderous rampage, Joseph fled Bethlehem with the child and his mother in the middle of the night.

The holy family's flight to Egypt parallels the plight of many first-century Jews who sought political asylum during Herod's reign. By AD 40, around one million Jews had relocated to the Egyptian city of Alexandria.[1] For Joseph and Mary, relocating to Egypt was a logical choice. From their doorstep in Bethlehem, Egypt would have been the closest region not under Herod's direct or indirect control. On their travel south toward Egypt, the holy family still would have needed to pass through Idumea—a region governed by members of Herod's family.[2] The family only returned to Nazareth after Herod was dead.

In the escape to and return from Egypt, Matthew sees a clear parallel to other instances in OT history when God's people fled to Egypt for their survival. When famine in the land forced Jacob and his sons to relocate to Egypt where God had providentially provided food through Joseph, God said, "Do not be afraid to go down to Egypt, for I will make you into a great nation there. I will go down with you to Egypt, and I will also bring you back" (Gen 46:3b–4a).[3]

Matthew understood the holy family's escape to Egypt to be the providential way God would fulfill Hos 11:1, which says, "Out of Egypt I called my son." We must not make the mistake of assuming Matthew thought Hosea predicted that the holy family would go to and return from Egypt. When the eighth-century prophet Hosea said, "Out of Egypt I called my son," the prophet was not looking ahead to the future but looking backward toward Israel's past.[4] Matthew found in Israel's history an event that typified Christ. Christ, who was from Israel and who represented Israel, reenacted this event, but with a notably different outcome.[5]

---

[1] Philo, *Against Flaccus* 6.42. For a contemporary exploration of this theme in the flight to Egypt, see D. Glenn Butner, Jr., *Jesus the Refugee: Ancient Injustice and Modern Solidarity* (Minneapolis: Fortress, 2023).

[2] France, *The Gospel of Matthew*, 79; see also Richard A. Horsley, *The Liberation of Christmas: The Infancy Narratives in Social Context* (New York: Crossroad, 1989), 72–74.

[3] See also 1 Kgs 11:17, 40; 2 Kgs 25:26; Jer 26:21; 42:13–44:30.

[4] Hays, *Echoes of Scripture in the Gospels*, 113, 139–40 (see introduction, n. 9).

[5] Hays, *Reading Backwards*, 39–41 (see chap. 2, n. 1).

Hosea ministered to the northern kingdom of Israel (Ephraim) during its final decades as a nation. This people had forgotten the covenant they made with God and committed spiritual adultery with the gods of neighboring nations. God depicted Israel's spiritual condition through Hosea's marriage to unfaithful Gomer. In the same way Hosea showed mercy to his unfaithful wife, God was going to show mercy to this wayward nation. In Hosea 11, God expressed his unconditional love for the rebellious northern kingdom. He compared his love for Israel to the love a father has for a prodigal son.

> When Israel was a child, I loved him,
> and out of Egypt I called my son.
> Israel called to the Egyptians
> even as Israel was leaving them.
> They kept sacrificing to the Baals
> and burning offerings to idols.
> It was I who taught Ephraim to walk,
> taking them by the hand,
> but they never knew that I healed them. . . .
> Israel will not return to the land of Egypt
> and Assyria will be his king,
> because they refused to repent. (Hos 11:1–3, 5)

God wanted Israel to remember how he had rescued them from slavery in Egypt. Even though God was their true parent, Israel had continued to worship and serve idols. But like any loving parent, God promised "tough love" for Israel. Although God vowed that he would never send Israel back to Egypt, he did warn them that their time of prosperity and blessing was about to come to an end. If Israel wanted to serve foreign gods, then they would also serve a foreign nation.

In a wave of successive deportations, Assyria took the ten tribes of the northern kingdom into captivity. Israel finally fell to Assyria in 722 BC. When the chronicler of 2 Kings looked back at why Israel fell to the Assyrians, his language closely resembles Hosea's prophecy: "This disaster happened because the people of Israel sinned against the LORD their God who had brought them out of the land of Egypt from the power of Pharaoh king of Egypt and because they worshiped other gods" (2 Kgs 17:7). But Assyria would eventually fall like the rest of Israel and Judah's enemies (Nah 3:18–19).

Instead of fulfilling a direct prediction, Matthew, under the inspiration of the Holy Spirit, discerns a pattern in the story of Israel that Jesus fulfills or completes. Put another way, Jesus reenacts the OT history of Israel and brings that story to a new and better ending. Where Israel failed in their disobedience, Israel's Messiah succeeded with perfect obedience.[6]

By quoting Hos 11:1, Matthew also tees up an important theme for the rest of his Gospel: Jesus is the new and better Moses. In the same way that baby Moses escaped the genocide designed by the Pharaoh for Hebrew boys, Jesus escaped the murder plot of the paranoid monarch named Herod. Throughout his Gospel, Matthew highlights various ways Jesus reenacts and improves on the ministry of Moses. Moses gave the law from God on Mount Sinai. But Jesus gave a new and better law in the Sermon on the Mount. Through Moses, God delivered the Israelites from bondage in Egypt. Through Jesus, God delivered all his people from their bondage to sin, death, and Satan.[7]

Answering Objections: Matthew Invented the Slaughter of the Innocents

Since the second century, skeptics have balked at Matthew's account of the death of the innocents (see Origen, *Against Celsus* 1.61). Critics are quick to point out that Josephus—the best ancient source for the life of Herod—never acknowledges this event. Although Josephus does not mention the Bethlehem incident, he

---

[6] See G. K. Beale, "The Use of Hosea 11:1 in Matthew 2:15: One More Time," *JETS* 55, no. 4 (2012): 697–715.

[7] For a helpful overview of this "new Moses" theme, see Quarles, *A Theology of Matthew*, 33–69 (see chap. 7, n. 13).

does document several comparable incidents. Josephus chronicled that Herod murdered anyone whom he perceived to be a threat to his power—including "the most intimate of his friends" (*Ant.* 15.7.8). One first-century Jewish author wrote, "He will kill both old and young, showing mercy to none" (*Assumption of Moses* 6:4).

Herod ordered executions of all the remaining members of the Hasmonean dynasty that formerly ruled in Judea, including his own wife Mariamne (*Ant.* 15.7.3–6), her brother (*Ant.* 15.3.3), her grandfather (*Ant.* 15.6.1–4), and her mother (*Ant.* 15.7.7–8). In his later years, an increasingly paranoid and physically ill Herod had his three oldest sons killed (*Ant.* 16.11.1–8; 17.7). Of this family dysfunction, Octavian allegedly joked, "It is better to be Herod's pig than his son" (Macrobius, *Saturnalia* 2.4.11).

Herod also contracted killings on his political enemies. On one occasion, he slayed the entire family of a man he believed was conspiring against him (*Ant.* 15.8; 17:3; Josephus, *Wars* 1.17; 1:22). Concerned that no one in the nation would mourn his death, Herod even devised a plan to have a group of imprisoned Jewish nobles executed upon his death to ensure that someone mourned when he died (even if they mourned for other people). Fortunately, these orders were never carried out (*Ant.* 17.6.5–6).

So why didn't Josephus write about the Bethlehem murders? Later tradition would put the death toll from this "massacre" in the tens of thousands, but biblical scholars today recognize that the number would have been much, much smaller. Scholars estimate that the population of first-century Bethlehem was somewhere between 300 and 1000, meaning the number of total male children under two would have been closer to a dozen or two—not tens of thousands.

Though this crime is no less horrific, the death of this smaller number better explains why ancient sources like Josephus may have overlooked or been ignorant of it. Contemporary historians working from memory alone would struggle to recall every mass shooting in the United States over the past decade. Unfortunately, prolonged exposure to such evil has a desensitizing effect. We tend to forget about some older atrocities that did not directly affect us when we always seem to be bombarded by new ones. Even if Josephus had known about the instance in Bethlehem, we could reasonably grasp why he failed to mention it.

As Josephus sums up his brutalities, Herod "prosecuted his own family members and friends and punished them as if they were enemies . . . out of a desire that he alone would have all the honor" as king (*Ant.* 15.6.4). Herod repeatedly proved that his ruthless ambition knew no bounds and never hesitated to kill anyone whom he perceived to be a threat to his power. The same tyrant who killed his own wife, children, and closest friends among countless others would not hesitate to kill a few dozen peasant children in Bethlehem if he perceived one of them to be a credible threat to his rule.

Jesus Reenacts the Exile

Then Herod, when he realized that he had been outwitted by the wise men, flew into a rage. He gave orders to massacre all the boys in and around Bethlehem who were two years old and under, in keeping with the time he had learned from the wise men. Then what was spoken through Jeremiah the prophet was fulfilled:

> **A voice was heard in Ramah,**
> **weeping, and great mourning,**
> **Rachel weeping for her children;**
> **and she refused to be consoled,**
> **because they are no more.** (Matt 2:16–18)

Matthew quotes Jer 31:15 in part because the mothers and fathers of Bethlehem would have wept for their murdered children. This unthinkably evil act by a mad tyrant certainly exposes the depths of human depravity and the brokenness of this world. As R. T. France observed, the link between Rachel's tears and Herod's rampage helps us "find reassurance in the thought that even human tragedy can be interpreted within the overall purpose of God."[8]

But the original context of this prophecy shows that Matthew is doing something more than just talking about evil and suffering in a generic way. In 587 BC, 135 years after Assyria took the tribes of the northern kingdom of Israel into captivity, most residents in the southern kingdom of Judah stood bound in chains and ready to be shipped off to Babylon. Ramah, the traditional burial site of Jacob's wife Rachel, was where their captors gathered the people of Judah to deport them (Jer 40:1).[9] The people of Judah—many of whom would have been descendants of Rachel—would be in exile for five decades.

When Matthew quotes "her children . . . are no more," he speaks of the murder of Bethlehem children. When Jeremiah uses the phrase "they are no more," he describes the kidnapping of a nation. For Jeremiah, not all hope is lost because "your children will return from the enemy's land" (Jer 31:16). Jeremiah's lamentation turns to joy and hopeful expectation as he promises that God will restore Judah from exile and bring his people back home. Most importantly, Jeremiah predicts a day when God will give his people a new covenant:

"Look, the days are coming"—this is the Lord's declaration— "when I will make a new covenant with the house of Israel and

---

[8] France, *The Gospel of Matthew*, 86.

[9] See France, *The Gospel of Matthew*, 88. France discusses the uncertainty surrounding Rachel's final resting place and suggests the possibility that she was buried outside of Bethlehem. See also 1 Sam 10:2; Gen 35:16–20; 48:7. On the other hand, Justin Martyr links "Ramah" to an Arabic city named Rama close to where he believed the magi were from (*Dialogue with Trypho* 78).

with the house of Judah. This one will not be like the covenant I made with their ancestors on the day I took them by the hand to lead them out of the land of Egypt—my covenant that they broke even though I am their master"—the LORD's declaration. "Instead, this is the covenant I will make with the house of Israel after those days"—the LORD's declaration. "I will put my teaching within them and write it on their hearts. I will be their God, and they will be my people. No longer will one teach his neighbor or his brother, saying, 'Know the LORD,' for they will all know me, from the least to the greatest of them"—this is the LORD's declaration. "For I will forgive their iniquity and never again remember their sin." (Jer 31:31–34; see also Ezek 36:24–27; Joel 2:28–29)

With his inclusion of Jer 31:15, Matthew points toward the new covenant God gave his people in Christ. New covenant people have forgiveness of sin and the law written on their hearts through the Holy Spirit (see Heb 10:14–17). Jesus had ushered in this new covenant through his blood (Matt 26:28). But the Evangelist also looks ahead to the future moment when God completely restores the broken world in which we now live. When we read about the mothers weeping in Jer 31:15, we must remember how that prophetic lament turned to joy:

> Keep your voice from weeping
> and your eyes from tears,
> for the reward for your work will come—
> this is the LORD's declaration—
> and your children will return from the enemy's land.
> There is hope for your future—
> this is the LORD's declaration—
> and your children will return to their own territory. (Jer 31:16–17)

The ultimate hope for the people of God is not in an earthly warrior king who would rid the land of Roman pretenders like Herod. Deposing

Herod would not bring the dead children of the mothers of Bethlehem back, but defeating death once and for all would. The ultimate hope for the people of God was an end to the spiritual exile of death through the cross and resurrection of Christ.

Jesus Returns to the Promised Land

After Herod died, an angel of the Lord appeared in a dream to Joseph in Egypt, saying, "Get up, take the child and his mother, and go to the land of Israel, because those who intended to kill the child are dead." So he got up, took the child and his mother, and entered the land of Israel. But when he heard that Archelaus was ruling over Judea in place of his father Herod, he was afraid to go there. And being warned in a dream, he withdrew to the region of Galilee. Then he went and settled in a town called Nazareth to fulfill what was spoken through the prophets, that he would be called a Nazarene. (Matt 2:19–23)

Matthew portrays Jesus's flight to Egypt and return to Nazareth as a symbolic reenactment of the exodus and the exile. Jesus lived out the story of Israel from the OT. But Matthew ends this sequence with a clear parallel to Moses's return to Egypt. God told Moses to return to Egypt because "all the men who wanted to kill you are dead" (Exod 4:19), but the angel told Joseph to leave Egypt "because those who intended to kill the child are dead" (Matt 2:19).[10] Whereas Moses returned to Egypt to rescue his people from slavery and bring them into the Promised Land, Jesus returned from Egypt to bring his people from the Promised Land into an even greater destination: the kingdom of God.[11]

---

[10] Matthew 2:19 is a direct quotation of the Greek version of Exod 4:19. See Quarles, *Theology of Matthew*, 37 (see chap. 7, n. 13).

[11] Weinandy, *Jesus Becoming Jesus*, 1:59 (see chap. 9, n. 11).

Legend and extrabiblical tradition paint the picture that Jesus spent many of his formative years in Egypt.[12] But despite claims of an extended stay in Egypt, Matthew twice notes that the holy family left Egypt after Herod the Great died (either in 4 BC or 1 BC). The holy family probably did not stay longer than a few months there and then quickly returned home to Nazareth. One conjectural proposal from the historian Paul Maier only has the family staying in Egypt for a few weeks.[13]

A Hypothetical Chronology of the Events Between Jesus's Birth and Herod's Death	
Event	**Number of Weeks After Jesus's Birth**
Birth of Jesus Luke 2:1–20	0
Circumcision of Jesus Luke 2:21	1
Purification of Mary and Presentation of Jesus Luke 2:22–38	6
Visit of the Magi Matt 2:9–11	7
Arrival in Egypt / Slaughter of the Innocents Matt 2:13–16	10 or 11

---

[12] *Arabic Gospel of the Infancy* 9–26; Origen, *Against Celsus* 1.28; *Toledot Yeshu*; Peter Schäfer, *Jesus in the Talmud* (Princeton, NJ: Princeton University Press, 2009), 15–24; Anne Rice, *Christ the Lord: Out of Egypt* (New York: Knopf, 2005). The "1260 days" (3½ years) of Rev 12:6 "the woman" spent in the "wilderness" is the likely basis of some of these traditions.

[13] The "Hypothetical Chronology" chart is adapted from Paul L. Maier, "The Date of the Nativity and the Chronology of Jesus' Life," in *Chronos, Kairos, Christos*, 127. I have amended Maier's chart to include the circumcision and to show progression of weeks after Jesus's birth.

Herod's Illness and Death
    Matt 2:19
    Josephus, *Ant.* 17.6–8
	13 or 14

Total Estimated Number of Weeks:	13 or 14 weeks

Joseph may have thought about taking the holy family back to
Bethlehem in Judea but changed his mind when he discovered that Herod's
son Archelaus ruled over it. Archelaus had a penchant for violent retaliation like his father. After the death of Herod, a group of Jews in Jerusalem
planned to overthrow the government. During the Passover, Archelaus
then sent a cohort of soldiers to diffuse the situation, but the people stoned
them. Archelaus ordered his army to respond in force, and his soldiers
killed three thousand people in Jerusalem in the middle of Passover week.[14]
After God warned him in a dream not to go back to Judea, Joseph took his
family back to Nazareth in Galilee where Herod Antipas reigned. Though
Antipas showed his own cruelty later in the Gospels, he was certainly the
lesser of two evils between these two sons of Herod.

Matthew claims that the holy family's arrival in Nazareth fulfills "what was spoken through the prophets, that he would be called a
Nazarene" (Matt 2:23). But what are we to make of this final prophetic
fulfillment? If Matthew quoted a direct prophecy from an OT text, its
meaning would be easy enough to discern: the Messiah would be born a
Nazarene. Yet this quotation is nowhere to be found in the OT (at least
in the specific way Matthew words it).

A few different OT texts have been proposed as potential sources
for partial quotation. One possibility is a vague reference to Judg 13:5–
7, which speaks of Samson's Nazarite vow. Yet to be from Nazareth is
not the same thing as taking the Nazarite vow. Furthermore, as France
observes, Jesus's reputation as a "wine drinker" (Matt 11:19) probably
precludes us from making that connection.[15]

---

[14] Josephus, *Ant.* 17.9.3.
[15] France, "The Formula-Quotations of Matthew 2," 131 (see chap. 13, n. 29).

Another possibility is from Isaiah 11, a passage that reveals what the reign of the future Messianic kingdom will be like:

> Then a shoot will grow from the stump of Jesse,
> and a branch from his roots will bear fruit. (Isa 11:1)

The Hebrew word translated as "branch" here is *nê-ṣer*. This Hebrew word sounds very much like "Nazareth" when pronounced. Matthew may be trying to connect Jesus's life experience raised as a Nazarene with this prophetic text (Matt 2:23; 21:11).

The setup to this "prophecy" resembles the formula Matthew has used throughout the nativity story to quote from OT prophets, but there are two key differences. First, Matthew notably uses the phrase "through the prophets" instead of "what was spoken by the prophet." Matthew indicates that he is speaking about the whole of biblical prophecy rather than quoting a single prophet or passage. Second, Matthew does not use the same word (the participle *legonotos*) to set up the quotation that he uses in the other Scripture quotations. Instead, Matthew uses the conjunction *hoti* (translated "that") in such a way that it can indicate "a paraphrase or a summary of what was said." From these two differences, France concludes "that what Matthew is here providing is not a quotation of a specific passage but rather a theme of prophecy."[16] A few contemporary translations (CSB, NIV, ESV) correctly recognize the change in Matthew's fulfillment formula and make the choice to set this up as a general prophetic fulfillment and not a direct quotation from a specific OT text.

Matthew does not suggest that Jesus's childhood in Nazareth is a direct fulfillment of a particular prophetic text. Instead, Matthew alludes to a prophetic tradition of the "branch person" that describes the Messiah as despised and rejected by his people (Ps 22:6–8; Isa 11:1; 49:7; 53:2–3; Dan 9:26).[17] As a town and culture generally loathed by most people

---

[16] France, *The Gospel of Matthew*, 91.
[17] Quarles, *Matthew*, 134; Carson, "Matthew," 243 (see chap. 2., n. 11).

in Israel, Nazareth becomes an appropriate hometown for the suffering Servant who was "despised and rejected by men" (Isa 53:3).

The Nations Rage Against the Virgin-Born King

The psalmist asked why the "nations rage" and "the peoples plot in vain" against the Lord and his Messiah (Ps 2:1–2). Unbelieving kings, dictators, and politicians still rebel against Christ because of the threat his sovereign rule poses to them. This was true in first century BC Judea, and it is true in twenty-first century Western culture.

Herod's murderous plot was the first of many attempts on the life of Jesus recorded in the Gospels. On the day when Jesus's ministry was inaugurated in Nazareth, people from the synagogue "got up, drove him out of town, and brought him to the edge of the hill that their town was built on, intending to hurl him over the cliff" (Luke 4:29). But something like a supernatural stupor fell over this lynch mob, and "he passed right through the crowd and went on his way" (Luke 4:30). On multiple occasions, religious leaders picked up stones to hurl at Jesus, but he was "hidden" from them (John 8:59; cf. 10:31). They plotted to kill Jesus out of jealousy toward him (Matt 12:14; 26:1–5).

God providentially protected Jesus from the harm of his enemies until the "hour had come for him to depart from this world" (John 13:1; cf. 12:23, 27; 17:1; Mark 14:35). Then, according to "God's determined plan and foreknowledge," he allowed "lawless people to nail him to a cross and kill him" (Acts 2:23).

Despite the great villainy of this drama, Matthew paints a picture of a virgin-born king who will rescue his people from slavery, who will bring them back out of exile, and who will lead them into the kingdom of God. Jesus summed up Israel's story and gave it a new and better ending. Whereas Israel forgot about the exodus and served other gods, the Messiah who came out of Egypt acted as a perfect representative for his nation. Even though Israel's suffering servant did not disobey God like Israel did, "he willingly submitted to death, and was counted among the rebels; yet he bore the sin of many and interceded for the rebels" (Isa 53:12).

Answering Objections: Luke Contradicts the Flight to Egypt

One statement in Luke's account appears to contradict large chunks of Matthew's story. In Luke 2:39, the Evangelist seems to suggest that Mary and Joseph packed their bags and headed straight back to Nazareth after Mary was purified and Jesus was dedicated to the Lord. If we only had Luke's account, then we would probably presume that to be exactly what happened.

But Matthew reported that "after [the magi] were gone," an angel of the Lord came to Joseph and told him to flee to Egypt where the child would be safe from Herod (Matt 2:13). Joseph and Mary only returned to Israel after Herod was dead (Matt 2:15, 19–20) and opted to return to Galilee because Joseph was warned about Herod's son Archelaus who was ruling down south in Judea (Matt 2:22–23).

So how do we explain the difference between Luke 2:39 and Matt 2:15–23? At least three options are available to us:

- Option #1—Matthew and Luke's timelines contradict one another. One or both Evangelists are wrong about the sequence of events. Although Matthew and Luke have different storytelling strategies and theological emphases, there are no explicit factual discrepancies between these accounts. Luke never claims that the family "immediately" made this trip after fulfilling their temple obligations (see Mark 1:12).
- Option #2—The events described in Matt 2:1–23 all happened within the first forty days of Jesus's life (before

Luke 2:22–24). The magi arrived at the house where Jesus was born when or shortly after the shepherds visited (see Martyr, *Dialogue with Trypho* 88). The holy family escaped to Egypt, but Herod died almost immediately after they crossed the border. This option would not work because it would have taken three to four weeks to make the one-way trip from Bethlehem to Egypt. Even presuming the holy family's time in Egypt was short, it still would have been a nearly two-month-long round trip.

- Option #3—The holy family took up residency in Bethlehem after the birth of Jesus. They made the day's journey to Jerusalem when Jesus was dedicated at forty days old and then returned to the house where they were staying in Bethlehem (Matt 2:11). Months, maybe even a year or more, passed before the magi visited Jesus. They returned to Nazareth after Herod's death. Luke did not mention the flight to Egypt either because he was unaware of the tradition or had theological reasons for glossing over it.

The third option presents the fewest difficulties for harmonizing Matthew's and Luke's stories. Luke may not have known about the flight to Egypt because he was unfamiliar with this story. Another possibility is that Luke, like many other ancient biographers, skips over large periods of time that he deems irrelevant to the story he tells. Luke 2:39–40 is part of a transitional statement that moves the narrative ahead from Jesus in the temple at forty days old to Jesus in the temple at twelve years old.

The similar statement "Jesus increased in wisdom and in stature" (Luke 2:52) is a transition statement from Jesus's childhood at twelve to the beginning of his adult ministry at or around thirty years old (Luke 3:23). If Luke leaves out twelve years and then eighteen years of Jesus's life, it is safe to assume that there are details he would have left out between the dedication of Jesus in the temple and the family's eventual return to Nazareth—including the escape to Egypt.

See Blomberg, *The Historical Reliability of the New Testament*, 61–62 (see chap. 2, n. for "Answering Objections: The Genealogies").

15

The Boy Grew Up and Became Strong

Luke 2:39–52

> The Word endured to be born in human fashion, although in his
> divine nature, he has no beginning, nor is he subject to time. He who
> as God is completely perfect, submitted himself to bodily growth.
> The one without a body now has limbs that grow and stretch toward
> adulthood. He who is all Wisdom was himself now filled with wisdom.
> —CYRIL OF ALEXANDRIA (c. 376–444)[1]

S top me if you have heard this version of the Christmas story in Sunday
school. The moment after he was wrapped in swaddling clothes, the
newborn Jesus looked over at Mary and started preaching like a grown
adult to his mother.

---

[1] Cyril of Alexandria, *Homilies on the Gospel of Luke* 5, paraphrased for clarity.

> When he was lying in his cradle he said to Mary his mother, "I am Jesus, the Son of God, the Word, whom you have delivered, just as the angel Gabriel announced to you. My Father has sent me for the salvation of the world." [2]

If you are not familiar with this retelling of the Christmas story, that's because it comes from a counterfeit gospel produced in the Middle Ages known as the *Arabic Gospel of the Infancy*. This infant Jesus only appeared to be a human child, but he spoke with a fully formed divine mind the moment he came out of the womb. Whoever wrote this "gospel" apparently had difficulty coming to terms with the idea that God the Son became a true human baby who cried, who slept, who ate, and who soiled himself. The so-called infancy gospels were written by people who were curious about Jesus's childhood, but because they had no connection to the apostles whatsoever, few in the early church took them seriously. These documents tell us more about popular religious imagination than the historical Jesus.

The idea that Jesus could be both God and human has always been a difficult pill to swallow. Where most critics of Christianity today dismiss the idea of Jesus's true divinity, many of the earliest opponents of the faith affirmed some version of his divinity but denied his true humanity. Many of the so-called gospels rejected by the early church scoffed at or completely misunderstood his human nature.

Luke's nativity story ends with a scene from Jesus's childhood at the age of twelve. It seems like a strange story to include—one episode from Jesus's preadolescence before his public ministry begins at his baptism eighteen years later. But this story serves an important purpose in Luke's Gospel: It shows how Jesus continues the story of the OT as the new and better Samuel. But this precious narrative also gives us the only biblical window we have into Jesus's maturation process.

---

[2] *Arabic Gospel of the Infancy* 1.

In My Father's House (Luke 2:41–51)

Every year his parents traveled to Jerusalem for the Passover Festival. When he was twelve years old, they went up according to the custom of the festival. After those days were over, as they were returning, the boy Jesus stayed behind in Jerusalem, but his parents did not know it. Assuming he was in the traveling party, they went a day's journey. Then they began looking for him among their relatives and friends. When they did not find him, they returned to Jerusalem to search for him. After three days, they found him in the temple sitting among the teachers, listening to them and asking them questions. And all those who heard him were astounded at his understanding and his answers. When his parents saw him, they were astonished, and his mother said to him, "Son, why have you treated us like this? Your father and I have been anxiously searching for you."

"Why were you searching for me?" he asked them. "Didn't you know that it was necessary for me to be in my Father's house?" But they did not understand what he said to them.

Then he went down with them and came to Nazareth and was obedient to them. His mother kept all these things in her heart. (Luke 2:41–51)

Contemporary readers may be tempted to judge Mary and Joseph for their failure to keep up with Jesus, but significant cultural differences between communal parenting in first-century Palestine and "helicopter parenting" in the twenty-first century could explain how Mary and Joseph lost their child. Families usually went on pilgrimages with large caravans made up of extended family members and other people from the community. Not only did these caravans provide protection from dangerous criminal elements, but they also reflected a collective communal approach to parenting quite foreign to modern Westerners.

A large caravan traveling from Jerusalem to Nazareth could have made that ninety-mile journey over the course of three days.[3] Were it presumed that Jesus was somewhere among the caravan, Mary and Joseph would not have worried about his location. When they discovered that Jesus was missing, they spent three days in the crowded city of Jerusalem looking for him. Eventually, they found Jesus in the temple, "sitting among the teachers, listening to them and asking them questions" (Luke 2:46). This incident illustrates several aspects of Jesus's maturing humanity.

First, Jesus displayed the virtue of studiousness and attentiveness to God's word.[4] In the temple, Jesus listened carefully to biblical teaching and asked good questions. Luke tells us that "all those who heard him were astounded at his understanding and his answers" (Luke 2:47). Luke does not claim what later infancy gospels would suggest: that the child Jesus "put to silence the elders and teachers of the people, expounding the heads of the law and the parables of the prophets."[5] Again, the authors of these heretical gospels had difficulty processing a truly human Jesus who grew in maturity and understanding.[6]

Second, Jesus had a clear sense of his identity as the Son of God. Theologians and biblical scholars have long wrestled with questions about how and when the incarnate Christ knew about his divine identity and messianic mission. When his parents finally found him in the Temple, Mary asked him how he could treat Joseph like this (Luke 2:48). Jesus responded that it was necessary for him to be in his "Father's house." Jesus knew that God, not Joseph, was his true Father. Mary and

---

[3] Craig S. Keener, *The IVP Bible Background Commentary—New Testament*, 2nd ed. (Downers Grove: IVP Academic, 2014), 186.

[4] Thomas Aquinas makes a helpful distinction between the virtue of studiousness and the vice of curiosity. See Thomas Aquinas, *Summa theologica* IIb q. 166–67.

[5] *Infancy Gospel of Thomas* 19.2.

[6] See also *Infancy Gospel of Thomas* 6–7.

Joseph were astonished by his statement—not because they had forgotten what happened twelve years ago, but because of Jesus's remarkable spiritual perception.[7]

Jesus honored his parents with perfect obedience. Though Jesus was separated from his parents when the family caravan left the city, Luke gives no indication whatsoever that Jesus did something wrong in their separation. Had Jesus failed to honor his father and mother, he would have violated the Ten Commandments and tarnished himself with sin (Exod 20:12; Deut 5:16). But Luke stresses Jesus "was obedient to them," so much so that his mother continued to reflect on these things for some time to come (Luke 2:51).

The Favor of God and People (Luke 2:40, 52)

The boy grew up and became strong, filled with wisdom, and God's grace was on him. . . . And Jesus increased in wisdom and stature, and in favor with God and with people. (Luke 2:40, 52)

The statements in Luke 2:40 and 2:52 serve as segues between the infancy of Jesus and his childhood and his childhood and the inauguration of his adult ministry. The description in 2:52 spans eighteen years of Jesus's life and gives no specifics about what happened in between the temple incident and his appearance at the Jordan River in Luke 3. The silence of Scripture about the so-called "missing years" of Jesus has led some to invent fanciful stories about Jesus traveling the world and learning from eastern sages.[8] But like ancient heretical gospels, these modern

---

[7] See Thomas Joseph White, *The Trinity: On the Nature and Mystery of the One God* (Washington, DC: Catholic University of America Press, 2022), 627–28. By adulthood, Christ was conscious of his Father, his Father's presence, his union with the Father, his filial identity as the Son of God, his own preexistence and divinity, the Spirit, the Spirit's anointing, and his role in sending the Spirit.

[8] The most famous of these counterfeit accounts was Levi H. Dowling's 1908 book *The Aquarian Gospel of Jesus Christ.*

fictions tell us more about the beliefs of their authors than they do the life of Jesus.

Although the transitional statement in Luke 2:52 leaves many unanswered questions about the "missing years of Jesus" on the table, it tells us everything we need to know about Jesus's transition to adulthood here. In the same way "the boy Samuel grew in stature and in favor with the LORD and with people" (1 Sam 2:26), "Jesus increased in wisdom and stature, and in favor with God and with people" (Luke 2:52). God the Son did not just appear to be human; he was united to true humanity with all its natural limitations. Just like Samuel, Jesus grew physically ("in stature"), mentally ("in wisdom"), spiritually ("in favor with God"), and socially ("in favor . . . with people").

But the acknowledgment of Jesus's true humanity raises interesting questions about his divinity. In what sense does the all-knowing and all-wise God increase in his wisdom? How can the God who exists outside of time and space occupy a human body that physically grows over time? Perhaps most puzzling: How is it possible for God to increase "in favor with God"?

The fourth-century theologian Gregory of Nazianzus devised a relatively simple solution to complex questions like these. In Scripture, some descriptions of God the Son talk about his *divine nature* whereas others describe his *human nature*. Every passage in Scripture that refers to Jesus's growth, anguish, or submission to the Father speaks of his human nature. Passages that speak of the Son's involvement in creation refer to his divine nature. Passages that describe the moral perfections of Christ speak about both his divine and human natures.

But whether Scripture speaks of his divine nature, his human nature, or both natures, Gregory observes, Scripture talks about one divine Person. When we read the NT descriptions of Christ, we should always ask whether an action attributed to him applies directly to his divine nature, his human nature, or both. Christian theologians call this interpretive practice *partitive exegesis*, from a word meaning one part of a whole. Partitive exegesis recognizes that some texts about Christ describe one aspect of his person (his humanity) whereas other texts speak of another aspect of his person (his divinity).[9]

In the incarnation, the omnipresent God who transcends space took up residence in a growing physical body. God the Son learned to crawl, toddle, and run. He went through growth spurts, puberty, and voice changes. Though the Son has every conceivable divine perfection, the incarnation did not guarantee physical perfection or superhuman athletic abilities. He subjected himself to physical weakness, the possibility of illness, and mortality.

But what are we to make of Luke's claim that Jesus "increased in wisdom"? What about instances in the Gospels where the Son appears to be ignorant of things in God's world or his plan (Mark 9:21; 13:32)? How could Jesus grow in his knowledge and wisdom and be all-knowing and all-wise? Or, as Jerome (c. 342–420) posed the question, "How does he who is Wisdom receive wisdom?"[10] God the Son also grew mentally in his human nature, though he never ceased to be all-knowing in his divine nature.

Jesus went through every stage of cognitive development essential to true humanity. As a toddler, he learned through sensory interaction with the world. He had to be taught the sounds, syntax, and vocabulary of the Aramaic language spoken by first-century Jews. Like any small child, he played with toys and thought about the world around him in very literal and concrete ways. But by twelve years old, Jesus was able to wrap his mind around complex abstract ideas. As Thomas Joseph White remarked, the mental growth he experienced from this point on included "ordinary activities of reflection, psychological maturation, progressive

---

[9] Gregory of Nazianzus, *Orations* 29.18–20. See John Behr, *The Nicene Faith*, Formation of Christian Theology, vol. 2 (Yonkers, NY: St. Vladmir's Seminary Press, 2019), 24–25. For a helpful overview of how to apply this principle in biblical exegesis, see R. B. Jamieson and Tyler R. Wittman, *Biblical Reasoning: Christological and Trinitarian Rules for Exegesis* (Grand Rapids: Baker, 2022), 153–78; Jamieson, *The Paradox of Sonship*, 31–36 (see chap. 5, n. 12).

[10] Jerome, *Homily on Psalm 15* (16).

learning, and thinking and speaking in the language and symbols of a given culture, making decisions and choices."[11]

We must not miss Luke's observation that "Jesus increased . . . in favor . . . with people." In his humanity, Christ underwent social development in which he learned how to relate to human beings who were made in his divine image. He acquired social skills and the ability to perform increasingly difficult tasks as he endured psychological maturation. However, without a fallen human nature and depraved desires, Christ's social development would have looked quite different from our own. Much of our early social growth is about overcoming impulsive, irrational, and selfish behavior. But Christ, who is Wisdom personified (Prov 8:22–31), would have learned how to relate to others in ways that embodied Israel's wisdom tradition.

> My son, don't forget my teaching,
> but let your heart keep my commands;
> for they will bring you
> many days, a full life, and well-being.
> Never let loyalty and faithfulness leave you.
> Tie them around your neck;
> write them on the tablet of your heart.
> Then you will find favor and high regard
> with God and people. (Prov 3:1–4)

Without a sin nature, Christ related to people in such a way that he naturally received their "high regard." Those who had difficulty understanding Jesus's mission—like his own brothers and sisters (John 7:1–7)—did so not because of a failure on his part but because of their own sinful shortcomings.

---

[11] White, *The Trinity*, 626; cf. Jean Galot, *Who is Christ? A Theology of the Incarnation*, trans. M. Angeline Bouchard (Chicago: Franciscan Herald, 1981), 371–75.

The most remarkable thing about Christ's development is how God "grew in favor with God." Jesus grew spiritually in his theological knowledge of God, his personal acquaintance with God, and his obedience to God. According to the author of Hebrews, Jesus, in his humanity, "offered prayers and appeals with loud cries and tears to the one who was able to save him from death, and he was heard because of his reverence. Although he was the Son, he learned obedience from what he suffered" (Heb 5:7–8; cf. Luke 22:42). This growth of Jesus in obedience implies two wills in Christ, the divine will and the human.[12] Christ learned how to submit his human will to God—the Father, the Spirit, and even the Son.[13]

As a human theologian, Jesus grew in his understanding of God. Obviously, human beings know God differently than God knows himself. God is the infinite and all-knowing Creator. He alone has perfect, infinite knowledge of himself (what theologians call his "archetypal theology"). We, on the other hand, are finite creatures limited in our knowledge and understanding. God only reveals to us what he knows we are capable of understanding about him. Our finite knowledge of God can only produce an imperfect copy of God's perfect, infinite knowledge of himself ("ectypal theology").[14]

---

[12] The doctrine of Christ's two wills, called *dyothelitism*, was affirmed at Constantinople III in AD 381. For a helpful contemporary assessment of this doctrine, see R. Lucas Stamps, "'Thy Will Be Done': A Dogmatic Defense of Dyothelitism in Light of Recent Monothelite Proposals" (PhD diss., The Southern Baptist Theological Seminary, 2014).

[13] White, *The Trinity*, 628–30.

[14] Special thanks to Tyler Wittman for this insight. See Jamieson and Wittman, *Biblical Reasoning*, 35–39. See also Franciscus Junius, *A Treatise on True Theology with the Life of Franciscus Junius*, trans. David C. Noe (Grand Rapids: Reformation Heritage, 2014), 107–20. Our ectypal knowledge of God "copies" God's perfect knowledge of himself. Junius delineates three types of ectypal theology: (1) the ectypal theology of the incarnate Son described in this section, (2) the ectypal theology of saints in heaven, and (3) the ectypal theology of people on earth, the most imperfect of the three. Although we have knowledge of God in this world, "now we see only a reflection as in a mirror," now we

But in the incarnation, God the Son experiences both the perfect, infinite knowledge of God in his divine nature (archetypal theology) and the imperfect, finite knowledge of God in his human nature (ectypal theology). Only God the Son knows what it is like to have perfect knowledge of God and to grow in his knowledge of God as a finite human being. Christ both gave the law of Moses and learned it for himself. As Jerome deftly perceived, Jesus advanced in wisdom as "his human nature was instructed by his own divinity."[15]

The Virgin-Born King Showed Us How to Grow Up

Like Jesus, Samuel was the rare combination of a prophet (1 Sam 3:20), priest (1 Sam 2:35), and ruler (1 Sam 7:6, 15). From childhood, Samuel lived in the Lord's presence. Unlike the wicked sons of Eli who "would not listen to their father" (1 Sam 2:25), "the boy Samuel grew in stature and in favor with the LORD and with people" (1 Sam 2:26). In adulthood, Samuel modeled faithful service to God and drew the respect of the people. Tragically, Samuel's own sons did not walk in the ways of the Lord like their father—"they turned toward dishonest profit, took bribes, and perverted justice" (1 Sam 8:3).

Like Samuel, Jesus, in his human nature, grew physically, mentally, socially, and spiritually. But where Samuel had his shortcomings and faults both as a leader in Israel and as a parent, Christ lived in perfect obedience to the Father. Because of this perfect obedience, "he became the source of eternal salvation for all who obey him" (Heb 5:9). Now those who belong to Christ can and should emulate his growth in understanding God and his Word, his growth in relationships to others, and his obedience to God's will.

---

only know "in part." But we long for the day when we "know fully," as we are "fully known" (1 Cor 13:12; cf. 1 John 3:2).

[15] Jerome, *Homily on Psalm 15 (16)*, quoted in *Luke*, Ancient Christian Commentary on Scripture, NT vol. 3, ed. Arthur A. Just (Downers Grove: IVP Academic, 2003), 57.

16

The Word Became Flesh

The Virgin-Born King in the Other Gospels

In these books . . . we found Jesus our Christ foretold as coming,
born of a virgin, growing up to man's estate, and healing every
disease and every sickness, and raising the dead, and being hated,
and unrecognized, and crucified, and dying, and rising again, and
ascending into heaven, and being, and being called, the Son of God.
                                        –JUSTIN MARTYR (c. 100–165)[1]

N either the Gospel of Mark nor the Gospel of John explicitly mention the circumstances surrounding the birth of Jesus. The sermons
of the apostles recorded in the book of Acts are replete with pronouncements about Jesus's death, burial, and resurrection but make nary a mention about his infancy. Though Paul makes a passing reference to the idea

---

[1] Justin Martyr, *First Apology* 31.

that Jesus was "born of a woman" (Gal 4:4), he nowhere proclaims that Jesus was conceived by supernatural means.

The apparent silence of the rest of the NT has led some modern theologians, like Emil Brunner (1889–1966), to reject the virginal conception:

> In the preaching of the Apostles, in the preaching of Paul and of John, as well as of the other writers of the New Testament, this idea does not play even a small part—it plays no part at all. Thus the doctrine of the Virgin Birth does not belong to the *Kerygma* [proclamation] of the Church of the New Testament. . . . We must assume, either, *that the Apostles were unaware of this view, or that they considered it unimportant, or even mistaken.*[2]

It is worth noting that the first generation of Christian theologians saw no difficulty with the silence of the rest of the NT on the virgin birth. When Ignatius, Justin Martyr, and Irenaeus wrote so much about the virgin birth in the early second century, they never suggested that Matthew or Luke were insufficient witnesses of this event or that they somehow contradicted the other Evangelists or apostles.

What Matthew and Luke write about the virgin birth is clear: Mary conceived Jesus by the power of the Holy Spirit (Matt 1:18; Luke 1:35). The Evangelists believed this event was anticipated in the OT. Of the clarity of Scripture on this topic, even the modernist Presbyterian theologian Charles Briggs (1841–1913) admitted,

> The virgin birth does . . . rest on the authority of two of the holy gospels, and that authority must be regarded as sufficient for those who recognize their divine inspiration. It has never been regarded by the Christian church as necessary that a doctrine should be sustained by a large number of passages. It is sufficient that the doctrine be clearly and unmistakably stated.

---

[2] Emil Brunner, *The Christian Doctrine of Creation and Redemption*, Dogmatics, vol. 2, trans. Olive Wyon (Eugene, OR: Wipf and Stock, 2014, 1952), 354, italics mine.

That is undoubtedly true of the virgin birth. It is impossible by any mode of explanation to remove that doctrine from these two passages of Holy Scripture.[3]

No Christian doctrine must be accounted for in every single biblical text, and there is no need for a minimum number of additional texts to affirm a doctrine where one text is sufficiently clear. "No one can dispute the existence of a biblical testimony to the virgin birth."[4]

The details of Christ's birth may only take up a very small portion of the total biblical word count, but they serve an enormously large role in the overarching story of the Bible. The infancy stories recorded in Matthew and Luke's Gospels serve as the canonical and narrative bridge between the Old and New Testaments. Although there may only be four chapters in the Bible that explicitly speak about the virgin birth, all Scripture testifies to the same Lord and Messiah who was born of a virgin. The witness to Christ in the other Gospels is completely consistent with the picture of Christ in the nativity stories.

Transmission of the Virgin Birth Tradition

The absence of a virgin-birth tradition in the Acts sermons, Paul's letters, and in the Gospel of Mark could be attributed to the later transmission of this story. The early church proclaimed the death and resurrection of Jesus before they proclaimed his virginal conception. Unlike the resurrection of Jesus, which had over 500 witnesses (1 Cor 15:6), the birth or infancy of Jesus was witnessed by fewer:

---

[3] Charles A. Briggs, "The Virgin Birth of Our Lord," *The American Journal of Theology* 12, no. 2 (1908), 193. Briggs was eventually excommunicated from the Presbyterian church for his rejection of plenary-verbal inspiration, but his views on the virgin birth would have been deemed to be too conservative for some of his modernist peers.

[4] Karl Barth, *Church Dogmatics* I.2, *The Doctrine of the Word of God* §13–15, study edition, trans. and ed. G. M. Bromiley and T. F. Torrance (London: T&T Clark, 2010), 185 [176].

- the magi from the east
- Simeon, Anna, and those who heard Anna's prophecy
- the shepherds
- anyone who may have been present in the house when Jesus was born
- Elizabeth and possibly Zechariah
- Mary and Joseph.

Even with a dozen or so witnesses to Jesus's birth or infancy, only Mary and Joseph had firsthand knowledge of the virginal conception. We could reasonably infer that Mary confided in Elizabeth and Zechariah about this miracle as well, even though Luke does not specifically tell us this.[5]

Joseph likely died before Jesus's adult ministry began, as did Simeon, Anna, Zechariah, and Elizabeth. Mary and Jesus's brothers and sisters may have been the original source of the nativity story traditions recorded in Matthew and Luke. But the family of Jesus would have had little reason to disclose these events until after the resurrection. The same holy family that fled to Egypt to provide safety for their son would not want to say anything about him that drew unwanted attention. Telling their neighbors in Nazareth that the Holy Spirit conceived Jesus could have invited skepticism and accusations of illegitimacy—or worse, threats of death from Herod's heirs.

In light of that, knowledge about Jesus's death and resurrection was likely public before knowledge of his conception and birth. This would explain why the apostles' sermons recorded in Acts do not mention the events of the nativity. (The author of Luke-Acts did not deny the nativity story.) Mary may have waited until after Pentecost to talk about these events, after Jesus's identity as the risen Lord became public knowledge. Empowered by the Spirit, Mary may have begun quietly sharing her story

---

[5] Orr, *The Virgin Birth of Christ*, 92–93 (see introduction, n. 6).

with those in the church who would listen, including her other children who only came to believe in Jesus after his resurrection.[6]

The Virgin-Born King in the Gospel of Mark

According to modern scholarship, the Gospel of Mark is likely the oldest of the four Gospels.[7] If this theory is true, Matthew and Luke probably used it in the composition of their own Gospels (see Luke 1:1). Besides the obvious absence of a nativity story, the structure of Mark's Gospel is very similar to Matthew and Luke. As Thomas Torrance points out, "Mark makes no explicit reference to the virgin birth, but then neither do Matthew and Luke from the same point in their narrative where Mark begins."[8]

Mark's silence about the virgin birth is by no means conclusive proof that he was ignorant of it or rejected it. Brevity is a key feature of Mark's Gospel. The Gospel reads like an action movie, moving at breakneck speed without a lot of detailed character development. Even Mark's word choices indicate his fast-moving narrative. He uses the adverb "immediately" (Gk. *euthys*) over forty times in the Gospel to advance scenes in his story. "Immediately the Spirit drove him into the wilderness" (Mark 1:12). "Immediately he called them" (Mark 1:20).

Moreover, Mark begins his Gospel with the baptism of Jesus (Mark 1:1–11) and ends abruptly with the women leaving Jesus's empty tomb in

---

[6] Machen, *The Virgin Birth*, 264–65 (see introduction, n. 6). For more on James's dramatic conversion after the resurrection, see John 7:2–5; 1 Cor 15:7; Acts 1:14; 15:13; Gal 1:19; 2:9.

[7] Although this is the majority opinion, some scholars argue for Matthean priority. See William R. Farmer, *The Gospel of Jesus: The Pastoral Relevance of the Synoptic Problem* (Louisville: WJK, 1994).

[8] Thomas F. Torrance, *Incarnation: The Person and Life of Christ*, ed., Robert T. Walker (Downers Grove: InterVarsity, 2015), 89.

fear (Mark 16:8).[9] Mark mentions nothing about the bodily appearances of Jesus after the resurrection, but this does not mean that Mark would deny such appearances took place.

Mark's emphasis on the divine sonship of Jesus runs on parallel tracks with the Christology of the nativity stories. Though they affirm the virgin birth, Matthew and Luke call Jesus the "son of Joseph" (Luke 3:23; see also John 1:45; 6:42) and the "carpenter's son" (Matt 13:55). But Mark never uses this phrase, nor does he mention Joseph. Instead, Mark only refers to Jesus as "the son of Mary" (Mark 6:3), the "Son of David" (Mark 10:47–48), and "the Son of God" (Mark 1:1; 15:39). The fact that Mark never calls Jesus the "son of Joseph" may be his subtle way of acknowledging the unique circumstances surrounding Jesus's birth.

Twice in this Gospel, God audibly declares Jesus to be his "beloved Son" (Mark 1:11; 9:7). God the Father is "well-pleased" with Jesus (Mark 1:11). The Father's declaration of Jesus's divine sonship in the transfiguration shows that Jesus is seen as superior to Moses and Elijah (Mark 9:2–13). The idea that Jesus had no human father is completely consistent with Mark's insistence on Jesus's divine sonship.

Unlike the other Evangelists, Mark never explains what it means for Jesus to be the divine Son of God, but he does repeatedly showcase Jesus's unique authority as God's Son. Jesus demonstrated that he has power over the natural world. When Jesus calmed an angry sea with his authoritative word, his disciples asked, "'Who then is this? Even the wind and the sea obey him!'" (Mark 4:41). Jesus has power over every human ailment—even death (Mark 1:29–34; 8:22–26; 10:46–52; cf. 5:21–43). Mark may say nothing about Mary's miraculous pregnancy in his Gospel, but such a miracle would perfectly cohere with the Evangelist's belief in Jesus's power over nature.

---

[9] Mark 16:9–20 is not in the earliest and most reliable Greek manuscripts. For an overview of the major perspectives on this text, see David Alan Black, ed., *Perspectives on the Ending of Mark: Four Views* (Nashville: B&H Academic, 2008).

The Virgin-Born King in the Gospel of John

Like Mark's Gospel, John's Gospel includes no nativity story. However, John admits that he was selective about which miracle stories or "signs" he chose to include in his Gospel: "Jesus performed many other signs in the presence of his disciples that are not written in this book" (John 20:30). John's Gospel even closes with this comment: "There are also many other things that Jesus did, which, if every one of them were written down, I suppose not even the world itself could contain the books that would be written" (John 21:25). For John, silence about a miraculous event in the life of Jesus is not necessarily a denial of it.

In the Beginning Was the Word (John 1:1–18)

Unlike Mark's Gospel, which opens at the beginning of Jesus's adult ministry, or Matthew's and Luke's Gospels, which open at the beginning of Jesus's earthly life, John's story goes all the way back to the very beginning—the beginning of time itself. With language clearly meant to remind readers of the first words of Genesis, John writes, "In the beginning was the Word, and the Word was with God, and the Word was God. He was with God in the beginning" (John 1:1–2; cf. Gen 1:1). Throughout the prologue of John 1:1–18, the Evangelist depicts Jesus as the eternal, preexistent Son of God who was made incarnate in true human flesh.

> In the beginning was the Word, and the Word was with God, and the Word was God. He was with God in the beginning. All things were created through him, and apart from him not one thing was created that has been created. In him was life, and that life was the light of men. That light shines in the darkness, and yet the darkness did not overcome it. (John 1:1–5)

John proclaims Christ to be different from every other person ever born. Before the world began, Christ was in the presence of God. Not only has he lived eternally in the presence of God; Jesus himself is God. Everything in the universe came into existence through Jesus. He is the source of all life and the true light of the world that dispels all darkness, death, and decay. The Lord Jesus is the "Word [who] became flesh and dwelt among us" (John 1:14a). Had Jesus never entered the world, we would never really know the "grace and truth" of the Father (John 1:14b). It is only through Jesus, "the one and only Son, who is himself God and is at the Father's side," that we can know God the Father (John 1:18).

John makes no mention of the mechanism of virginal conception, but he certainly celebrates its outcome: The eternal, creative Word of God became flesh and resided with us. The God who created every human being became one himself. The God who is beyond space and time entered it, taking up physical space in a real place, in a real culture, and at a real moment in human history. The "event" through which this incarnation took place is the virgin birth.[10]

> ## Answering Objections: The Virgin Birth Contradicts the Preexistence and Incarnation of Christ
>
> Emil Brunner and Wolfhart Pannenberg (1928–2014), two of the most influential theologians of the twentieth century, contended that the virgin birth tradition in Matthew and Luke's nativity stories contradicted the doctrine of Christ's preexistence in John's Gospel and the letters of Paul. Brunner even proposed that the prologue to John's Gospel (John 1:1–18) was written in direct opposition to the nativity stories of Matthew and Luke (*The Christian Doctrine of Creation and Redemption*, 352–53).
>
> Brunner and Pannenberg asserted that Matthew's and Luke's nativity stories present an alternative to, not an explanation of the incarnation of the Word of God. As Brunner and Pannenberg read them, the nativity stories were not about how the eternal Son of

---

[10] Karl Barth, *Credo* (New York: Charles Scribner's Sons, 1962), 62.

God became man but how the Son of God was created in time. If this were so, then John's prologue and the nativity stories would contradict one another, because John plainly teaches that Jesus existed before becoming flesh (John 1:14; 8:58; 17:4–5).

But do Matthew and Luke tell the story of how the Son of God came to exist? This preposterous claim has no basis in the text. These texts describe the enthronement of the Son of God among humanity but not the beginning of his divine existence. How can we know this?

First, the Gospel writers use the language of divine visitation to describe the entrance of Christ into the world. Matthew has the incarnation of God in mind when he calls Jesus "Immanuel" and explicitly defines this name as "God with us" (Matt 1:23). In his prophetic praise, Simeon states, "The dawn from on high will visit us" (Luke 1:78). Christ the eternal dayspring does not come from below, but from "on high." He descended to be among us; he did not originate in a human form as we do.

Second, the preexistence of the Son is implied in Matthew's quotation of Mic 5:2. This text says, "His times of coming forth are from long ago, From the days of eternity" (NASB). Micah was clear that the coming Messiah existed before he appeared in Bethlehem. The Messiah existed with the "Ancient of Days" in eternity past and was "given dominion and a glory and a kingdom, so that those of every people, nation, and language should serve him" (Dan 7:13–14).

Third, Matthew's and Luke's Gospels contain other indications of Jesus's preexistence. Jesus claimed to be David's Lord spoken of in Ps 110:1 (Matt 22:41–45; Luke 20:41–44)—an odd notion if Jesus did not begin to exist until after the virgin birth.

Finally, the very nature of the virginal conception implies that Jesus existed before his conception. If human life ordinarily begins at conception, then it stands to reason that an individual conceived by supernatural means does not necessarily conform to this rule.

Simon Gathercole adds, "One would expect a supernatural being to enter the human realm in a supernatural way; if one begins with the Son's preexistence, then his humanity must have started somewhere" (*The Preexistent Son*, 285). If we say that Christ's humanity began through natural conception, we run the risk of presuming that his humanity could exist independently of his divine nature, which would put us in danger of the heresies of adoptionism or Nestorianism (see chs. 19, 20). Furthermore, no human father could be the originator of the incarnate Word.

As D. A. Carson makes clear, "There is no logical or theological reason to think that virginal conception and preexistence preclude each other" ("Matthew," 98). Rather than contradicting John's description of the preincarnate "Word made flesh," the nativity stories explain how that event transpired in time and space. John and Paul tell us that God the Son became incarnate among us; Matthew and Luke show us how.

See Simon J. Gathercole, *The Preexistent Son: Recovering the Christologies of Matthew, Mark, and Luke* (Grand Rapids: Eerdmans, 2006), 238–42.

Born, Not of Natural Descent (John 1:13)

He was in the world, and the world was created through him, and yet the world did not recognize him. He came to his own, and his own people did not receive him. But to all who did receive him, he gave them the right to be children of God, to those who believe in his name, who were born, not of natural descent, or of the will of the flesh, or of the will of man, but of God. (John 1:10–13)

The first Christian theologians contended that John 1:13 directly referenced the virginal conception of Jesus. They interpreted this verse to mean that Jesus himself "was not born of natural descent, or of human family planning, but God's will alone."[11] Even if John 1:13 is not a direct reference to Jesus's virginal conception, one could see why the church fathers interpreted this text as a reference to the incarnation. God, not Joseph, initiated Mary's miraculous conception. It was God's will—not man's will—that Christ would enter the world when he did. However, the case for this interpretation is largely dependent on an alternate Greek spelling with little support in the earliest surviving copies of the Greek New Testament. In every surviving Greek manuscript dating from the second century on, the pronoun "who" and the verb "born" are plural.[12]

If John originally meant for this pronoun and verb to be plural, then John 1:13 is about God's sovereign purpose in calling out and adopting us as his children. Simply put, this means we are not natural-born followers of Jesus, nor are we Christians simply by virtue of having Christian parents. We are born again not by human family planning but by faith in Christ through the power of the Holy Spirit. This traditional interpretation is perfectly consistent with what John and other New Testament texts say about the "new birth" Christians receive through the Holy Spirit (see John 3:3, 5–8; 1 John 3:9; 5:4; cf. Eph. 2:1–10; Jas 1:18; 1 Pet 1:23).

Both the singular and plural readings are consistent with historical Christian orthodoxy. Jesus was not born of human family planning. Nor are we born again in the Spirit by human reproduction, as Jesus explains to Nicodemus in John 3:3–8. Both readings may be consistent with the whole of Christian teaching, but only one is original. With most modern interpreters of John, I contend that the plural reading of John 1:13 is the

---

[11] See Justin Martyr, *Dialogue with Trypho* 54, 63; Clement of Alexandria, *Stromata* 2.13; Irenaeus, *Against Heresies* 3.16.2; 3.19.2; Hippolytus, *The Refutation of All Heresies* 6.4; Tertullian, *On the Flesh of Christ* 19. For a survey of these interpretations, see Jean Galot, *Etre né de Dieu: Jean 1, 13* (Rome: Institut Biblique Pontifical, 1969), 64–79.

[12] *hoi . . . egennēthēsan.* One early Latin translation from around Ephesus (the area where the Gospel of John was likely written) uses the singular. Several Syriac translations use the singular verb "was born" but retain the plural "who" pronoun. See John W. Pryor, "Of the Virgin Birth or the Birth of Christians? The Text of John 1:13 Once More," *Novum Testamentum* 27, no. 4 (1985): 296–97.

best reading. However, it seems that John's description of the new birth in John 1:13 presumes belief in the virgin birth.

The same Holy Spirit who caused Mary to conceive apart from human initiative is the same Holy Spirit who gives us the new birth apart from human initiative. The virginal conception by the Holy Spirit thus becomes a picture of our own salvation. No one was looking for a virgin-born messiah, nor could any man plan such a divine feat. The same is true for our salvation. No one was looking for it, nor could any man plan it or will it.[13]

The Manna from Heaven (John 6:22–59)

Another possible allusion to the virgin birth may be found in the heavenly manna sayings of Jesus in John 6. Following Jesus's feeding of the five thousand in John 6:1–15, a crowd went looking for Jesus, presumably out of a desire to be fed by him again. This prompted Jesus to begin teaching about "food that lasts for eternal life" (John 6:27).

The crowd asked Jesus for another sign, like the manna God provided Israel in the wilderness. But Jesus insisted that Moses's manna was not the true bread from heaven that the Father gives: "For the bread of God is the one who comes down from heaven and gives life to the world. . . . *I* am the bread of life. . . . No one who comes to *me* will ever be hungry, and no one who believes in *me* will ever be thirsty again" (John 6:33, 35, emphasis mine).

Jesus added, "I have come down from heaven, not to do my own will, but the will of him who sent me" (John 6:38). Do not miss the bold claim here: Jesus claims to have existed in heaven before he existed on earth. The religious leaders responded, "Isn't this Jesus the son of Joseph, whose

---

[13] C. E. B. Cranfield, "Some Reflections on the Subject of the Virgin Birth," *Scottish Journal of Theology* 41, no. 2 (1988): 179; cf. C. K. Barrett, *The Gospel According to St. John*, 2nd ed. (Louisville: WJK, 1978), 164.

father and mother we know? How can he now say, 'I have come down from heaven'?" (John 6:42).

How can Jesus be both the bread who came down from heaven and the son of Joseph? John uses *dramatic irony* here to draw attention to Jesus's unique origin as the virgin-born Messiah.[14] With dramatic irony, the audience of the Gospel knows more than the characters in the story: We know that Jesus did come from heaven and is, in the adoptive sense, the son of Joseph. As C. K. Barrett explains, "John nowhere affirms belief in the virgin birth of Jesus, but it is probable that he knew and accepted the doctrine . . . and that he here ironically alludes to it—if the objectors had known the truth about Jesus' parentage they would have been compelled to recognize that it was entirely congruent with his having come down from heaven."[15]

Where Does Jesus Come From? (John 7:40–44; 8:14, 23)

> When some from the crowd heard these words, they said, "This truly is the Prophet." Others said, "This is the Messiah." But some said, "Surely the Messiah doesn't come from Galilee, does he? Doesn't the Scripture say that the Messiah comes from David's offspring and from the town of Bethlehem, where David lived?" So the crowd was divided because of him. Some of them wanted to seize him, but no one laid hands on him. (John 7:40–44)

The question of Jesus's identity and origin proved to be a source of contention between the people and the religious leaders. After Jesus foretold the coming of the Spirit, some of the people were ready to label him

---

[14] The classic example of dramatic irony we learn in high school literature classes comes from *Romeo and Juliet*. The audience knows Juliet is not dead because she took the potion that made her comatose, but a lovesick Romeo does not know this, and he drinks a fatal poison to take his own life.

[15] Barrett, *The Gospel According to St. John*, 295.

"the Prophet" from Deut 18:15.[16] Others wanted to call him Messiah, but there was confusion about how Jesus could be the Messiah if he grew up in the Galilean town of Nazareth. They were familiar with the promise of Micah who said that the Shepherd over Israel would be born in Bethlehem (John 7:42). Elsewhere in his Gospel, John indicated a popular prejudice against Nazarenes (John 1:46).

Craig Keener contends that the original hearers of John's Gospel would already be familiar with the nativity stories in Matthew and Luke by the time John's Gospel was written. Again, John employs dramatic irony for his readers who already know where Jesus came from. The characters in the story debate whether Jesus came from Bethlehem or Jerusalem, but John wants us to know that Jesus really came from heaven.[17] This irony becomes even clearer in the next chapter, where Jesus twice indicated that his origins are not from this world at all: "My testimony is true, because I know where I came from and where I'm going. But you don't know where I come from or where I'm going" (John 8:14). "You are from below . . . I am from above. You are of this world; I am not of this world" (John 8:23). Jesus's self-testimony is plain: He did not come into the world the same way other men do—a claim that coheres perfectly with the virginal conception in Luke 1:35 and Matt 1:18.

The Consistent Witness of the Gospels

All four Gospels are pronouncements of the good news about King Jesus. All four share a common message about the Messiah who revealed God to us, who suffered on the cross in the place of sinners, and who rose in victory over sin and death. First, the whole NT builds on the idea that Jesus was the descendant of David—an idea very clearly expressed

---

[16] See also Acts 3:22–26.
[17] Craig S. Keener, *The Gospel of John: A Commentary* (Grand Rapids: Baker Academic, 2010), 1:730.

in Matthew's and Luke's nativity stories.[18] Second, Jesus modeled perfect obedience and never committed sin—an idea that could only be explained by a supernatural birth. Third, Jesus is both the son of Mary and the Word from heaven. Only the narrative of the virginal conception can explain both ideas prevalent in John's Gospel.[19]

Were John read in isolation of the other Gospels, the reader would never know how the Word was made flesh. Were Matthew and Luke read in isolation of John, the reader might not fully understand the meaning of Jesus's miraculous birth. What John tells us about Jesus's identity and origin helps us make much more sense of the baby lying in the manger. The prologue of John's Gospel fits together with Matthew's and Luke's nativity stories like puzzle pieces from the same larger picture. In isolation, each piece of the puzzle is incomplete or impossible to identify, but together, they create a seamless picture of the virgin-born king who is the Word from God made flesh. "The Word [who] became flesh and dwelt among us" in John's Gospel truly is "Immanuel" from Matthew's nativity story.

---

[18] Herman Bavinck, *Reformed Dogmatics*, vol. 3, *Sin and Salvation in Christ*, ed. John Bolt, trans. John Vriend (Grand Rapids: Baker, 2006), 289. See also Matt 1:1, 20; 9:27; 12:23; 15:22; 20:30–31; 21:9, 15; 22:42–45; Mark 10:47; 11:10; 12:35–37; Luke 1:27, 32, 69; 18:38–39; 20:41–44; John 7:42; Acts 2:30; 13:23; Rom 1:3; 2 Tim 2:8; Heb 7:14; Rev 3:7; 5:5; 22:16.

[19] Bavinck, *Reformed Dogmatics*, 290.

17

Born of a Woman

The Virgin-Born King in the Letters of Paul

"God sent his Son," Paul says, not born of a man and a woman
but "born of a woman" only; that is, born of a virgin.
—CYRIL OF JERUSALEM (c. AD 313–386)[1]

The only explicit reference Paul makes to the birth of Jesus is in Gal 4:4–5: "When the time came to completion, God sent his Son, born of a woman, born under the law, to redeem those under the law, so that we might receive adoption as sons." Paul says Jesus was born as a man under the law of Moses to buy back other men who were under the same law. He makes no specific claim about how Jesus was conceived.

---

[1] Cyril of Jerusalem, *Catechetical Lectures* 12.31.

Paul never addressed the virgin birth directly, but did he affirm it? Was he even aware of the virgin birth tradition? These questions present no easy answers—and much of what we say here will be conjecture and guesswork. Although we cannot know with certainty whether Paul knew about the virgin birth, much of what Paul says about Christ seems to presume a miraculous incarnation event that could only be explained by a virginal conception. At the very least, Paul's doctrine of the "last Adam" and "the man from heaven" coheres well with the nativity stories recorded in Matthew and Luke.

Did Paul Know About the Virgin Birth?

When it comes to Paul's knowledge of the virgin birth tradition recorded in Matthew and Luke, we have three basic options:

1. Paul knew about the virgin birth tradition and rejected it.
2. Paul did not know about the virgin birth tradition.
3. Paul knew about the virgin birth tradition and presumed it in his teachings about Christ.

Any argument made for any one of these positions will be an argument from silence, and each option presents its own difficulties.

Option #1—Paul rejected the virgin birth tradition. The least convincing option is the idea that Paul knew about the virgin birth tradition and denied it. One possible line of support for claiming that Paul spurned the virgin birth might be his appeal to Jesus's Davidic ancestry. Paul names Jesus the "descendant of David according to the flesh" (Rom 1:3; see also Rom 9:5; 2 Tim 2:8). But the authors of the nativity stories in Matthew and Luke also affirm this lineage and see no inconsistency with their claims that Jesus was conceived by the Holy Spirit.

If Paul had known about the virgin birth and rejected it, we probably would have more evidence of that in his letters. After all, Paul condemns a wide range of heretical teachings he believes are contrary to the gospel of Christ. The apostle warned the Corinthian Christians about receiving false teachers who proclaim "another Jesus, whom we did not preach" and "a different gospel" (2 Cor 11:4). Paul often used his letters to rebuke doctrine contrary to the Jesus and the gospel he preached:

- In Galatians, Paul addressed those trying to distort the gospel by adding the requirements of the law of Moses (Gal 1:6–9; 5:1–6).
- In 1 Corinthians 15, Paul denounced a teaching that denied the future bodily resurrection of believers (1 Cor 15:12).
- Paul directs the book of Colossians toward a legalistic heresy (Col 2:4–23) that apparently downplayed the true divinity of Jesus (hence Paul's defense of this doctrine in Col 1:15–23).

Had Paul opposed the virgin birth doctrine, we might expect to see something like a defense of Jesus's natural conception somewhere in his letters. Admittedly, such an argument stems from silence, but it seems unlikely that Paul would have been both a vocal supporter of Luke's ministry (see Col 4:14; 2 Tim 4:11; Phlm 1:24) and openly opposed to his teaching.

Option #2—Paul did not know about the virgin birth. Paul's silence on the virgin birth has led many scholars—including some conservative scholars—to believe that Paul was ignorant about the virgin birth whenever he wrote his letters.[2] Those who hold this position argue that Paul's letters predate the widespread acceptance of the virginal conception in the early church.

The fact that Paul does not directly address the virgin birth is not conclusive proof that he knew nothing of it. Outside of his discussion of the cross and resurrection, Paul spoke very little about specific episodes from the life of Christ. (One notable exception to this rule was the apostle's discussion about the Last Supper in 1 Cor 11:17–26.) Paul wrote nothing about Jesus healing the sick, feeding the multitudes, performing exorcisms, or raising the dead.

Few interpreters would take Paul's silence on these events to mean he did not know about them or denied them. Paul primarily wrote letters

---

[2] Tim Perry, *Mary for Evangelicals: Toward an Understanding of the Mother of Our Lord* (Downers Grove: IVP Academic, 2006), 30.

of encouragement, correction, and instruction to established churches throughout the Roman Empire. He did not have to detail specific instances from Jesus's life that already would have been well known to these churches.

Option #3—Paul presumed the virgin birth. Although it is certainly possible that Paul did not know about the virginal conception when he began writing his letters, he likely knew about this tradition toward the end of his ministry. The logic behind this claim is simple:

- Luke probably wrote Acts before Paul died (c. AD 64–67).[3]
- Luke wrote Acts as a sequel to his Gospel (Acts 1:1–2), meaning the Gospel of Luke was already in circulation when Paul died.
- The nativity stories recorded in Luke 1–2 were always part of Luke's Gospel.
- Therefore, the nativity stories were circulated in Christian churches before Paul died.

Furthermore, given the close partnership between Paul and Luke, it seems plausible that Paul would have been familiar with what the nativity story preserved in Luke's Gospel. In 1 Tim 5:18, Paul even appeals to a saying of Jesus only recorded in Luke 10:7 and calls it "Scripture"![4]

Possible Allusions to the Virgin Birth Tradition in Paul's Letters

Presuming Paul knew about the virgin birth tradition his missionary associate Luke wrote about, we can ask whether there are any indications of this tradition in his letters. Do texts that speak of the incarnation point to the virginal conception or something like it? Do references to

---

[3] Although this is a common view among evangelical NT scholars, it is not universally agreed on by all NT scholarship. This view stems from the ending of Acts 28:30–31. According to this view, Luke did not write about Paul's martyrdom because it had not yet occurred.

[4] Orr, *The Virgin Birth of Christ*, 115 (see introduction, n. 6).

Jesus's birth in Paul's letters indicate familiarity with the same nativity tradition Luke had? Here are a few passages that may help us answer these questions.

Galatians 4:4–5

> When the time came to completion, God sent his Son, born of a woman, born under the law, to redeem those under the law, so that we might receive adoption as sons. (Gal 4:4–5)

Critics may ask, "Why doesn't Paul just say, 'born of a virgin'?" Yes, he says "born of a woman," but he also excludes the normal male role in reproduction. It is also possible that the phrase "born of a woman" simply describes Jesus's true humanity, not his virginal conception. After all, Jesus uses a similar phrase to describe John the Baptist (see Matt 11:11; Luke 7:28).

With Paul, we recognize that Jesus was born in a normal way. But the key difference between Jesus and other men born of women is in his identity as the Son of God "sent forth" from heaven. The Son of God was born of a woman and born under the law of Moses to redeem us and secure our own adoption as the sons and daughters of God. Or, as Irenaeus put it, "The Son of God became the Son of man, that man, having been taken into the Word, and receiving the adoption, might become the son of God."[5]

But there is one striking difference in Paul's vocabulary: In all of his letters, Paul never uses the normal NT words for human birth in reference to Jesus (*gennaó, gennétos*). He uses these words to chronicle the birth of Jacob and Esau (Rom 9:11), Ishmael (Gal 4:23), and Isaac (Gal 4:29). But whenever he refers to Jesus's entrance into the world, he uses a word that means "to become" (*ginomai*).

---

[5] Irenaeus, *Against Heresies* 3.19.1.

Romans 1:1–4

> Paul, a servant of Christ Jesus, called to be an apostle, set apart
> for the gospel of God, which he promised beforehand through
> his prophets in the holy Scriptures, concerning his Son, who was
> descended from David according to the flesh and was declared
> to be the Son of God in power according to the Spirit of holi-
> ness by his resurrection from the dead, Jesus Christ our Lord.
> (Rom 1:1–4 ESV)

In the opening statement of his letter to the Romans, Paul defines
the "gospel of God" as the news that was promised by the prophets concerning Jesus. Paul confirms that Jesus fulfills OT prophecy in his descent
from David "according to the flesh" and in his resurrection from the dead
by which he "was declared to be the Son of God in power." The resurrection did not make Jesus the Son of God; the Spirit used this event to
establish him publicly as the Son of God.[6]

James Orr draws several interesting parallels between this salutation
and the angelic annunciation to Mary recorded in Luke 1:31–33, 35.[7]

Luke	Paul
"give birth to a son" (Luke 1:31)	"born" or "having become" (*genomenou*, Rom 1:3)
"his father David" (Luke 1:32)	"who was descended from David" (Rom 1:3 ESV) or more literally, "having come out of the seed of David"
"The Holy Spirit will come upon you" (Luke 1:35)	"according to the Spirit of holiness" (Rom 1:4 ESV)

---

[6] Thomas R. Schreiner, *Romans* (Grand Rapids: Baker Academic, 1998),
41–42.

[7] Adapted from Orr, *The Virgin Birth of Christ*, 121.

"He will be great and will be called the Son of the Most High. . . . The holy one to be born will be called the Son of God" (Luke 1:32, 35)	"declared to be the Son of God in power" (Rom 1:4 ESV)
"the power of the Most High" (Luke 1:35)	"in power" (Rom 1:4 ESV)

These texts do not prove that Luke used Paul or that Paul used Luke. But their comparison shows parallel lines of thinking in Paul and Luke. Both emphasize the prophetic fulfillment of Jesus taking David's throne. Both texts highlight Jesus's human nature. Both underscore the Spirit's activity—one in the conception of Jesus, the other in his resurrection. Neither the virginal conception nor the resurrection made Jesus the Son of God, but both events declared his divine identity in power.

At the very least, Paul's statement that Jesus "descended from David according to the flesh" (Rom 1:3 ESV) indicates that Paul may have shared a source for Jesus's genealogy with Luke or Matthew.[8]

1 Timothy 3:16

> And most certainly, the mystery of godliness is great:
> He was manifested in the flesh,
> vindicated in the Spirit,
> seen by angels,
> preached among the nations,
> believed on in the world,
> taken up in glory. (1 Tim 3:16)

---

[8] Thomas C. Oden, *Systematic Theology*, vol. 2, *The Word of Life* (San Francisco: Harper, 1989), 143.

In the middle of a discussion about the moral and spiritual qualifica-
tions of pastors and deacons (1 Tim 3:1–16), Paul cites what appears to
be an early hymn about Christ's incarnation. Christians should conduct
themselves a certain way in the church, the argument goes, because God
has provided a "pillar and foundation of the truth" for us in the incarnation of Jesus (1 Tim 3:15). As Thomas Oden explains, "How we ought
to act is set in the context of how God has acted toward humanity in the
ministry of his Son."[9]

A few scholars have suggested that the phrase "the mystery of god-
liness" may have been Paul's veiled way of speaking about the virginal
conception to protect it against accusations of demonic activity. Many
ancient Jews explained the origin of demons from Gen 6:4, which says
that "the Nephilim [fallen ones] were on the earth . . . when the sons of
God came to the daughters of mankind, who bore children for them."
In other words, demons were born when angels had sex with women.
This interpretation of the Nephilim comes from a Jewish book written between the OT and NT called *The Book of Enoch*. "Enoch" (or the
author imitating the man described in Gen 5:24) called this conception
between spiritual beings and human women a work of "ungodliness"
(*asebia*, *1 Enoch* 1:9; see also Jude 1:14–15).

According to the Finnish theologian Antti Laato, Paul affirmed the
virgin birth but did not speak directly of it out of the concern that his
readers would accuse Christ of an "ungodly" origin like the Nephilim.
Contrasted with the "ungodliness" of these angels, "the mystery of godli-
ness" would have been insider language to the church familiar with the
story of how the incarnation took place. Laato contends that Paul uses
the same strategy in Phil 2:7 when he simply describes the incarnation as
the Son "taking on the likeness of humanity."[10] No explanation will sat-

---

[9] Thomas C. Oden, *First and Second Timothy and Titus*, Interpretation
(Louisville: WJK, 1989), 44.

[10] Antti Laato, "Celsus, Toledot Yeshu and Early Traces of Apology for the
Virgin Birth of Jesus," Jewish Studies in Nordic Countries Today, *Scripta Instituti*

isfy every inquirer about why Paul never spoke about how God became human, but Laato's intriguing thesis merits further consideration.

The Virgin-Born Man from Heaven

We can endlessly speculate about whether Paul ever indirectly addressed the virginal conception. But one thing is certain: Paul has much to say about the same divine-human person who was conceived in a virgin's womb. On two occasions, Paul contrasts Adam with Christ. In Rom 5:12–21, he juxtaposes the sin of Adam that brought judgment on the world with the righteous act of Christ that led to justification for everyone. In 1 Cor 15:35–49, Paul distinguishes between the earthly body we inherit from the first Adam and the spiritual body we inherit from the "last Adam"—the risen Lord (1 Cor 15:45). Adam is called "a man of dust" (a callback to the way God created Adam in Gen 2:7) whereas Christ, the "second man," is "from heaven" (1 Cor 15:47).

The second-century theologian Irenaeus linked the virgin birth and Paul's teaching on the second Adam—a connection that has baffled and flustered modern critics.[11] But the internal logic of such a connection is sound. Like Christ, Adam had no father but God (see Luke 3:23, 38). Like Christ, Adam came into this world without the guilt of sin or the effects of depravity. For Paul, Adam represents the failure of the old human race to obey God, but Christ represents a new beginning (see also Matt 1:1). It is at least conceivable that Paul knew that the only way Christ could be both "born of a woman" and a new human representative was through a virginal conception.

Paul's rich theology of the incarnation overlays remarkably well with the nativity stories in Matthew and Luke. Christ Jesus existed "in the

---

Donneriani Aboensis 27 (2016): 74–76. See also Jukka Thurén, *Korinttilaiskirjeet, Tessalonikalaiskirjeet, Paimenkirjeet* (Helsinki: Kustannus oy Arkki, 2008), 512–15.

[11] See Hans von Campenhausen, *The Virgin Birth in the Theology of the Ancient Church*, trans. Frank Clarke (London: SCM, 1954), 39–40.

form of God" but did not exploit his rightful authority as God (Phil 2:6). Instead, he assumed the "form of a servant," the Servant of the Lord prophesied by Isaiah (Isa 42:1) and raised up in Simeon's arms (Luke 2:28). Paul declares that Jesus took on "the likeness of humanity" (Phil 2:7). Without an alternate explanation for how he was "made" in the form of the servant, it is safe to assume the only way this could have happened was through the conception of the Holy Spirit.

The humility spoken of in an abstract way in Phil 2:8 takes on flesh and bones in the story of a baby laid in a manger. The exaltation of the Son expressed in Phil 2:9–11 seems to fulfill Gabriel's promise that Christ "will be called the Son of the Most High" (Luke 1:32) whose "kingdom will have no end" (Luke 1:33). To the glory of his true Father, "Jesus," the name angels commanded Mary and Joseph to give this child, would forever be on the tongues of every creature.

18

The Serpent Crushed

Genesis 3:14–15; Revelation 12:1–17

> The enemy would not have been justly conquered unless it
> had been a man made of woman who conquered him. For
> it was by a woman that he had power over man from the
> beginning, setting himself up in opposition to man.
> —IRENAEUS OF LYONS[1]

If you have never done so, take a few moments to read the first three
chapters of Genesis with the last three chapters of Revelation side by
side. The opening and closing chapters of the Bible fold together like a
long tablecloth where each corner and seam matches up perfectly. These
chapters are like mirror images of one another, further illustrating the
supernatural character of biblical inspiration.

---

[1] Irenaeus, *Against Heresies* 5.21.1.

- The same triune God who created the heavens and the earth
  in Genesis 1 brings a new heaven and new earth forward in
  Revelation 21.
- The same triune God who expelled humanity from the temple-
  like garden of Eden welcomes humanity back to the garden-like
  temple in the New Jerusalem.
- Humanity is denied access to the tree of life in Gen 3:22, but in
  Rev 22:2, the leaves of the tree of life are made available for the
  "healing of the nations."
- The serpent who made hell on earth in Genesis 3 is cast from
  earth into hell in Revelation 20.
- God cursed the ground in Gen 3:17 but declared that there
  "would no longer be any curse" in Rev 22:3.
- The God who banished Adam and Eve from his presence in
  Genesis 3 sits enthroned among his people in Revelation 22.

From the very beginning of the biblical story, its redemptive end is
anticipated. The story of the whole Bible bends like an arc—from creation to fall, from fall to redemption, and from redemption to new creation. At the center of this arc stands the Lord Jesus, whose redemptive
work made the new creation and the final defeat of evil possible. God's
promise in Gen 3:15 that the "seed of the woman" would crush the serpent establishes a pattern for the final redemption portrayed in the book
of Revelation. For this reason, biblical interpreters often refer to this text
as "the first gospel" (protoevangelium) or "the first glimmer of gospel hope."

Genesis 3:15 lays the groundwork for a "cosmic Christmas story" in
Revelation 12, where John dramatically retells the entire biblical story
through word pictures. At the center of this story is another version of
Christ's nativity. But unlike the nativity stories of the Gospels that focus
on the how and when of Jesus's birth, the nativity story of Revelation 12
focuses on the why: the seed of the woman was delivered to crush the
serpent and rescue his people.

The First Glimmer of Gospel Hope (Gen 3:14–15)

The promise of Gen 3:15 appears in a series of what we might call "divine curse words." No, God was not being profane in his speech. Through his "curses," God executed just judgment on the created order for human sinfulness. Before their act of rebellion, Adam and Eve lived in blissful ignorance of good and evil. But after they listened to their serpentine tempter, they would have an intimate acquaintance with suffering and death.

God never cursed the man and woman who bore his image but promised trouble in his work, her childbearing, and their marriage. God cursed the ground, ensuring that man would labor and toil all the days of his life. Yet the most significant "curse" God delivered was against the serpent who tempted our first parents:

> Because you have done this,
> you are cursed more than any livestock
> and more than any wild animal.
> You will move on your belly
> and eat dust all the days of your life.
> I will put hostility between you and the woman,
> and between your offspring [seed] and her offspring [seed].
> He will strike your head,
> and you will strike his heel. (Gen 3:14–15)

On one level, this curse is simply a description of the animosity between man and creation in a fallen and broken world. As bearers of the divine image, human beings were created to rule over every creature (Gen 1:28), but in a created world subjected to futility (Rom 8:20), dangers now lurk around every corner for us. Natural evils like cancer, coronavirus, floods, heart attacks, hurricanes, tornadoes, wildfires, and venomous snake bites flow out of this curse. In such a dangerous world, our human fragility and mortality are exposed like prey before a bloodthirsty predator.

On another level, this promise establishes a pattern leading to the ultimate defeat of evil in redemption history. Though Genesis 3 never directly refers to the serpent as Satan—that name appears later in the OT (1 Chr 21:1; Job 1:6–12; 2:1–7; Zech 3:1–2)—Revelation clearly identifies "the ancient serpent" with "the devil and Satan. the one who deceives the whole world" (Rev 12:9). In Gen 3:15, God promises the serpent that the "seed" of the woman will always be at war with the serpent and that one day, the offspring will finally deliver the striking blow to the serpent's head.

Unlike many of the other OT texts we have explored to this point, Gen 3:15 is never directly quoted in the NT. We do not have a NT quotation followed by an inspired author saying something like "this happened to fulfill the Scripture." This verse is not, strictly speaking, a prediction of a future event like the virgin birth of Jesus, but it establishes a pattern that gets constantly revisited across the rest of Genesis, the other books of Moses, and the entire canon.[2] The immediate context of Genesis suggests that the "seed of the woman" refers to the people of God (plural) who live in opposition to the "seed of the serpent."[3]

Cain murdered his brother and was "cursed" like the serpent (Gen 4:11). Eve gave birth to Seth, another "seed" (Gen 4:25). God promised Abraham that all families of the earth would be blessed through the "seed" of Abraham, anticipating the serpent's final defeat through the woman's seed (Gen 12:3; cf. 22:17–18).[4] Paul plainly identified this "seed" as Christ (Gal 3:16). The law was given to expose our sin "until the Seed to whom the promise was made would come" (Gal 3:19). Paul told Roman Christians that "the God of peace will soon crush Satan under your feet" (Rom 16:20)—meaning that God would soon give the offspring of the woman, his holy people, total victory over Satan. This

---

[2] Hamilton, *Typology*, 6–17 (see chap. 4, n. 3).
[3] Daniel P. Fuller, *The Unity of the Bible: Unfolding God's Plan for Humanity* (Grand Rapids: Zondervan, 1992), 223–47.
[4] Hamilton, *Typology*, 16.

dramatic conflict reaches a crescendo in the incarnation wherein the evil powers of this world are soundly defeated by the Lord's Messiah.

The people who rebel against God are the children of the serpent (John 8:44–47; 1 John 3:8–15). Those who serve the Lord belong to the "seed" (plural) of the woman. The woman's offspring and the serpent's offspring are locked in mortal combat. The children of the serpent may inflict temporary suffering on the people of God, but the ultimate defeat of the serpent himself by the Seed of the woman (singular) ensures their victory.[5]

The Cosmic Christmas Story (Rev 12:1–17)

The chain reaction set off in Gen 3:15 culminates in the book of Revelation, where the offspring of the woman finally, fatally crushes the serpent's head. The "cosmic Christmas story" of Revelation 12 borrows heavily from the imagery of Gen 3:15 to tell the story of Christ's work of redemption and the ultimate victory secured for the people of God.

Rise the Woman's Conquering Seed (Rev 12:1–6)

A great sign appeared in heaven: a woman clothed with the sun, with the moon under her feet and a crown of twelve stars on her head. She was pregnant and cried out in labor and agony as she was about to give birth. Then another sign appeared in heaven: There was a great fiery red dragon having seven heads and ten horns, and on its heads were seven crowns. Its tail swept away a third of the stars in heaven and hurled them to the earth. And the dragon stood in front of the woman who was about to give birth, so that when she did give birth it might devour her child. She gave birth to a Son, a male who is going to rule all nations with an iron rod. Her child was caught up to God and to

---

[5] See Hamilton, *Typology*, 14.

his throne. The woman fled into the wilderness, where she had a place prepared by God, to be nourished there for 1,260 days. (Rev 12:1–6)

Who is this mystery woman "clothed with the sun" and wearing a "crown of twelve stars on her head"? Since medieval Christianity, Roman Catholic commentators have identified this "woman" as Mary, calling her the "Queen of Heaven." Although this symbolic "woman" gives birth to the Christ child as Mary did in human history, we should not confuse her with the historical individual Mary of Nazareth. Unlike this "woman," Mary was never persecuted after the birth of Christ (see Rev 12:13).

The "woman" who gives birth to Jesus here stands in for the true people of God in the OT and NT. Like the "seed of the woman" in Gen 3:15, the "offspring" (or "seed," *spermatos*) of this "woman" are "those who keep the commands of God and hold firmly to the testimony about Jesus" (Rev 12:17). The crown of twelve stars she wears on her head is a picture of Israel's twelve tribes and the future rule the people of God will have with him when Christ returns.[6]

The people of God are compared to a pregnant woman who "cried out in labor and agony as she was about to give birth" (Rev 12:2). John here pictures the people of God who eagerly waited for God to fulfill his covenant promises through the advent of the Messiah. The "great fiery red dragon having seven heads and ten horns" (Rev 12:3) represents both the earthly kingdoms of men who oppose God and his people and the evil spiritual power behind those earthly kingdoms—the serpent himself (Rev 12:9; see also Dan 7:23–27).[7] The imagery of the dragon sweeping "away a third of the stars in heaven and hurled them to the earth" is borrowed from Dan 8:10. Daniel's prophecy spoke of the future persecution of God's people by Antiochus IV Epiphanes, the Seleucid king who

---

[6] G. K. Beale, *The Book of Revelation*, NIGTC (Grand Rapids: Eerdmans, 1999), 626–27.

[7] Beale, 632–34.

killed tens of thousands of Jews (2 Macc 5:11–14) and who desecrated the temple by slaughtering a pig on the altar (Diodorus 34.1).

This dragon representing the evil empires of men and Satan himself stood patiently by the "woman" in labor, looking to "devour her child" (Rev 12:4). Satan had always used evil earthly powers to prevent God from fulfilling his promises to crush the serpent through the seed of the woman, to bless the nations through the seed of Abraham, and to ensure that an heir of David would rule forever. The Pharaoh plotted to kill the sons of Israel (Exod 1:8–20). Haman wanted to annihilate all the Jewish people (Esth 3:6, 13). Had God not providentially used Esther to rescue her people from this representative of the dragon (Esth 4–7), the covenant promises fulfilled by the Messiah would never have come to fruition. Herod the Great also embodied the dragon who sought to kill the child immediately after he was born to the woman (Matthew 2). These earthly rulers falsely believed they were acting in their own best interests, but they were really pawns in a larger demonic plot to thwart the serpent's certain and promised crushing defeat.

The "woman" gave birth to a Son—the seed of the woman—again indicating that God had fulfilled his covenant promises to Abraham and the people of God. Across his writings, John exclusively uses this word for "son" (*huion*) to refer to Jesus.[8] The claim that the son will "rule all nations with an iron rod" is a clear reference to Psalm 2, where the "Anointed One" (2:2) who is called the Son of God (2:7) will reign over all nations on the earth (2:8) and break the evil kingdoms of the world with an "iron scepter" (2:9). The reign of the son with an iron rod fulfills the promise of Christ's eternal kingdom made to David (2 Sam 7:16) and Mary (Luke 1:32–33). Now all kingdoms were made subject to Christ:

> The kingdom of the world has become the kingdom
> of our Lord and of his Christ,
> and he will reign forever and ever. (Rev 11:15)

---

[8] John Christopher Thomas and Frank D. Macchia, *Revelation* (Grand Rapids: Eerdmans, 2016), 218.

When the Son's rule had been established, he "was caught up to God and to his throne" (Rev 12:5). Here John speaks of the ascension of Christ depicted in Luke 24:50–51 and Acts 1:9–10 (see also Eph 4:8; 1 Tim 3:16).

After the Son ascended to the throne of God, the "woman fled into the wilderness, where she had a place prepared by God, to be nourished there" (Rev 12:6). This imagery invokes God's provision of manna in the wilderness (Exodus 16) and possibly, the flight of the holy family into Egypt where God provided protection from Herod (Matt 2:13–15). Christians may debate the meaning of the 1,260 days (or three-and-a-half years), but the most important element is God's protection and provision of his people.[9]

Bruise in Us the Serpent's Head (Rev 12:7–17)

Then war broke out in heaven: Michael and his angels fought against the dragon. The dragon and his angels also fought, but he could not prevail, and there was no place for them in heaven any longer. So the great dragon was thrown out—the ancient serpent, who is called the devil and Satan, the one who deceives the whole world. He was thrown to earth, and his angels with him. Then I heard a loud voice in heaven say,

The salvation and the power
and the kingdom of our God
and the authority of his Christ
have now come,
because the accuser of our brothers and sisters,
who accuses them

---

[9] Robert H. Mounce, *The Book of Revelation*, NICNT (Grand Rapids: Eerdmans, 1977), 239.

before our God day and night,
has been thrown down.
They conquered him
by the blood of the Lamb
and by the word of their testimony;
for they did not love their lives
to the point of death.
Therefore rejoice, you heavens,
and you who dwell in them!
Woe to the earth and the sea,
because the devil has come down to you
with great fury,
because he knows his time is short.

When the dragon saw that he had been thrown down to the earth, he persecuted the woman who had given birth to the male child. The woman was given two wings of a great eagle, so that she could fly from the serpent's presence to her place in the wilderness, where she was nourished for a time, times, and half a time. From his mouth the serpent spewed water like a river flowing after the woman, to sweep her away with a flood. But the earth helped the woman. The earth opened its mouth and swallowed up the river that the dragon had spewed from his mouth. So the dragon was furious with the woman and went off to wage war against the rest of her offspring [seed]—those who keep the commands of God and hold firmly to the testimony about Jesus. (Rev 12:7–17)

John describes a war in heaven between the archangel Michael and the serpentine dragon prince (see Dan 12:1; Jude 1:9). The serpent of Gen 3:15 has been conquered and crushed by the son of the woman. The "serpent spewed water like a river . . . to sweep her away with a flood" (Rev 12:15). He waged war against God's people—the faithful seed of the woman (Rev 12:17). This satanic war might include the devastation wrought against Israel by foreign enemies and the persecution of the church throughout history. John elsewhere reminds us that God honors and protects the martyrs who came out of the "great tribulation" (Rev 7:14; see also Rev 6:9–11; 7:9–17). No matter what trouble may come, the serpent's fate is sealed. "The Lord Jesus will destroy him with the breath of his mouth and will bring him to nothing at the appearance of his coming" (2 Thess 2:8).

As believers, we share in Christ's victory over Satan. Christ is the singular seed of the woman who crushes the serpent, but the people of God are the plural seed—the woman's seed described in Rev 12:17. We have "conquered him by the blood of the Lamb and by the word of [our] testimony" (Rev 12:11). As Paul promised believers in Roman house churches, the God of peace has crushed the serpent under our feet (Rom 16:20).

The devil may have come down to us (Rev 12:12). He may accuse us of evils God no longer holds against us (Rev 12:10). The ancient serpent may taunt us and persecute us through worldly powers and kingdoms that hate God and his people. But he knows full well that "his time is short" (Rev 12:12) and his final blow is looming.

The Virgin-Born King Has Conquered

Interpreters of Revelation often get lost in the insignificant details, feuding over the minor characters and subplots in the book. But this book has one primary purpose: to unveil the risen and exalted Lord Jesus Christ. The Gospels depict Jesus as the servant born to a virgin, laid in a manger, crucified, and raised on the third day. But Revelation paints a picture of Jesus with "eyes like a fiery flame" (Rev 1:14), "a sharp double-edged sword" coming from his mouth (Rev 1:16a), and a face "shining like the sun at full strength" (Rev 1:16b). Unlike the "Gentle Jesus, meek and mild" of the first advent, Revelation puts the blazing glory of the Son on display for all to see.

Only Matthew and Luke relay the historical event of Jesus's conception and birth, but we can only discover the full significance of this event by seeing it in the light of the whole biblical story. From Genesis to Revelation, we see that the birth of Jesus was not an arbitrary act of God—but an event that looked back to the garden of Eden and forward to the New Jerusalem.

— Part Two —

The Virgin-Born King in Christian Theology and Practice

19

The Church Fathers Who Saved Christmas

The Virgin-Born King in Early Christology

So then, brothers and sisters, stand firm and hold to the traditions you were taught, whether by what we said or what we wrote.

—2 THESSALONIANS 2:15

Many holiday movies and TV specials revolve around the same silly "saving Christmas" trope. In these stories, something like a blizzard or a global shortage of "Christmas spirit" (whatever that may be) is hindering Santa Claus from making his annual deliveries. The hero of the story, whether he be a certain red-nosed reindeer, an overgrown elf, or Ernest P. Worrell, must do something to help Santa accomplish his mission, otherwise Christmas is cancelled.

253

Church history tells an entirely different kind of story about the holiday that almost was not. The real heroes who "saved Christmas" (if one could do such a thing) were those early church theologians who defended the biblical doctrine of Christ from false teachers on the naughty list. Heresies that denied the true divinity of Jesus, the true humanity of Jesus, or both his deity and his humanity multiplied throughout the second, third, and fourth centuries. The NT teaching about the virgin birth was often at the center of these theological controversies. Many who denied the orthodox doctrine of Christ likewise denied or redefined the virgin birth.

The Rise of Orthodoxy: Second- and Third-Century Developments

Heretics wrote theology before the Christians who later came to be known as *orthodox* (from a Greek word meaning "right belief"). This historical observation has led some skeptical scholars to the conclusion that Christianity originally was more like a cafeteria of competing views about Jesus than a single "faith that was delivered to the saints once for all" (Jude 1:3). For skeptics who subscribe to this "cafeteria" theory of early Christianity, the doctrine of Christ that eventually came to be known as "orthodox" only became the predominant view after it gained political power and influence.[1] Critical historians have also indicated that the diversity of views about the virgin birth among heretical groups proves that it was not a widely established tradition.[2]

---

[1] This theory, widely known as the "Bauer thesis," was first developed by the German NT scholar Walter Bauer (1877–1960). Bart Ehrman has popularized this view in recent years in works like *Lost Christianities: The Battles for Scripture and the Faiths We Never Knew* (New York: Oxford University Press, 2005). For a critique of the Bauer thesis from an evangelical perspective, see Andreas J. Köstenberger and Michael J. Kruger, *The Heresy of Orthodoxy: How Contemporary Culture's Fascination with Diversity Has Reshaped Our Understanding of Early Christianity* (Wheaton, IL: Crossway, 2010).

[2] von Campenhausen, *The Virgin Birth in the Theology of the Ancient Church*, 22–23 (see chap. 17, n. 11).

But the church historian Harold O. J. Brown demonstrated how muddy this kind of thinking can be. If orthodox Christians were not already convinced that Jesus was truly God and truly man according to the Scriptures, then why were they so offended when false teachers blatantly rejected these ideas? "Heresy," Brown argued, "presupposes orthodoxy. . . . Orthodoxy was there from the beginning, and heresy reflected it."[3] In the same way that we cannot really appreciate how healthy we are until we have been sick, the early church needed the sickness of false teaching to help them express the healthiness of sound doctrine.

Much like today, the Christian theologians of the second and third centuries battled for the truthfulness of Christian doctrine against those who opposed it outside of the church or those who would seek to pervert it within the church. Heresies that denied or redefined Jesus's virgin birth forced theologians like Ignatius (d. 118), Irenaeus (c. 130–202), and Tertullian (c. 155–240) to articulate the importance of the nativity stories for Christian theology and practice.

Adoptionist Heresies: Jesus Was Born a Mere Mortal

One of the most prevalent theological errors in the early centuries of Christianity was *adoptionism*. Although adoptionism came in various flavors, all versions of this heresy rejected the eternal sonship of Jesus. Adoptionists of every stripe believed that Jesus was a saintly man whom God "adopted" as his Son, either at his birth, his baptism, or his resurrection.[4]

The Ebionites (from a Hebrew word meaning "poor ones") were a second-century Jewish sect who claimed that Jesus was a prophet like

---

[3] Harold O. J. Brown, *Heresies: Heresy and Orthodoxy in the History of the Church* (Peabody, MA: Hendrickson, 2003), 42.

[4] The best contemporary treatment of this doctrine can be found in Michael F. Bird, *Jesus the Eternal Son: Answering Adoptionist Christology* (Grand Rapids: Eerdmans, 2017).

Moses but denied that he was the eternal Son of God.[5] Some in this group
believed that Jesus was conceived naturally by Joseph and Mary; whereas,
others contended that Jesus was "possessed" by an angel during Mary's
virginal conception.[6] The Ebionites produced their own "gospel," a highly
redacted version of Matthew that altogether removed his nativity story.[7]

Some adoptionists, like the lay teacher Theodotus of Byzantium,
may have affirmed the virgin birth, but all adoptionists betrayed its biblical significance.[8] Jesus would be "called the Son of the Most High" (Luke
1:32), not because he was a mere man whom God adopted as a son. The
biblical nativity stories depict Jesus as "the dawn from on high" who came
to "visit us" in the incarnation (Luke 1:78). Christ did not become the
Son of God in time; he was the Son of God before time began.

As Irenaeus correctly observed, those who teach adoptionism have
ironically denied the gift of adoption God makes available to all of us
by the incarnation of his Son: "For it was for this end that the Word of
God was made man, and He who was the Son of God became the Son
of man, that man, having been taken into the Word, and receiving the
adoption, might become the son of God. For by no other means could
we have attained incorruptibility and immortality."[9] If Jesus were a mere
man who was adopted by God because he lived a sinless life, what hope

---

[5] See Epiphanius, *Panarion* 30.17. Some early accounts suggest that the
Ebionites sold all their earthly possessions and lived in voluntary poverty.

[6] Origen, *Against Celsus* 5.61; see also James Papandrea, *The Earliest
Christologies: Five Images of Christ in the Postapostolic Age* (Downers Grove: IVP
Academic, 2016), 23–32.

[7] Epiphanius, *Panarion* 30.13. Lest a critical scholar suggest the Ebionites
were merely following an earlier version of Matthew before the nativity story tradition was circulated, John is described as "the son of Zechariah and Elizabeth"
(Epiphanius, *Panarion* 30.13.6), names that depend on Luke's nativity tradition.

[8] Ancient sources disagree about Theodotus's view of the virgin birth.
Hippolytus claimed Theodotus affirmed some version of this teaching
(*Refutation of All Heresies* 7.23; 7.35.2; 10.19). Epiphanius claimed Theodotus
taught Jesus was a "mere man begotten of a man's seed" (*Panarion* 54.1.8).

[9] Irenaeus, *Against Heresies* 3.19.1.

would we who are sinners have? But if Christ was God the Son who became man to rescue us from our sin, then we too can become adopted sons and daughters of God.

Docetic Heresies: Jesus Was Not Born at All

Another early heresy made the opposite error: the Docetists denied the true humanity of Jesus. *Docetism* (from a Greek word meaning "to seem" or "to appear") taught that Jesus was a *spirit-being* or a *phantom* who only appeared to be human. Think Jesus "the friendly ghost." An early predecessor to this Docetic heresy prompted John to write letters to the churches of Asia Minor (1 John 4:1–6; 2 John 1:7). Later Docetists not only denied that Jesus was born of a virgin, but they also denied that he was born at all.[10] In response to this Docetic teaching, Ignatius taught believers at the beginning of the second century to confess that Jesus was "truly born of a virgin, was baptized by John . . . and was truly, under Pontius Pilate and Herod the tetrarch, nailed [to the cross] for us in His flesh."[11]

The second-century teacher Marcion of Sinope held a Docetic view of Christ (and even claimed that Jesus came from a different god than the "evil" God of Israel).[12] Marcion rejected the OT and only accepted some of Paul's letters as his "canon." Marcion produced his own version of Luke's Gospel that cut out any passages from Luke that contradicted his strange view of Christ—including the nativity story in Luke 1–2 and the genealogy of Jesus in Luke 3. Marcion's version of Luke opened like this: "In the fifteenth year of Tiberius Caesar [see Luke 3:1], *God descended into Capernaum*, a city of Galilee [see Luke 4:31]."[13]

---

[10] Irenaeus 3.22.1.

[11] Ignatius, *Epistle to the Smyrnaeans* 1; cf. Ignatius, *Epistle to the Trallians* 9.

[12] See Irenaeus, *Against Heresies* 4.33.2; Tertullian, *Against Marcion* 3.11; 4.7.

[13] See Ernest Evans, ed., *Tertullian Adversus Marcionem* (Oxford: Clarendon, 1972), 2:643 (emphasis mine).

In response to Marcion's claim that Jesus just dropped in without a real human body, Tertullian offered this savage burn: "You may, I assure you, more easily find a man born without a heart or without brains, like Marcion himself, than [a man] without a body, like Marcion's Christ."[14]

Gnosticism: Christ "Passed Through Mary"

To borrow a phrase from *This is Spinal Tap*, Gnosticism took all the bad ideas of Docetism and "turned them up to eleven." They too denied the true humanity of Christ, but also muddied the waters with other unbiblical ideas about the virgin birth, human sexuality, and salvation. The Gnostics, who got their name from a Greek word meaning "knowledge" (*gnosis*), taught that we are "saved" from this physical world by secret spiritual knowledge known only to an elite few.

Gnostics created their own "gospels" and scriptures that mixed elements from Greek philosophy, pagan mythology, and biblical stories. They recast the creator God of Genesis 1–2 as "the Craftsman," an incompetent junior deity in the pantheon of gods called "aeons." This Craftsman entrapped our souls in these physical bodies.[15] For some Gnostics, the serpent of Genesis 3 became the hero of the story because he offered "knowledge" (*gnosis*) for how we could escape these physical bodies.[16] For most Gnostics, Christ came from the supreme god to show us how to escape this physical world.

Because they were insistent that Christ could not be contained within a physical body like ours, Gnostic teachers offered several alternative explanations for what happened in the virgin birth. In the late first century, Cerinthus (c. 50–100) claimed the man Jesus and the spiritual being Christ were two distinct entities. Cerinthus denied the virgin

---

[14] Tertullian, *Against Marcion* 4.10.

[15] Ancient and scholarly literature usually refers to this Craftsman as "the Demiurge" (from the Greek word *dēmiurgós*).

[16] See *The Testimony of Truth* 46:15–49:10.

birth, insisting that Mary and Joseph conceived the man Jesus through sexual intercourse. However, the spirit-being called Christ came down from the supreme god in the form of a dove and possessed the man Jesus at his baptism.[17]

Other Gnostic teachers did not deny the virgin birth as much as they transformed it into a completely unrecognizable doctrine. Ascetic Gnostics discouraged sexual activity because of its close ties to the "prisons" of our physical bodies. These Gnostics used the virgin birth to rail against all forms of sexual pleasure.[18] They also insisted that Christ was not truly conceived in Mary: "John was begotten by means of a womb worn with age, but Christ *passed through a virgin's womb*."[19]

In the modern world where reproductive science has outpaced measured ethical reflection, a pregnant woman can now legitimately be asked, "Is the baby yours or someone else's?" The development of in vitro fertilization paved the way for gestational surrogacy, meaning that women can carry and deliver children with whom they share no genetic link.[20] In their rejection of Jesus's true humanity, gnostic teachers claimed Mary was merely a surrogate, that "Christ passed through Mary just as water flows through a tube."[21] These Gnostics taught that Jesus shared no genetic link with Mary.

Unlike their ascetic cousins, the libertine Gnostics practiced sexual debauchery because they believed the body was soon going away. *The Gospel of Philip*, a third-century libertine Gnostic "gospel," redefined

---

[17] Irenaeus, *Against Heresies* 1.26.

[18] *The Testimony of Truth* 39:25–40:5. Gnostics extolled Jesus's virginity as one of his chief virtues. See *The Second Apocalypse of James* 58:15–20. All quotations from Gnostic texts in this section come from James M. Robinson, ed., *The Nag Hammadi Library in English*, 3rd ed. (Leiden: Brill, 1988).

[19] *The Testimony of Truth* 45:15, (italics mine).

[20] For the record, I do not believe every instance of IVF is unethical but do worry about dangers it poses to human embryos considered by many to be dispensable genetic material. I am also grateful for women who have chosen to "adopt" IVF-created embryos who would otherwise be discarded.

[21] Irenaeus, *Against Heresies* 1.7; cf. 3.11.3.

the "virginal" conception by sexualizing it in a way more akin to pagan mythology than the Bible. This text asks how Mary could have conceived a child by the Holy Spirit when, its author claims, the Holy Spirit is a female spiritual force.[22] Instead, the author suggests that "the father of all" brought Jesus into being through a sexual union with Mary in the heavenly bridal chamber.[23] Irenaeus pointed out several fatal flaws in Gnostic approaches to the nativity.

First, Irenaeus questions the logic of the claim that "Christ passed through Mary just as water flows through a tube."[24] Irenaeus asks, "Why did he come down into her if he were to take nothing of her?" If Mary did not generate Christ's human nature in her womb, why feign the appearance of a human birth in the first place?[25]

Second, Irenaeus argued that only a true human nature from Mary can explain Jesus's appearance, his hunger, his thirst, his temptation, and his suffering.[26] If Christ only appeared to be a human and took nothing from Mary's humanity, then he was not made man and "he did no great thing in what he suffered and endured."[27] If Mary only bore a "heavenly flesh" created to resemble our fallen humanity, then the cross of Christ did nothing for us. A human nature generated by Mary ensured that we had genuine representation before God.

---

[22] *The Gospel of Philip* 55:24–25.

[23] *The Gospel of Philip* 71:10, 15. See also Hippolytus, *Refutation of All Heresies* 6.30.

[24] Irenaeus, *Against Heresies* 1.7; cf. 3.11.3.

[25] Irenaeus 3.22.2. A version of this heresy resurfaced after the Protestant Reformation when the Anabaptist theologian Melchior Hoffman (1495–1543) embraced what was called a "heavenly flesh" or "celestial flesh" Christology. Hoffmann, and later, the General Baptist Matthew Caffyn (1628–1714), taught that Christ escaped having a sin nature because he took no flesh from Mary. See also Calvin's response to Menno Simons in *Institutes*, 1:474–78 [2.13.1–2] (see chap. 8, n. 24).

[26] Irenaeus, *Against Heresies* 3.19.2–3.

[27] Irenaeus, *Against Heresies* 3.22.1.

Finally, if Jesus was not truly human, Irenaeus argued, we are still under the curse of sin and death. Christ took on true humanity through the virginal conception so that the human race could be "recapitulated," or, to use a more contemporary expression, "rebooted." The immortal and incorruptible Word took on human mortality and corruptibility so that he might defeat them once and for all on our behalf.

The Virgin Birth in the First Creedal Formulations

The theologians of the second and third centuries insisted that the Bible should be read with a set of theological guidelines they called the "rule of faith." Think of this like a mental canon of Christian doctrines. If you were discipled in the early church, you received the same "faith that was delivered to the saints once for all" (Jude 1:3). This "rule" summarizes what the apostles taught in the NT. With the "rule of faith," the early church preached the gospel, instructed converts, refuted heretics, interpreted Scripture, and set boundaries for essential Christian belief.[28] As Irenaeus summarizes what Christians teach in the rule, we believe

> in one God, the Father Almighty, Maker of heaven, and earth . . . and in one Christ Jesus, the Son of God, who became incarnate for our salvation; and in the Holy Spirit, who proclaimed through the prophets the dispensations of God, and the advents, and the birth from a virgin, and the passion, and the resurrection from the dead, and the ascension into heaven in the flesh of the beloved Christ Jesus, our Lord, and His [future] manifestation from heaven in the glory of the Father "to gather all things in one" (Eph 1:10). . . .[29]

---

[28] See Everett Ferguson, *The Rule of Faith: A Guide* (Eugene, OR: Cascade, 2015), 67–81.

[29] Irenaeus, *Against Heresies* 1.10.1.

For Irenaeus, denial of any of these tenets was a denial of the faith given to us by the apostles. Justin Martyr likewise professed that Jesus was "was born of a virgin as a man, and was named Jesus, and was crucified, and died, and rose again, and ascended into heaven."[30]

Although elements of the rule of faith are contained in the writings of theologians like Ignatius, Irenaeus, and Tertullian, the church recognized the need for a way to express what they believed in a concise, portable manner. They needed an "elevator pitch" for the whole biblical story and Christian doctrine. So, they began creating *creeds* or confessional statements of belief (from the Latin word *credo*, meaning "I believe"). The NT contains several creedal formulations that were likely used in the worship of the early church.[31]

These shorthand expressions of faith proved incredibly useful in worship, evangelism, and discipleship. Churches used these creeds as a corporate confession of shared belief. Disciples learned and affirmed these creeds before taking their faith public in baptism.[32] Creeds also provided a way for believers to share their faith with non-Christians in succinct ways. One such creed was the Roman Symbol (c. AD 200), the basis for the later Apostles' Creed. This early creed wrapped up the basic plot of Scripture with an overtly trinitarian shape.

> I believe in God the Father Almighty;
> and in Christ Jesus His only Son, our Lord,
> Who was born of the Holy Spirit and the Virgin Mary,

---

[30] Justin Martyr, *First Apology* 46; cf. J. N. D. Kelly, *Early Christian Creeds* (London: Longman, 1960), 70–76.

[31] James D. G. Dunn and Anthony Thiselton identify several example of creedal formulas used in the writings of Paul: Rom 1:3–4; 3:25; 4:24–25; 5:6, 8; 7:4; 8:11, 32; 10:9; 1 Cor 6:14; 8:6, 11; 11:23; 12:3; 15:3–7; 2 Cor 4:14; 5:14–15; Gal 1:1; 4:5; Eph 4:5; Phil 2:5–11; Col 2:6; 1 Thess 1:10; 4:14; 5:10; 1 Tim 1:15; 2:6; 4:8–9; 2 Tim 2:11; Titus 3:5–8. See James D. G. Dunn, *The Theology of Paul the Apostle* (Grand Rapids: Eerdmans, 1998), 174–77; Anthony C. Thiselton, *The Hermeneutics of Doctrine* (Grand Rapids: Eerdmans, 2007), 13–14.

[32] Hippolytus, *Apostolic Tradition* 21.

Who under Pontius Pilate was crucified and buried,
   on the third day rose again from the dead,
   ascended to heaven,
   sits at the right hand of the Father,
   whence He will come to judge the living and the dead;
and in the Holy Spirit,
the holy Church,
the remission of sins,
the resurrection of the flesh
(the life everlasting).

Orthodoxy Defined: Fourth-Century Developments

By the end of the third century, the influence of heresies like adoptionism and Gnosticism began to wane. Those who professed Christ agreed, at least in principle, that Jesus was, in some sense, divine, and in some sense human. But leaders in the church struggled to define the meaning of Jesus's divinity and humanity. In the fourth century, new heresies like Arianism, semi-Arianism, and Apollinarianism forced the church to give clear definitions to these concepts.

To answer these abuses of biblical truth, theologians were forced to develop new theological terms that faithfully expressed the judgments of Scripture, even if they did not use the exact language of Scripture.[33] They invented new terms like "Trinity," "consubstantial," and "hypostatic union" to express what the Bible teaches about the nature of God and the nature of Christ. As the historian Richard Hanson observed, the "theologians of the Christian Church were slowly driven to a realization that

---

[33] On these "judgments," see David S. Yeago, "The New Testament and Nicene Dogma: A Contribution to the Recovery of Theological Exegesis," in *Theological Interpretation of Scripture: Classic and Contemporary Readings*, ed. Stephen E. Fowl (Cambridge, MA: Blackwell, 1997), 87–100.

the deepest questions that face Christianity cannot be answered in purely biblical language, because *the questions are about the meaning of biblical language itself.*[34]

Arianism: Christ Was a Created God

A few decades into the fourth century, an Alexandrian pastor named Arius gained a substantial following when he began preaching that Jesus was created by God and subordinate to him. Controversy ensued when Arius was defrocked and excommunicated for heresy. The conflict eventually reached the ears of Constantine, the emperor of Rome who had only recently made Christianity legal in the Roman Empire. In AD 325, Constantine, desiring to keep his new religion intact, convened an empire-wide council of bishops to discuss the Arian controversy.

Arius and his supporters could not understand what all the fuss was about. They were not like the Gnostic and adoptionist teachers who added to or took away from the Scriptures. Arius believed Jesus was "divine" in the sense that he was like God. Arius did not believe Jesus was "adopted" in his earthly ministry. He may have believed that God used Jesus to create the universe, but for Arius, Jesus was a created demigod, not the eternal Son of God.[35]

But the bishops at Nicaea insisted that Jesus was not just like God; he was the same as God. The key term from Nicaea was *homoousion*, meaning "same substance." The pro-Arian party preferred the term *homoiousion*, which meant "similar substance." The Nicene Fathers used *homoousion* to proclaim Jesus was the same as God, not a demigod. At the end of their deliberations, they affirmed Arius's excommunication and

---

[34] R. P. C. Hanson, *The Search for the Christian Doctrine of God: The Arian Controversy, 318–381* (New York: T&T Clark, 1988), xxi.

[35] See Rhyne R. Putman, "Before and After Nicaea: Arianism as a Test Case for the Ongoing Development of Heresy," *Criswell Theological Review* 18, no. 1 (2020): 3–22.

formulated what we might call the "first draft" of the Nicene Creed. This simple (and still incomplete) statement of faith articulated what orthodox Christians in the early fourth century believed about the Trinity and the divinity of Christ.

This first pass at the creed said nothing about the virgin birth, likely because no one in the controversy denied it. This draft also said painfully little about the person of the Holy Spirit, which forced fourth-century theologians like Basil of Caesarea (AD 330–79) to develop this doctrine further when the Spirit's deity and personhood were questioned. But in the decades that followed Nicaea, even the defenders of this creed were susceptible to theological errors that denied the true humanity of Christ.

The Apollinarian Error: Jesus's Body Was Only an Avatar

A Laodicean bishop named Apollinaris (c. 315–92) who affirmed the first version of the Nicene Creed taught that Christ never assumed a complete human nature.[36] Christ is, according to Apollinaris, "neither whole human being nor God but a mixture of God and human being."[37] Concerned about the possibility of Christ having two personalities, Apollinaris claimed that the Word took on a human body ("flesh") without taking on a true human mind. For Apollinaris, Christ was not God made man but a "flesh-bearing God."[38]

What does this mean for Apollinaris's understanding of the virgin birth? The Spirit may have caused Mary to conceive the "flesh" that the Son bore, but the Son never became truly human. Without a true human

---

[36] Gregory of Nazianzus, *First Letter to Cledonius* 14. Apollinaris affirmed some notion of the Trinity, but Gregory of Nazianzus suspects a streak of functional subordinationism in Apollinarian teaching.

[37] Apollinaris, *Fragments of Other Writings* 113. These translations of Apollinaris's writings appear in Mark DelCogliano, ed., *The Cambridge Edition of Early Christian Writings*, vol. 3, *Christ: Through the Nestorian Controversy* (New York: Cambridge University Press, 2022), 301–38.

[38] Apollinaris, *Fragments of Other Writings* 109.

mind that "increased in wisdom" (Luke 2:52), the man Jesus was like an avatar Christ controlled from heaven. The "human being was formed and then God put him on to wear."[39] Mary was once more reduced to a surrogate mother. In Apollinaris's own words, "For anyone who calls the one who came from Mary a human being, and the one who was crucified a human being, changes him from God into a human being instead."[40] Those who claim that the Word became man are "man-worshippers."[41]

Gregory of Nazianzus did not mince words in his response to this Apollinarian teaching: "Whoever says that he was channeled, as it were, through the Virgin but not formed within her divinely and humanly . . . is . . . godless." If the virgin only bore the fleshly vessel of the Word and not a true man, "this is not God's birth but the avoidance of birth." Much like Irenaeus's response to the Gnostics, Gregory rejected the notion of Mary as a mere flesh surrogate: "Whoever says that his flesh descended from heaven, but had no source here amongst us, is to be anathema."[42]

The Apollinarian might object that God the Son could not assume a human mind because the human mind is under condemnation. But Gregory insists that the fallenness of the human mind is even more reason for the Word to take on a true human mind. From the human mind we choose to obey God's commandments or disobey them. Adam made the choice to sin with his mind and brought all other human minds under his condemnation. So, Gregory argued, "The very thing that transgressed stood in special need of salvation." The Word assumed a true human mind so he could save our minds.[43] For Christ could not heal those

---

[39] Gregory of Nazianzus, *First Letter to Cledonius* 5, in *On God and Christ: The Five Theological Orations and Two Letters to Cledonius*, trans. Frederick Williams and Lionel Wickham (Yonkers, NY: St. Vladimir's Seminary Press, 2002).

[40] Apollinaris, *On the Faith of the Incarnation* 9.

[41] Gregory of Nazianzus, *First Letter to Cledonius* 8.

[42] Gregory of Nazianzus 5.

[43] Gregory of Nazianzus 9.

aspects of humanity that he did not assume, "but what is united with God is also being saved."[44]

The Council of Constantinople condemned the Apollinarian heresy in 381.[45] The council also revised the Nicene Creed, addressing many of the heresies that surfaced in the intervening decades between these councils. But this updated version of the creed added a new phrase that ensured that Mary was truly identified as the mother of God incarnate and not simply his surrogate: the "Lord Jesus Christ . . . who for us men, and for our salvation, came down from heaven, and became incarnate by the Holy Spirit of the virgin Mary, and was made human."

Celebrating the Virgin-Born King in the Creeds

Some in my free church tradition are reluctant to embrace the creeds of the early church, asserting (rather ironically) that "we have no creed but the Bible."[46] Along these lines, one might ask, why were creeds needed if biblical truth was a sufficient source of Christian revelation?

Although Scripture is a wholly sufficient source of the knowledge of God and the only standard for theological truth we have, Scripture must still be interpreted (see Neh 8:1–8; Ezra 7:10; Acts 8:30–31). The fifth-century Gallic theologian Vincent of Lérins believed Scripture to be "sufficient for every purpose" but also recognized the many different ways it can be interpreted: "By its very depth the Holy Scripture is not received by all in one and the same sense, but its declarations are subject

---

[44] Gregory of Nazianzus 5.

[45] The Council of Constantinople, Canon 1.

[46] See Albert Mohler, Jr., *The Apostles' Creed: Discovering Authentic Christianity in an Age of Counterfeits* (Nashville: Nelson, 2019), 42. Dr. Mohler, president of The Southern Baptist Theological Seminary in Louisville, Kentucky, recalled a moment in our denomination's history when a "no creed but the Bible" Baptist said that a theology professor "who might also be led by the Scripture not to believe in the virgin birth should not be fired." He went on to ask how one could reasonably come to such a conclusion when Scripture gives a clear witness to the virgin birth.

to interpretation, now in one way, now in another, so that, it would appear, we can find almost as many interpretations as there are men."[47] We cannot simply quote Scripture back to false teachers who "twist them to their own destruction" (2 Pet 3:16).

To help people avoid heretical misunderstandings of Scripture in the church, we disciple them in sound doctrine. We "proclaim things consistent with sound teaching" (Titus 2:1). One way we can do this well is to teach people in our churches the creeds of the whole church—what we call *ecumenical creeds*—and the confessions of our particular faith traditions (like *The Westminster Confession* or *The Baptist Faith and Message*). These are not substitutes for Scripture but helpful guides in understanding what Scripture teaches. When it comes to creeds in the life of the church, Christians can make several theological mistakes.

First, they can ignore the creeds completely, writing them off as unnecessary. But many Christians could avoid heresies that deny Jesus's true humanity or divinity or that confuse the persons of the Trinity if they were discipled and instructed in these creeds. I use creeds like the Apostles Creed to introduce Christian beliefs to new believers or students who are unfamiliar with the faith.

Second, some professing Christians may give lip service to the creeds in their respective traditions without believing what they profess. Liberal theologians who deny the virgin birth or the deity of Jesus will often profess these creeds in ecclesial settings. They treat these words as empty symbols, like a fight song at a college football game. They certainly do not think of these creeds as the boundaries of orthodoxy that distinguish between those who are in the faith and those who are outside it.

Finally, some Christians mistakenly presume that the creeds provide everything we need to know about the Christian faith. We should avoid a theological minimalism that suggests that any doctrines not discussed or outlined in the creeds are unimportant or irrelevant to the Christian life. The fact that ancient creeds do not have explicit statements about

---

[47] Vincent of Lérins, *The Commonitory* §2.2.

doctrines like the inerrancy of Scripture or the substitutionary atonement of Christ does not mean these doctrines are inconsequential to the Christian faith.

Since the second century, Christians have professed the virgin birth in their creedal formulations. We would do well not to ignore what they so boldly professed. Karl Barth made this case:

> The Church knew well what it was doing when it posted this doctrine on guard, as it were, at the door of the mystery of Christmas. It can never be in favour of anyone thinking he can hurry past this guard. It will remind him that he is walking along a private road at his own cost and risk. It will warn him against doing so. It will proclaim as a church ordinance that to affirm the doctrine of the Virgin birth is a part of real Christian faith.[48]

---

[48] Barth, *CD* I.2, study edition, 190 [181] (see chap. 16, n. 4).

20

One and the Same Son

The Unity of the Virgin-Born King

How could this happen to me, that the mother
of my Lord should come to me?

–Luke 1:43

With the issues of Jesus's true divinity and humanity virtually settled at the councils of Nicaea in AD 325 and Constantinople in AD 381, the church could turn its attention to another important question: How do the human and divine natures of Jesus relate to one another?

Does Jesus wear his divinity and humanity like summer and winter clothes, changing in and out of these natures whenever the situation calls for it? Did the Word of God control Jesus's body from heaven like an avatar? Did God put Jesus's humanity and divinity in a blender and create a new mixed nature—a third kind of thing? Did Jesus simply give up being God when he took on human nature? (Spoiler alert: All those options are problematic.)

Theologians who affirmed both the divinity and humanity of Jesus had significant disagreements about how to understand the relationship between these natures. The doctrine of the virgin birth took center stage in one such fifth-century debate. Both parties involved in the controversy affirmed the virgin birth, but they wrestled over its implications for the person of Christ. The controversy forced these Christian theologians to develop a clear and well-defined statement about the relationship between these two natures. The present chapter explores what they said about the virgin-born king and how they arrived at their conclusions.

Is Mary "the Mother of God"?

By the mid-fourth century, Christians throughout the world had come to know Mary as the *Theotokos*—the "God-bearer" or the "mother of God."[1] For many, this title was a no-brainer, the logical corollary of what Christians already believed about Christ's true identity. In the virginal conception of Jesus, Mary literally gave birth to God the eternal Son.

In AD 428, Nestorius (c. 386–451), the newly appointed archbishop of Constantinople, turned the theological world upside down when he declared that Mary should not be called *Theotokos*. He offered the names "Christ-bearer" and "Man-bearer" as potential alternatives for Mary's title. Nestorius had no problem acknowledging Mary as the mother of Christ's human nature but found the title "mother of God" to be disconcerting and potentially blasphemous. Nestorius also questioned the propriety of saying "God suffered on the cross," insisting that only the human nature of Christ suffered this way.[2]

---

[1] See Alexander's AD 320 anti-Arian address in Theodotus, *Church History* 1.4; Athanasius, *Four Discourses Against the Arians* 3.29. Socrates Scholasticus claimed Origen used this term in the third century (*Ecclesiastical History* 7.32), cited in Perry, *Mary for Evangelicals*, 142–43 (see chap. 17, n. 2).

[2] See Nestorius, "First Sermon Against the *Theotokos*." Before Nestorius, Theodore of Mopsuestia (c. 350–428) raised a similar objection: "It is madness

For his rejection of Mary's title as God-bearer, opponents of Nestorius quickly accused him of serious heresy. To be clear, the Nestorian heresy was not really about Mary at all. Rather, by suggesting that Mary was only the mother of Jesus's human nature, Nestorius was accused of making too sharp of a distinction between the divine and human natures of Jesus. This led to the rumor that Nestorius taught that Christ is two distinct persons: a divine person and a human person.

Nestorius may have wholeheartedly affirmed the deity and humanity of Jesus, but his careless and imprecise use of language put him in hot water with other bishops across the Roman Empire. Some of the things Nestorius said were interpreted to mean that Christ was two persons, though it is debatable whether he actually believed this. At one point, Nestorius claimed that two *prosōpa* are united in Jesus. The problem is that the word *prosōpon* can mean "person" or "outward appearance" (i.e., more literally, a "face").[3]

Did Nestorius mean to say Jesus was two persons or that he merely had two outward appearances? We may never know the answer to this question on this side of eternity. But what we do know is that the heresy of calling Christ two separate persons came to be known as Nestorianism. Whether or not Nestorius embraced the heresy associated with his name, this teaching endured for centuries to come.[4]

Church politics loomed large over the charges leveled against Nestorius. At the Council of Ephesus in AD 431, Cyril of Alexandria, Nestorius's chief accuser, presided over what could be interpreted as a kangaroo court of underhanded politics. Nestorius's allies were prevented

---

to say that God is born of the Virgin. . . . Not God, but the temple in which God dwelt, is born of Mary" (cited in *NPNF*[2] 14:208).

[3] The uncharitable reading of Nestorius's critics led them to believe he was claiming the former.

[4] The first churches planted in China held to a Nestorian doctrine of Christ. Historians date these churches between the seventh and tenth centuries. The oldest physical evidence for these churches is the Xi'an Stele (or Nestorian Stele) that was erected in AD 781.

from getting to the meeting on time because of flooded roadways, and Cyril never gave his fellow bishop a chance to answer for himself. We can question Cyril's motives and pass judgment on how poorly he conducted the Council of Ephesus, but we must also ask whether he made the right judgment condemning Nestorius's ideas.

Was Nestorius dangerously close to denying the union between God the Son and the man Christ Jesus? Over the last century of theological scholarship, Nestorius has gained a more favorable hearing that has suggested that he did not subscribe to the heresy associated with his name. But even a fair reassessment of Nestorius's work reminds us that sloppy theological language can often create more problems than it solves.

Why the Term Theotokos Confounds Us

Nestorius rejected the term *Theotokos* in large part because he did not understand its original intention. The growing devotion to Mary in medieval theology further complicated this confusion. Devotees of Mary came to view her as the "Queen of Heaven" who protects the church and who intercedes on their behalf as a "co-redemptrix."[5] These churches even sang and prayed to her. No wonder the founder of Islam seemed to think that Christians worshipped Mary as the third person of the Trinity.[6]

One could easily see where the confusion over the term "mother of God" takes place. When we call Jesus the "Son of God," we mean that he is the Second Person of the Trinity—the eternally begotten Son of God. The grammatically similar phrase "mother of God" might suggest

---

[5] For an overview of these teachings from a Roman Catholic perspective, see Scott Hahn, *Hail, Holy Queen: The Mother of God in the Word of God* (New York: Doubleday, 2001).

[6] In Qur'an 5:116, Isa (Jesus) objects to those who worship him and Mary as divine: "And imagine when thereafter Allah will say: 'Jesus, son of Mary, did you say to people: "Take me and my mother for gods beside Allah"? and he will answer: "Glory to You! It was not for me to say what I had no right to. Had I said so, You would surely have known it."

that Mary is equal to the Father, Son, and Holy Spirit the way the "Son of God" is equal to the Father and the Spirit. Worse, the title "mother of God" might lead some to believe that Mary is somehow above God in authority. Nestorius seemed especially concerned to address this potential misunderstanding about Mary:

> Does God have a mother? A Greek without reproach introducing mothers for the gods! Is Paul then a liar when he says of the deity of Christ, "without father, without mother, without genealogy" [Heb 7:3]? Mary, my friend, did not give birth to the Godhead (for "what is born of flesh is flesh" [John 3:6]). A creature did not produce him who is uncreatable. . . . A creature did not produce the Creator, rather she gave birth to the human being, the instrument of the Godhead. The Holy Spirit did not create God the Logos [God the Word]. . . . Rather, he formed out of the Virgin a temple for God the Logos, a temple in which he dwelt.[7]

Nestorius may have had the noble motive of protecting us from Mary worship, but his language was dangerously imprecise. He wanted to preserve the distinctions between Jesus's human and divine natures and to avoid an unhelpful and equally dangerous notion related to Mary.

Some Protestant and evangelical theologians have voiced similar concerns about calling Mary the mother of God. In a late twentieth-century book defending the virgin birth, one evangelical theologian wrote about the *Theotokos* controversy in such a way that it sounded as if he were channeling Nestorius:

> To be the mother of God, one must of necessity exist before God. This, of course, is impossible. God is eternal; He had no beginning. It is true that Jesus Christ was both God and man, but He

---

[7] Nestorius, "First Sermon Against the *Theotokos*," quoted in *The Christological Controversy*, trans. and ed. Richard A. Norris, Jr. (Philadelphia: Fortress, 1980), 124–25.

was God long before Mary's conception. Mary rightfully mothered the humanity of Jesus, but not His deity. It is true that God was within her womb, but she did not cause that to happen.[8]

From a certain point of view, this concern makes sense. Mothers normally precede their sons chronologically and in authority. But the term *Theotokos* says nothing about Mary chronologically preceeding God the Son or being eternal with God. On the contrary, *Theotokos* means that Mary bore the eternal Word of God in her body from the moment he was joined to a human nature at his conception. As Cyril explained, "The idea is not that he found the beginning of his existence inside the holy Virgin."[9]

Why the Term Theotokos is Fitting

The title *Theotokos* later came to be associated with an improper and unbiblical devotion to Mary as another redeemer and intercessor. But for its earliest adopters, the title "mother of God" was not a statement about Mary as much as it was a statement about the person of Christ. *Theotokos* was simply a way of affirming the unity of Christ's person. In Cyril's words, "The one Lord Jesus Christ must not be divided into two Sons." Mary was called *Theotokos* because the Word of God was "born of a woman as a human being."[10]

This term also had a biblical basis. When Mary visited her in Luke 1:39–45, Elizabeth called Mary "the mother of my Lord" (1:43). Note, Elizabeth did not call Mary the "mother of the human person who is joined to my Lord." She had no difficulty stating that Mary was carrying God in her womb.

---

[8] Gromacki, *The Virgin Birth*, 104 (see chap. 8, n. 11).

[9] Cyril of Alexandria, "Second Letter to Nestorius," quoted in *The Christological Controversy*, 133.

[10] Cyril, 134.

Defenders of the *Theotokos* insisted that whatever we say about Jesus's human nature can also be attributed to God the Son. The logic of calling Mary the God-bearer works like this:

1. Jesus Christ is truly God.
2. The virgin Mary bore Jesus Christ in her body and gave birth to him.
3. Therefore, the virgin Mary bore God in her body and gave birth to him.

Mary bore God the Son in her body. Although the title God-bearer does rightly apply to Mary, we could also apply the title "God-killer" to Pilate with the same kind of logic:

1. Jesus Christ is truly God.
2. Jesus Christ suffered death under Pontius Pilate.
3. God suffered death under Pontius Pilate.

Here someone might object, God is eternal. Death is the cessation of biological life. God, who is Spirit, cannot die the way human beings die. We must also avoid the *modalistic heresy* of the "Father sufferers" who insisted that God the Father died on the cross. We also deny that the Holy Spirit suffered this way. But God the Son did experience human death at the hands of Pontius Pilate.

Scripture presents us with several other quandaries like this. The devil tempted Jesus in the wilderness for forty days after his baptism (Matt 4:1–11; Mark 1:12–13; Luke 4). The author of Hebrews adds that Jesus was "tempted in every way as we are, yet without sin" (Heb 4:15). But James explicitly states, "God is not tempted by evil" (Jas 1:13). So, if Jesus is truly God, and God cannot be tempted by evil, in what sense can we say that Christ was tempted? Some might throw their hands up and cry, "Mystery!" Others may shake their fists and chant, "Contradiction!" This sort of impasse might cause some to reject the divinity of Jesus, the authority of Scripture, or both.

Two Important Concepts

Two concepts embraced by the early church help us navigate these difficulties. First, Cyril and the Council of Ephesus (AD 431) used the term *hypostatic union* to describe the way the divine and human natures came together in the same person (or *hypóstasis*) of Jesus Christ. Christ was not a human person who took on a divine nature (the adoptionist view), nor was he a divine person who took on another whole human person (the Nestorian view). Had Christ been joined to an already formed human person created by Mary and Joseph through human sexual reproduction, he would be an alien entity that "possessed" the son of Mary and Joseph (a Gnostic view). Instead, Christ was the divine Person who took on a true human nature.

According to the doctrine of the hypostatic union, the divine Person was acting in and through the true human nature to which he had been united. Because Christ was born of a virgin, his humanity has never existed independently of his divinity. Whenever Jesus of Nazareth acted, God the Son acted, because they were the same person. In Christ, God the Son personalized a true human nature.[11]

The second important concept to grasp is the *communication of attributes* in Christ. The communication of attributes means that the qualities we ascribe to Jesus's divine nature and the qualities we ascribe to his human nature describe the same Person.[12] Whether we speak of some-

---

[11] Christian theologians use two other terms to express these ideas: *anhypostasis* and *enhypostasis*. *Anhypostasis* (meaning "no person") is simply a way of saying that Jesus was not united with an already existing human person (which would lead to the error of teaching there were two persons in Christ). Since the Second Council of Constantinople (AD 553), Christian theologians have employed the term *enhypostasis* (meaning "in-personal") to describe the way the person of Christ subsists as man in a real human nature. For a fuller discussion of the differences between these terms, see Stephen J. Wellum, *God the Son Incarnate: The Doctrine of Christ* (Wheaton, IL: Crossway, 2016), 316–24.

[12] This term is well known by the Latin phrase *communicatio idiomatum*. For explorations of this doctrine's implications for biblical interpretation, see Jamieson and Wittman, *Biblical Reasoning*, 126–52 (see chap. 15, n. 9).

thing Jesus does in his divine nature or his human nature, we are still speaking about the same Person.

The communication of attributes helps us understand how Christ can be said to be both all-knowing (in his divine nature) and increasing in wisdom (in his human nature). Christ is both God who cannot be tempted and human who was tempted in every way that we are! In his divine nature, God the Son is immutable and unchanging—the "same yesterday, today, and forever" (Heb 13:8). There was never a time when God the Son did not exist. But the human nature of Jesus was conceived and born in time, and Mary bore that person in her body.

If Mary did not bear God the Son in her body, Elizabeth was wrong when she called Mary the mother of her Lord (Luke 1:43). If Mary did not bear God in her body, Gabriel wrongly told Joseph that her son would save his people from sin. If Mary did not give birth to God the Son, then the shepherds and the wise men worshipped the Bethlehem baby in error.

The definition formulated by the Council of Chalcedon (AD 451) provides a concise summary of the relationship between these two natures in one Person.

> We, then, following the holy Fathers, all with one consent, teach men to confess one and the same Son, our Lord Jesus Christ, the same perfect in his divine nature and also perfect in his human nature.

The fathers at Chalcedon recognized that whenever we are talking about God the Son, we are talking about one "subject"—the divine Person with two distinct natures. Against the heresy associated with Nestorius, the Council at Chalcedon insisted that Jesus is "one and the same Son." In other words, Jesus is one Person, not two. Against the error of Eutyches (c. 380–456) who said that Jesus possessed a single, new hybrid nature, the Council of Chalcedon said that Jesus has two distinct natures. They declared that Jesus is truly God and truly human in every sense of those words. He shares the same essence with the Father and the same essence with humanity. He is like us in every way except for the fact that he is without sin.

> [He was] begotten before all ages of the Father according to the divine nature. And in these latter days, for us and for our salvation, [he was] born of the virgin Mary, the mother of God [*Theotokos*], according to the human nature.

In our theological grammar, all these descriptions of Jesus are different verbs but describe the same subject. In his divine nature, the Son is "begotten before all ages" of the Father. In his human nature, the Son was born of the virgin Mary, the mother of God.

> [He is] one and the same Christ, Son, Lord, Only-begotten, to be acknowledged in two natures, without confusion, without change, without division or separation. The distinction of [his] natures being by no means taken away by the union. . . . The property of each nature [is] being preserved, and concurring in one Person and one Subsistence, not parted or divided into two persons, but one and the same Son, only begotten: God the Word, the Lord Jesus Christ.

In the incarnation and virginal conception of Jesus, God the Son was permanently united to a human nature. We can speak about God the Son as subject with different verbs, according to whatever nature we are describing. These natures are distinct, but they cannot be separated or divided into two subjects or persons. The divine nature did not grow, change, or die, but God the Son experienced growth, change, and death in his true human nature.[13]

---

[13] The doctrine described here is called the *extra Calvinisticum*, and it directly contradicts Luther's idea that the human nature of Jesus is present everywhere. Luther had a muddled understanding of the "communication of attributes" (*communicatio idiomatum*). In Luther's understanding, every description we give to the human nature of Jesus can also be applied to the divine nature. See Luther, "On the Councils and the Church," trans. Charles M. Jacobs

The Two Births of the Same Son

Toward the end of the fourth century, Augustine, the bishop of Hippo, preached a powerful Christmas Day sermon about the "two births of Christ." Though it predated the Nestorian controversy by several decades, Augustine beautifully explained the wonder of the one Son who experienced two "births" in his divine and human natures.

> Born of his mother, he commended this day to the ages, while born of his Father he created all ages. That birth could have no mother, while this one required no man as father. To sum up, Christ was born both of a Father and of a mother; both without a father and without a mother; of a Father as God, of a mother as man; without a mother as God, without a father as man. . . .
>
> The one who holds the world in being was lying in a manger; he was simultaneously [a] speechless infant and [the] Word. The heavens cannot contain him, a woman carried him in her bosom. She was ruling our ruler, carrying the one in whom we are, suckling our bread. O manifest infirmity and wondrous humility in which was thus concealed total divinity! Omnipotence was ruling the mother on whom infancy was depending; was nourishing on truth the mother whose breasts it was sucking. May he bring his gifts to perfection in us, since he did not shrink from making his own our tiny beginnings; and may he make us into children of God, since for our sake he was willing to be made a child of man.[14]

---

and Eric W. Gritsch, in *Luther's Works*, vol. 41, ed. Jaroslav Pelikan (Philadelphia: Fortress, 1966), 100–101.

[14] Augustine, "Sermon 184," in *Sermons*, trans. Edmund Hill, ed. John E. Rotelle, ser. 3, vol. 6, *The Works of St. Augustine: A Translation for the 21st Century* (New Rochelle, NY: New City Press, 1993), 18–19.

21

The Fittingness of the Virgin Birth

The Virgin-Born King as the Revealer of God

> The Virgin birth denotes particularly the mystery of
> revelation. It denotes the fact that God stands at the
> start where real revelation takes place—God and not the
> arbitrary cleverness, capability, or piety of man.
>
> —KARL BARTH[1]

The nativity stories of the Gospels depict Jesus as Immanuel, the rightful heir to David's throne, and the one who saves us from our sins. But was it really necessary for Jesus to be born of a virgin? How we answer that question all depends on what we mean by "necessary."

---

[1] Barth, *CD* I.2, study edition, 192 [182] (see chap. 16, n. 4).

The word "necessary" yields a wide range of meanings. For example, certain laws of nature are described as *physically necessary*. If I were to jump out of a plane, I would plummet to the earth below because I am necessarily bound to the laws of gravity. What goes up must come down. Laws of nature like gravity, Newton's three laws of motion, and many others are said to be physically necessary because they occur regularly in nature.

Obviously, no law of nature says that virgins must have babies, so the unique event that is the virgin birth of Jesus would not fit the description of something that is physically necessary. In fact, the virgin birth was only possible because God interrupted the regular way tiny humans are made in nature.

If something is *legally necessary*, then it is compulsory activity mandated by the government. If I want to drive legally in the state of Arkansas, then it is legally necessary for me to get a driver's license from the Department of Motor Vehicles in this state or another. The DMV may say it is legally necessary for me to provide proof of citizenship, residence, and insurance to acquire a driver's license. But neither the DMV nor the state of Arkansas can force me to get a driver's license if I do not plan to operate a motor vehicle. The virgin birth certainly does not fit this definition of legal necessity.

Some truths are *logically necessary*. Triangles necessarily have three sides. Take away a side and your *tri*-angle just becomes an angle. The statement "2+2=4" is true by logical necessity. I can easily imagine an improbable universe where pigs fly and I look just like Channing Tatum, but I cannot possibly conceive of a world with four-sided triangles or a world where 2+2=5. Why? Because some truths are logically necessary in every possible world. If we could possibly imagine a world in which God did not send his Son through a virgin, the virgin birth is not logically necessary.

A *necessary being* is a being who must exist in every conceivable universe. We can all admit that mosquitoes and snakes are unnecessary creatures by this definition! But truth be told, human beings are not necessary either. We can imagine worlds God could have created that would keep on ticking fine without us. The same is true for every other creature in the universe. Only one being is necessary: the ground and source of everything else that exists. God must exist because nothing else can exist without him. But was the virgin birth necessary for God?

In some sense, all talk about what God must do is nonsensical. God is sovereign, meaning he answers to no one else.[2] He is omnipotent, meaning all power is at his disposal. Though he cannot and will not do anything contrary to his holy character, he is free to do whatever he pleases (Ps 115:3). For example, nothing in God's nature required him to create the world in which we presently live. God could have created a world with an entirely different set of physical laws, a world in which we were silicon-based life-forms instead of carbon-based life-forms. In fact, God did not have to create a world at all.[3]

As sinful people, we may have desperately needed salvation, but God was under no compulsion to save us from our sins. God would have been completely within his rights to end the human experiment after Adam and Eve rebelled in the garden of Eden. Thankfully, out of the great love he has for his creatures, God did act to save us from sin, but he certainly was not obligated to do so. As Karl Barth explained, "We know of no divine necessity on the basis of which the Word *had* to become flesh. And we have absolutely no knowledge of any human possibility on the basis of which the Word *could* become flesh."[4]

Anselm argued that the only way God could have saved sinful humanity was through the incarnation of the God-man. His logic was simple: Only God can atone for sins, but only human beings need atonement. Therefore "it is necessary for the God-man to make it."[5] Put another way,

---

[2] See Anselm, *Why God Became Man* 2.18.

[3] Thomas Aquinas, *Summa Contra Gentiles* 1.81.2; Aquinas, *Summa theologica* I, q. 44, a. 2.

[4] Barth, *Credo*, 65 (see chap. 16, n. 10).

[5] See Anselm, *Why God Became Man* 2.6–7. In recent decades, some Christian theologians have made the case that Jesus would have been made incarnate regardless of whether God allowed the fall of man to happen. See Edwin Chr.

God was never required to save us, but he freely chose to do this for us. In the world he chose to create, the incarnation of the Son provided the only way sinful people could be forgiven.

Was the virgin birth the only way God the Son could have become man? Athanasius argued that the Son could have appeared bodily in other ways if he chose to do so.[6] Anselm said that Jesus would still be the God-man if God created his human nature from the dirt as he did with Adam. But if God came into the world this way, he could not represent the descendants of Adam because he would not share their lineage.[7] The Son could have come to earth the first time with the same glory and splendor that will accompany him when he returns (Acts 1:11; Rev 1:7). Although that kind of display certainly would have drawn a lot of attention, Jesus would never have become the man of sorrows acquainted with our grief (Isa 53:3).

But on this point let us be crystal clear: The virgin birth did not make Jesus divine. As the eternally begotten Son of God, Jesus Christ is the "same yesterday, today, and forever" (Heb 13:8). He is and always was the eternal Son of God. And although God the Son was joined to a true human nature in the incarnation, the church fathers suggested that he still could have become human without the virginal conception.

But Christian theologians do not affirm this doctrine because we believe God the Son could not have become human any other way. We affirm the virgin birth because it was the only divinely ordained means by which Christ's divine and human natures were united in one person. We affirm the virgin birth because it was the most fitting way for the God-man to enter our world. Most importantly, we affirm this doctrine because God chose to reveal himself to us in this way in the incarnation and in his inspired and inerrant written word.

---

van Driel, *Incarnation Anyway: Arguments for Supralapsarian Christology* (New York: Oxford University Press, 2008).

[6] Athanasius, *On the Incarnation* 8.

[7] Anselm, *Why God Became Man* 2.8.

The Fitting Sign of Our Salvation

Rather than speaking about the absolute necessity of the virgin birth, theologians like Irenaeus, Augustine, Anselm, Aquinas, and Barth have written much about its *fittingness* as a "sign of our salvation."[8] When they call the virgin birth "fitting," they mean that it was the most appropriate way for God to reveal himself in Christ and reconcile himself to us.

After all, Scripture repeatedly calls the virgin birth a "sign" that points us to the presence and saving power of God. Ahaz is told that "the Lord himself will give you a sign" (Isa 7:14). The angel told the shepherds to look for "the sign" of "a baby wrapped tightly in cloth and lying in a manger" (Luke 2:12).

Signs are a regular part of human communication, but they usually point to something besides the sign itself. When you are driving down the interstate at night and see a glowing pair of yellow arches, you do not stop and stare at the sign itself. The sign is directing you to the greasy burger joint somewhere in the vicinity. The golden arches are the sign, but the fast-food restaurant is the thing signified by the sign.

Though it is one of the most pervasive signs in twenty-first-century Western culture, very few people stop to think about the meaning of the twin-tailed siren of the sea on our Starbucks Coffee cups. The sign of this beautiful creature from Greek mythology is luring you to the overpriced coffee she signifies.

God had used "signs" all throughout Scripture that pointed toward some aspect of what he was doing in the world: the "sign of the covenant" he made with Noah in the rainbow (Gen 9:12, 17), the "sign of the covenant" he made with Abraham in male circumcision (Gen 17:11), the various "signs" of the plagues on Egypt God used to free his people (Exod

---

[8] Irenaeus, *Against Heresies* 3.20.3; 3.21.1; cf. Barth, *CD* I.2, study edition, 185–86 [176–77]. For a helpful overview of this theme in Barth and the tradition, see Dustin Resch, *Barth's Interpretation of the Virgin Birth: A Sign of Mystery* (New York: Routledge, 2016).

4:30; 7:3), and numerous "signs" God gave through the prophets of Israel and Judah (Isa 66:19; Jer 44:29; Ezek 24:24; Dan 6:27).

But the virgin birth was different from every other sign God had given to Israel at this point in their history. Those other signs pointed away from themselves toward something else God was doing. The virgin birth, on the other hand, was a sign that pointed back to itself. The virgin birth revealed the mystery of God incarnate. The unusual way God took on humanity called attention to the fact that God had taken on true humanity.[9]

The sign of the virgin birth, like the sign of Jesus's resurrection from the dead, did not establish the divinity of God the Son. It declared his divinity. As Barth explained, "The mystery [of the incarnation] does not rest upon the miracle [of the virgin birth]. The miracle rests upon the mystery. The miracle bears witness to the mystery, and the mystery is attested by the miracle."[10] Just as the Bethlehem star guided the magi to Jesus, the virgin birth points us to the God who seeks to reconcile us to himself. Instead of thinking about the virgin birth as an absolute necessity, we think of it as a fitting sign that reveals the identity and saving purposes of God.

First, the virginal conception was a fitting sign that we are saved by God's grace alone. Were the incarnation the result of ordinary human planning, then one might argue that our salvation resulted from Mary and Joseph's decision to procreate. In this case, man did something to bring about his own salvation. "But," Irenaeus wrote, "since an unlooked-for salvation was to be provided for men through the help of God, so also was the unlooked-for birth from a virgin accomplished."[11] Though they did not earn it or deserve it, Mary and Joseph were recipients of God's favor and grace (Luke 1:28).

Our salvation by God's free grace echoes the Spirit's gracious activity in the virgin birth: "But to all who did receive him, he gave them the right

---

[9] Barth, *CD* I.2, study edition, 214 [202].

[10] Barth, 215 [202].

[11] Irenaeus, *Against Heresies* 3.21.6.

to be children of God, to those who believe in his name, who were born, not of natural descent, or of the will of the flesh, or of the will of man, but of God" (John 1:12–13). Irenaeus wrote, "We understand that His advent in human nature was not by the will of a man, but by the will of God."[12] If human beings could do nothing to rescue themselves from the power of sin, it was fitting that God caused a virgin to conceive the Savior without human planning or intervention.

Second, the virgin birth demonstrates that divine revelation is only God's initiative. Human beings do not seek out God (Ps 14:2; Rom 3:11), but he has chosen to reveal himself through the Son (John 1:18; Col 1:15). God alone has enabled us to share in the light of his revelation (Col 1:12). Irenaeus says this is also true of the sign of Jesus's conception: Joseph took no part in it, and Mary merely complied with the will of God.[13] The virgin birth points to the truth that only God could save us and that only God has acted to save us. As Barth explains, the virgin birth denotes that "God has acted solely through God" and that "God can likewise be known solely through God."[14]

Third, the virgin birth is a sign of Jesus's uniqueness as the natural, only-begotten Son of God. In one sense, every human being is a child of God by virtue of the fact that we were all created by God (Acts 17:28–29). In quite another sense, we were not born God's children at all. Before God rescued us from sin, we "were by nature children of wrath" (Eph 2:3 ESV) and children of the devil (John 8:44). But to everyone who receives Jesus as Lord, God gives them "the right to be children of God" (John 1:12).

---

[12] Irenaeus 3.21.7; cf. Thomas Aquinas, *Summa theologica* IIIa q. 28, a. 1.

[13] Irenaeus, *Against Heresies* 3.21.7. Irenaeus interpreted Dan 2:34 as a prophetic sign of this truth. Nebuchadnezzar dreamed of a statue, which Daniel understood to represent the various kingdoms of men. The statue is cut and reshaped "without a hand touching it" (Dan 2:34). Human beings are ultimately powerless to control the destiny of their kingdoms.

[14] Barth, *CD* I.2, 177.

The virgin birth signals that Jesus is unlike every other human being ever born. We are by nature the children of sinful human fathers who must be adopted as God's children. But Christ was naturally the Son of God who adopted a sinful human father for himself. As Thomas Aquinas explained, "For since Christ is the true and natural son of God, it was not fitting that He should have any other father than God: lest the dignity belonging to God be transferred to another."[15]

Fourth, the virgin birth is a sign of the supremacy of Christ. Irenaeus wrote, "Jesus Christ was not a mere man, begotten from Joseph in the ordinary course of nature, but was very God, begotten of the Father most high, and very man, born of the Virgin."[16] If Jesus were the biological son of Joseph, Irenaeus argued, he would have been an inferior Savior. "If He were the son of Joseph, how could He be greater than Solomon, or greater than Jonah, or greater than David, when He was generated from the same seed, and was a descendant of these men?"[17] But if Jesus were not the son of Mary, there would be no adequate way of explaining his true humanity.[18] A mere man could not save us, and neither could a spiritual being without a true human nature.[19]

Fifth, the virgin birth is a witness to Christ's identity as the divine "Son of Man." One of Jesus's favorite self-descriptions in the Gospels is the "Son of Man." This title appears frequently in all four Gospels. This title refers to Jesus's divine identity as the Son of Man who rules from God's throne in Dan 7:13–14, but paradoxically, it literally describes a human being. Someone who is the son of a human is himself a human. Jean Galot (1919–2008) believed the virgin birth was an important witness to this title: "The virginal conception of Jesus . . . resulted in a child who was at once begotten from above and the son of a woman. It manifested the

---

[15] Thomas Aquinas, *Summa theologica* IIIa q. 28, a. 1.
[16] Irenaeus, *Against Heresies* 3.19.
[17] Irenaeus 3.21.8.
[18] Irenaeus 3.19.2.
[19] Irenaeus 3.20.3.

divine sonship within a human sonship. . . . Mary . . . is the woman who has made it possible for Jesus to call himself the Son of Man."[20]

Finally, the virgin birth is a fitting sign of Christ's preexistence. Most Christian theologians and philosophers look to conception—when the sperm fertilizes the egg—as the moment human life begins. But Jesus's life did not begin to exist at his virginal conception. In fact, Jesus did not begin to exist at all. Scripture is emphatically clear that Jesus existed before the incarnation (John 1:18; 3:13; 6:38; 8:58; 17:3). Jesus existed before the creation of the world (John 1:1–3; 17:5; Col 1:15–17; Heb 1:2–3). The Nicene Creed (AD 381) declares that Jesus is "begotten of the Father before all worlds . . . begotten, not made, of the same substance as the Father." There was never a time when the Son did not exist. Rather than contradicting the preexistence of Jesus, the virgin birth bears witness to the fact that his life did not begin at conception like ours.

The Virgin Birth Is Essential Revelation

Many theologians reject the virgin birth because they do not believe it to be necessary to affirm the true deity and humanity of Jesus. But this logic is fatally flawed. Like every other contingency in human history, just because a Christian doctrine is not logically necessary does not make it untrue. God did not need to create this world to prove his omnipotence, but he did. God could have left us in our sins, but freely chose to offer his Son as our substitute. God did not have to send his Son through a virgin's womb, but he did ordain the incarnation through this supernatural means.

The Bible plainly, unequivocally tells us a virgin conceived a baby. As J. Gresham Machen notes, "The Bible teaches the virgin birth of Christ; a man who accepts the virgin birth may continue to hold to the full truthfulness of the Bible; a man who rejects it cannot possibly do

---

[20] Galot, *Who Is Christ?*, 135–36 (see chap. 15, n. 11).

so. That much at least should be perfectly plain."[21] But the one who rejects the virgin birth not only rejects what Scripture plainly teaches about it; he also rejects an important aspect of God's self-revelation in the incarnation event. The virginal conception of Jesus was one of the important ways God revealed himself to the world. This miracle speaks volumes about the identity of Jesus, the character of God, and the nature of our salvation.

---

[21] Machen, *The Virgin Birth*, 387 (see introduction, n. 6).

22

Veil'd In Flesh the Godhead See

The Virgin-Born King and the Doctrine of the Trinity

Understand the incarnation and the virgin birth in the same way, as
indivisibly wrought by one and the same working of Father and Son,
not leaving out, of course, the Holy Spirit, of whom it is said in so
many words that [Mary] was found to be with child of the Holy Spirit.

—AUGUSTINE OF HIPPO[1]

Few topics make believers scratch their heads more than the doctrine
of the Trinity. How can God be both one and three? How do the

---

[1] Augustine, *The Trinity* (*De Trinitate*), trans. Edmund Hill, ed. John E.
Rotelle, ser. 1, vol. 5, *The Works of St. Augustine: A Translation for the 21st Century*
(Hyde Park, NY: New City Press, 1991), 2.2.9.

Father, the Son, and the Spirit relate to one another? To be sure, this biblical teaching is mysterious and difficult. Studying the doctrine of the Trinity may be hard work, but it promises great reward for followers of Christ. As Augustine put it, "For nowhere else is a mistake more dangerous, or the search more laborious, or discovery more advantageous."[2] The doctrine of the Trinity stretches our minds, floods our hearts with joyful adoration, and moves our hands and feet to active obedience.

So, what does the doctrine of the Trinity have to do with the Christmas story? The short answer is: everything. Christmas is the celebration of the moment in time when God the Father sent God the Son into the world by the power of God the Holy Spirit to accomplish the revealing and reconciling work of the triune God. The biblical nativity stories invite us to reflect on the eternal relations between the three persons of the Trinity and how the three persons work together to accomplish God's saving work in the world.

The Bible and the Trinity

If you were to look up the word "Trinity" with the search tool in your favorite Bible app, you would be met with a message like this: "Sorry, we didn't find any results for your search." Why? Because the term "Trinity" is nowhere to be found in any remotely accurate translation of the Bible. The word "Trinity" may be a term that only pops up a little later in the Christian tradition, but the triune God is all over the Bible. In the words of B. B. Warfield, "The whole book is Trinitarian to the core; all its teaching is built on the assumption of the Trinity; and its allusions to the Trinity are frequent, cursory, easy and confident."[3] The Bible contains all the ingredients of the Christian doctrine of the Trinity.

---

[2] Augustine 1.1.5.

[3] Benjamin B. Warfield, "Trinity," in *The International Standard Bible Encyclopedia*, ed. James Orr (Grand Rapids: Eerdmans, 1974), 4:3014–15.

First, the Bible teaches that there is only one true God. In the OT, God rescued Israel from the Egyptians "so that [they] would know that the LORD is God; there is no other besides him" (Deut 4:35). "Yahweh" or "the LORD" was more than the official God of Israel's worship; he is the one true God over all creation. God made this truth plain through the prophet Isaiah:

> No god was formed before me,
> and there will be none after me.
> I—I am the LORD.
> Besides me, there is no Savior. (Isa 43:10–11)

Elsewhere this God plainly states, "There is no God but me" (Isa 44:6b). Though NT authors frequently refer to God as the Father, the Son, and the Holy Spirit, they also believed that there is only one true God (Mark 12:29; 1 Cor 8:4–6; Eph 4:6; 1 Tim 2:5–6; Jas 2:19).

Second, the Bible teaches that the Father, the Son, and the Holy Spirit are truly God. The name of God in the OT ("Yahweh" or "The LORD") is synonymous with "the name of the Father and of the Son and of the Holy Spirit" in the NT (Matt 28:19). The title "LORD" rightly applies to the Father (2 Cor 6:18), the Son (1 Cor 8:6; Eph 1:3), and the Holy Spirit (2 Cor 3:17). Though the Father, Son, and Holy Spirit can all be properly called "LORD," we do not serve three lords.

We know Jesus is truly God because he shares the same divine nature with the Father and the Holy Spirit. Biblical authors repeatedly refer to Jesus with divine names like "God" (Rom 9:5; 2 Pet 1:1), "Son of God" (1 John 5:20), "Lord" (Rom 10:9, 13; Phil 2:11), "the Word" (John 1:1–18), and "Son of Man" (Mark 14:62). The early church preached Jesus as the exalted Messiah who stands at the right hand of God (Acts 2:32–33; 7:55).

We also know about Jesus's divinity through his action in the world. Christ does things only God can do. The world was created through Jesus (John 1:3; Col 1:16; Heb 1:2). Jesus can forgive sins against God (Mark 2:5–11). Christ will judge the world for its sin (John 9:39; 2 Cor 5:10).

Scripture teaches that Jesus is worthy of worship as God (Matt 28:9; John 9:38; Heb 1:6; Revelation 5).

Though the NT does not say in so many words that "the Holy Spirit is the third person of the Trinity," the name "Holy Spirit" is used interchangeably with God (Acts 5:3–4; 1 Cor 3:16–17; 6:19–20; 2 Cor 3:17–18). The Holy Spirit is also shown to share in God's eternal nature (Heb 9:14), sovereignty (1 Cor 12:4–11), and creative power (Gen 1:2; Job 26:13; Ps 104:30). The Holy Spirit, like the Father and the Son, created the world and has acted to redeem it. Because the Holy Spirit is God, he is deserving of all the same praise, glory, and honor that is given to the Father and the Son.

Third, the Bible teaches that God the Father, God the Son, and God the Holy Spirit are three distinct eternal persons. Simply put, God the Father is not God the Son. God the Son is not God the Holy Spirit. God the Holy Spirit is not God the Father. We must not reduce the Father, Son, and Spirit to different "roles" performed by the one true God.

God the Father is eternally the "Father of our Lord Jesus Christ" (Rom 15:6; Col 1:3). Christ is the "only begotten" Son of the Father (John 1:14, 18; 3:16, 18; 1 John 4:9 KJV). God the Holy Spirit is "sent" or "poured out" by the Father (Acts 2:17–18; Rom 5:5; Gal 4:6) and the Son (John 14:26; 15:26; 20:22; Titus 3:6). These relations within the Trinity are the only way we can properly distinguish between the persons of the Godhead.

God is and always has been three distinct persons: the Father, the Son, and the Holy Spirit. We must also resist the temptation to define the persons of the Trinity like human persons.[4] Human persons are complex individuals who have their own minds, wills, and personalities. The Trinity does not consist of three separate beings with three minds, three

---

[4] For a helpful overview of the issues with confusing human and divine persons, see Giles Emery, *The Trinity: An Introduction to the Catholic Doctrine on the Triune God*, trans. Matthew Levering (Washington, DC: The Catholic University of America Press, 2011), 83–110.

wills, and three personalities. This communal approach to the Trinity sounds a lot like *tri-theism*, or the worship of three gods. As Scott Swain explains, "The multiplication of divine persons within the one God does not amount to the multiplication of divine beings, divine minds, divine wills, or divine powers. In the one God all of these things—the divine being, the divine mind, the divine will, and the divine power—are one and indivisible. For us there is one God, one Lord, one Spirit."[5]

The only way we can properly distinguish between the three persons of the Trinity is in their eternal relations as Father, Son, and Holy Spirit.[6] Each person of the Godhead eternally exists in relation to the other two persons. Each person has his own property in these relations.

1. God the Father eternally begets (not creates) the Son. We call this relation the *paternity* of the Father.
2. The Son is eternally begotten by the Father. Throughout eternity God the Son has existed in relation to the Father as his Son, but unlike human father-son relationships, there is no creation or beginning in the eternal begetting of God the Son. We call this relation the *filiation* of the Son (from a Latin word meaning "son").
3. God the Holy Spirit eternally exists as the divine person who is breathed forth by the Father and the Son.[7] We call the "breathing out" of the Spirit *spiration*.

These relations are eternal, essential to God, and unchanging. Even if God had chosen not to create the world or to reveal himself to us, these eternal relations would remain the same within the Trinity.

---

[5] Scott R. Swain, *The Trinity: An Introduction* (Wheaton, IL: Crossway, 2020), 60.

[6] Stephen R. Holmes, *The Quest for the Trinity: The Doctrine of God in Scripture, History, and Modernity* (Downers Grove: IVP Academic, 2012), 146.

[7] The Hebrew and Greek words for "spirit" (*ruach, pneuma*) can also be translated "breath."

All three persons of the Godhead share in *one divine nature*—the essential attributes of God. All three persons have the attributes of God: perfect power, perfect knowledge, perfect wisdom, perfect love, etc. But God is not like a puzzle where all these pieces fit together to make him who he is. He is simple, meaning he is not composed of parts. Nor is God like the man walking through the grocery store trying to carry all the items he can without getting a shopping cart. God does not hold on to attributes that are external to his being. Instead, God simply is his perfect attributes. These perfections are essential to his being.

The Father, Son, and Holy Spirit share in one nature, but they also share in *one being*. My son Ben and my daughter Annie both share in one human nature. They both have all the essential attributes that every human possesses, but they are also two different beings with very different personalities, different appearances, different interests, etc. When we talk about humanity, two distinct, numerical beings can share one nature. In the case of a simple God without division or parts, one nature ensures one being. The Father, the Son, and the Holy Spirit share the same essential attributes but do not count as three beings or three gods. All three persons in the Trinity share *one substance*, meaning three divine persons "count" as one being. Consequently, we worship the Father, the Son, and the Holy Spirit as one God. Each divine person is truly the one God in his fullness, not a "third" of God.

The Work of the Triune God in the Virgin Birth

Christian theologians since Augustine have made a clear distinction between who God is in the eternal relations within the Godhead and who God has revealed himself to be in creation and redemption history. This distinction is important for our doctrine of the incarnation: The Son may have taken on the form of a servant in human history (Phil 2:6–7), but this act does not mean he is subordinate to the Father in eternity. The fact that God the Son took on the likeness of a baby in the manger does not mean he is of a lesser glory or station than the Father who sent him or the Spirit who caused his conception in true humanity.[8]

Remember that the relations between the Father, Son, and Spirit are eternal, essential to God, and unchanging. We sometimes call these eternal relations the *internal works of God*.[9] But God's creative and saving acts in the world are the *external works of God*.[10] Although we must not conflate what God does in history with who he is in eternity, the redemptive activity of God in history reflects who he is in eternity. The triune God at work in the incarnation of Jesus reveals the mystery of who God has been in all eternity. The Son who relates eternally to the Father as the begotten Son became the human Son in time. The Spirit who always proceeds from the Father and the Son in eternity was sent by the Father and Son on the day of Pentecost.

God Doesn't Tag Team

Sometimes people talk about the three persons of the Trinity as if they were a three-man tag team. In the OT, the Father was in the ring doing all the work, occasionally spotted by the Son. In the Gospels, the Father tagged and exchanged places with Jesus. At the ascension, Jesus tagged out, and the Spirit entered the ring. When the end comes, the Spirit will tag out and exchange places with Jesus once more. But this picture, which sounds a lot like the work of three separate gods, does not remotely resemble biblical orthodoxy.

Theologians use the term "inseparable operations" to describe the way all three persons are at work in every single external work of God

---

[8] Augustine, The Trinity 1.3.14.

[9] *Ad intra*, a Latin phrase meaning "at the interior," describes the works *within* God.

[10] *Ad extra*, a Latin phase meaning "at the extremity," describes the works of God *outside of himself* in the world.

in the world.[11] The inseparable operations of the Trinity must not be compared to the "teamwork" of three agents working together toward a common goal. Rather, in the inseparable operations of the Trinity, one substance (God) who is three persons singularly acts in this world to achieve his ends.[12] In the inseparable operations, because the three persons share a *single will*, they also share singular "verbs."

Simply put, every time God acts in the world, the whole Trinity acts. The Trinity created the world. The Trinity rescued Israel from Egypt. The Trinity gave Moses the law on Mt. Sinai. The Trinity made a covenant with David. The Trinity spoke through prophets like Jeremiah and Ezekiel in a time of exile. Whenever and wherever in human history God has been at work, the whole Godhead has been involved.

The nativity stories recorded in Matthew and Luke also put the inseparable operations of God on display. The triune God revealed himself to Mary through the angelic messenger he sent. The triune God extended his favor to Mary and told her that she would bear the "Son of the Most High" and the long-awaited heir of David's throne. Even though she was a virgin, she would conceive a child by the power of the triune God.

All three persons of the Godhead indivisibly willed and acted to redeem his people through the incarnation of the Son. In the inseparable external work of the triune God, the Father sent his only begotten Son into the world through the power of the Holy Spirit. Augustine remarks, "Father and Son have but one will and are indivisible in their working." He then adds that we must "understand the incarnation and the virgin birth in the same way, as indivisibly wrought by one and the same working of Father and Son, not leaving out, of course, the Holy Spirit."[13]

---

[11] The Latin phrase for this teaching is *opera Trinitatis ad extra indivisa sunt* ("the external operations of the Trinity are indivisible"). See Adonis Vidu, *The Same God Who Works All Things: Inseparable Operations in Trinitarian Theology* (Downers Grove: Eerdmans, 2021).

[12] Augustine, *The Trinity* 1.2.8.

[13] Augustine, *The Trinity* 2.2.9.

We may distinguish between the works of the Father, Son, and Holy Spirit, but we cannot separate them or attribute them to three different wills or three different gods. The creation of the Son's human nature in Mary is rightly appropriated to the Holy Spirit in Scripture. Mary became "pregnant from the Holy Spirit" (Matt 1:18). But the Son also said of the Father, "You prepared a body for me" (Heb 10:5; cf. Ps 40:6). The Son prepared his human nature as well. He himself willed to take on a human nature (John 3:13; 6:38).[14] Or, as Athanasius described it, "Although being himself powerful and the creator of the universe, he prepared for himself in the Virgin the body as a temple, and made it his own, as an instrument, by making himself known and dwelling in it."[15] The conception of the Son in Mary's womb rightly belongs to the inseparable operations of the Godhead.

The Father Was Not Born of a Virgin

Although there is no division of God's work in the world, some works are specifically ascribed to an individual person within the Godhead. For example, the triune God can rightly be called "Savior" (Pss 17:7; 42:11; 43:5; 140:7; Luke 1:47; 1 Tim 1:1), but we are also correct when we specifically call Jesus the "Savior" (Luke 2:11; Acts 5:31; 13:23; Phil 3:20). The triune God gave us his written Word, but we can also say the Holy Spirit inspired the writing of Scripture (2 Tim 3:16; 2 Pet 1:21). We call these person-specific designations *divine appropriations*.

The clearest example of divine appropriations is in the incarnation. As Maximus the Confessor (c. 580–662) expounded on this mystery, "The Father himself did not become incarnate but rather approved the incarnation of the Son. Moreover, the whole Holy Spirit exists by essence

---

[14] Bavinck, *Reformed Dogmatics*, 3:290 (see chap. 16, n. 18).

[15] Athanasius, *On the Incarnation* 8.

in the whole Son, but he too did not become incarnate but rather cooperated in the Son's ineffable incarnation for our sake."[16]

The nativity stories supply us with a helpful example of divine appropriation. The triune God willed and empowered a virgin to conceive, but the biblical text specifically attributes the virgin birth to the overshadowing power of the Holy Spirit (Luke 1:35; Matt 1:20).[17] Augustine states that even when one person is specifically ascribed to doing something in the world, the whole Trinity is still at work. Peter Lombard (AD 1100–60) adds, "The frequent mention of the Holy Spirit does not exclude the Father or the Son from that work; it is rather the case that, by the naming of the one, the three are understood, as it often happens with reference to other works."[18]

The persons of the Trinity have distinct activities in the saving work of God. As Augustine makes plain, the Trinity was not "born of the virgin Mary, crucified and buried under Pontius Pilate, rose again on the third day and ascended into heaven, but the Son alone."[19] Only God the Son was born of Mary. Only God the Spirit overshadowed her. Only God the Father relates to Jesus in a father-son relationship.

Born in Time, Forever Born in Eternity

Specific persons in the Trinity are tasked with distinct activities in salvation. The Father sent the Son into the world through the Spirit's action of the virginal conception. The Father and Son sent the Holy Spirit to indwell and empower believers on Pentecost (Acts 2:1–11). Augustine

---

[16] Maximus, *Ad Thalassium* 60, in *On the Cosmic Mystery of Jesus Christ: Selected Writings from St Maximus the Confessor*, trans. Paul M. Blowers and Robert Louis Wilkin (Yonkers, NY: St Vladimir's Seminary Press, 2003), 121. By contrast, Praxeas, a second-century heretic charged with modalism, claimed that "the Father Himself came down into the Virgin" (Tertullian, *Against Praxeas* 1).

[17] Augustine, *The Enchiridion* 38.

[18] Peter Lombard, *The Sentences* 3.4.1.

[19] Augustine, *The Trinity* 1.2.7.

called these sending activities the *divine missions*.[20] The Son and the Spirit have always been in this world in one sense—they are God who is present to all his creation. But in the missions, the sending of the Son and the Spirit could be seen and perceived by his people. Augustine called them "visible missions."

Although these missions are distinct from the eternal relations within the Godhead, these missions reveal the eternal relations. For example, in the eternal relations of the Trinity, the Spirit always proceeds from the Father and the Son, for all eternity. But in the divine missions, the Spirit was sent by the Father and the Son in time. Christ is, in the words of Peter Lombard, "forever being born from the Father" in his eternal relations to the Father. Christ is in eternity "forever born."[21] But Christ was born in time of the virgin Mary.

Conclusion

The nativity story gives us a unique window into the activity of the triune God. Here we see all three persons inseparably but distinctively working together to bring about the incarnation of the Son. The Spirit may have caused Mary to conceive, but Jesus is the Son of the Father, not the Spirit. The sending of the Son in time reflects the proceeding of the Son in eternity.

Truths related to the Trinity are admittedly mysterious. Augustine reminded us that if finite human minds could fully comprehend these matters, we would not really be talking about God.[22] He is an infinite Creator, and we are finite creatures. On this side of heaven, we may not be able to comprehend these truths fully, but we must affirm what the Bible

---

[20] Augustine, *The Trinity* 2.2.9. The word *missions* comes from a Latin word *missio*, which means "sent."

[21] Christ is always being begotten by the Father. Christ is, in the words of Peter Lombard, "forever born." Peter Lombard, *Sentences* 1.9.4. For this helpful discovery, special thanks to Fred Sanders, Professor of Theology, Biola University.

[22] Augustine, *Sermons* 67.5 [117.3.5], *NPNF*[1] 6:459.

teaches about them. We cannot deny that there is one true God. We who are orthodox will not deny that the Father is God, that the Son is God, and that the Holy Spirit is God. We must also not confuse the persons of the Trinity because the Bible nowhere affords us that opportunity.

23

And Heav'n and Nature Sing

The Virgin-Born King in Creation and Science

> Here God will not hold to the order of creation but make a new one. A virgin shall conceive, and that shall be a 'sign' or miracle.
> —MARTIN LUTHER[1]

Years ago, some seminary colleagues and I went to lunch with a world-renowned biblical scholar who was in town for a conference.

This scholar had made quite the name for himself—and a small fortune—writing popular books aimed at debunking traditional Christian beliefs.

While we gorged ourselves on New Orleans cuisine, one of the men around the table began to press this skeptical scholar about some of his

---

[1] Luther, *Preb. üb. Lc.* 1²⁶ᶠᶠ, 1552, *E.A.* 6, 195, cited in Barth, *CD* I.2, 178 (see chap. 16, n. 4).

claims, particularly some of the things he had written about the resurrection accounts in the Gospels.

When confronted with some of my colleague's counterarguments, the biblical scholar piped up and responded, "I hear what you're saying. I have heard those arguments before. But let me be clear: Jesus could not possibly have been raised from the dead *because dead men cannot be raised*."

No matter what rationale or evidence was offered, this skeptic had already made up his mind. He began his argument against the resurrection of Jesus with the assumption that such resurrections cannot happen. This type of faulty reasoning is properly called "question-begging."

Along similar lines, many critics of the virgin birth dismiss this event right out of the gate because they presuppose *naturalism*—the atheistic worldview that denies the existence of anything beyond this natural world. Naturalists view the universe as a closed, self-contained system with no possibility of God, angels, demons, or nonmaterial things. Because they believe the universe is a self-contained system, they refuse the possibility of miracles. They regularly follow David Hume's (1711–1776) lead in defining a miracle as an impossible "violation of the laws of nature."[2]

The biblical accounts of the virginal conception of Jesus present an altogether different worldview. Matthew and Luke would agree with anyone else that angelic appearances, roaming stars, and virgins having babies are events that do not normally occur in nature. (If these ancient authors did not find these happenings unusual, they would not have bothered writing about them the way they did.) But instead of thinking about the universe as a closed, self-sustaining system formed by random natural causes, the biblical authors viewed the world as *creation*. In other words, this world only exists because an all-powerful, all-knowing, and all-loving God desired to create it (Rev 4:11). This world is God's domain, and he does what he pleases in it.

Miracles or "signs" like the virgin birth are not outside of what this God can do because, in their understanding, "nothing will be impossible

---

[2] David Hume, *An Enquiry Concerning Human Understanding*, §10.1.

with God" (Luke 1:37). In the nativity stories, the Evangelists give us a model for how to reflect on God's creative power. Christian theologians throughout the centuries have built on ideas latent here in the nativity accounts.

When Heaven Interrupts Nature

The naturalist objection to the virginal conception of Jesus is the same objection made to his healing ministry, his turning water into wine, and his resurrection: Miracles cannot and do not happen in this world because nothing and no one exists outside of the natural universe. In 1947, C. S. Lewis published a book-length response to this claim entitled *Miracles*. Here Lewis exposed some of the fundamental problems with naturalism and the ways naturalists misunderstand the Christian concept of miracles. The virgin birth plays a crucial role in his argument.

First, Lewis demonstrated the incoherence of the naturalist worldview with his "argument from reason."[3] If everything we think and believe is the product of physical causes in our brains, Lewis argued, then the whole idea of human reason is itself an illusion put on by our brains. If all human reasoning is an illusion, then belief in naturalism is also an irrational illusion put on by the material brain. Furthermore, the naturalist view of human reason makes it impossible to distinguish between "good" and "evil." The idea that we "ought" to do anything is nonsensical if all our moral reasoning is the product of chemical processes in our brains.[4]

Second, Lewis challenged the naturalist claim that ancient Christian belief in miracles was merely the product of a superstitious, prescientific worldview. Many naturalists contend that modern science has made it impossible

---

[3] See C. S. Lewis, *Miracles* (New York: HarperCollins, 2000), 17–36. For a thorough defense of Lewis's argument, see Victor Reppert, *C .S. Lewis's Dangerous Idea: In Defense of the Argument from Reason* (Downers Grove: IVP Academic, 2003).

[4] See Lewis, *Miracles*, ch. 5.

to believe in miracles. Unlike ancient civilizations, the argument goes, we know the laws of nature so we know miracles cannot happen.[5] Lewis illustrated this bias against ancient cultures with a conversation he had with a naturalist about the virginal conception of Jesus.

> "Miracles," said my friend. "Oh, come. Science has knocked the bottom out of all that. We know that Nature is governed by fixed laws."
>
> "Didn't people always know that?" said I.
>
> "Good Lord, no," said he. "For instance, take a story like the Virgin Birth. We know now that such a thing couldn't happen. We know there *must* be a male spermatozoon."
>
> "But look here," said I, "St Joseph—"
>
> "Who's he?" asked my friend.
>
> "He was the husband of the Virgin Mary. If you'll read the story in the Bible you'll find that when he saw his fiancée was going to have a baby he decided to cry off the marriage. Why did he do that?"
>
> "Wouldn't most men?"
>
> "Any man would," said I, "provided he knew the laws of Nature—in other words, provided he knew that a girl doesn't ordinarily have a baby unless she's been sleeping with a man. But according to your theory people in the old days didn't know that Nature was governed by fixed laws. I'm pointing out that the story shows that St Joseph knew *that* law just as well as you do."
>
> "But he came to believe in the Virgin Birth afterwards, didn't he?"
>
> "Quite. But he didn't do so because he was under any illusion as to where babies came from in the ordinary course of Nature. He believed in the Virgin Birth as something *super*-natural. He knew Nature works in fixed, regular ways: but he also believed

---

[5] Lewis, *Miracles*, ch. 7.

that there existed something *beyond* Nature which could interfere with her workings—from outside, so to speak."[6]

Modern science is certainly able to tell us more about the natural world than a prescientific worldview. We may know more about embryonic development than people did two millennia ago. But ancient people understood the birds and the bees. They knew where babies come from. To insist that they were gullible and naïve simply because they lived in a less scientifically developed age is to practice what Lewis calls "chronological snobbery."[7]

Finally, Lewis proposed a new and better definition of the "miracle." The naturalist asserts, with Hume, that miracles are scientifically impossible because they "violate" the laws of nature. But miracles are not violations of the laws of nature. The "laws of nature" merely describe what regularly happens in nature. These laws do not dictate or prescribe what nature does. Lewis helpfully defined miracles as interferences in the natural world by a supernatural power outside of nature.[8]

On occasion God may interrupt the natural order of things by using his creative power in this world, but this divine interruption is always followed by nature continuing to run its course. According to Lewis, God does not suspend natural law as much as he inserts new events into the established patterns of nature that he himself created. Miracles are the product of God's intervening activity, but because they happen in the world he created, they will conform to natural law once they are activated. Water turned into wine still makes people drunk. Those whom Jesus healed eventually got sick again. Lazarus may have been raised from the dead, but he died again later.

---

[6] C. S. Lewis, *God in the Dock* (Grand Rapids: Eerdmans, 1970), 72–73; cf. Lewis, *Miracles*, 73–75.

[7] C. S. Lewis, *Surprised by Joy: The Shape of My Early Life* (New York: Harcourt Brace, 1955), 200–201.

[8] Lewis, *Miracles*, 5.

Aside from the unusual way Mary conceived Jesus, her pregnancy was quite normal. From the germinal stage of human development until birth, God the Son experienced every stage of human embryonic development. And just like every other mother in the ancient world, Mary went through normal labor pains and delivered a baby through her birth canal. The orthodox assertion of Jesus's true humanity means that Jesus, although supernaturally conceived, entered the world of nature he created and conformed to its regular patterns.

The miracle of the virginal conception was a divine intervention in human history that, once initiated, followed the normal laws of nature. Had Joseph conceived a child, it would be an abomination to nature (because men are not equipped with uteruses). But following the divine interruption of her conception, Mary's pregnancy conformed to all natural laws. Her body was designed to carry a baby, and it did just that. As Lewis explained, "If God creates a miraculous spermatozoon in the body of a virgin, it does not proceed to break any laws. The laws at once take it over. Nature is ready. Pregnancy follows, according to all the normal laws, and nine months later a child is born."[9]

Think about the ways we pray for our friends and family members who are facing physical illnesses or injuries. These prayers stem from three foundational assumptions about God.

First, we believe God is all-powerful; he is almighty. God can do any logically possible thing that will not contradict or violate his character.[10] This means that God is at least capable of interrupting nature with miracles.

Second, we believe God providentially rules over all creation. Sometimes this providential rule means "just letting things happen," meaning God never directly causes evil but does allow it and even wills it (see Gen 50:20; Acts 2:23). Other times this providential rule means God directly

---

[9] Lewis, *Miracles*, 94.

[10] The caveat "any logically possible thing" suggests that logic flows out of the being of God. This disclaimer means God cannot make a rock so large he cannot pick it up, nor can God, who is a necessary being, cease to exist.

intervenes in nature or human affairs. Whether God allows calamity to happen or causes it, he is ultimately in control of all things that transpire in the world. Nothing surprises him or catches him off guard.

Third, we believe that God desires good things for those who love him and who are called according to his purpose. Oftentimes the good thing God wants most for his people is not the same good thing we request (like physical healing on this side of our future resurrection). But we trust God to do what is best in every circumstance because we trust his character.

When he hears our prayers for healing, God may choose to let the physical illness run its natural course in death. God may allow the human body that he designed to fight off the illness, and to do the healing work for which he prepared it. God may provide a physician or a surgeon with extraordinary wisdom and good judgment in treating the illness or injury. All good things—even medical science—are a gift from God (see Jas 1:17). God may also directly intervene and interrupt a natural process with a creative act. This kind of action, strictly speaking, is what constitutes a miracle. Miracles like these cannot be explained by natural causes or mechanisms.

Can We Explain the Virgin Birth Scientifically?

Some have attempted to explain how the virgin birth could have worked in the natural world.[11] Although there is only one instance of a virgin-born human in history, nonhuman virgin births occur regularly in nature. *Parthenogenesis* (from two Greek words meaning *virgin* and *beginning*) is a form of asexual reproduction that occurs in the kingdoms of plants and animals.

---

[11] See R. J. Berry, "The Virgin Birth of Christ," *Science and Christian Belief* 8 (1996): 101–10. See also Augustine, *Contra Faustum* 20.11. Against Faustus the Manichean, Augustine argues that the virginal conception of Jesus is not a work of nature but the will of God.

In parthenogenesis, female species can reproduce without a male or the fertilization of the egg. Animals and plants can reproduce this way, and some species only reproduce this way. Snakes, birds, lizards, sharks, Komodo dragons, spiders, and various types of insects can multiply and fill the earth through parthenogenesis.

However, no mammals are known to reproduce asexually in nature. But parthenogenesis can be simulated in a laboratory setting. And although it raises serious ethical questions, some scientists have even made human stem cells from parthenogenetic blastocysts. In plain speech, scientists have created embryos created from unfertilized eggs.[12]

In nature, save for that one time in Nazareth, all human life begins when a male sperm unites with a female ovum, creating a fertilized egg. We get our DNA from our mommies and daddies. Were humans created by parthenogenesis, they would only have the DNA of their mothers. Orthodox theologians insist that Jesus's human nature does come forth from Mary's ovum, meaning he did carry Mary's DNA.

But there is another difficulty. Our sex is determined by the pair of chromosomes we have. We have either male chromosomes (XY) or female chromosomes (XX). Females always provide one X chromosome, and males provide either the X or the Y chromosome. So, here is the rub: Natural parthenogenesis cannot account for the virginal conception because Jesus could not have been born male without a Y chromosome from a human father—at least in a natural process.[13] But this is not in and of itself a defeater for the virgin conception. If we believe Adam was

---

[12] See Qingyun Mai, et. al, "Derivation of Human Embryonic Stem Cell Lines from Parthenogenetic Blastocysts," *Cell Research* 17 (2007): 1008–19; Elena S. Revazova, et. al, "HLA Homozygous Stem Cell Lines Derived from Human Parthenogenetic Blastocysts," *Cloning & Stem Cells* 10, no. 1 (2008): 11–24.

[13] Arthur Peacocke, "DNA of Our DNA," in *The Birth of Jesus: Biblical and Theological Reflections*, ed. George J. Brooke (Edinburgh: T&T Clark, 2000), 63; cf. Lincoln, *Born of a Virgin*, 264, 280–81 (see chap. 5, n. for "Answering Objections: The Virginal Conception").

created by God without a Y chromosome from a natural father, then God could have created Jesus as a male without a chromosome from a human father as well.

Although the virginal conception of Christ is, strictly speaking, an instance of asexual reproduction, we should not think of it like naturally occurring asexual reproduction. In the same way that we cannot explain by science how water molecules could be transformed into wine or how a putrid Lazarus carcass came back to life, science cannot provide a natural explanation for the virginal conception. As Thomas Torrance insists, the virgin birth "cannot be understood *biologically*. If you ask biological questions of the virgin birth you will only get biological answers, and to ask biological questions only is to presuppose from the start that there is nothing more here than [a] normal biological process."[14] Machen adds that such attempts to explain this miracle scientifically "are contrary to sound sense."[15]

On this side of eternity, we will never know how this worked. Maybe God the Holy Spirit fertilized Mary's ovum without a sperm. Maybe God created a sperm in the likeness of David that inseminated Mary's ovum. He may have done something entirely different. What we can know is that the Holy Spirit somehow interrupted the normal process of human reproduction to create the true human nature of Jesus within Mary's womb.[16]

Nature Rise and Worship Him

The way we understand creation shapes the way we view miraculous events like the virgin birth. If we believe that the natural universe is all there is (what atheistic materialists believe), then miraculous interventions

---

[14] Torrance, *Incarnation*, 95 (see chap. 16, n. 8).

[15] Machen, *The Virgin Birth of Christ*, 390 (see introduction, n. 6).

[16] Oliver D. Crisp, *God Incarnate: Explorations in Christology* (New York: T&T Clark, 2009), 79–87.

in the natural order of things are impossible. If we believe that God and the universe are one and the same thing (the view of New Age pantheists), then miracles are unnecessary. If we believe the universe was created by a god uninvolved with our affairs (what Deists believe), then miracles, although not impossible, are highly unlikely. But if we believe that a wise, loving, and omnipotent God created the universe "from nothing" (*ex nihilo*), then we recognize God's power to intervene in nature any way he pleases.

In the virginal conception, the Creator created a human nature for Christ from material he had already created (Mary's ovum) and from nothing (thus giving Christ that Y chromosome). Church fathers like Athanasius contended that Christ's "body is from Mary."[17] The birth of Jesus was not, Thomas Torrance observes, "an entirely new act of creation on the part of God, but rather a recreation within our human existence."[18]

But as important as the miracle of the virgin birth is in the biblical story, its importance is secondary to the miracle Lewis called "the Grand Miracle." The greatest miracle of all was God becoming man. This grand miracle was "the central event in the history of the earth."[19] The virginal conception of Jesus was the God-ordained means to this wonderful end. The one who created the universe (John 1:3; Col 1:16; Heb 1:2) entered into creation by taking on a created human nature (John 1:14). Pay close attention here: We are not saying Christ was created. We assert that the uncreated God joined himself to a true human nature he himself created.

This miraculous event is a sign of Christ's identity as Messiah and Lord, but it is, as B. B. Warfield also made note, a sign or witness to his great creative power:

> He who walked the earth as its Lord, and whom the very winds and waves obeyed; who could not be holden of the grave, but burst the bonds of death and ascended into the heavens in the

---

[17] Athanasius, *To Epictetus* 4.1.

[18] Torrance, *Incarnation*, 99.

[19] Lewis, *Miracles*, 174.

sight of man: he who now sits at the right hand of God and sheds down his gift of salvation through his Spirit upon the men of his choice—it were impossible that such a one should have entered the world undistinguished among common men. His supernatural birth is given already, in a word, in his supernatural life and his supernatural work, and forms an indispensable element in the supernatural religion which he founded.[20]

Answering Objections: "Mary Should Have Had an Abortion"

Following the landmark 2022 decision of the US Supreme Court that overturned *Roe v. Wade*, an Australian journalist posted a picture of herself on Instagram that incited outrage. In the photograph, she gleefully embraced a protest sign that read, "MARY (The Virgin) should've had an abortion." At the request of her employer, she took down the post and then publicly apologized, insisting that she never meant to offend members of the "religious community."

Signs like these, which have appeared at pro-choice rallies and protests for over a decade now, represent a heresy unique to this post-sexual-revolution world. According to this new heresy, the unborn Jesus, regardless of whether he was conceived by the Holy Spirit, was not truly human. Because Jesus was not truly human, Mary would have been completely within her rights to terminate the fruit of her womb.

Many abortion advocates today will assert that unborn children are merely "fetuses," not human beings or persons. They assert that they are merely following "the science." The assumption for many is that these unborn children are not afforded basic human dignity until after they have travelled through the birth canal. The Bible

---

[20] Benjamin W. Bacon, Andrew C. Zenos, Rush Rhees, and B. B. Warfield, "The Supernatural Birth of Jesus," *American Journal of Theology* 10, no. 1 (1906): 24.

gives no such room for such a view of unborn human children. In
Luke's nativity story, John the Baptist is said to "be filled with the
Holy Spirit while still in his mother's womb" (Luke 1:15). The same
unborn "baby leaped for joy" inside his mother (Luke 1:44).

Note: Elizabeth does not call Mary "the woman carrying the
fetus who has the potential of becoming my Lord." Instead, she
calls her the "mother of my Lord" (Luke 1:43) because this Spirit-
filled woman recognizes Mary's unborn child to be truly human and
truly divine. In the worldview of biblical authors and these women,
the "fruit of the womb" (*karpos tēs koilias*) was more than a clump
of fetal tissue. They spoke rather literally about the "babies" they
carried. Luke employs the same Greek word for "baby" (*brephos*)
when he speaks about John that he uses elsewhere to describe the
newborn Christ in swaddling clothes (Luke 2:12). He also uses this
term to describe those infants who were murdered by intentional
exposure to the elements (Acts 7:19).

Contemporary attempts to justify human abortion by appealing to biblical texts like Exod 21:22–23 are wholly incompatible
with the biblical worldview. In ancient Israel, childlessness was
considered a curse (Lev 20:20–21; 1 Sam 15:33; Job 24:21; Prov
30:16; Jer 15:7; 18:21). Human stillbirth was a horrific thought to
people (Num 12:12). Children were considered a God-given blessing that secured a future for his people (Pss 113:9; 127:3–5; Gal
4:27). Jesus valued children immensely (Matt 18:14; 19:14). God
creates children in the womb and knows them intimately there (Ps
139:13–16; Jer 1:5).

Scripture also repeatedly warns against the sacrifice of children. To sacrifice a child is to "profane the name of your God" (Lev
18:21). Child sacrifice was called "whoring after Molech" and was
punishable by death (Lev 20:5 ESV). God hates child sacrifice; it
is an abomination to him (Deut 12:31). Those who sacrifice their

children do so unto demons (Ps 106:37). Contemporary abortions for the sake of convenience, financial prosperity, or hedonistic pleasure are no different than the sacrifice of children to Molech for the same ends.

Even the Christmas story itself serves as a warning against the murder of innocent children. Herod's slaughter of the innocents (Matt 2:16–18) was the client-king's failed attempt to squelch the prophesied plan of God. It was a violation of God's commandment not to murder (Gen 9:6; Exod 20:13; 21:12). It also demonstrated that God alone is sovereign over life. He alone has the right to give life and take it (Deut 32:39; 1 Sam 2:6).

Lastly, a denial of Christ's true humanity from the moment of conception opens one up to the possibility of Christological heresies denounced by the early church. If Jesus was only a soulless human fetus until a later stage in Mary's pregnancy or until after Mary gave birth, that would imply some form of Apollinarism in which the Word was controlling that body until he took possession of it. If Jesus only became the divine Person at birth, then his human nature existed independently of him (which resembles the heresy of adoptionism). One cannot deny the true humanity of unborn children and hold an orthodox view of the person of Christ.

See Crisp, *God Incarnate*, 103–21.

24

Born to Give Them Second Birth

The Virgin-Born King as the New Adam

Adam's Likeness, LORD, efface,
Stamp thy Image in its Place,
Second Adam from above,
Reinstate us in thy Love.
—"HYMN FOR CHRISTMAS-DAY," CHARLES WESLEY (1707–88)

No modern Christmas hymn communicates the wonder of the incarnation quite like "Hark! The Herald Angels Sing!" John and Charles Wesley published the first version of this carol, "Hymn for Christmas-Day," in 1739. But when their friend George Whitefield published a revised version two decades later, he had the foresight to change the already archaic opening line "HARK how all the Welkin rings" to the more familiar "HARK! the Herald Angels sing."

Though the angels get all the attention in the hymn's opening line, the song is really about the newborn king who reconciles sinners to God through the incarnation. The hymn describes the newborn king who was born of a virgin as the eternal Lord of heaven who in time has become Immanuel for us:

Christ by highest Heav'n ador'd,
Christ the everlasting Lord;
Late in Time behold-him come,
Offspring of the Virgin's Womb.

Veil'd in Flesh the Godhead see,
Hail th' incarnate Deity!
Pleas'd as Man with Men t'appear,
Jesus our Emmanuel here.

The authors provide a threefold reason why the incarnation was necessary. Christ was born "that men may no more die," "to raise the sons of earth," and "to give them second birth." For Wesley and Whitefield, the birth of Christ anticipates his death and resurrection. Many hymnals unfortunately leave out the third and fourth verses, which connect Christ's birth with his saving purpose, and these lyrics draw on many of the biblical themes we have explored to this point:

Come, Desire of Nations, come,
Fix in us thy heav'nly Home;
Rise the Woman's conqu'ring Seed,
Bruise in us the Serpent's Head.

Adam's Likeness now efface,
Stamp thy Image in its Place;
Second Adam from above,
Work it in us by thy Love.

The biblical nativity stories also anticipate the cross of Christ from the very beginning. They depict Jesus, the virgin-born king, as "the

Savior" (Luke 2:11) who "will save his people from their sins" (Matt 1:21). Through Christ, God has "provided redemption for his people" (Luke 1:68). This chapter is an exploration of the relationship between Christ's saving work and the unique way he came into the world. We must address some popular misconceptions about the virgin birth and human sinfulness and look to the history of Christian teaching for some better answers. Finally, we conclude by reflecting on the relationship between the manger and the cross in the gospel narratives.

Adam's Likeness Now Efface

The Bible teaches (and our experience confirms) that all people everywhere are sinners. As the preacher of Ecclesiastes writes, "There is certainly no one righteous on the earth who does good and never sins" (Eccl 7:20). Human nature is *totally depraved*—inclined toward evil and selfish behavior. In the words of the psalmist,

> There is no one who does good.
> The LORD looks down from heaven on the human race
> to see if there is one who is wise,
> one who seeks God.
> All have turned away;
> all alike have become corrupt.
> There is no one who does good,
> not even one. (Ps 14:1b–3)

People do not gradually become depraved over time. Scripture is clear that we begin life depraved and inclined toward sin: "I was guilty when I was born; I was sinful when my mother conceived me" (Ps 51:5). All people "fall short of the glory of God" (Rom 3:23). We are all guilty before God and deserving of his righteous judgment (Rom 6:23). God's anger is rightly directed toward our sin (Jer 4:4; 15:14). Before we were adopted as sons and daughters of God, we were by nature enemies of God (Rom 5:10; cf. Lam 2:4–5).

The Bible plainly teaches that all people are sinners because of Adam's sinful action (Rom 5:12–21), but there is no consensus among Christian theologians as to how exactly Adam's sin affects us. The fourth-century British monk Pelagius taught that all human beings are born morally neutral and capable of doing good without any special intervention on God's part. For Pelagius, Adam's sin does not directly affect us in any way apart from leaving us with a poor example. Human beings could hypothetically do what is right and good on their own, without any need for Christ to save or redeem them from their sins. Pelagius's ideas were condemned as heretical at the Council of Carthage in AD 418.

Pelagius's chief critic was Augustine of Hippo, the most influential theologian of Western Christianity. Augustine believed that we inherit our souls from our parents like we inherit our biological features from them (a view of human souls called *traducianism*). According to his understanding, our souls were present in Adam when he disobeyed God. Because our souls were with Adam when he sinned, we share in Adam's depravity and his guilt—his original sin. Augustine's position on the transmission of sin is sometimes called *natural headship*. We received our depraved natures from parents who transmitted them to us sexually.[1]

The sixteenth-century reformer John Calvin argued for another position known as *federal headship*. Calvin did not believe that we were guilty because parts of our souls were present in Adam. Instead, he thought that God created a new soul with every individual (a view of human souls called *soul creationism*). Calvin understood Adam to be God's appointed representative of the human race (like an elected representative in a federal government). According to this view, God made a "covenant of

---

[1] Augustine's view is based in part on a literal understanding of Ps 51:5, which read like this in the Latin translation he used: "For behold I was conceived in iniquities; and in sins did my mother conceive me" (Ps 50:7 DRA, Vulgate). The original text of the psalm does not suggest that the psalmist was sinful because his mother conceived him but that he was sinful from his conception.

works" with our representative.[2] Were Adam to live in perfect obedience to God, he could continue to live. Were Adam to disobey, he would bring death on himself and all his heirs. The human race suffers with sin and death because our first federal head betrayed the covenant of works made with God.

Although the Bible does not explicitly tell us which, if any, of these theories is correct, biblical authors stress that death and human sinfulness and guilt are a consequence of Adam's rebellious action. As Paul explains, "Just as sin entered the world through one man, and death through sin, in this way death spread to all people, because all sinned" (Rom 5:12).

Stamp Thy Image in Its Place

Sin has contaminated the entire human race, save for one individual: Jesus Christ. NT authors universally agree with this truth. Luke tells us that the favor of God was on Jesus as he grew up (Luke 2:52). Jesus was tempted by the devil but resisted every temptation (Matt 4:1–11; Mark 1:12–13; Luke 4:1–13). Those who knew him best said that he "did not commit sin, and no deceit was found in his mouth" (1 Pet 2:22) and that "there is no sin in him" (1 John 3:5). For Paul, Christ came "in the likeness of sinful flesh as a sin offering" (Rom 8:3), though he personally "did not know sin" (2 Cor 5:21).

The author of Hebrews tells us that Jesus was exactly the "kind of high priest we need: holy, innocent, undefiled, separated from sinners, and exalted above the heavens" (Heb 7:26). This high priest "has been tempted in every way as we are, yet without sin" (Heb 4:15). Like OT sacrifices without blemish (Lev 3:1, 6; 9:2–3; 23:12; Ezek 46:6), Christ "through the eternal Spirit offered himself without blemish to God" (Heb 9:14).

---

[2] Calvin, *Institutes* 2.14 (see chap. 8, n. 24).

So, how did Christ avoid the effects of sin wrought by Adam's dis-obedience in his incarnation? Many who have held to Augustine's view of natural headship—that human sin is transmitted through sexual reproduction—have argued that Jesus could not have been truly human and sinless apart from the virgin birth.[3] As Maximus the Confessor expressed this belief, "There is no human being who is sinless, since everyone is subject to the law of sexual procreation that was introduced after man's true creaturely origin in consequence of his sin."[4] Later theo-logians developed the idea that Mary herself had to be conceived without original sin through the miracle known as the "immaculate conception."[5] Neither of these doctrinal claims have direct biblical support. Both also presume speculative and unbiblical ideas about marriage and sex.[6]

Scripture's silence on the relationship between the virginal concep-tion and Adamic sin should give us some pause about establishing its necessity for Christ's sinlessness.[7] That being said, Scripture affirms both Jesus's virginal conception and his sinless human nature. So, it is wholly appropriate to infer some relationship between these two ideas, even if we are reluctant to say that the virgin birth was the only way Christ could have been sinless. As James Orr argued, even if Jesus were conceived some other way, some type of miracle would have been needed to allevi-ate the effects of Adam's sin on Jesus's human nature.[8] The idea of a man

---

[3] Anselm, *Why God Became Man* 2.16; Thomas Aquinas, *Summa theologica* IIIa q. 31, a. 7.

[4] Maximus, *Ad Thalassium* 21.

[5] See Pius IX, *Ineffabilis Deus* (December 8, 1854). This doctrine became official Roman Catholic dogma in 1854.

[6] Shenk provides a brilliant critique of these views in *The Virgin Birth of Christ*, 44–67 (see chap. 2, n. for "Answering Objections: The Genealogies").

[7] Michael F. Bird, *What Christians Ought to Believe: An Introduction to Christian Doctrine Through the Apostles' Creed* (Grand Rapids: Zondervan, 2016), 104–105.

[8] Orr, *The Virgin Birth of Christ*, 189 (see introduction, n. 6).

born without sin in this broken and fallen world is just as miraculous as the idea of a man born of a virgin.[9]

Yet as Calvin carefully explains, the divinely ordained mechanism of the virginal conception is not what ultimately keeps Christ from the corruption of Adam. Rather, the work of the Spirit does this: "For we make Christ free of all stain not just because he was begotten of his mother without copulation with man, but because he was sanctified by the Spirit in that the generation might be pure and undefiled as would have been true before Adam's fall."[10] Gabriel appears to speak of this sanctifying work in his announcement to Mary: "The Holy Spirit will come upon you . . . therefore the child to be born will be called holy" (Luke 1:35 ESV). The holiness of God the Son was by itself enough to ensure that the human nature he personalized in the incarnation was holy as he was.

Although the virginal conception was not, strictly speaking, necessary for Jesus to be sinless, it was a visible reminder that Jesus did not suffer from sin the same way every other human person does. As Calvin observed, the virginal conception did not make Jesus sinless; it drew attention to Jesus's sinlessness. "The manner of conception . . . assures us that we have a Mediator separate from sinners."[11]

Second Adam from Above

What role, then, did the virginal conception play in our salvation? Irenaeus was the first to explain their relationship in his theory of *recapitulation*. Irenaeus builds this doctrine on these themes from the writings of Paul. To *recapitulate* (or to *recap*) means to "summarize," "sum up" or to "state again." This language comes from Eph 1:10, which talks about

---

[9] Wellum, *God the Son Incarnate*, 236.

[10] Calvin, *Institutes*, 1:481 [2.13.4].

[11] John Calvin, *Commentary on a Harmony of the Evangelists Matthew, Mark, and Luke*, vol. 1, trans. William Pringle (Edinburgh, 1845), 44, quoted in Resch, *Barth's Interpretation of the Virgin Birth*, 25 (see chap. 21, n. 8).

God's plan to "sum up all things in Christ, both things in heaven and things on earth."[12] In his life of perfect obedience, Christ has summed up or recapped Adam and the whole history of humanity. Whereas the old human race was under Adam as its head, the new human race has placed itself under Christ.

The original lead of the human story (Adam) has been recast with the new lead actor (Christ). Those who place themselves under Christ have become new characters in a new story. Jesus has effectively "rebooted" Adam's race. Christ has, "in His work of recapitulation, summed up all things, both waging war against our enemy, and crushing him who had at the beginning led us away captives in Adam, and trampled upon his head."[13] Christ has dealt a fatal blow to the serpent by his obedience, his death on the cross, and his redemption of all who were formerly united to the first Adam.

A little context from Paul's thought is necessary here. In Rom 5:12–21, Paul contrasts Adam's sin with Christ's righteousness. Paul calls Adam a "type" of Christ (Rom 5:14). A "type" (*typos*) can refer to a literal mark or an indentation on a physical surface, but the Bible also uses this word to describe a pattern or an example of someone or something to come later. Adam, like Christ, entered the world without a human father. Adam and Christ are both called "[the] son of God" (Luke 3:38) but in distinct ways. Adam, like Christ, entered the world without the guilt of sin or the inclination to sin. Adam, like Christ, was the chosen representative for all humanity.

But for all Adam and Christ had in common, their actions had very different consequences. Sin and death entered the world through Adam's disobedience. All who continue to sin are cobelligerents in Adam's disobedience and share in his condemnation. But where Adam's disobedient act brought sin and death to humanity, Christ's righteous action on the

---

[12] Author's own translation. The Greek verb for *recapitulate* or "sum up" is a form of the word *anakephalaioó*.

[13] Irenaeus, *Against Heresies* 5.21.1.

cross brought justification and life for everyone who believes. "For if by the one man's trespass the many died, how much more have the grace of God and the gift that comes through the grace of the one man Jesus Christ overflowed to the many" (Rom 5:15b).

Paul picks the Adam-Christ contrast back up in his discussion of the resurrection in 1 Corinthians 15. Again, Adam's sin brought the consequence of death. Christ's resurrection from the dead secures our own future resurrection. "For just as in Adam all die, so also in Christ all will be made alive" (1 Cor 15:22). The Adam-Christ comparison is also in the background of 2 Cor 5:16–21, where Paul speaks about Christ's "ministry of reconciliation." Christ is "the one who did not know sin." Christ, like Adam, came into this world without sin, but unlike Adam, Christ remained perfectly obedient, even to the point of death. Those who are united to Christ by faith are reconciled to God and are made "the righteousness of God" (2 Cor 5:21). Our guilt by association with Adam and the old creation ends, and we become "a new creation" in Christ (2 Cor 5:17).

Irenaeus was the first theologian to draw out the importance of the virgin birth for the relationship between the two Adams. Irenaeus interprets Paul's statement "when the fulness of time had come, God sent forth his Son, born of a woman" (Gal 4:4 ESV) as the fulfillment of God's promise to put enmity between the seed of the woman and the seed of the serpent in Gen 3:15. The enemy could never be vanquished until the man "born of a woman" had conquered him. In the same way that Adam

> had his substance from untilled and as yet virgin soil . . . and was formed by the hand of God, that is, by the Word of God, "for all things were made by Him," and the Lord took dust from the earth and formed man; so did He who is the Word, recapitulating Adam in Himself, rightly receive a birth, enabling Him to gather up Adam [into Himself], from Mary, who was as yet a virgin. If, then, the first Adam had a man for his father, and was

born of human seed, it were reasonable to say that the second
Adam was begotten of Joseph.[14]

For Irenaeus, Jesus could never really recap Adam's role if he were
Joseph's (Adam's) biological son. It was only fitting that Christ become
the beginning of a new race of men.[15] If Jesus's human nature were created from the dust like Adam, there might remain some question as to
whether he was the same creature as human beings or the beginning of
a new and better species.[16] Assuming flesh from Mary meant that he
could be both the new Adam and one and the same with the present
human race.[17]

God and Sinners Reconciled

Although Irenaeus provides us with a helpful way of thinking of the big
picture story, his theory does not directly address why Jesus had to die.
So, we must also consider Christ's atoning death in the place of sinners.
Irenaeus's view that Christ had recapped the human race and triumphed
over Satan coheres well with the later views of Anselm and Calvin that
Christ ultimately died to pay our punishment. Christ was born a spotless
sacrifice without sin. But his faithful service as the New Adam (or what
we call his *active obedience*) ensured that he could pay the penalty of sin
for us on the cross (his *passive obedience*).[18] This spotless Lamb of God

---

[14] Irenaeus, *Against Heresies* 3.21.10.

[15] As Herman Bavinck (1854–1921) expressed this doctrine, "He did not
descend from Adam but was the Son of the Father, chosen from eternity to be
the head of a new covenant." Bavinck, *Reformed Dogmatics*, 3:294 (see chap. 16,
n. 18).

[16] Irenaeus, *Against Heresies* 3.21.10. As Thomas Torrance adds, "This creation then was not a *creatio ex nihilo*, but a *creatio ex virgine*, presupposing the
first creation and beginning the new creation." Torrance, *Incarnation*, 100 (see
chap. 16, n. 8).

[17] Irenaeus, *Against Heresies* 3.22.1.

[18] R. Lucas Stamps, "Irenaeus and Recapitulation," *Credo*, February 3, 2012,
https://credomag.com/2012/02/irenaeus-and-recapitulation/.

was "pierced because of our rebellion, crushed because of our iniquities," and the "punishment for our peace was on him" (Isa 53:5).

According to Luke, the same Christ who was "attested . . . by God with miracles, wonders, and signs" was ultimately "delivered up according to God's determined plan and foreknowledge," nailed to a cross and killed by lawless men (Acts 2:22–23). The virginal conception was one of many signs that pointed to his divine identity, but it ultimately served the larger purpose in his sacrificial, atoning death in the place of sinners.

The nativity story anticipates the death and resurrection of Jesus as well. The same one "born king of the Jews" (Matt 2:2) and spared from Herod's rage later stood before the Roman governor Pilate, who asked him, "Are you the king of the Jews?" (Matt 27:11). When Jesus was an infant, Gentiles fell to their knees and worshipped him (Matt 2:11), but when Jesus was an adult, Gentiles "knelt down before him and mocked him" as the "king of the Jews" (Matt 27:29). When they crucified him, they gave him the same title he was given in infancy: "This is Jesus, the King of the Jews" (Matt 27:37).

Some may find it morbid to speak about the death of Christ when we speak of his birth, to talk about how that child in the manger would eventually die an excruciating death. But understand this: The cross was never "plan-B" in the incarnation of Christ. Jesus was not the failed revolutionary Albert Schweitzer imagined him to be. The "Lamb of God" was born for the distinct purpose of taking "away the sin of the world" (John 1:29). "Christ Jesus came into the world to save sinners" (1 Tim 1:15). With his invocation of "*Tetelestai*"—"it is finished" (John 19:30)—what Jesus voiced from the cross was not the lament of agonizing defeat but the declaration of a mission accomplished.

But our salvation could not be completely rendered without another life-giving miracle: the resurrection of Jesus. The Gospels end much like they begin, with angels delivering incredible news to faithful women of God. God miraculously brought life to a virgin's womb, and later, a rich man's virgin tomb (John 19:41). The same Holy Spirit who caused Mary to conceive Jesus had now raised him from the dead (see Rom 1:4; 8:11;

1 Tim 3:16; 1 Pet 3:18). Christ's resurrection from the dead completes the sign of Jesus's virgin birth by communicating to us the identity of the child who was born to Mary.[19]

The same Spirit who caused a virgin to conceive and raised Christ from the dead now creates in us a new life through the new birth (John 1:13; 3:3; 2 Cor 5:17). "Because of his great mercy he has given us new birth into a living hope through the resurrection of Jesus Christ from the dead and into an inheritance that is imperishable, undefiled, and unfading, kept in heaven for you" (1 Pet 1:3b–4).

---

[19] Thomas F. Torrance, *Atonement: The Person and Work of Christ*, ed. Robert T. Walker (Downers Grove: IVP Academic, 2009), 218–22.

25

Joy to the World

The Two Advents of the Virgin-Born King

Let the sea and all that fills it,
the world and those who live in it, resound.
Let the rivers clap their hands;
let the mountains shout together for joy
before the Lord,
for he is coming to judge the earth.
He will judge the world righteously
and the peoples fairly.

—Psalm 98:7–9

When Isaac Watts penned "Joy to the World" in 1719, the last thing on his mind was writing one of the most beloved Christmas carols of all time. He probably was not thinking about the birth of Christ at all. Interacting with Ps 98:4–9, Watts imagined how humanity and creation will respond in the future when the Lord comes to the earth again in his glorious second coming:

> Joy to the world! the Lord is come!
>   Let earth receive her King;
> Let every heart prepare him room,
>   And heav'n and nature sing.

> Joy to the earth! the Savior reigns!
>   Let men their songs employ,
> While fields and floods, rocks, hills, and plains,
>   Repeat the sounding joy.

> No more let sins and sorrows grow,
>   Nor thorns infest the ground;
> He comes to make his blessings flow
>   Far as the curse is found.

> He rules the world with truth and grace,
>   And makes the nations prove
> The glories of his righteousness,
>   And wonders of his love.

Notice why heaven and nature are singing here, why fields and floods repeat the sounding joy. They are not singing or rejoicing because Jesus has been born. Nature is celebrating its future release from the curse of Adam's sin! "No more let sins and sorrows grow, nor thorns infest the ground." Christ has come again to make his blessings flow as "far as the curse is found." In that future moment, all creation will join together in a chorus of praise because Christ has finally returned to vanquish sin, sorrow, and death. Joy to the world indeed!

Even if the words of "Joy to the World" are not really about the birth of Christ, they remind us that Christ came into our world in the past to redeem our future. The biblical nativity stories do the same thing. They narrate how the Word became flesh, assumed the form of a servant, and became Immanuel for us in a virgin's womb. But they also anticipate the future enthronement and rule of the eternal king, when through Christ God will restore creation and bring blessing and peace to his people. The first advent of Christ sets the stage for what will inevitably follow in his second advent.

God Rules as King

We cannot begin to wrap our minds around the mission and message of Jesus without having a firm grasp on what he meant by the "kingdom of God" (or in Matthew's Gospel, the "kingdom of heaven"). Jesus said his purpose was "to proclaim the good news about the kingdom of God" (Luke 4:43). As Matthew summarized Jesus's ministry, he went "to all the towns and villages, teaching in their synagogues, preaching the good news of the kingdom, and healing every disease and every sickness" (Matt 9:35). The "good news" or "gospel" is about the kingdom.

So, what is this "kingdom" Jesus refers to? The kingdom of God is not like the Magic Kingdom in Orlando or even the kingdom of Israel. The kingdom of heaven is not a geopolitical territory. It is also important to not confuse the kingdom of heaven with the eternal home of believers in heaven. The operative word Jesus uses here is "kingdom" or "kingship," which describes the activity of God from heaven. Whenever Jesus speaks about the "kingdom of God" or the "kingdom of heaven," he describes the sovereign rule of God over all things and the hearts of his people. This rule of God is both internal and external. It is internal in the sense that God rules over the hearts of all believers who know Christ as Lord. The kingdom is also external because God rules over everything and everyone in this world—even those who do not yet acknowledge his rule.[1]

Jesus launched the kingdom of God with his first coming in the incarnation. To be clear, God has always reigned as the sovereign king

---

[1] Quarles, *A Theology of Matthew*, 86–87 (see chap. 7, n. 13).

over all creation because everything and everyone already belongs to him (see 1 Chr 29:11–12).[2] But when Jesus came into the world, he revealed to us what the kingdom of God was like and made a way for us to enter it. Jesus showed us that the kingdom of God was not drawn around geographical boundaries like the kingdoms of men. God may rule over all people, but not everyone belongs to his kingdom. Not everyone lives as if God is their king. But those who do live under God's rule love him and seek his kingdom first in every aspect of their lives.

Jesus had much to say about how we "enter" the kingdom of God. We come under God's kingdom when we do his will (Matt 7:21) and keep his commandments (Matt 19:17). We cannot come under God's rule unless we exercise childlike trust (Matt 18:3; Mark 10:5). We "enter" God's kingdom by renouncing the wealth and riches of this world as sources of ultimate satisfaction (Matt 19:23–24; Mark 10:25; Luke 18:24–25). Because we are sinners who cannot save ourselves, we can only enter the kingdom of God when we recognize Christ as Lord and entrust our lives to him in faith (Rom 10:9–13). Through Christ's finished work on the cross, God "has rescued us from the domain of darkness and transferred us into the kingdom of the Son he loves" (Col 1:13).

Yet an important tension punctuates Jesus's entire teaching about the kingdom of God: The kingdom of God is already here but has not yet come. Jesus told us to repent because "the kingdom of heaven is at hand" (Matt 3:2 ESV; see also Matt 4:17; 10:7; Mark 1:15). The idiom "at hand" means something near to us. We can reach out and touch the kingdom of God now because it is at hand, already present in our midst (Luke 17:21). Because of Jesus's birth, life, teaching, death for sinners, and resurrection, we can now live under the kingdom of God.

---

[2] As Abraham Kuyper (1837–1920) described this external kingdom, "There is not a square inch in the whole domain of our human existence over which Christ, who is Sovereign over *all*, does not cry: 'Mine!'" Abraham Kuyper, "Sphere Sovereignty," in *Abraham Kuyper: A Centennial Reader*, ed. James D. Bratt (Grand Rapids: Eerdmans, 1998), 461.

But this kingdom will not be fully realized until Christ "comes in his glory" and sits "on his glorious throne" (Matt 25:31). Then and only then will Gabriel's promise to the virgin finally be fulfilled: "He will be great and will be called the Son of the Most High, and the Lord God will give him the throne of his father David. He will reign over the house of Jacob forever, and his kingdom will have no end" (Luke 1:32–33).

Isaiah promised that a "child will be born for us, a son will be given to us" (Isa 9:6) and that "he will reign on the throne of David and over his kingdom" (Isa 9:7). Immanuel has already been born for us, but we still await the future kingdom of the Prince of Peace. In the future, the present "kingdom of the world" will be seized by the "kingdom of our Lord and of his Christ, and he will reign forever and ever" (Rev 11:15). Isaiah gives us a clear picture of what this future reign of Christ will look like:

> Then a shoot will grow from the stump of Jesse,
> and a branch from his roots will bear fruit.
> The Spirit of the LORD will rest on him—
> a Spirit of wisdom and understanding,
> a Spirit of counsel and strength,
> a Spirit of knowledge and of the fear of the LORD.
> His delight will be in the fear of the LORD.
> He will not judge
> by what he sees with his eyes,
> he will not execute justice
> by what he hears with his ears,
> but he will judge the poor righteously
> and execute justice for the oppressed of the land.
> He will strike the land
> with a scepter from his mouth,
> and he will kill the wicked
> with a command from his lips.
> Righteousness will be a belt around his hips;
> faithfulness will be a belt around his waist.

The wolf will dwell with the lamb,

and the leopard will lie down with the goat.

The calf, the young lion, and the fattened calf will be together,

and a child will lead them.

The cow and the bear will graze,

their young ones will lie down together,

and the lion will eat straw like cattle.

An infant will play beside the cobra's pit,

and a toddler will put his hand into a snake's den.

They will not harm or destroy each other

on my entire holy mountain,

for the land will be as full

of the knowledge of the Lord

as the sea is filled with water.

On that day the root of Jesse

will stand as a banner for the peoples.

The nations will look to him for guidance,

and his resting place will be glorious. (Isaiah 11)

The "Righteous Branch" of David "will reign wisely as king and administer justice and righteousness" (Jer 23:5; see also Jer 33:15). The sevenfold Spirit of God will rest on him (Isa 11:1–2; Rev 1:4).[3] The "mountains [will] shout together for joy before the Lord" (Ps 98:8b–9) and the "desert . . . will also rejoice with joy and singing" (Isa 35:1b–2). The curse on creation will finally be lifted, and creation will be at perfect peace (Isa 11:6–10). The peace between God and men that a host of heaven promised a group of shepherds will finally be seen by all (Luke 2:14).

---

[3] See Brandon D. Smith, *The Trinity in the Book of Revelation: Seeing Father, Son, and Holy Spirit in John's Apocalypse* (Downers Grove: IVP Academic, 2022), 151–65.

The Church Between Two Advents

In his first advent, Christ launched the church. In Christ, God made a new people for himself—a people made up of Jews and Gentiles alike. This incarnate Word has saved "his people from their sins" (Matt 1:21) and given "peace on earth to people he favors" (Luke 2:14). By his blood, this Lamb of God has "purchased people . . . from every tribe and language and people and nation." He "made them a kingdom and priests to our God" (Rev 5:9–10; cf. Rev 1:6). These people, Christ's church, constitute the body (1 Cor 12:12–30) and bride of Christ (Rev 19:7; 21:9). Though the church is called a "kingdom" of priests, we must not confuse the church with the kingdom of God. Instead, the church was created by God to be a witness to the kingdom and the instrument of the kingdom on the earth.[4]

The church lives between two advents—in a period of time the Bible calls "the last days." The "last days" began 2,000 years ago at Pentecost (Acts 2:17) and will end when the Lord appears again. In these last days, evil men rage against God and his people (2 Tim 3:1–9; 2 Pet 3:3–7; Jas 5:1–6). But we know that Christ will soon bring about "the restoration of all things, which God spoke about through his holy prophets from the beginning" (Acts 3:21). Christ did not leave us as orphans in this period of time between his two advents: he has given us the Holy Spirit and his peace (John 14:18, 26–27).

In the second advent, Christ will finally and completely deliver his church from sin, sickness, and suffering. Christ "will appear a second time, not to bear sin, but to bring salvation to those who are waiting for him" (Heb 9:28). He will reward "all those who have loved his appearing" with the crown of righteousness (2 Tim 4:8). We will marvel at him and glorify him when our faith becomes sight (2 Thess 1:10). For those who belong to his church, "the appearing of the glory of our great God and Savior,

---

[4] See George Eldon Ladd, *Jesus and the Kingdom: The Eschatology of Biblical Realism* (New York: Harper & Row, 1964), 259–73.

Jesus Christ" is our "blessed hope" (Titus 2:13). We all long for the heavenly celebration that will ensue when we all party like it's Rev 19:9 at "the
marriage feast of the Lamb!"

In his second advent, the kingdom of God will be realized and brought to a
state of perfection for all to see. When he returns bodily and visibly to judge
this world, everyone will finally recognize him as God and King. When
Christ judges the world, it will be known to all that God's people were
on the "right side of history" all along. The Messiah will vindicate the
afflicted and crush the opposition (Ps 72:1–4). Those who do not know
Christ will "beat their chests," mourning their disobedience and judgment (Matt 24:30). But those who know Christ will receive a precious
reward as his co-regents:

> Truly I tell you, in the renewal of all things, when the Son of
> Man sits on his glorious throne, you who have followed me will
> also sit on twelve thrones, judging the twelve tribes of Israel. And
> everyone who has left houses or brothers or sisters or father or
> mother or children or fields because of my name will receive a
> hundred times more and will inherit eternal life. But many who
> are first will be last, and the last first. (Matt 19:28–30; cf. Obad
> 21; Luke 22:30; Rev 4:4–10)

The apostle Paul describes the future event following the resurrection when the kingdom of the Davidic Messiah is given back to God.

> Then comes the end, when he hands over the kingdom to God
> the Father, when he abolishes all rule and all authority and power.
> For he must reign until he puts all his enemies under his feet.
> The last enemy to be abolished is death. For **God has put every-**
> **thing under his feet.** Now when it says "everything" is put under
> him, it is obvious that he who puts everything under him is the
> exception. When everything is subject to Christ, then the Son
> himself will also be subject to the one who subjected everything
> to him, so that God may be all in all. (1 Cor 15:24–28)

Some interpreters have used this text to suggest that God the Son is or somehow will be subordinate to the Father in eternity future. This interpretation is fraught with problems because it suggests that God the Son is a lesser rank than the Father.

Remember that some biblical texts about Christ describe his divine nature, some his human nature, and others both natures. Whether a text refers to the human nature of Christ or to his divine nature, these texts refer to the same divine-human Person. Partitive exegesis helps us distinguish between which texts relate to his divinity and which relate to his humanity. We must understand this future event to describe Christ in his humanity finally abolishing all human authority and power, handing the keys of the kingdom back to God "so that God may be all in all" (1 Cor 15:28). The paradox of the incarnation is that God the eternal Son became the human Son of God in time. Christ became a human son and a human king to redeem broken and sinful humanity. God the Son became a human ruler so that all human authority would come under God again.[5] Even with the human nature of Jesus placed under submission to God, Jesus will, as Gabriel promised, "reign over the house of Jacob forever, and his kingdom will have no end" (Luke 1:33).[6]

My Redeemer Will Stand on the Earth

Under the old covenant, prophets of Israel were only given glimpses into the glory that awaited the world in the incarnation of Christ. The virgin birth was a fitting sign of the uniqueness of Christ, but only a young virgin really knew she conceived apart from marital congress. The incarnation was a sign witnessed only by a relatively small portion of

---

[5] See Basil of Caesarea, *Against Eunomius* 1.16; Augustine, *On the Trinity* 1.15, 20. See also D. Glenn Butner, Jr., *The Son Who Learned Obedience: A Theological Case Against the Eternal Submission of the Son* (Eugene, OR: Pickwick, 2018), 162–72.

[6] Emery, *The Trinity*, 74 (see chap. 22, n. 4).

human beings throughout history, but "blessed are those who have not seen and yet believe" (John 20:29). Only about 500 people saw the sign of the resurrection for themselves (1 Cor 15:6). But there is a final sign coming, when

> **He is coming with the clouds,**
> and **every eye will see him,**
> **even those who pierced him.**
> **And all the tribes** of the earth
> **will mourn over him.** (Rev 1:7; cf. Zech 12:10)

Though we suffer in this present life, we can confess with Job hopeful expectation that we will see our embodied Redeemer standing on the earth at the end of this age:

> I know that my Redeemer lives,
> and at the end he will stand on the dust.
> Even after my skin has been destroyed,
> yet I will see God in my flesh.
> I will see him myself;
> my eyes will look at him, and not as a stranger.
> My heart longs within me. (Job 19:25–27)

The signs that began in Israel and were manifested in the earthly ministry of Jesus will culminate in his glorious revealing (1 Thess 5:23; 1 John 2:28). Unlike the first coming through a virgin womb, no one will be able to deny this manifestation of God the Son. No one will be able to hide. Every eye will see, and every ear will hear. "Every knee will bow—in heaven and on earth and under the earth—and every tongue will confess that Jesus Christ is Lord, to the glory of God the Father" (Phil 2:10–11).

Conclusion

Come Let Us Adore Him

You are good, and you do what is good; teach me your statutes.
–Psalm 119:68

C hristian theology involves critical and organized reflection on God's self-revelation for the purpose of growing in Christ and making disciples. The doctrinal truths gleaned from the study of theology grow God's people in knowledge, spiritual maturity, and obedience.[1] In other words, with Christian doctrine, head knowledge becomes heart knowledge.

At the end of this exploration of the nativity stories in the NT and the Christmas story in the Christian tradition, I would suggest that any reflection on the person and work of Christ is about these ends. We learn about Christ so that we can learn to treasure Christ as his followers. The good news of Christ's virginal conception plays a vital role in our formation as his disciples.

---

[1] See Rhyne R. Putman, *The Method of Christian Theology: A Basic Introduction* (Nashville: B&H Academic, 2021), 44.

First, the good news about the virginal conception of Jesus reshapes the way we see the whole biblical story. From Genesis to Revelation, Scripture reveals one overarching story about the triune God that reaches its dramatic climax in the incarnation of Christ Jesus. In the first act of this story, the same Creator God who created life in a virgin's womb created this world with his infinite power and wisdom. In the second act, God chose a people for himself in Israel and made a series of covenants and promises to the nation and individuals within it, all of which are fulfilled by the baby born in Bethlehem. In the third act, God himself entered humanity and forever became Immanuel, God with us in true humanity. In the fourth act, Immanuel has commissioned his people to proclaim the good news of the coming kingdom—not only to Israel but also the same Gentiles to whom he manifested himself as a child. Even though he is in heaven, the incarnate Lord is still mysteriously God with us in the church. In the fifth and final act of the biblical story, the kingdom of the virgin-born king will be known by all people everywhere in his second glorious advent.

Second, the good news about the virginal conception of Jesus reshapes the way we answer life's biggest questions. The question "Who am I?" is a question about what it means to be human. Although Jesus certainly did not come into the world the same way ordinary human beings do, he put what true, created humanity was meant to be on display for us. He revealed what it meant to grow in wisdom, in stature, and in favor with God and others. He showed us what our own redeemed humanity could look like without the corruption of sin and death. And he showed us the life that lies ahead of us in his eternal kingdom.

The question "Where am I?" addresses the type of world in which we live. Do we live in a world without purpose or design, where everything that happens is a result of random chance? Or do we live in a world where the major events and minutiae of history are orchestrated by God to accomplish his intentions for it? The nativity stories of the NT show us that nothing in this world is outside of the control of God. The natural processes of human reproduction, the affairs of kings and emperors, and individual lives are guided by his caring and providential hand.

The question "What's wrong?" helps us navigate the existential crisis we all find ourselves in when we look at the world around us that is broken by sin, sickness, evil, and death. The nativity stories are set in a world where men and women lived with hope and expectation that God would finally break this cycle of suffering and injustice. Even as an infant, Jesus faced great danger from those who opposed his rule as king.

The question "What's the solution?" asks what hope we have in this fallen world. The nativity stories are clear: Christ did not come into this world to offer us political salvation. He entered a virgin womb to reveal God's kingdom to us and to reverse the curse for us. Through his suffering on our behalf, Christ has taken the penalty of our sin for us and become the head of a new human race that exists for his glory.

Third, the story of the virginal conception reshapes our ethics and the way we live our lives as followers of Jesus. Many in early and medieval Christianity understood the primary moral takeaway of the virginal conception to be God's desire for us to be chaste or abstinent—even refraining from sex in marriage. But the primary way Mary succeeded as the "New Eve" where the "Old Eve" failed was not in her perpetual sexual chastity but in her unflinching obedience to God's request of her: "I am the Lord's servant. . . . May it happen to me as you have said" (Luke 1:38).

The nativity stories feature many other characters whose faithfulness we should seek to emulate.[2] Joseph modeled obedience to God as a husband and father. The shepherds give us a strategy for evangelism: to encounter Jesus, to exalt Jesus, and to tell people the good news about Jesus. Simeon and Anna show us what life in the Spirit looks like as we eagerly await the advent of the Lord. The magi who brought their gifts before Christ show us that God can save anyone—even godless pagans.

---

[2] See Daniel Darling, *The Characters of Christmas: The Unlikely People Caught Up in the Story of Jesus* (Chicago: Moody, 2019).

The nativity stories color our views of human dignity. If God used shepherds spurned by society to be his witnesses, we should recognize in every human image bearer an opportunity to serve God with gladness. God showed that Zechariah and Elizabeth had dignity and worth, even in their advanced age and childlessness. If the Lord of glory was himself a true human being from the moment of conception, so too are other unborn children. If John the Baptist leapt for joy in the presence of Christ, we know that God cares for unborn image bearers in the world today.

Finally, the good news of the virgin-born king reshapes the affections of our heart and our devotional practices. Luke's story emphasizes the affectionate response of those who encounter Christ. Mary magnified the Lord and rejoiced in his attributes and activity with the totality of her being—her heart, her mind, and her speech. She treasured the truths of God's Word and God's work in her heart and mind. Elizabeth radiated joy when the Holy Spirit filled her. Zechariah blessed the God of Israel for his faithfulness to the covenant promises made to Israel. Enthusiastic shepherds glorified and praised God for "all the things they had seen and heard" (Luke 2:20). The sight of Jesus was enough to make Simeon content enough to die happy because nothing else in this world mattered to him after he held that baby boy in his arms. Anna thanked God for hearing the cries of his people.

In advent and Christmas seasons, we have an opportunity to reflect on what God has done for us in the virgin-born king and what he will do for us in the future. We rehearse the OT story, reliving the expectation of Israel as we await the final consummation of God's kingdom in Christ. At the heart of the Christmas story is a profoundly theological message about the triune God and his great salvation. We do not study these things lightly or treat them as mere intellectual curiosities. Instead, with transformed minds and hearts, we offer the same kind of affectionate response of praise that was offered by those who first encountered him.

O come, let us adore him,
O come, let us adore him,
O come, let us adore him,
Christ the Lord.

For he alone is worthy,
For he alone is worthy,
For he alone is worthy,
Christ the Lord.

Let's praise his name together,
Let's praise his name together,
Let's praise his name together,
Christ the Lord.

We'll give him all the glory,
We'll give him all the glory,
We'll give him all the glory,
Christ the Lord.

Appendix 1

A Harmony of the Nativity Stories

A fact must be established by the testimony of two or three witnesses.

—DEUTERONOMY 19:15B

We can read the Gospels in one of two basic ways: *vertically* or *horizontally*. Vertical readings study one Gospel at a time, examining the book from top to bottom. This is the normal way we read books of the Bible (or any other work of literature). Vertical approaches take a deep dive into an individual Gospel and focus on its purpose, arrangement, and unique themes. A vertical reading of Matthew might trace this Gospel's unique emphasis on the way Jesus fulfilled OT prophecy or the importance of discipleship. A vertical reading of Luke may highlight this Gospel's exclusive focus on the work of the Spirit among God's new people.

By contrast, horizontal readings of the Gospels read stories from the Gospels side by side to compare their similarities and differences.

Horizontal readings can help us discover the distinctive theological themes of the Gospels—i.e., why one Evangelist makes a big deal of something in the story that the other Evangelists downplay or overlook.

The historical investigation of the Gospels also requires horizontal reading. By reading the parallel stories of the Gospels, we can piece together an account of what really happened "behind the text." Horizontal readings are especially useful in the task of *harmonizing the Gospels*—showing how the stories from Jesus's life across all four Gospels fit together. Although harmonization can be misused, this task is especially important for the nativity stories often accused of contradictions and wholesale fabrications. Demonstrating that the nativity narratives do not contradict one another does not conclusively prove their historicity, but two contradictory accounts cannot be true. If Matthew and Luke provide truthful accounts of the details surrounding Jesus's birth, their accounts will be compatible with one another.

To get the full picture of what the Bible teaches about the virginal conception and birth of Jesus, we will need to approach these stories horizontally, side by side. As J. Gresham Machen noted, neither nativity story completely makes sense without the other.[1] Without Luke's Gospel, we would have no idea about Mary's feelings or motivations. Without Matthew's account, it would be unclear to us why Joseph would want to hang around after discovering this pregnancy. Without both accounts, we would struggle to understand the timeline of when Mary knew and why Joseph did not know right away. Only Luke's Gospel tells us when and how Jesus was born. Only Luke tells us about the response of faithful Jewish people to the news of Jesus's birth. Matthew alone explains the hostile political climate that Jesus would have faced if the rumor got out that the Messiah was born in Bethlehem.

---

[1] Machen, *The Virgin Birth of Christ*, 195–96 (see introduction, n. 6).

Text	Description
Luke 1:5–23	Gabriel announced the conception and birth of John to Zechariah in the temple.
Luke 1:24–25	Elizabeth conceived John and went into seclusion for five months.
Luke 1:26–38	In Nazareth, Gabriel announced the conception and birth of Jesus to Mary.
Luke 1:39–56	Mary stayed with her relative Elizabeth for the first three months of her pregnancy.
Matt 1:18–19	Mary returned to Nazareth where Joseph learned about her pregnancy.
Matt 1:20–24a	Joseph was visited by an angel in a dream who told him that Mary's child is from the Holy Spirit.
Matt 1:24b–25	Joseph and Mary were married but did not consummate their marriage at that time.
Luke 1:57–80	John was born, and Zechariah spoke the *Benedictus*.
Luke 2:1–7	Joseph and Mary traveled to Bethlehem for the census. While they were there, Mary gave birth to Jesus and laid him in a manger.
Luke 2:8–20	The angels announced the birth of Jesus to the shepherds, and the shepherds confirmed that report.
Luke 2:21	Jesus was circumcised and named eight days after his birth.
Luke 2:22–38	Jesus was presented in the temple forty days after his birth. Mary underwent the purification ritual. Simeon and Anna prophesied over Jesus. We presume Luke 2:39 does not mean that the holy family immediately returned to Nazareth. Instead, the holy family stayed in Bethlehem until the flight to Egypt in Matt 2:13–15.

Matt 2:1–8	The magi arrived in Jerusalem looking for the child who was born to be the king of the Jews. They met King Herod, who inquired about where the Messiah was supposed to be born.
Matt 2:9–11	The magi were led to the house in Bethlehem where the holy family was staying.
Matt 2:12	After being warned by God, the magi returned east but avoided crossing paths with Herod.
Matt 2:13–15	After being warned by God in a dream, Joseph fled with Mary and Jesus to Egypt.
Matt 2:16–18	Herod ordered the slaughter of all male children in and around Bethlehem who were two years old or younger.
Matt 2:19–23 Luke 2:39–40	After the death of Herod the Great, Joseph and the holy family returned to Nazareth.
Luke 2:41–52	The holy family visited Jerusalem for the Passover when Jesus was twelve years old. They returned to Nazareth after Jesus was discovered in the temple.

Appendix 2

Marian Dogma and the Sufficiency of Scripture

> All Scripture is inspired by God and is profitable for teaching, for
> rebuking, for correcting, for training in righteousness, so that the
> man of God may be complete, equipped for every good work.
> —2 Timothy 3:16–17

We cannot speak of the impact of the virgin birth on the Christian tradition without some mention of Marian dogmas—those unique doctrines mainly held by the Roman Catholic and Eastern Orthodox churches that specifically pertain to the virgin Mary. Protestant and evangelical Christians typically reject these doctrines because we have different conceptions of theological method, the authority of Scripture, and church tradition.

Early Christian theologians called Mary the "God-Bearer" or "Mother of God" (*Theotokos*) because she bore God the Son in her body, but this designation was less about Mary and more about the baby she carried in her womb. That distinction gradually changed over time.

Medieval theologians formulated more doctrines about Mary herself, what theologians call "Mariology."[1] To explain how Jesus was protected from the original sin of Adam, medieval theologians developed the idea that Mary herself was conceived by her parents without sin in the *immaculate conception*.

To explain how a woman who lived without the effects of sin would transition to heaven, Catholics later developed the idea of the *assumption of Mary*. This doctrine taught that she was taken up into heaven in a manner like Jesus's ascension so that her body never would have decayed or turned into ashes.[2] In the previous two centuries, Roman Catholic popes have declared these doctrines to be infallible dogma that all Catholics must affirm.

But the doctrine most relevant to our present topic is the Marian dogma of *perpetual virginity*. All orthodox Christians acknowledge that Mary conceived Jesus as a virgin before giving birth to him (*virginitas ante partum*). But Roman Catholic, Eastern Orthodox, and some Protestant and evangelical Christians also assert that Mary miraculously retained her virginity during birth (*virginitas in partu*) and remained a virgin for the rest of her life after the birth of Jesus (*virginitas post partum*). This view runs deep in the tradition. Many patristic and medieval theologians affirmed Mary's status as the "ever-virgin."[3] And perhaps to the

---

[1] See von Campenhausen, *The Virgin Birth in the Theology of the Ancient Church*, 71–86; Jaroslav Pelikan, *Mary Through the Centuries: Her Place in the History of Culture*, rev. ed. (New Haven, CT: Yale University Press, 1998).

[2] Pius XII, *Munificentissimus Deus* (November 1, 1950). See also Matthew Levering, *Mary's Bodily Assumption* (Notre Dame, IN: University of Notre Dame Press, 2014). Catholics disagree about whether she died before her body was assumed into heaven. Eastern Orthodox churches teach a similar yet distinctive doctrine: the "dormition of Mary." The dormition of Mary is the idea that Mary died peacefully before being resurrected like Jesus and ascending to heaven. See Brian J. Daley, ed., *On the Dormition of Mary: Early Patristic Homilies* (Yonkers, NY: St Vladmir's Seminary Press, 1997).

[3] See Clement of Alexandria, *Stromata* 7.16; Origen, *Commentary on Romans* 3.10; Jerome, *Against Helvidius*; Gregory of Nazianzus, *Moral Poems*

surprise of many of their theological heirs, so did Protestant Reformers like Luther, Zwingli, and (possibly) Calvin.[4]

The debate over Mary's perpetual virginity can be highly contentious—especially between Roman Catholic and Protestant polemicists. Because I learn much from Roman Catholic thinkers, I certainly do not intend to provoke such hostility here. My primary concern is to talk about differences in our respective theological methodologies and doctrines of Scripture. The perpetual virginity doctrine presents an interesting test case for this comparison because of its strong footing in extrabiblical tradition.

The doctrine of the perpetual virginity appeared first in noncanonical religious texts like *The First Gospel of James* or *The Odes of Solomon*. Its first appearances in theological writings, in the work of Alexandrian theologians Clement (c. 150–215) and Origen (c. 185–253), appeal explicitly to *The First Gospel of James* as an authority on this matter. This doctrine took even longer to develop in Western, Latin speaking Christianity. Figures like Tertullian celebrated the virginity of Mary prior to the birth of Jesus but also celebrated the holy, monogamous consummation of Mary and Joseph's marriage after Jesus's birth.[5]

Was Jesus's Birth Miraculous?

The primary miracle of Matthew's and Luke's nativity stories is the virginal conception of Jesus, but those who affirm the perpetual virginity of

---

1; Gregory of Nyssa, *On Virginity*; Gregory of Nyssa, *Homily on the Nativity*; Augustine, *Sermon* 186.1; Gregory the Great, *Morals on the Book of Job* 24.3; Thomas Aquinas, *Summa theologica* IIIa q. 28, a. 2–4; Pseudo-Athanasius, *On Virginity* 77–81.

[4] Martin Luther, "That Jesus Was Born a Jew," trans. Walther I. Brandt in *LW* 45, 205–6; Ulrich Zwingli, "Ein predig von der reinen gotzgebärerin Maria," *Zwingli Opera* (Berlin, 1905), 1:399–428, esp. 424–28; Calvin, *Calvin's Commentaries*, 16/1, 107 (see chap. 13, n. 2).

[5] Tertullian, *On Monogamy*.

Mary also contend that Mary supernaturally gave birth without painful labor—a true miracle in a time before epidurals or modern anesthesia. They also argue that Jesus somehow passed through Mary's birth canal without breaking her hymen because they believe the hymen to be the physical token of female virginity (see Deut 22:15–17).

Because the Gospels are silent about this matter, defenders of Mary's perpetual virginity must appeal to other passages in support of their position. Passages about the new Jerusalem and the heavenly temple are often understood as allegories about Mary's perpetual virginity and painless birth (Isa 66:7; Ezek 44:2).[6] Roman Catholics also appeal to Gen 3:16, which indicates that labor pains are a consequence of the curse on creation:

> I will intensify your labor pains;
> you will bear children with painful effort.
> Your desire will be for your husband,
> yet he will rule over you.

For many Roman Catholic interpreters, Eve's curse was reversed in the birth of Jesus. Eve was a sinner, and consequently, her labor was painful. Mary's labor, on the other hand, was painless because as the "New Eve," she was protected from the effects of sin in her "immaculate conception."[7]

Popular religious texts in the early second century like the *Ascension of Isaiah* (c. AD 150) and *The Odes of Solomon* (c. AD 125) promoted the idea that Mary had a miraculous, pain-free delivery (*in partu*). In the *Ascension of Isaiah*, the infant Jesus miraculously appears in the home of Mary and Joseph. Mary's womb was instantaneously vacated, and no

---

[6] See Irenaeus, *On Apostolic Preaching* 54; Gregory of Nyssa, *On the Song of Songs* 13.

[7] See Irenaeus, *Against Heresies* 3.22.1. The idea that Mary was the "New Eve" has its origins in second-century patristic teaching.

midwife was needed.[8] A similar account of Mary's painless labor without a handmaiden appears in the poetry collection *The Odes of Solomon.*[9]

Yet the most important source for the perpetual virginity doctrine is a mid-second-century apocryphal gospel called *The First Gospel of James* (not to be confused with the New Testament letter of James). This forged gospel claims James, the brother of Jesus, as its author (*Prot. Jas* 24). Part of this book acts as a prequel to Matthew's and Luke's nativity stories, providing an account of Mary's family, her own miraculous conception, and her childhood service in the temple. The other part of the book provides alternate accounts of the annunciation, Joseph's discovery, Jesus's birth, the visit of the magi, and Herod's slaughter of the innocents. The book features many fantastic elements, like time literally standing still (*Prot. Jas* 18), Zechariah's blood being turned to stone (*Prot. Jas* 24), and a mountain that opens to receive Elizabeth and baby John (*Prot. Jas* 22).

The clear but unstated purpose of this book is to defend Mary's perpetual virginity. The author depicts Joseph as an older widower who agrees to wed the young virgin Mary, but the relationship is more akin to legal guardianship than a marriage. The author claims that Joseph had grown sons from a previous marriage, providing a half-baked explanation for how Mary could remain a virgin and Jesus still have "brothers" (though it does not account for Jesus's sisters).

In this account, Mary and Joseph traveled to Bethlehem with Joseph's sons. There is no mention of an inn or a crowded guest room. Mary and Joseph sought shelter in a nearby cave when her contractions began. Joseph went to find a midwife to help him deliver the child, but when they returned,

> A luminous cloud overshadowed the cave. And the midwife said: My soul has been magnified this day, because my eyes have seen

---

[8] *Ascension of Isaiah* 11.2–16; cf. Perry, *Mary for Evangelicals,* 124 (see chap. 17, n. 2).

[9] *Odes of Solomon* 19.1–9.

strange things—because salvation has been brought forth to Israel. And immediately the cloud disappeared out of the cave, and a great light shone in the cave, so that the eyes could not bear it. And in a little that light gradually decreased, until the infant appeared, and went and took the breast from His mother Mary. (*Prot. Jas* 19)

Luke spoke of the Holy Spirit overshadowing Mary like a cloud (Luke 1:35), but the author here describes a literal cloud overshadowing the cave where Jesus was born. When the cloud was lifted, Jesus was somehow beamed up to Mary's breast. The implication? Jesus was not delivered through Mary's birth canal at all. He simply appeared on the other side of Mary's womb, like when he appeared behind closed doors after the resurrection (see John 20:19).

The astonished midwife went to report this miraculous birth to her friend Salome. Salome balked at the story in doubting Thomas-like fashion, saying, "Unless I thrust in my finger, and search the parts, I will not believe that a virgin has brought forth." (*Prot. Jas* 19:19; cf. John 20:25). So, Salome and the midwife returned to Mary and instructed her to position herself for a gynecological examination. When Salome attempted to inspect Mary, her hand was consumed with fire. Salome then repented for her unbelief, and an angel of the Lord healed her hand.

As Tim Perry rightly notes, texts like these may give us a better window into the popular beliefs of the church than the more well-known theological texts of Ignatius, Irenaeus, and Justin Martyr (the same is still true today: the local Walmart stocks the "Christian literature" racks in their stores with prosperity preachers, *Left Behind*, and novels about Amish women, not serious works in biblical studies or Christian theology[10]). Although these texts have little or no historical value in understanding what actually happened to Jesus and the holy family, they do

---

[10] Perry, *Mary for Evangelicals*, 123–26.

convey more evidence that the virginal conception tradition was widespread by the mid-second century.

Luke, the only biblical author to provide an account of Jesus's actual birth, says nothing about a miraculous delivery whatsoever. Had he believed that this occurred, it seems likely that he would have included it in his account of this specific event. Furthermore, his inclusion of Mary's purification sacrifice contradicts the idea that Mary had anything other than a natural birth. The Levitical law specifically states that a new mother "will continue in purification from her bleeding" at least forty days (Lev 12:2–4). If Mary did not bleed or deliver Jesus naturally, she would have no need for the purification ritual that followed Jesus's birth (Luke 2:22–24). The extrabiblical tradition of Jesus's supernatural birth simply does not coincide with the facts of the biblical narrative. This miraculous birth story also reads more like the gnostic idea that Christ simply "passed through Mary" than a perspective that preserves Jesus's true humanity.

Were Joseph and Mary Really Married?

Defenders of Mary's perpetual virginity contend that Joseph and Mary's marriage was merely a legal arrangement, a legal fiction of sorts. Joseph and Mary were not "husband" and "wife" in the traditional sense of those words because they never consummated their marriage (see Gen 2:24–25; 4:1; 24:67).

The primary biblical text used in this debate is Matt 1:24–25, where the Evangelist states that Joseph "took his wife but knew her not until she had given birth to a son" (ESV). The natural reading of this text would suggest that Joseph took Mary to live with him but did not have sex with her until after Jesus was born. After Jesus's birth (or the forty days of her purification were complete), Joseph and Mary began a normal sexual relationship that produced several other children.

In his fourth-century defense of Mary's perpetual virginity, Jerome mounted a complex argument against this reading that hangs on the word "until" (*heós*).[11] Jerome observed that "until" (*heós*) can denote either (1) a fixed time with a definite end point or (2) an indefinite period with no end in sight. Matthew uses "until" (*heós*) both ways. He notes that Joseph stayed in Egypt "until Herod's death" (Matt 2:15), indicating that Joseph's stay in Egypt had a termination point in Herod's death. In Matt 28:20, Jesus promises his disciples that he is always with us, "until (*heós*) the end of the world." Of this indefinite usage, Jerome rightly observes, Jesus did not say that he would be with us until the end of the world and then abandon us.[12]

When Matthew says Joseph "did not know" or "did not have sexual relations" with Mary, does the Evangelist use "until" with a definite end in sight (until after Jesus was born) or indefinitely (even after Jesus was born)? Catholic apologists often answer with the latter: Joseph never knew Mary, even after Jesus was born. By contrast, evangelical scholars have convincingly argued that the particular Greek phrase used in Matt 1:25 (*heós hou*) always has a temporal connotation in the NT.[13] But as Catholic NT scholar Raymond Brown rightly noted, this question of Mary's sexual status after giving birth to Jesus was not Matthew's primary concern in this text. In this immediate context, the Evangelist was simply trying to show how Jesus fulfilled the prophetic words of Isa 7:14.[14]

Who Were Jesus's "Brothers" and "Sisters"?

Proponents of Mary's perpetual virginity also teach that Mary remained a virgin for the rest of her life, even after the birth (*post partu*) of her

---

[11] Jerome, *Against Helvidius* 6–7; cf. John Chrysostom, *Homily on Matthew* 5.3.

[12] See Jerome, *Against Helvidius* 6. Jerome also uses this indefinite sense of "until" to explain the enduring reign of Christ in 1 Cor 15:25.

[13] See Eric Svendsen, *Who is My Mother? The Role and Status of the Mother of Jesus in the New Testament and Roman Catholicism* (Amityville, NY: Calvary, 2007), 52. See also Matt 13:33; 18:34; Luke 22:18; 24:49; John 13:38; Acts 21:26; 23:12, 21; 25:21.

[14] Brown, *Birth of the Messiah*, 132 (see chap. 1, n. 6).

"firstborn son" (Luke 2:7). They may appeal to Jesus's instruction from the cross to the beloved disciple to take Mary into his home (John 19:25–27). Why, the advocate of perpetual virginity might ask, would Jesus ask that of the beloved disciple if Mary had other children? We might answer that Jesus preferred one of his inner circle to care for Mary when John himself tells us that her other children were not yet believers (John 7:5). But the greater difficulty for perpetual virginity proponents are the numerous references to Jesus's "brothers" and "sisters" in the New Testament (see Matt 13:55–56; Mark 3:31–32; 6:3; Luke 8:19; John 7:3–5; 1 Cor 9:5; Gal 1:19).

Although the Roman Catholic Church officially teaches that Jesus is Mary's only child, there are divergent opinions as to the precise identity of these "brothers" and "sisters."[15] Following *The First Gospel of James*, one group maintains that the "brothers" mentioned in the Gospels were Jesus's stepbrothers—children from Joseph's previous marriage. This position is wholly reliant on extrabiblical tradition and impossible to justify exegetically from the biblical text.

Jerome contended that references to the "brothers" and "sisters" of Jesus were references to cousins or other relatives outside of Jesus's nuclear family.[16] Jerome suggested that these brothers and sisters may in fact be the children of Mary's sister (who also happened to be named Mary?) or Mary, the wife of Clopas. Jerome correctly observed that "firstborn" language in Scripture is equally applicable to only children. He was also

---

[15] *Catechism of the Catholic Church*, 2nd ed. (New York: Doubleday, 2012), 140–41 (§499–501).

[16] Jerome, *Against Helvidius* 11–16; cf. Thomas Aquinas, *Summa theologica* IIIa q. 28, a. 3. See also Luther, *Sermons on the Gospel of St. John* (1537–1540), trans. Martin H. Bertram in LW 22, 214; Calvin, *Calvin's Commentaries*, 16/2, 215; Turretin, *Institutes of Elenctic Theology*, vol. 2, trans. George Musgrave Giger, ed. James T. Dennison, Jr. (Phillipsburg, NJ: P&R, 1994), 686–90. Luther, Calvin, and Turretin (1623–1687) held similar views to Jerome and Aquinas's. Others throughout church history, like Tertullian, denied Mary's perpetual virginity and asserted that these were Jesus's literal siblings. See Tertullian, *On the Flesh of Christ* 7.

right to say that terms like "brother" or "sister" have broader uses than just nuclear siblings. The Bible metaphorically refers to national kinsmen as "brothers" (Deut 15:12; 17:15; Rom 9:3–4). When we talk about "brothers" or "sisters" in Christ, we are talking about spiritual, not biological relationships (Ps 133:1; Rom 8:29).

But several holes in Jerome's argument render his explanation implausible. First, the Greek word for "brother" (*adelphos*) may have literal and metaphorical uses in the New Testament, but nowhere else does it refer to a "relative" or "cousin." Instead, the Evangelists use other words for "relatives" (*suggenes*) and "cousins" (*anepsios*).[17]

Second, stories in the Gospels that refer to Jesus's "brothers" and "sisters" make more sense if these individuals are siblings from his nuclear family than they would if they were cousins or more distant relatives.

> He went to his hometown and began to teach them in their synagogue, so that they were astonished and said, "Where did this man get this wisdom and these miraculous powers? Isn't this the carpenter's son? Isn't his mother called Mary, and his brothers James, Joseph, Simon, and Judas? And his sisters, aren't they all with us? So where does he get all these things?" And they were offended by him. (Matt 13:54–57)

Jesus found no love for his prophetic ministry in Nazareth. His hometown people were highly skeptical of the notion of Jesus as the Messiah because they knew just how ordinary and human Christ was. They watched him grow up. They knew his family and could call them by name. Why would they group Jesus's parents together with his cousins or distant relatives? They lumped Jesus together with James, Joseph, Simon, Judas, and his sisters because they grew up in the same household. In another text,

---

[17] In Luke 21:16, Jesus refers to both brothers (*adelphōn*) and relatives (*syngenōn*) in the same context.

His mother and his brothers came, and standing outside, they sent word to him and called him. A crowd was sitting around him and told him, "Look, your mother, your brothers, and your sisters are outside asking for you."

He replied to them, "Who are my mother and my brothers?" Looking at those sitting in a circle around him, he said, "Here are my mother and my brothers! Whoever does the will of God is my brother and sister and mother." (Mark 3:31–35)

The Evangelists do not tell us exactly what Jesus's mother and brothers wanted, just that they could not get to Jesus because of the crowds (see also Matt 12:46–50; Luke 8:19–21). Perhaps they wanted to give him advice about how they thought he should run his ministry (see John 7:1–4). Perhaps they were embarrassed by him. Or, speaking from my personal experience, maybe they just felt what every pastor's kid feels on Sunday after church is over: "When are you going to get out of here so we can eat?"

But the main point is clear: those closest to Jesus did not understand him or believe him (see John 7:5).[18] Jesus contrasts his nuclear family with his spiritual family. If Jerome were correct in assuming that "brothers" referred to cousins or distant relatives, the impact of Jesus's teaching here would be lost. "Whoever does the will of God is my cousin, my distant relative, and my mother"? With his lordship, Jesus divides allegiances and demands first place in our lives—even over immediate family members (see Matt 10:32–39). Our conformity to the will of God means we have intimacy in the family of God as coheirs with Christ—a metaphor that loses its force if we are relegated to the status of Jesus's cousins.

---

[18] Tertullian, *On the Flesh of Christ* 7.

The Perpetual Virginity of Mary in Early Church Tradition[19]

Text / Theologian	Mary's virginity before birth (*virginitas ante partu*)	Mary's virginity during birth (*virginitas in partu*)	Mary's virginity after birth (*virginitas post partu*)	Sinlessness of Mary
Ignatius (c. d. AD 118)	Yes	N/A	N/A (Jerome claimed that Ignatius affirmed this teaching)	N/A
Ascension of Isaiah (c. AD 150?)	Yes	Yes	N/A	N/A
Odes of Solomon (c. AD 125?)	Yes	Yes	N/A	Yes (see *Ode* 33.5)
Justin Martyr (c. AD 100–165)	Yes	N/A	N/A (Jerome claimed that Justin affirmed this teaching)	N/A
Irenaeus (c. AD 130–202)	Yes	N/A	N/A (Jerome claimed that Irenaeus affirmed this teaching)	No; describes Mary as impatient

---

[19] This chart is largely based on the synthesis of these materials found in Perry, *Mary for Evangelicals*, 119–47.

First Gospel of James (c. AD 150)	Yes	Yes	Yes; or at least it is strongly implied in its explanation of Jesus's brothers as stepbrothers from Joseph's previous marriage	Yes; or at least it is strongly implied in the miraculous conception of Mary herself
Clement of Alexandria (c. AD 150–215)	Yes	Yes; appears to grant authority to *The First Gospel of James*	Yes; appeals to *The First Gospel of James*	N/A
Tertullian (c. AD 155–220)	Yes	No	No; Mary modeled holiness in conjugal matrimony	No; accuses Mary of occasional unbelief
Origen (c. AD 185–253)	Yes	No	Yes; appeals to *The First Gospel of James*	No
Athanasius (c. AD 295–373)	Yes	No	Yes	Maybe

Sola Scriptura and Christian Tradition

Unlike their Roman Catholic and Eastern Orthodox counterparts, Protestant and evangelical Christians subscribe to *sola Scriptura* ("Scripture alone"). *Sola Scriptura* was a guiding principle of the Protestant Reformation, and it completely sets our approach to the Bible and Christian theology apart from those other traditions. But whereas this principle is widely cherished by Protestants and evangelicals, it is also widely misunderstood inside and outside of Protestantism.

When the Protestant Reformers like Luther, Zwingli, and Calvin pushed the theology of the church back to the Bible, they did not reject all forms of tradition. The Reformers regularly and favorably quoted from the creeds, fathers, and doctors of the church. *Sola Scriptura* does not mean we cannot learn theological truth from tradition or other sources like experience or reason. The Protestant principle of *sola Scriptura* means that Scripture is the supreme source of Christian revelation and the only standard by which our knowledge of God can be evaluated.[20] Scripture is the written Word of God—God's words through human words. It is the only inerrant and infallible source of knowledge about God.

Traditions such as creeds, confessions, or other writings may be authoritative for Protestants in one sense, but tradition is only authoritative to the degree that it accurately reflects biblical teaching. When we speak of the authority of a pastor, we do not mean the pastor has authority in and of himself or that his authority is equal to or superior to biblical authority. Tradition, like pastors, can have a kind of delegated authority. They speak for God when and only when they speak God's word.

Roman Catholic and Eastern Orthodox churches often seem to suggest the inverse: Church tradition is often viewed as the final authority by which doctrine is evaluated. They believe that the church "authorized" the canon of Scripture. They believe that the church holds the keys to the proper interpretation of Scripture. They assert that tradition must be revered just like Scripture. The *Catechism of the Catholic Church* openly

---

[20] See James Leo Garrett, *Systematic Theology*, vol. 1, 3rd ed. (North Richland Hills, TX: BIBAL, 2007), 206–9. Garrett used the phrase *suprema Scriptura* to explain this Protestant belief.

affirms this: "Both Scripture and Tradition must be accepted and honored with equal sentiments of devotion and reverence."[21]

Catholic apologists frequently point out that Luther, Zwingli, and Calvin upheld Mary's perpetual virginity. Luther and Zwingli certainly affirmed this doctrine, and Calvin was at least open to the possibility. But to quote these Reformers who came out of a background of Marian devotion to support this doctrine is to miss the main point of their method. We revere the tradition and show appreciation for retrieving it—as I hope is evidenced across this book—but we always return to the fount, back to the original sources (*ad fontes*). Tradition can and should be corrected where it does not conform to Scripture—even tradition that we receive from Protestant Reformers.

Protestants and Catholics not only disagree about how tradition is authoritative; they also disagree about what sources of tradition are valuable and authoritative. Protestants and evangelicals treat the Bible as the only source of special revelation we can access today. For Protestants, tradition is simply the church's interpretation of the Bible, "the rule of faith" if you will. But for many Catholics and Orthodox Christians since medieval Christianity, tradition is another source of revelation alongside Scripture.[22] These additional sources of revelation can include oral or written traditions ascribed to the apostles, "histories" recorded by the faithful, and other truths God reveals through the Church.[23]

The dependence on an apocryphal gospel like *The First Gospel of James* in the development of the doctrine of Mary's perpetual virginity strongly indicates a view that apocryphal tradition is weighed alongside

---

[21] *Catechism of the Catholic Church*, 2nd ed. (New York: Doubleday, 2012), 31 (§82).

[22] For a thorough evaluation of one-source (Tradition I) and two-source theories (Tradition II) of revelation and tradition, see Heiko A. Oberman, *Forerunners of the Reformation: The Shape of Medieval Thought*, trans. Paul L. Nyhus (New York: Holt, Rinehart, and Winston, 1966), 51–120.

[23] John Brevicoxa, "A Treatise on Faith, the Church, the Roman Pontiff, and the General Council," in Oberman, *Forerunners of the Reformation*, 72–73.

Scripture as another source of revelation. To be fair, the Roman Catholic church does not acknowledge this book as inspired Scripture. Jerome, one of the primary proponents of perpetual virginity, rejected the canonical status of *The First Gospel* as Scripture—largely because it contradicted his own view that Jesus's "brothers" like James were really his cousins.[24] Nevertheless, Roman Catholics show dependence on this book for the names of Mary's parents—both of whom share a feast day in the liturgical calendar. Defenders of the perpetual virginity doctrine often appeal to *The First Gospel of James* in support of this teaching.

Herein lies the rub: When Protestants talk about tradition, they speak about the way the church has interpreted biblical texts through the centuries. We do not readily embrace extrabiblical historical claims as authoritative—particularly miracles or supernatural events that are not recorded in Scripture. We may hold some appreciation for written traditions outside of Scripture, such as traditions surrounding the martyrdom of apostles, but we always hold these things lightly, knowing they are not inerrant like Scripture. Peter may or may not have been crucified upside down, as reported in the apocryphal book *The Acts of Peter* 40.11. Although there is some apologetic value in martyrdom traditions like this one, they do not rise to the level of importance of, say, doctrines about Christ and his conception. If they are true, great! If not, the Christian faith keeps on ticking.[25]

Protestants have no difficulty accepting creeds or confessions that make claims about the meaning of Scripture, even when councils must invent new theological terms and conceptual categories to describe its contents (e.g., the Trinity, the hypostatic union, etc.). These are not new revelations but explanations of the revelation contained in Scripture. But Protestants are reluctant to take as authoritative claims about events in

---

[24] J. K. Elliot, *The Apocryphal New Testament* (New York: Oxford University Press, 1994), 50–51.

[25] See Sean McDowell, *The Fate of the Apostles: Examining the Martyrdom Accounts of the Closest Followers of Jesus* (New York: Routledge, 2018).

redemption history that are not explicitly mentioned in the canon of Scripture. Consequently, no Protestant feels the compulsion to affirm the miraculous delivery of Jesus or Mary's immaculate conception or bodily assumption because these are claims about the events of redemption history outside the scope of revelation.

Marriage, Singleness, and Concupiscence

The doctrine of Mary's perpetual virginity grew out of an ascetic church culture where virginity was prized as a superior virtue, the ultimate example of physical and emotional self-denial for the glory of God. In his defense of this doctrine, Jerome argued that virginity is morally and spiritually superior to the state of marriage.[26]

Compare that with the sometimes embarrassingly cavalier attitude toward sex in Protestant evangelical circles. Years ago, an evangelical megachurch pastor did a live, twenty-four-hour broadcast where he and his wife lay in bed together on the roof of their church facility. The same pastor openly encouraged every married couple in his church to have sex every day for a month's time.

These two extremes—the denial of the goodness of married sex and the somewhat crass parading of married sensuality—represent two very different ways of thinking about marriage, singleness, and sex.

The tension between God-honoring sex in the context of marriage and the honor given to faithful singles has been with the church since the very beginning. Paul had to address those in Corinth who said, "It is good for a man not to have sexual relations with a woman" (1 Cor 7:1). Instead of affirming this proposition, Paul said "each man should have sexual relations with his own wife, and each woman should have sexual relations with her own husband" in order to avoid sexual immorality (1 Cor 7:2). Granting an exception for a brief time of prayer and fasting, Paul encouraged regular sexual relations between husband and wife (1 Cor 7:5).

---

[26] Jerome, *Against Helvidius* 19–22.

Paul's encouragement of married sex was a concession—not a blanket command for all people (1 Cor 7:6). The apostle spoke of his own "gift" of celibacy/singleness, wishing that everyone could be gifted in the same way he was (1 Cor 7:7). He encouraged those who did not have strong sexual desires to remain unmarried (1 Cor 7:8), not because such sexual desire is inherently sinful but because they can serve God "without distraction" outside of marriage (1 Cor 7:35). From Paul's perspective, the choice between marriage and singleness is not a one-size-fits-all equation. All persons are expected to follow God's commands regarding sexual immorality (1 Thess 4:3–8). But marriage is not for everyone, nor is the gift of celibacy.

Whereas modern Protestants and evangelicals do not blush to talk about sex for the sake of pleasure and intimacy in marriage, many early church theologians, like Augustine, would have winced at such talk. For Augustine, married intercourse was not sinful so long as it came out of a desire to produce children. He regarded sex between spouses for the sake of pleasure to be a sin—a lesser sin, but still sin.[27] The operative word here is *concupiscence*, which describes any disordered or sinful desire. Anytime a married couple engages in sex without the desire to produce children, it is concupiscence.

Although Augustine and Jerome insisted that they were not speaking disparagingly of marriage, they also seemed to speak of it as a necessary evil. Marriage is clearly of lesser glory than virginity and self-denial for the Lord's service. But is this assumption a biblical one? Protestant interpreters of Scripture usually say "no." From the beginning of creation, God ordained married sexuality as a gift. The first command given to man was to "be fruitful and multiply" (Gen 1:28). But the poetic description of sexual attraction and sexual desire in Gen 2:22–25 makes no mention of childbearing. Prior to the fall, Adam and Eve appeared to enjoy sex for the sake of married intimacy and pleasure.

The Song of Songs may have larger implications for understanding the relationship between God and his people, but this spiritual significance

---

[27] Augustine, *On Marriage and Concupiscence* 17.

builds on the literal meaning of a song between lovers who celebrate the gift of sex and intimacy. Scripture doesn't condemn the Shulammite maiden for her desire for the king to kiss her and bring her to his bedroom (Song 1:2–4). Elsewhere in Proverbs, a father encourages his son to take pleasure in his wife's body—even past her childbearing years. "Take pleasure in the wife of your youth . . . let her breasts always satisfy you; be lost in her love forever" (Prov 5:18, 19). Notably, none of these passages that celebrate married sexuality mention conceiving children.

Setting aside the question of Mary's sinlessness, we can safely say that were she to have had marital relations with her husband, this practice would not have been condemned as sin by Scripture. If we cannot make the case from Scripture that the consummation of Mary and Joseph's marriage would have been sinful, we likewise can make no biblical case that the normal, God-ordained pattern for married sexuality would somehow defile the purity of Mary's womb, the ark that carried the new covenant. Procreation was a divine ordinance even before the original Eve disobeyed (Gen 1:28).

And contrary to the views of Jerome and Thomas Aquinas, we have no textual or historical reason to think that Mary and her betrothed husband took vows of virginity before entering into the covenant of marriage.[28] As Tertullian suggested, faithful monogamy between man and woman can be an equally important calling.[29]

Conclusion

Some Christians find the doctrine of Mary's perpetual virginity appealing because of its typological significance. In some sense, Mary has become the "ark" of the new covenant as the glory of the Lord resided in her womb. Mary is also described as another Eve. But unlike the first mother

---

[28] See Jerome, *Against Helvidius* 19–21; Thomas Aquinas, *Summa theologica* IIIa q. 28, a. 4.

[29] Tertullian, *On Monogamy*.

who succumbed to the temptation of the servant, the mother of Christ faithfully obeyed God when she was told she would bear his Son. There is admittedly something attractive to this imagery.

However, this doctrine also has deep roots in an extrabiblical tradition that makes revelatory and biographical claims about the life of Jesus's mother. It goes far beyond the bounds of what Scripture claims about the life of Mary and other members of the holy family. If Scripture is a sufficient source of revelation for evangelical interpreters of Scripture, we must resist appeals to forms of tradition that add to the substantial content of Christian belief. Appealing to extrabiblical traditions like *The First Gospel of James* is methodologically different from appealing to tradition like creeds or confessions that help us understand Scripture on its own terms.

The doctrine of perpetual virginity also presumes a negative view of human sexuality that more closely reflects Greco-Roman aestheticism than the Jewish views of marriage and sex. Furthermore, the idea that Mary gave birth to Jesus without pain or physically affecting her own body has a gnostic quality that detracts from the true humanity of Jesus in the incarnation. We have no biblical warrant to assume that Jesus's birth was anything but natural.

For the time being, I am convinced that arguments in favor of Mary's perpetual virginity doctrine are simply not compelling in the light of other biblical data. References to Jesus's brothers and sisters are probably best taken at face value. Despite what Roman Catholic interpreters may claim, the plain reading of Matt 1:25 indicates that Joseph and Mary did eventually consummate their marriage. Yet because Scripture does not explicitly address the matter, there is room for disagreement between brothers and sisters in Christ.

The biblical doctrine of the virginal conception is not really about sex in the first place—especially the gift of married sex created by God. Instead, the virginal conception is a sign of the uniqueness of Christ as the God-man, born without a human father, conceived by the Holy Spirit apart from the will of man.

BIBLIOGRAPHY

Allison, Gregg. *Roman Catholic Theology and Practice: An Evangelical Assessment.* Wheaton, IL: Crossway, 2014.

Allison, Gregg and Andreas J. Köstenberger. *The Holy Spirit.* Theology for the People of God. Nashville: B&H Academic, 2020.

Anselm of Canterbury.

Athanasius.

Augustine. *The Trinity (De Trinitate).* Translated by Edmund Hill and edited by John E. Rotelle. Hyde Park, NY: New City, 1991.

———. *Sermons to the People.* Translated and edited by William Griffin. New York: Doubleday, 2002.

Bacon, Benjamin W., Andrew C. Zenos, Rush Rhees, and Benjamin B. Warfield. "The Supernatural Birth of Jesus." *American Journal of Theology* 10, no. 1 (1906): 1–30.

Bailey, Kenneth E. *Jesus Through Middle Eastern Eyes: Cultural Studies in the Gospels.* Downers Grove: IVP Academic, 2008.

Barrett, C. K. *The Gospel According to St. John.* 2nd ed. Louisville: Westminster John Knox, 1978.

Barrett, Matthew. *Canon, Covenant, and Christology: Rethinking Jesus and the Scriptures of Israel.* Downers Grove: IVP Academic, 2020.

Barth, Karl. *Church Dogmatics* I.2. *The Doctrine of the Word of God* §13–15. Study edition. Translated and edited by G. M. Bromiley and T. F. Torrance. London: T&T Clark, 2010.

———. *Credo.* New York: Charles Scribner's Sons, 1962.

Bartholomew, Craig G. and Michael W. Goheen. *The Drama of Scripture: Finding Our Place in the Biblical Story*. Grand Rapids: Baker, 2004.

Batson, Jerry W. "Nazareth, Nazarene." In *Holman Illustrated Bible Dictionary*, edited by Chad Brand, et al., 1177–78. Nashville: Holman Bible Publishers, 2003.

Bauckham, Richard. *Gospel Women: Studies of the Named Women in the Gospels*. Grand Rapids: Eerdmans, 2002.

———. "Tamar's Ancestry and Rahab's Marriage: Two Problems in the Matthean Genealogy." *Novum Testamentum* 37.4 (1995): 313–29.

Beale, G. K. *The Book of Revelation*. NIGTC. Grand Rapids: Eerdmans, 1999.

———. *Handbook on the New Testament Use of the Old Testament: Exegesis and Interpretation*. Grand Rapids: Baker, 2012.

———. "The Use of Hosea 11:1 in Matthew 2:15: One More Time." *JETS* 55.4 (2012): 697–715.

Behr, John. *The Nicene Faith*. Formation of Christian Theology. Vol. 2. Yonkers, NY: St. Vladmir's Seminary Press, 2019.

Bernier, Jonathan. *Rethinking the Dates of the New Testament: The Evidence for Early Composition*. Grand Rapids: Baker, 2022.

Berry, R. J. "The Virgin Birth of Christ." *Science and Christian Belief* 8 (1996): 101–10.

Bird, Michael F. *Evangelical Theology*. 2nd ed. Grand Rapids: Zondervan, 2020.

———. *Jesus the Eternal Son: Answering Adoptionist Christology*. Grand Rapids: Eerdmans, 2017.

———. *What Christians Ought to Believe: An Introduction to Christian Doctrine Through the Apostles' Creed*. Grand Rapids: Zondervan, 2016.

Black, David Alan, ed. *Perspectives on the Ending of Mark: Four Views*. Nashville: B&H Academic, 2008.

Blomberg, Craig L. *The Historical Reliability of the New Testament*. Nashville: B&H Academic, 2016.

Bock, Darrell L. *Luke 1:1–9:50*. Baker Exegetical Commentary on the New Testament. Grand Rapids: Baker, 1994.

————. *A Theology of Luke and Acts: God's Promised Program, Realized for All Nations*. Grand Rapids: Zondervan, 2012.

Boethius, *Consolation of Philosophy*. Translated by Joel C. Relihan. Indianapolis: Hackett, 2001.

Borg, Marcus and John Dominic Crossan. *The First Christmas: What the Gospels Really Teach About Jesus's Birth*. New York: HarperOne, 2009.

Boslooper, Thomas. *The Virgin Birth*. Philadelphia: Westminster, 1962.

Boyce, Mary. *Zoroastrians: Their Religious Beliefs and Practices*. New York: Routledge, 1979.

Bradshaw, Paul. "The Dating of Christmas: The Early Church." In *The Oxford Handbook of Christmas*. Edited by Timothy Larsen. Oxford: Oxford University Press, 2020.

Briggs, Charles Augustus. "The Virgin Birth of Our Lord." *The American Journal of Theology* 12, no. 2 (1908): 189–210.

Brindle, Wayne. "The Census and Quirinius: Luke 2:2." *JETS* 27, no. 1 (1984): 43–52.

Brown, Harold O. J. *Heresies: Heresy and Orthodoxy in the History of the Church*. Peabody, MA: Hendrickson, 2003.

Brown, Raymond E. *The Birth of the Messiah: A Commentary on the Infancy Narratives in the Gospels of Matthew and Luke*. Rev. ed. New York: Doubleday, 1993.

————. "Note: Luke's Description of the Virginal Conception." *Theological Studies* 35, no. 2 (1974): 360–61.

————. *The Virginal Conception and Bodily Resurrection of Jesus*. New York: Paulus, 1973.

Brunner, Emil. *The Christian Doctrine of Creation and Redemption, Dogmatics*. Vol. 2. Translated by Olive Wyon. Eugene, OR: Wipf and Stock, 2014.

Butner, D. Glenn, Jr. *Jesus the Refugee: Ancient Injustice and Modern Solidarity*. Minneapolis: Fortress, 2023.

————. *The Son Who Learned Obedience: A Theological Case Against the Eternal Submission of the Son*. Eugene, OR: Pickwick, 2018.

Calvin, John. *Calvin: Commentaries*. Edited by Joseph Haroutunian. Louisville: Westminster John Knox, 1958.

———. *Commentary on a Harmony of the Evangelists Matthew, Mark, and Luke*. Vol. 1. Translated by William Pringle. Edinburgh, 1845.

———. *Institutes of the Christian Religion*. Edited by John T. McNeill and translated by Ford Lewis Battles. 2 vols. Philadelphia: Westminster, 1960.

Campbell, Joseph. *The Hero with a Thousand Faces*. 3rd ed. Novato, CA: New World Library, 2008.

Carson, D. A. "Matthew." In *Matthew and Mark*. Edited by Tremper Longman III and David E. Garland, 23–670. The Expositor's Bible Commentary. Grand Rapids: Zondervan, 2010.

Carter, Craig A. *Interpreting Scripture with the Great Tradition: Recovering the Genius of Premodern Exegesis*. Grand Rapids: Baker, 2018.

Chilton, Bruce. *Rabbi Jesus: An Intimate Biography*. New York: Doubleday, 2000.

Clarke, Adam. *The New Testament*. Vol. 1, Matthew–Acts. New York, 1855.

Cole, Dennis R. *Numbers*. Nashville: B&H Academic, 2000.

Comfort, Philip Wesley. *A Commentary on the Manuscripts and Text of the New Testament*. Grand Rapids: Kregel, 2015.

Cranfield, C. E. B. "Some Reflections on the Subject of the Virgin Birth." *Scottish Journal of Theology* 42, no. 2 (1988): 177–90.

Crisp, Oliver D. *Analyzing Doctrine: Toward a Systematic Theology*. Waco, TX: Baylor University Press, 2019.

———. *God Incarnate: Explorations in Christology*. New York: T&T Clark, 2009.

Dahl, Nils. *Jesus in the Memory of the Early Church*. Minneapolis: Augsburg, 1976.

Darling, Daniel. *The Characters of Christmas: The Unlikely People Caught Up in the Story of Jesus*. Chicago: Moody, 2019.

Davies, W. D. and Dale C. Allison, Jr. *Matthew 1–7*. International Critical Commentary. New York: T&T Clark, 2004.

DelCogliano, Mark, ed. *The Cambridge Edition of Early Christian Writings*. Vol. 3. *Christ: Through the Nestorian Controversy*. New York: Cambridge University Press, 2022.

Dowling, Levi H. *The Aquarian Gospel of Jesus Christ*. Los Angeles, 1908.

Duby, Steven J. *Jesus and the God of Classical Theism: Biblical Christology in Light of the Doctrine of God*. Grand Rapids: Baker Academic, 2022.

Dunn, James D. G. *Jesus Remembered*. Grand Rapids: Eerdmans, 2003.

———. *The Theology of Paul the Apostle*. Grand Rapids: Eerdmans, 1998.

Edwards, Jonathan. "To Be More Blessed Than Mary." In *Come, Thou Long-Expected Jesus: Experiencing the Peace and Promise of Christmas*. Edited by Nancy Guthrie. 55–60. Wheaton, IL: Crossway, 2008.

Ehrman, Bart D. *Lost Christianities: The Battles for Scripture and the Faiths We Never Knew*. New York: Oxford University Press, 2005.

Elliot, T. S. *Collected Poems 1909–1962*. New York: Harcourt Brace, 1963.

Emerson, Matthew Y. *"He Descended to the Dead": An Evangelical Theology of Holy Saturday*. Downers Grove: IVP Academic, 2019.

Emery, Giles. *The Trinity: An Introduction to the Catholic Doctrine on the Triune God*. Translated by Matthew Levering. Washington, DC: The Catholic University of America Press, 2011.

Evans, Craig A. "Mark's Incipit and the Priene Calendar Inscription: From Jewish Gospel to Greco-Roman Gospel." *Journal of Greco-Roman Christianity and Judaism* 1 (2000): 67–81.

Evans, Ernest, ed. *Tertullian Adversus Marcionem*. Oxford: Clarendon, 1972.

Eykel, Eric Vanden. *The Magi: Who They Were, How They've Been Remembered, and Why They Still Fascinate*. Minneapolis: Fortress, 2022.

Farmer, William R. *The Gospel of Jesus: The Pastoral Relevance of the Synoptic Problem*. Louisville: Westminster John Knox, 1994.

Farris, Stephen C. "On Discerning Semitic Sources in Luke 1–2." In *Gospel Perspectives: Studies of History and Tradition in the Four Gospels*. Vol. 2. Edited by R. T. France and David Wenham, 201–37. Eugene, OR: Wipf and Stock, 1981.

Ferguson, Everett. *The Rule of Faith: A Guide.* Eugene, OR: Cascade, 2015.

Ferrari-D'Ochchieppo, Konradin. "The Star of the Magi and Babylonian Astronomy." In *Chronos, Kairos, Christos: Nativity and Chronological Studies Presented to Jack Finegan.* Edited by Jerry Vardaman and Edwin M. Yamauchi, 41–53. Winona Lake, IN: Eisenbrauns, 1989.

Fitzmyer, Joseph A. "The Virginal Conception of Jesus in the New Testament." *Theological Studies* 34 (1973): 542–74.

France, R. T. "The Formula-Quotations of Matthew 2 and the Problem of Communication." In *The Right Doctrine from the Wrong Texts? Essays on the Use of the Old Testament in the New.* Edited by G. K. Beale, 114–34. Grand Rapids: Baker, 1994.

———. *Matthew.* New International Commentary on the New Testament. Grand Rapids: Eerdmans, 2007.

———. *Matthew: Evangelist and Teacher.* Exeter, UK: Paternoster, 1992.

Fuller, Daniel P. *The Unity of the Bible: Unfolding God's Plan for Humanity.* Grand Rapids: Zondervan, 1992.

Galot, Jean. *Etre ne' de Dieu: Jean 1, 13.* Rome: Institut Biblique Pontifical, 1969.

———. *Who is Christ? A Theology of the Incarnation.* Translated by M. Angeline Bouchard. Chicago: Franciscan Herald, 1981.

Gambero, Luigi, ed. *Mary and the Fathers of the Church: The Blessed Virgin Mary in Patristic Thought.* Translated by Thomas Buffer. San Francisco: Ignatius, 1999.

Gathercole, Simon J. *The Preexistent Son: Recovering the Christologies of Matthew, Mark, and Luke.* Grand Rapids: Eerdmans, 2006.

Gentry, Peter J. *Kingdom Through Covenant: A Biblical-Theological Understanding of the Covenants.* Wheaton, IL: Crossway, 2012.

Gladd, Benjamin L. *From the Manger to the Throne: A Theology of Luke.* Wheaton, IL: Crossway, 2022.

Gregory of Nazianzus. *On God and Christ: The Five Theological Orations and Two Letters to Cledonius.* Translated by Frederick Williams and Lionel Wickham. Yonkers, NY: St Vladmir's Seminary Press, 2002.

Gribetz, Sarit Kattan. "Toledot Yeshu." In *Early New Testament Apocrypha*. Ancient Literature for New Testament Studies. Vol. 9. Edited by J. Christopher Edwards, 154–74. Grand Rapids: Zondervan, 2022.

Gromacki, Robert. *The Virgin Birth: A Biblical Study of the Deity of Christ*. 2nd ed. Grand Rapids: Kregel, 2002.

Gundry, Robert H. *Matthew: A Commentary on His Literary and Theological Art*. Grand Rapids: Eerdmans, 1982.

Hahn, Scott. *Hail, Holy Queen: The Mother of God in the Word of God*. New York: Doubleday, 2001.

Hamilton, James M., Jr. *Typology: Understanding the Bible's Promise-Shaped Patterns—How Old Testament Expectations are Fulfilled in Christ*. Grand Rapids: Zondervan, 2022.

———. "'The Virgin Will Conceive': Typological Fulfillment in Matthew 1:18–23." In *Built Upon the Rock: Studies in the Gospel of Matthew*. Edited by Daniel M. Gurtner and John Nolland, 228–47. Grand Rapids: Eerdmans, 2008.

Hamilton, Victor P. "Marriage (Old Testament and Ancient Near East)." In *The Anchor Yale Bible Dictionary*. Edited by David Noel Freedman, 4:559–69. New York: Doubleday, 1992.

Hanson, R. P. C. *The Search for the Christian Doctrine of God: The Arian Controversy, 318–81*. New York: T&T Clark, 1988.

Hays, Richard B. *Echoes of Scripture in the Gospels*. Waco, TX: Baylor University Press, 2016.

———. *Reading Backwards: Figural Christology and the Fourfold Gospel Witness*. Waco, TX: Baylor University Press, 2014.

Hereth, Blake. "Mary, Did You Consent?" *Religious Studies* 58, no. 4 (2021): 677–700.

Holmes, Stephen R. *The Quest for the Trinity: The Doctrine of God in Scripture, History, and Modernity*. Downers Grove: IVP Academic, 2012.

Horsley, Richard A. *The Liberation of Christmas: The Infancy Narratives in Social Context*. New York: Crossroad, 1989.

Hume, David. *An Enquiry Concerning Human Understanding*. Edited by Eric Steinberg. Indianapolis: Hackett, 1993.

Incomplete Commentary on Matthew (*Opus imperfectum*). Translated by James A. Kellerman and edited by Thomas C. Oden. *Ancient Christian Texts*. Vol. 1. Downers Grove: IVP Academic, 2010.

Jamieson, R. B. *The Paradox of Sonship: Christology in the Epistle to the Hebrews*. Downers Grove: IVP Academic, 2021.

Jamieson, R. B. and Tyler R. Wittman. *Biblical Reasoning: Christological and Trinitarian Rules for Exegesis*. Grand Rapids: Baker, 2022.

Jipp, Joshua W. "Luke's Scriptural Suffering Messiah: A Search for Precedent, a Search for Identity." *Catholic Biblical Quarterly* 72, no. 2 (April 2010): 255–74.

Junius, Franciscus. *A Treatise on True Theology with the Life of Franciscus Junius*. Translated by David C. Noe. Grand Rapids: Reformation Heritage, 2014.

Just, Arthur A. *Luke*. Ancient Christian Commentary on Scripture. NT Vol. 3. Downers Grove: IVP Academic, 2003.

Keener, Craig S. *The Gospel of John: A Commentary*. Grand Rapids: Baker Academic, 2010.

———. *The Gospel of Matthew: A Socio-Rhetorical Commentary*. Grand Rapids: Eerdmans, 2009.

———. *The IVP Bible Background Commentary—New Testament*. Rev. ed. Downers Grove: InterVarsity, 2014.

Kelly, J. N. D. *Early Christian Creeds*. London: Longman, 1960.

Komoszweski, J. Ed, M. James Sawyer, and Daniel B. Wallace. *Reinventing Jesus*. Grand Rapids: Kregel, 2006.

Köstenberger, Andreas J. and Alexander E. Stewart. *The First Days of Jesus*. Wheaton, IL: Crossway, 2015.

Köstenberger, Andreas, J., L. Scott Kellum, and Charles L. Quarles. *The Cradle, the Cross, and the Crown*. Nashville: B&H Academic, 2009.

Köstenberger, Andreas J. and Michael J. Kruger. *The Heresy of Orthodoxy: How Contemporary Culture's Fascination with Diversity Has Reshaped Our Understanding of Early Christianity*. Wheaton, IL: Crossway, 2010.

Kreitzer, Beth, ed. *Luke*. Reformation Commentary on Scripture. NT Vol. 3. Downers Grove: InterVarsity, 2015.

Kupp, David D. *Matthew's Emmanuel: Divine Presence and God's People in the First Gospel*. Society for New Testament Studies Monograph Series, 90. New York: Cambridge University Press, 1997.

Kuyper, Abraham. *Abraham Kuyper: A Centennial Reader*. Edited by James D. Bratt. Grand Rapids: Eerdmans, 1998.

Laato, Antti. "Celsus, Toledot Yeshu and Early Traces of Apology for the Virgin Birth of Jesus." Jewish Studies in Nordic Countries Today. *Scripta Instituti Donneriani Aboensis* 27 (2016): 61–80.

Ladd, George Eldon. *Jesus and the Kingdom: The Eschatology of Biblical Realism*. New York: Harper & Row, 1964.

Lee, Jason K. and William M. Marsh, eds. *Matthew*, Reformation Commentary on Scripture. NT Vol. 1. Downers Grove: InterVarsity, 2021.

Leithart, Peter J. *The Gospel of Matthew Through New Eyes*. Vol. 1. *Jesus as the New Israel*. West Monroe, LA: Athanasius Press, 2018.

Letham, Robert. *Systematic Theology*. Wheaton, IL: Crossway, 2019.

Lewis, C. S. *God in the Dock*. Grand Rapids: Eerdmans, 1970.

———. *Mere Christianity*. New York: HarperCollins, 2001.

———. *Miracles*. New York: HarperCollins, 2000.

———. *Surprised by Joy: The Shape of My Early Life*. New York: Harcourt Brace, 1955.

Levertov, Denise. *A Door in the Hive*. New York: New Directions, 1989.

Liddon, H. P. *Magnificat: Sermons in St. Paul's*. London: Rivington's, 1890.

Lincoln, Andrew T. *Born of a Virgin? Reconceiving Jesus in the Bible, Tradition, and Theology*. Grand Rapids: Eerdmans, 2013.

Loisy, Alfred. *Les évangiles synoptiques*. Ceffonds: Chez l'Auteur, 1907.

Luther, Martin. "The Magnificat." In *Luther's Works*. Vol. 21. Edited by Jaroslav Pelikan and translated by A. T. W. Steinhaeuser, 295–354. St. Louis: Concordia, 1956.

———. "On the Councils and the Church." In *Luther's Works*. Vol. 41. Edited by Jaroslav Pelikan and translated by Charles M. Jacobs and Eric W. Gritsch, 95–106. Philadelphia: Fortress, 1966.

MacArthur, John. *Luke 1–5*. MacArthur New Testament Commentary. Vol. 7. Chicago: Moody, 2007.

Machen, J. Gresham. *The Virgin Birth of Christ*. New York: Harper & Row, 1930.

Mai, Qingyun, et. al, "Derivation of Human Embryonic Stem Cell Lines from Parthenogenetic Blastocysts." *Cell Research* 17 (2007): 1008–19.

Maier, Paul L. "The Date of the Nativity and the Chronology of Jesus' Life." In *Chronos, Kairos, Christos: Nativity and Chronological Studies Presented to Jack Finegan*. Edited by Jerry Vardaman and Edwin M. Yamauchi, 113–32. Winona Lake, IN: Eisenbrauns, 1989.

———. *In the Fullness of Time: A Historian Looks at Christmas, Easter, and the Early Church*. Rev. ed. Grand Rapids: Kregel, 1998.

Marshall, I. Howard. *The Gospel of Luke*. NIGNT. Grand Rapids: Eerdmans, 1978.

Maximus the Confessor. *The Life of the Virgin*. Translated by Stephen J. Shoemaker. New Haven, CT: Yale University Press, 2012.

———. *On the Cosmic Mystery of Christ: Selected Writings from St Maximus the Confessor*. Translated by Paul M. Blowers and Robert Louis Wilkin. Yonkers, NY: St Vladmir's Seminary Press, 2003.

McCabe, Herbert. *God Matters*. London: Continuum, 2005.

McDowell, Sean. *The Fate of the Apostles: Examining the Martyrdom Accounts of the Closest Followers of Jesus*. New York: Routledge, 2018.

McKnight, Scot. *The Real Mary: Why Evangelical Christians Can Embrace the Mother of Jesus*. Brewster, MA: Paraclete, 2006.

Minear, Paul S. "Luke's Use of the Birth Stories." In *Studies in Luke-Acts*. Edited by Leander E. Keck and J. Louis Martyn, 111–30. Philadelphia: Fortress, 1980.

Mohler, R. Albert, Jr. *The Apostles' Creed: Discovering Authentic Christianity in an Age of Counterfeits*. Nashville: Nelson, 2019.

Morris, Leon. *Luke*. TNTC. Rev. ed. Downers Grove: InterVarsity, 1988.

Moule, C. F. D. *The Origin of Christology.* New York: Cambridge University Press, 1977.

Mounce, Robert H. *The Book of Revelation.* NICNT. Grand Rapids: Eerdmans, 1977.

Naselli, Andrew David. *The Serpent and the Serpent Slayer.* Wheaton, IL: Crossway, 2020.

Nicholl, Colin R. *The Great Christ Comet: Revealing the True Star of Bethlehem.* Wheaton, IL: Crossway, 2015.

Nolland, John. *Luke 1–9:20.* WBC 35a Nashville: Thomas Nelson, 1989.

Norris, Richard A., Jr., trans and ed. *The Christological Controversy.* Philadelphia: Fortress, 1980.

O'Connor, Flannery. "Southern Fiction." In *Mysteries and Manners: Occasional Prose.* Edited by Sally and Robert Fitzgerald, 36–50. New York: Farrar, Straus, & Giroux, 1957.

Oden, Thomas C. *First and Second Timothy and Titus.* Interpretation. Louisville: Westminster John Knox, 1989.

———. *The Word of Life.* Vol. 2 of *Systemic Theology.* San Francisco: Harper, 1989.

Orr, James. *The Virgin Birth of Christ.* New York: Charles Scribner's Sons, 1907.

Ortlund, Gavin. *Theological Retrieval for Evangelicals: Why We Need Our Past to Have a Future.* Wheaton, IL: Crossway, 2019.

Ortlund, Raymond C., Jr. *Isaiah: God Saves Sinners.* Preaching the Word. Edited by R. Kent Hughes. Wheaton, IL: Crossway, 2005.

Osborne, Grant R. *Luke: Verse by Verse.* Bellingham, WA: Lexham Press, 2018.

———. *Matthew.* Exegetical Commentary on the New Testament. Grand Rapids: Zondervan, 2010.

Pao, David and Eckhart Schnabel. "Luke." In *Commentary on the New Testament Use of the Old Testament.* Edited by G. K. Beale and D. A. Carson, 251–414. Grand Rapids: Baker, 2007.

Papandrea, James. *The Earliest Christologies: Five Images of Christ in the Postapostolic Age.* Downers Grove: IVP Academic, 2016.

Parrinder, Geoffrey. *Son of Joseph: The Parentage of Jesus*. Edinburgh: T&T Clark, 1992.

Peacocke, Arthur. "DNA of our DNA." In *The Birth of Jesus: Biblical and Theological Reflections*. Edited by George J. Brooke, 59–70. Edinburgh: T&T Clark, 2000.

Peeler, Amy. *Women and the Gender of God*. Grand Rapids: Eerdmans, 2022.

Pelikan, Jaroslav. *Mary Through the Centuries: Her Place in the History of Culture*. Rev. ed. New Haven, CT: Yale University Press, 1998.

Perry, Tim. *Mary for Evangelicals: Toward an Understanding of the Mother of Our Lord*. Downers Grove: InterVarsity, 2006.

Perrin, Nicholas. *Luke*. TNTC. Downers Grove: InterVarsity, 2022.

Prior, Karen Swallow. "'Let It Be': Mary's Radical Declaration of Consent." *The Atlantic*. December 24, 2012. https://www.theatlantic.com/sexes/archive/2012/12/let-it-be-marys-radical-declaration-of-consent/266616/.

Pryor, John W. "Of the Virgin Birth or the Birth of Christians? The Text of John 1:13 Once More," *Novum Testamentum* 27, no. 4 (1985): 296–318.

Putman, Rhyne R. "Before and After Nicaea: Arianism as a Test Case for the Ongoing Development of Heresy," *Criswell Theological Review* 18, no. 1 (2020): 3–22.

———. *In Defense of Doctrine: Evangelicalism, Theology, and Scripture*. Minneapolis: Fortress, 2015.

———. *The Method of Christian Theology: A Basic Introduction*. Nashville: B&H Academic, 2021.

Quarles, Charles L. "Jesus as *Mamzer*: A Response to Bruce Chilton's Reconstruction of the Circumstances Surrounding Jesus' Birth in *Rabbi Jesus*." *Bulletin for Biblical Research* 14, no. 2 (2004): 243–55.

———. *Matthew*. Evangelical Biblical Theology Commentary. Bellingham, WA: Lexham, 2023.

———. "Midrash as Creative Historiography: Portrait of a Misnomer." *JETS* 39, no. 3 (September 1996): 457–64.

———. *A Theology of Matthew: Jesus Revealed as Deliverer, King, and Incarnate Creator*. Explorations in Biblical Theology. Phillipsburg, NJ: P&R, 2013.

———. "Why Not 'Beginning from Bethlehem'?" In *Memories of Jesus: A Critical Appraisal of James D. G. Dunn's* Jesus Remembered. Edited by Robert B. Stewart and Gary Habermas, 173–96. Nashville: B&H Academic, 2010.

Reppert, Victor. *C .S. Lewis's Dangerous Idea: In Defense of the Argument from Reason*. Downers Grove: IVP Academic, 2003.

Resch, Dustin. *Barth's Interpretation of the Virgin Birth: A Sign of Mystery*. New York: Routledge, 2016.

Reimarus, Hermann Samuel. *Reimarus Fragments*. Edited by Charles H. Talbert and translated by Ralph S. Fraser. London: SCM, 1970.

Revazova, Elena S., et. al. "HLA Homozygous Stem Cell Lines Derived from Human Parthenogenetic Blastocysts." *Cloning & Stem Cells* 10, no. 1 (2008): 11–24.

Rice, Anne. *Christ the Lord: Out of Egypt*. New York: Knopf, 2005.

Richter, Sandra L. *The Epic of Eden: A Christian Entry into the Old Testament*. Downers Grove: InterVarsity, 2008.

Roberts, Kyle. *A Complicated Pregnancy: Whether Mary Was a Virgin and Why It Matters*. Minneapolis: Fortress, 2017.

Robertson, A. T. *The Mother of Jesus: Her Problems and Her Glory*. New York: George H. Doran, 1925.

Robinson, James M., ed. *The Nag Hammadi Library in English*. 3rd ed. Leiden: Brill, 1988.

Rose, Jenny. *Zoroastrianism*. New York: I. B. Tauris, 2010.

Rowe, C. Kavin. *Early Narrative Christology: The Lord in the Gospel of Luke*. New York: Walter de Gruyter, 2006.

Rutledge, Fleming. *Advent*. Grand Rapids: Eerdmans, 2018.

Sanders, Fred. *The Triune God*. Grand Rapids: Zondervan, 2016.

Schaberg, Jane. *The Illegitimacy of Jesus: A Feminist Interpretation of the Infancy Narratives*. New York: Harper & Row, 1987.

Schäfer, Peter. *Jesus in the Talmud*. Princeton, NJ: Princeton University Press, 2009.

Schleiermacher, Friedrich. *Christian Faith*. Translated by Terrence N. Tice, Catherine L. Kelsey, and Edwina Lawler. 2 vols. Louisville: Westminster John Knox, 2016.

Schmidt, Thomas C. "Calculating December 25 as the Birth of Jesus in Hippolytus' *Canon* and *Chronicon*." *Vigiliae Christianae* 69, no. 5 (2015): 542–63.

Schreiner, Patrick. *The Ascension of Christ: Recovering a Neglected Doctrine*. Bellingham, WA: Lexham, 2020.

———. *Matthew, Disciple and Scribe: The First Gospel and Its Portrait of Jesus*. Grand Rapids: Baker, 2019.

Schreiner, Thomas R. *Romans*. Grand Rapids: Baker Academic, 1998.

Schürer, Emil. *The History of the Jewish People in the Age of Jesus Christ*. Rev. ed. Edited by Geza Vermes, Fergus Millar, and Matthew Black. New York: T&T Clark, 2014.

Shenk, Richard A. *The Virgin Birth of Christ*. Milton Keynes, UK: Paternoster, 2016.

Silva, Moisés, ed. *New International Dictionary of New Testament Theology and Exegesis*. 2nd ed. 5 vols. Grand Rapids: Zondervan, 2014.

Simonetti, Manlio. *Biblical Interpretation in the Early Church: An Historical Introduction to Patristic Exegesis*. Translated by John A. Hughes. Edited by Anders Bergquist and Markus Bockmuehl. New York: T&T Clark, 1994.

———., ed. *Matthew*. Ancient Christian Commentary on Scripture. NT Vol. 1a. Downers Grove: IVP Academic, 2001.

Smith, Brandon D. *The Biblical Trinity: Encountering the Father, Son, and Holy Spirit in Scripture*. Bellingham, WA: Lexham, 2023.

———. *The Trinity in the Book of Revelation: Seeing Father, Son, and Holy Spirit in John's Apocalypse*. Downers Grove: IVP Academic, 2022.

Spong, John Shelby. *Born of a Woman: A Bishop Rethinks the Birth of Jesus*. New York: Harper Collins, 1992.

Stamps, R. Lucas. "Irenaeus and Recapitulation." *Credo*, February 3, 2012. https://credomag.com/2012/02/irenaeus-and-recapitulation/.

———. "'Thy Will Be Done': A Dogmatic Defense of Dyothelitism in Light of Recent Monothelite Proposals." PhD diss., The Southern Baptist Theological Seminary, 2014.

Stauffer, Ethelbert. *Jesus and His Story*. Translated by Richard and Clara Winston. New York: Knopf, 1974.

Strauss, David F. *Das Leben Jesu*. 2 vols. Tübingen, 1835.

Strauss, Mark L. *Four Portraits, One Jesus*. 2nd ed. Grand Rapids: Zondervan, 2020.

Swain, Scott R. *The Trinity: An Introduction*. Wheaton, IL: Crossway, 2020.

———. *The Trinity and the Bible: On Theological Interpretation*. Bellingham, WA: Lexham Press, 2021.

Swain, Scott R. and Michael Allen. *Reformed Catholicity: The Promise of Retrieval for Theology and Biblical Interpretation*. Grand Rapids: Baker, 2015.

Thiselton, Anthony C. *The Hermeneutics of Doctrine*. Grand Rapids: Eerdmans, 2007.

Thomas, John Christopher and Frank D. Macchia. *Revelation*. Grand Rapids: Eerdmans, 2016.

Thorley, John. "When Was Jesus Born?" *Greece & Rome* 28, no. 1 (1981): 81–89.

Thurén, Jukka. *Korinttilaiskirjeet, Tessalonikalaiskirjeet, Paimenkirjeet*. Helsinki: Kustannus oy Arkki, 2008.

Torrance, Thomas F. *Atonement: The Person and Work of Christ*. Edited by Robert T. Walker. Downers Grove: IVP Academic, 2009.

———. *Incarnation: The Person and Life of Christ*. Edited by Robert T. Walker. Downers Grove: IVP Academic, 2015.

Turretin, Francis. *Institutes of Elenctic Theology*. Vol. 2. Translated by George Musgrave Giger. Edited by James T. Dennison, Jr. Phillipsburg, NJ: P&R, 1994.

van Driel, Edwin Chr. *Incarnation Anyway: Arguments for Supralapsarian Christology*. New York: Oxford University Press, 2008.

van Unnik, W. C. "Once More St. Luke's Prologue." *Neotestamentica* 7 (1973): 7–26.

Vidu, Adonis. *The Divine Missions: An Introduction*. Eugene, OR: Cascade, 2021.

————. *The Same God Who Works All Things: Inseparable Operations in Trinitarian Theology*. Grand Rapids: Eerdmans, 2021.

von Balthasar, Hans Urs and Joseph Ratzinger. *Mary: The Church at the Source*. Translated by Adrian Walker. San Francisco: Ignatius, 2005.

von Campenhausen, Hans. *The Virgin Birth in the Theology of the Ancient Church*. Translated by Frank Clarke. London: SCM, 1954.

Walton, John H. *The Lost World of Genesis One: Ancient Cosmology and the Origins Debate*. Downers Grove: InterVarsity, 2009.

Warfield, Benjamin B. "Trinity." In *The International Standard Bible Encyclopedia*. Edited by James Orr, 4:3014–15. Grand Rapids: Eerdmans, 1974.

Weinandy, Thomas C. *Jesus Becoming Jesus: A Theological Interpretation of the Synoptic Gospels*. Vol. 1. Washington, DC: Catholic University of America Press, 2018.

Wellum, Stephen J. *God the Son Incarnate: The Doctrine of Christ*. Wheaton, IL: Crossway, 2016.

White, Thomas Joseph. *The Trinity: On the Nature and Mystery of the One God*. Washington, DC: Catholic University of America Press, 2022.

Wilhite, David E. *The Gospel According to Heretics: Discovering Orthodoxy Through Early Christological Conflicts*. Grand Rapids: Baker, 2015.

Williamson, Paul R. "Covenant." In *Dictionary of the Old Testament: Pentateuch*. Edited by T. Desmond Alexander and David W. Baker, 139–55. Downers Grove: InterVarsity, 2003.

Witherington III, Ben. "Birth of Jesus." In *Dictionary of Jesus and the Gospels*. Edited by Joel B. Green, Scot McKnight, and I. Howard Marshall, 60–74. Downers Grove: InterVarsity, 1992.

Wright, Christopher J. H. *Knowing Jesus Through the Old Testament.* Downers Grove: InterVarsity, 1992.

Wright, N. T. *Jesus and the Victory of God.* Minneapolis: Fortress, 1996.

———. *The Kingdom New Testament: A Contemporary Translation.* Grand Rapids: Zondervan, 2011.

———. *The New Testament and the People of God.* Minneapolis: Fortress, 1996.

———. *Who Was Jesus?* Grand Rapids: Eerdmans, 2014.

———. "Yet the Sun Will Rise Again: Reflections on the Exile and Restoration in Second Temple Judaism, Jesus, Paul, and the Church Today." In *Exile: A Conversation with N. T. Wright.* Edited by James M. Scott, 19–81. Downers Grove: InterVarsity, 2017.

Yamauchi, Edwin. *Persia and the Bible.* Grand Rapids: Baker, 1997.

Yarnell, Malcolm B., III. *Who is the Holy Spirit? Biblical Insights into His Divine Person.* Nashville: B&H Academic, 2019.

Yeago, David S. "The New Testament and Nicene Dogma: A Contribution to the Recovery of Theological Exegesis." In *Theological Interpretation of Scripture: Classic and Contemporary Readings.* Edited by Stephen E. Fowl, 87–100. Cambridge, MA: Blackwell, 1997.

NAME INDEX

A

Anselm, 285–87, 328
Apollinaris, 265–66
Arius, 264–65
Athanasius, 120, 286, 301, 314, 363
Augustine, 97, 281, 287, 293–94, 298, 300, 302–3, 311, 322, 368

B

Barrett, C. K., 225
Barth, Karl, 269, 283, 285, 287–89
Basil of Caesarea, 265
Bauer, Walter, 254
Bavinck, Herman, 328
Bock, Darrell L., 36, 67, 141
Boethius, 123
Boslooper, Thomas, 24
Briggs, Charles, 214
Brown, Harold O. J., 255
Brown, Raymond, 358
Brunner, Emil, 214, 220
Bucer, Martin, 149

C

Caffyn, Matthew, 260
Calvin, John, 10, 121, 173, 322, 325, 328, 353, 364–65
Carson, D. A., 222
Carter, Craig, 111

Celsus, 100
Cerinthus, 258–59
Chadwick, James, 137
Clarke, Adam, 140
Clement, 353, 363
Constantine, 129, 264
Cyril of Alexandria, 203, 273–74, 276, 278
Cyril of Jerusalem, 229

D

Duby, Stephen, 121
Dunn, James D. G., 262

E

Edwards, Jonathan, 93–94
Ehrman, Bart, 254
Eliot, T. S., 171
Epiphanius, 256
Eutyches, 279
Eykel, Eric Vanden, 174

F

Flavius Josephus, 58
Fosdick, Harry Emerson, 6
France, R. T., 192, 196

G

Garrett, James Leo, 364
Gathercole, Simon, 222

Gladd, Benjamin, 168
Gregory of Nazianzus, 208, 265–66

H

Hamilton, James, 60, 114
Hanson, Richard, 263–64
Hippolytus of Rome, 140, 256
Hoffman, Melchior, 260
Hopkins, John Henry Jr., 172
Hume, David, 306

I

Ignatius of Antioch, 184, 214, 255,
    257, 262, 356, 362
Irenaeus, 15, 111, 181, 214, 233, 237,
    239, 255–56, 260–62, 287–90,
    325, 327–28, 356, 362

J

Jerome, 209, 212, 357–62, 366–69
Josephus, 126–28, 178, 189–91
Judas Maccabeus, 32
Julian, 40
Junius, Franciscus, 211
Justin Martyr, 111, 192, 213–14, 262,
    356, 362

K

Keener, Craig, 226
Kennedy, John F., 34
Köstenberger, Andreas, 145
Kuyper, Abraham, 334

L

Laato, Antti, 236
Levertov, Denise, 69
Lewis, C. S., 123, 307–9, 314
Liddon, H. P., 92
Lincoln, Andrew T., 78–79
Lombard, Peter, 302–3
Lucas, George, 23
Luther, Martin, 29, 83, 90, 280, 305,
    353, 364–65

M

Machen, J. Gresham, 291, 313, 348
Maier, Paul, 195
Marcion, 257–58
Maximus the Confessor, 301, 324
McCabe, Herbert, 46
Mohler, Albert Jr., 267

N

Nestorius, 272–75, 279

O

O'Connor, Flannery, 2
Oden, Thomas, 236
Origen, 353, 363
Orr, James, 234, 324
Ortlund, Ray Jr., 116

P

Pannenberg, Wolfhart, 220
Peeler, Amy, 89
Pelagius, 322
Perrin, Nicholas, 85
Perry, Tim, 356
Praxeas, 302

Q

Quarles, Charles, 22, 104, 107

R

Reagan, Ronald, 34
Richter, Sandra, 169
Robertson, A. T., 91–92
Rowe, C. Kavin, 86
Rutledge, Fleming, 135

S

Schaberg, Jane, 100
Schweitzer, Albert, 329
Spong, John Shelby, 80
Stauffer, Ethelbert, 126
Stewart, Alexander, 145
Strauss, Mark, 40

Suetonius, 175
Swain, Scott R., 9, 297

T

Tertullian, 255, 258, 262, 353, 363, 369
Theodore of Mopsuestia, 272
Theodotus of Byzantium, 256
Thiselton, Anthony, 262
Thomas Aquinas, 97, 206, 287, 290, 369
Torrance, Thomas, 217, 313–14, 328

V

Vermigli, Peter Martyr, 95
Vincent of Lérins, 267

W

Warfield, B. B., 294, 314
Watts, Isaac, 331
Weinandy, Thomas, 134
Wesley, Charles, 319–20
Wesley, John, 319
Whitefield, George, 319–20
White, Thomas Joseph, 209
Wright, N. T., 128

Z

Zwingli, Ulrich, 353, 364–65

SUBJECT INDEX

A

abortion, 315–17
Adam, 326–28
adoptionism, 255–56
adultery, 97–99
Advent, 159–60
angels, 59–60, 139, 141, 143–44, 186, 306
anhypostasis, 278
animals, 131–33
Anna, 160, 165
Annunciation, 70, 73–74, 300
Apollinarism, 265–67, 317
Archelaus, 196
Arianism, 264–65
atonement, 5, 156, 158, 269, 285

B

Balaam, 176–77
Bauer thesis, 254
Bethlehem, 125, 129–30, 179, 190
Bible
    canon, 9
    story of, 9–10, 240, 342
blessing, 86–87, 90, 93–94, 163, 183, 188, 316, 332–33

C

cave tradition, 129
census, 125–29, 349
Christian life, 343
Christmas, 1–2, 253–54, 294
church, 118–19, 337
circumcision, 150–52, 195, 287
clean and unclean, 154
communication of attributes, 278–80
cosmic Christmas story, 243–48
Council of Carthage, 322
Council of Chalcedon, 279–80
Council of Constantinople, 267
Council of Ephesus, 273–74, 278
covenant, 30–31, 152
    Abrahamic, 33–34, 245
    Davidic, 34–35, 38
    new, 192–93
creation, 76, 208, 306, 313
creeds, 262–63, 267–69
curse, 157–58, 241

D

Davidic king, 49, 114, 116, 182
demons, 236, 306, 317
depravity, 192, 237, 321–22
divine revelation, 183, 289, 292
Docetism, 257–58
dragon, 185, 243–47
dreams, 101–2, 182–83
dyothelitism, 211

E

Ebionites, 255–56
ectypal theology, 211–12
enhypostasis, 278
epiphany, 172
ethics, 343–44
evangelism, 262, 343

F

federal headship, 322–23
flight to Egypt, 186–87, 199–201
fulfillment
    multiple, 112, 115–16
    predictive, 114
    singular, 111–12
    typological, 114, 116
Fundamentalist-Modernist contro-
    versy, 5–6

G

Gabriel, 22, 57, 59, 62–64, 67, 70–76,
    80–81, 85, 90, 102, 143, 146, 204,
    238, 279, 325, 335, 339, 349
gematria, 38
genealogy, 30–31, 35–37, 39–42,
    46–47
Gentile redemption, 163, 168, 183
Gnosticism, 258–61
God
    attributes, 310–11
    faithfulness, 93
    glory, 141, 143–44
    knowledge of, 211–12
    magnifying, 84, 89
    nature, 285
    presence, 34, 108, 113, 116, 145
    promise to Israel, 49, 93
    protection, 246
    providence, 91
    reconciliation with, 4
    servant, 135
    sovereignty, 135, 342
good news, 141–42, 144, 146–47, 164,
    226, 333, 341–44

gospel of John, 219–20, 226
gospel of Luke, 17–18
    historical context, 124–25
    methodology, 19, 21–22
gospel of Mark, 217–18
gospel of Matthew, 19–20, 31, 105
gospels, 129, 141–42, 144, 146–47,
    234, 258, 347
    consistency, 226–27
    eyewitness accounts, 16–17, 21–22
    harmonization, 348–50
    purpose, 17
Great Commission, 118

H

heresy, 255
Herod, 127, 177–80, 183, 186–87,
    189–99
holy, 153–54
Holy Spirit, 76, 78, 86, 111, 160, 162–
    63, 193, 224, 265, 296–98, 301–2,
    325, 329, 337
homoousion, 264
hope, 193–94
human dignity, 315, 344–45
humility, 71, 89–90, 119, 238, 281
hypostatic union, 263, 278, 366

I

image bearers, 241, 344
Immanuel, 113, 116, 118–19, 221
infancy gospels, 204, 206
innkeeper, 129–30
inspiration, 8
Israel, 25, 32, 37, 48, 61, 103, 163, 183,
    187–88, 198, 244
    consolation, 161–62, 167
    exile, 188–89, 192
    kings, 47–48

J

Jesus
    ancestry, 56, 99–100
        Bathsheba, 54–55

Rahab, 52–53
Ruth, 53–54
Tamar, 50–52
ascension, 246
birth, 3, 133–34, 140, 155–56,
229–30, 255
location, 129–32
witnesses, 215
brothers and sisters, 358–60
childhood, 204–6
comparison to John the Baptist,
58–59
death, 91, 164, 213, 215–16, 277,
320–21, 328–29
dedication, 153–54, 156–57
divine nature, 208, 271, 275
divinity, 4, 119–20, 208–9, 220,
265, 279, 288, 295–96
fulfillment in, 9, 25, 38, 50, 67, 74,
105–8, 111–12, 115, 150, 158,
167, 187, 189, 196–98, 234–35
head of the church, 118
humanity, 204, 206, 208–10, 222,
260–61, 266, 279, 286, 317,
339, 342
human nature, 120, 208, 212, 265,
271, 275, 278, 280, 314, 324,
328
identity, 225
in Revelation, 248–49
in the temple, 206
incarnation, 16, 117–18, 120, 220–
23, 236–37, 280, 298–302,
303, 320, 333–34, 339
king of the Jews, 329
kingship, 56, 335–36
knowledge of, 10–11
last Adam, 237–38, 326–28
light to Gentiles, 182
Lord, 86, 142–43, 314
manna sayings, 224–25
Messiah, 30–33, 74, 142, 162–64,
226, 314
ministry, 333

miracles, 219
"missing years", 207–8
mission, 25, 333
Nazarene, 196–98
new and better Moses, 189
obedience, 158, 207, 211–12, 227,
326–28
opposition to, 198–99
origin, 225–26
poverty, 156
preexistence, 221, 224–25, 291
presence, 119, 121–22
prophecy about ministry, 163–70
resurrection, 194, 306, 329–30
return, 332, 337–38, 340
Savior, 142
sinless, 210, 227, 323–25
Son of Abraham, 30, 33
Son of David, 30, 226
Son of God, 74–75, 206–7, 218–
19, 233–34, 245, 256, 274,
286, 289
Son of Man, 290–91
supremacy, 290
temptation, 277
John the Baptist, 58–59, 66
birth, 64–67
birth announcement, 62–64
Joseph
ancestry, 41
character, 96, 99
naming of Jesus, 102, 152
obedience, 101–3, 343
response, 3, 95–97, 99
Judah, exile, 192
justification, 237, 327

K
kenotic Christology, 119–20
kingdom of God, 91–92, 194, 333–36,
338

L
last days, 337

law, 150–51, 153–55, 157–58, 229
laws of nature, 309–11
Lord's Supper, 119

M

magi, 171–72, 175, 177, 180–81,
    183–84
    gifts, 181–82
    identity, 173–75
Magnificat, 84–85, 87–93
Mariology, 352
marriage, 367–69
Mary
    assumption, 352
    betrothal to Joseph, 97–98
    blessed, 90, 93
    devotion to, 5, 90, 274, 276
    dormition, 352
    effect of Jesus's ministry, 164–65
    immaculate conception, 324, 352,
        354
    marriage to Joseph, 357–58
    Mother of God, 272–74
    obedience, 3, 80, 343
    painless labor, 354–55
    perpetual virginity, 155–56, 352–
        58, 358, 362–63, 365, 369
    perspective in nativity story,
        22–23, 85–86
    purification, 153–56, 357
    response to Annunciation, 70–72,
        75, 79–80
    visit to Elizabeth, 85–86, 276
Messiah, 139, 179, 221
midrash, 107
miracles, 306, 309, 314
miraculous conception
    Isaac, 60–61
    Samson, 61–62

N

nativity stories, 2–3, 20, 24, 129, 186,
    216, 332–33, 342
    interpretation, 7–8

    purpose in Luke, 25
    truthfulness, 6, 16, 27, 348
natural headship, 322, 324
naturalism, 306–9
Nazareth, 70–71
Nestorianism, 222, 273–74
new birth, 223–24, 330
Nicene Creed, 265, 267, 291

O

original sin, 5, 322, 324, 352
orthodoxy, 254–55, 263–64

P

pagan mythology, 23–24
Palestine, 126–27, 130–32, 205
parthenogenesis, 311–12
partitive exegesis, 208–9, 339
Passover, 130, 140, 157, 196, 205, 350
peace, 144–45
people of God, 25, 152, 242, 244
perichoresis, 118
prayer, 18, 63, 90, 165, 310–11, 367
    of Hannah, 87–88
progressive revelation, 8–9
promise fulfillment, 4
prophecy
    Hosea, 188–89
    Isaiah, 108–14
    Jeremiah, 192–93
prophets, 7, 9, 25, 33, 58, 62, 65, 67,
    73, 106, 166, 194, 196–97, 206,
    234, 261, 288, 300, 337, 339
protoevangelium, 240

Q

quest for the historical Jesus, 5
questions, 342
Quirinius, 124, 126–28

R

rape, 75, 80–81, 98, 100
reason, 307
recapitulation, 325–26

reconciliation, 327
redemption, 91, 166, 169–70, 240
redemptive plan, 25, 50, 158
redemptive promise, 242
resurrection, 1, 4–5, 7, 16, 27, 33, 61,
    91, 147, 164, 194, 213, 215–18,
    231, 234–35, 255, 261, 263, 288,
    306–7, 311, 320, 327, 329–30, 334,
    338, 340, 356
return to Nazareth, 194–98
Roman Symbol, 1, 262–63
rule of faith, 4, 261

S

sacrificial system, 154
salvation, 4, 89, 103–4, 163, 168, 224,
    285, 288–89, 302–3, 329, 343
Samuel, 59, 87, 138, 157, 208, 212
Satan, 104, 116, 189, 242, 245–46,
    248, 328
Scripture
    interpretation, 267
    sufficiency, 370
seed, 242–45
sensus plenior, 117
serpent, 240–48, 258, 326–27
servant songs, 167–68
sex, 367–69
shepherd imagery, 138–39
shepherds, 137, 139–41, 146–47
sign, 143, 287, 306, 339–40
Simeon, 160–65
sin, 89, 156, 321–23, 326–27, 343
    Adam's, 322–23, 327
singleness, 367–69
slaughter of the innocents, 189–92
sola Scriptura, 363–66
soul creationism, 322
spiritual gifts, 119
star, 175–76, 180

T

theology, 16, 123, 237, 254, 274, 341,
    356, 364

Theotokos, 272, 274–77, 280, 351
time, 123–24
tradition, 364–66
traducianism, 322
Trinity, 11, 263, 265, 293–304, 366
    divine appropriations, 301–2
    divine missions, 303
    eternal relations, 297–98
    inseparable operations, 299–300
    persons, 118, 268, 296–97
type, 326

V

virgin, 114
virgin birth, 3, 23–24, 55, 214–15, 217,
    220–22, 254, 259, 265, 291–92,
    301–2, 339
    creeds, 261–63
    fittingness, 287–91
    necessary, 283–86
    objections, 306
    Paul's knowledge, 230–32
    scientific explanation, 311–13
    sign, 287–90
    tradition, 215–17, 232–37
virginal conception, 3–4, 23, 55,
    75–78, 100, 108, 114–16, 214, 216,
    221–23, 227, 237–38, 280, 301,
    310, 314, 324–25, 329, 341–42,
    370
    historical acceptance, 4–6
    objection, 78–79, 307
virginity, 5, 367–69

W

war in heaven, 247–48
wisdom, 208, 210
women, 50–55
worship, 181

SCRIPTURE INDEX

Genesis

1 *240*
1:1 *8, 219*
1–2 *168, 258*
1:2 *76, 296*
1–2:3 *37*
1:28 *241, 368–69*
2:7 *76, 237*
2:22–25 *368*
2:24–25 *357*
3 *240, 242, 258*
3:14–15 *241*
3:15 *240–44, 247, 327*
3:16 *354*
3:17 *240*
3:22 *240*
4:1 *78, 357*
4:2 *138*
4:4 *138*
4:11 *242*
4:25 *242*
5:24 *236*
6:2–4 *73*
6:4 *236*
9:1–17 *31*
9:6 *317*
9:12 *287*
9:17 *287*
11:30 *62*
12:1–5 *33*

12:2 *33*
12:3 *33, 242*
12:16 *138*
12–21:7 *60*
14:18–20 *73*
14:22 *73*
15:5 *33*
16:4–5 *60*
16:10 *60*
16:11 *60, 77*
17:3 *72*
17:9–12a *152*
17:11 *287*
17:13b–14 *152*
18:2–3 *72*
18:10 *60*
18:11–13 *64*
18:12 *60*
18:13–14 *60*
18:14 *77*
21:1–7 *33*
21:10 *60*
22:1–19 *80*
22:8 *80*
22:17–18 *242*
22:18 *80*
24 *72*
24:16 *114*
24:67 *357*
25:21 *60, 62*

28:12 *101, 144*
29:1–30 *72*
29:31 *60, 62*
30:13 *90*
30:22–23 *78*
35:16–20 *192*
35:19 *179*
37 *50*
37:5–9 *101*
37:9 *101*
37:19 *101*
37:26–27 *51*
38 *50–51*
38:1–2 *51*
38:9 *51*
38:26 *52*
38:27–30 *52*
39–50 *50*
40 *101*
41:1–36 *101*
44:18–34 *51*
46:3b–4a *187*
46:34 *138*
48:5–6 *36*
48:7 *179, 192*
48:15 *138*
49:24 *138*
50:20 *310*

Exodus
1:8–20 *245*
2:2 *85*
3:2 *138*
3:5 *153*
4:19 *194*
4:30 *287*
6:6 *91*
7:3 *288*
11–13:16 *157*
13:1 *157*
13:15 *157*
13:16 *157*
13:21–22 *180*
14:19 *180*

14:24 *180*
15:13 *169*
15:20 *165*
16 *246*
19–24 *31*
20:12 *207*
20:13 *317*
21:12 *317*
21:22–23 *316*
22:16–17 *114*
28:41 *31*
29:37 *153*
33:9–10 *180*
33:18–23 *141*
40:9 *153*
40:34 *76*

Leviticus
3:1 *323*
3:6 *323*
4:5 *32*
4:16 *31–32*
5:7–10 *156*
6:22 *31–32*
9:2–3 *323*
10:10 *153*
12:2 *154*
12:2–4 *357*
12:3 *151, 155*
12:5 *155*
12:6 *155*
12:8 *155–56*
18:21 *316*
19:9–10 *53*
20:1–5 *108*
20:5 *316*
20:10 *55, 79, 98*
20:20–21 *316*
20:26 *153*
21:3 *114*
21:14 *114*
23:9–14 *157*
23:12 *323*
25:33 *169*

25:47–49 *53*
25:48 *169*
27:9 *153*

Numbers

5 *98*
5:11–31 *79*
5:21–22 *98*
6:1–21 *62*
12:5 *180*
12:12 *316*
18:14–15 *157*
18:17 *153*
22–24 *177*
23:7 *176*
24:16 *73*
24:17–19 *176*

Deuteronomy

4:19 *174*
4:34 *91*
4:35 *295*
5:15 *91*
5:16 *207*
6:6–7 *155*
6:16 *110*
6:20–25 *155*
7:8 *169*
7:19 *91*
12:31 *108, 316*
14:1 *73*
15:12 *360*
17:15 *360*
18:9–12 *174*
18:9–14 *178*
18:15 *226*
19:15b *347*
22:15–17 *155, 354*
22:19 *114*
22:23 *114*
22:23–24 *98*
22:25–27 *98*
22:25–29 *81*
22:28 *114*

23:2 *99*
25:5–10 *36, 41, 51*
31:15 *180*
32:39 *317*

Joshua

2:8–13 *52*
2:11 *52*
6:22–25 *52*
10:12–13 *180*
19:15 *179*
24:3 *33*

Judges

2:11–19 *61*
4:4–14 *165*
11:29–40 *132*
11:31 *132*
13 *61, 103*
13:3 *61, 77*
13:5 *61, 77, 103, 107*
13:5–7 *196*
13:7 *77, 107*
13:22 *72*
16:21–31 *62*
19:24 *114*
21:12 *114*

Ruth

1:14–15 *53*
2:2 *53*
2:20 *53*
3:8–9 *53*
3:8–13 *169*
3:11 *53*
4:1–14 *169*
4:11 *125, 179*
4:11–12 *54*
4:18–22 *54*

1 Samuel

1:1–27 *59*
1:11 *82, 87, 157*
2:1 *87*

2:1–10 *64, 87*
2:2 *87*
2:4 *88*
2:5 *88*
2:6 *317*
2:7 *88*
2:10 *32*
2:25 *212*
2:26 *208, 212*
2:30 *64*
2:35 *212*
7:6 *212*
7:15 *212*
8:3 *212*
9:15–16 *31*
10:2 *192*
12:3 *31*
12:5 *31*
15:33 *316*
16:6 *32*
16:11–12 *138*
16:18 *125*
17:12 *125*
17:15 *125*
24:6 *31–32*
24:10 *31*
28:24 *132*

2 Samuel

5:2 *179*
5:14 *39*
7:3 *34*
7:8b–9 *34*
7:12–16 *35, 74*
7:14 *47*
7:16 *245*
7:23 *169*
8:2 *176*
8:14 *176*
11:1–24 *54*
11:3 *54*
11:26–27 *54*
12:15–24 *54*

13:2 *114*
13:18 *114*
23:34 *54*

1 Kings

1:28–31 *54*
2:27 *106*
4:29–31 *47*
8:15 *106*
9:15–23 *47*
10:10 *182*
11 *47*
11:6 *47*
11:11–13 *47*
11:14–25 *48*
11:14–40 *35*
11:17 *187*
11:26–40 *48*
11:39 *47*
11:40 *187*
12:1–24 *48*
12:25–33 *48*
14:1–20 *48*
14:21–31 *48*
17:19 *132*
19:18 *166*

2 Kings

16:2–4 *109*
16:7 *110*
17:7 *189*
21:6 *108*
22:14–20 *165*
24:9 *48*
25:26 *187*

1 Chronicles

3:5 *39, 54*
3:11–12 *36*
14:4 *39*
17:11–14 *35*
21:1 *242*
29:11–12 *334*

2 Chronicles

6:4 *106*
10–12 *48*
28:1 *112*
28:1–5 *109*
28:5–6 *109*
28:16 *109*
28:21 *110*
28:23 *110*
36:9 *48*
36:21–22 *106*

Ezra

1:1 *106*
3:2–5:1 *49*
7:10 *267*

Nehemiah

6:14 *165*
8:1–8 *267*

Esther

2:2–3 *114*
2:7 *36*
2:15 *36*
2:19 *114*
3:6 *245*
3:13 *245*
4–7 *245*

Job

1:6 *73*
1:6–12 *242*
2:1 *73*
2:1–7 *242*
10:8–12 *78*
19:25–27 *340*
24:21 *316*
26:13 *296*
31:15 *78*
38:7 *73*

Psalms

2 *245*
2:1–2 *198*
2:2 *31, 245*
2:6–9 *73*
2:7 *75, 245*
2:8 *245*
2:9 *245*
7:17 *73*
9:9 *81*
11:4 *153*
14:1b–3 *321*
14:2 *289*
17:7 *301*
22:6–8 *197*
23 *138*
25:22 *169*
26:11 *169*
34:3 *94*
40:6 *301*
42:11 *301*
43:5 *301*
45:14 *114*
47:2 *73*
48:1 *73*
49:15 *169*
50:7 *322*
50:10 *156*
50:12 *156*
51:5 *321–22*
72 *173*
72:1–4 *338*
72:4 *81*
72:10–11 *173*
75:2 *73*
76:1 *73*
78:63 *114*
80:1 *138*
82:3 *81*
85:10 *73*
86:10 *73*
86:16b *82*

89:13 *91*
91:4 *76*
98:4–9 *331*
98:7–9 *331*
98:8b–9 *336*
100:3 *78*
103:4 *169*
103:17 *88*
103:19–21 *144*
104:30 *296*
106:10 *169*
106:37 *317*
106:37–38 *108*
110:1 *221*
111:9 *88*
113:9 *316*
115:3 *285*
119:68 *341*
119:105 *67*
119:134 *169*
127:3–5 *316*
130:8 *103*
132:11–12 *49*
133:1 *360*
134:5 *73*
135:5 *73*
136:12 *91*
138:2 *153*
138:6 *89*
139:13–16 *78, 316*
140:7 *76, 301*
148:2 *144*

Proverbs

3:1–4 *210*
5:18 *369*
5:19 *369*
7:6–26 *47*
8:22–31 *210*
30:16 *316*
31:10 *53*
31:10–31 *53*
31:28 *90*

Ecclesiastes

5:1–3 *64*
5:2 *64*
7:20 *321*

Song of Songs

1:2–4 *369*
3:6 *181*
4:6 *181*
4:14 *181*

Isaiah

6:1–5 *144*
7:1–25 *109*
7:4 *109*
7:6 *109*
7:7b *109*
7–9 *182*
7:9b *109*
7:10–11 *110*
7:12 *110*
7:14 *106–8, 111, 113–17, 287, 358*
7:14a *110*
7:14b–17 *110*
8:3 *165*
8:3–4 *113*
8:4 *182*
8:14 *164*
9 *113*
9:1 *113–14*
9:1–7 *163*
9:2 *184*
9:6 *114, 125, 335*
9:6–7 *35, 74, 114*
9:7 *114, 335*
11 *197, 336*
11:1 *107, 197*
11:1–2 *336*
11:6–10 *336*
35:1b–2 *336*
39 *161*
40 *162*

40:1–2 *161*
40:3 *57, 66*
40:3–5 *58, 63*
40:11 *138*
40–55 *163, 167*
41:2 *161*
42:1 *167–68, 238*
42:1–9 *167*
43:10–11 *295*
44:6b *295*
44:24–45:13 *162*
47:13 *178*
47:13–14 *174*
49 *165*
49:1 *167*
49:1–13 *167*
49:2 *165*
49:5 *163*
49:5–6 *167*
49:6 *103, 163, 168, 172*
49:7 *197*
50:4–11 *168*
50:6 *168*
51:5 *91*
51:9 *91*
52:9–10 *167*
52:10 *91*
52:13–53:12 *168*
53 *71, 111*
53:2–3 *71, 197*
53:3 *198, 286*
53:5 *329*
53:5–6 *157*
53:7–8 *168*
53:12 *168, 199*
60:1–3 *182*
60:6 *182*
64:11 *153*
66:7 *354*
66:19 *288*

Jeremiah

1:5 *78, 316*
4:4 *321*

6:21 *164*
15:7 *316*
15:14 *321*
18:21 *316*
22:24–30 *42*
22:30 *48*
23:5 *336*
23:5–6 *49*
26:21 *187*
31:15 *107, 192–93*
31:16 *192*
31:16–17 *193*
31:31–34 *193*
33:15 *336*
36:29–31 *48*
36:30 *42*
40:1 *192*
42:13–44:30 *187*
44:29 *288*

Lamentations

2:4–5 *321*
3:25–26 *159*

Ezekiel

1:28 *141*
16:4 *133*
24:24 *288*
34:23–24 *139*
36:24–27 *66, 193*
36:29 *103*
44:2 *354*
46:6 *323*

Daniel

2:2 *175*
2:10 *175*
2:19 *101*
2:34 *289*
4:24 *73*
6:27 *288*
7:13–14 *221, 290*
7:14 *74*
7:23–27 *244*

8–10 *63*
8:10 *244*
8:17 *63, 72*
9:20–21 *63*
9:23 *63*
9:26 *197*
10:15 *63*
12:1 *247*

Hosea

1:10 *73*
11 *188*
11:1 *107, 187, 189*
11:1–3 *188*
11:5 *188*

Joel

2:27 *113*
2:28–29 *162, 193*

Amos

1:1–2 *138*

Obadiah

21 *338*

Micah

4:6–8 *139*
5:2 *107, 115, 125, 139, 179, 221*
5:4 *139*

Nahum

3:18–19 *189*

Zephaniah

3:11 *153*
3:15 *103*

Haggai

1–2 *49*

Zechariah

2:10–11 *113*
2:12 *153*

3:1–2 *242*
4 *49*
9:9–10 *32*
12:7 *32*
12:10 *340*

Malachi

2:14 *97*
3:1 *57–58, 66*
4:5 *58*
4:5–6 *63*

Matthew

1:1 *31, 227, 237*
1:1–17 *39, 106*
1–2 *107*
1:2–6a *36*
1:2–17 *39*
1:6b *39, 54*
1:6b–11 *36*
1:8 *36*
1:12–16 *37*
1:16 *20, 41*
1:17 *35–36*
1:18 *20, 79, 95–96, 214, 226, 301*
1:18–2:23 *3*
1:18–19 *96, 349*
1:18–25 *106–7*
1:19 *98–99*
1:20 *20, 227, 302*
1:20–21 *20, 101*
1:20–24a *349*
1:20b-21 *102*
1:21 *20, 73, 103, 152, 164, 321,
    337*
1:22–23 *105*
1:23 *20, 37, 221*
1:24–25 *20, 101, 357*
1:24b–25 *349*
1:25 *20, 358, 370*
2 *139, 179, 245*
2:1 *20, 171, 176*
2:1–2 *172*
2:1–8 *350*

2:1–12 *107*
2:1–23 *199*
2:2 *174–75, 181, 329*
2:3 *178*
2:3–8 *177*
2:7 *179*
2:8 *180–81*
2:9 *180*
2:9–11 *151, 180, 195, 350*
2:11 *200, 329*
2:12 *182, 350*
2:12–23 *186*
2:13 *199*
2:13–15 *107, 186, 246, 349, 350*
2:13–16 *195*
2:15 *199, 358*
2:15–23 *199*
2:16 *179*
2:16–18 *107, 178, 191, 317, 350*
2:19 *194, 196*
2:19–20 *199*
2:19–23 *107, 194, 350*
2:22–23 *199*
2:23 *20, 196–97*
3:2 *334*
3:3 *106*
4:1–11 *277, 323*
4:7 *110*
4:14 *106*
4:17 *334*
5:3 *91*
5:5 *91*
5:7 *90*
5:10 *91*
5:14–15 *133*
5:17–18 *158*
5:27–32 *99*
7:21 *334*
7:23 *157*
8:17 *106*
9:11 *53*
9:27 *227*
9:35 *333*
10:7 *334*

10:32–39 *361*
10:34 *164*
10:35–39 *164*
11:10 *106*
11:11 *233*
11:13 *62*
11:19 *196*
12:14 *198*
12:17 *106*
12:18–21 *167*
12:23 *227*
12:46–50 *361*
13:14 *106*
13:33 *358*
13:35 *106*
13:54–57 *360*
13:55 *102, 218*
13:55–56 *359*
14:1–12 *58*
15:7 *106*
15:22 *227*
17:11–13 *63*
18 *118*
18:3 *334*
18:14 *316*
18:15–20 *118*
18:20 *118*
18:34 *358*
19:1–11 *99*
19:14 *316*
19:17 *334*
19:23–24 *334*
19:28–30 *338*
20:30–31 *227*
21:4 *106*
21:9 *227*
21:11 *197*
21:15 *227*
21:31–32 *53*
21:42 *7*
22:29 *7*
22:41–45 *221*
22:42–45 *227*
23:28 *157*

24:30 *74, 338*
25:1–13 *98*
25:31 *335*
26:1–5 *198*
26:26 *119*
26:28 *193*
26:31 *106*
26:64 *74*
27:9 *106*
27:11 *329*
27:19 *101*
27:29 *329*
27:37 *329*
27:61 *71*
28:1 *71*
28:9 *296*
28:18 *119*
28:19 *118, 295*
28:20 *119, 358*

Mark

1:1 *142, 218*
1:1–11 *217*
1:2–3 *57*
1:11 *218*
1:12 *199, 217*
1:12–13 *277, 323*
1:15 *334*
1:20 *217*
1:29–34 *218*
2:5–11 *295*
3:21 *165*
3:31–32 *359*
3:31–35 *361*
4:41 *218*
5:21–43 *218*
6:3 *218, 359*
6:14–29 *58*
8:22–26 *218*
9:2–13 *218*
9:7 *218*
9:21 *209*
10:5 *334*
10:25 *334*

10:45 *168*
10:46–52 *218*
10:47 *227*
10:47–48 *40, 218*
11:10 *227*
12:29 *295*
12:35–37 *227*
13:32 *209*
13:36 *144*
14:35 *198*
14:49 *7*
14:62 *74, 295*
15:39 *218*
15:40 *71*
16:8 *218*
16:9–20 *218*

Luke

1:1 *25, 217*
1:1–4 *18, 128*
1–2 *21, 25, 232, 257*
1:2 *19, 21*
1:3 *21*
1:4 *27*
1:5 *20, 58*
1:5–2:52 *3*
1:5–20 *59*
1:5–23 *349*
1:5–25 *62*
1:6 *142, 161*
1:6–7 *62*
1:7 *63*
1:9 *142*
1:9–11 *63*
1:11–12 *63*
1:12 *72*
1:13 *63*
1:15 *67, 316*
1:15a *63*
1:15b *63*
1:16 *63, 142*
1:17 *63*
1:18 *64, 75*
1:20 *63–64*

1:21–25 *59*
1:22 *63*
1:24–25 *349*
1:25 *64*
1:26–30 *70*
1:26–33 *59*
1:26–38 *70, 349*
1:27 *20, 41, 71, 227*
1:28 *72, 77, 288*
1:28-38 *102*
1:29 *72*
1:29–30 *63*
1:30 *72*
1:30-31 *102*
1:30–31 *77*
1:30–35 *20*
1:31 *20, 77, 81, 152, 234*
1:31–33 *73, 234*
1:32 *20, 67, 142, 164, 227, 234–
   35, 238, 256*
1:32–33 *245, 335*
1:33 *25, 90, 238, 339*
1:34 *20, 71*
1:34–35 *78*
1:34–37 *59, 75*
1:35 *20, 81, 102, 157, 214, 226,
   234–35, 302, 325, 356*
1:35a *77*
1:36 *62, 85*
1:36a *77*
1:37 *77, 85, 307*
1:38 *79, 81, 86, 343*
1:39 *146*
1:39–40 *85*
1:39–45 *62, 85, 276*
1:39–56 *349*
1:41 *86*
1:41–45 *86*
1:42a *86*
1:42b *86*
1:43 *86, 89, 143, 271, 276, 279,
   316*
1:44 *316*
1:45 *86*

1:45–46 *86*
1:46–47 *87*
1:46–50 *88*
1:46–55 *24, 84, 87*
1:47 *301*
1:48 *82, 87–89*
1:48–50 *88*
1:49 *87–88*
1:50 *88*
1:51–53 *90–91*
1:52 *88*
1:53 *88*
1:54–55 *92*
1:56 *85, 95*
1:57–66 *59*
1:57–79 *64*
1:57–80 *62, 349*
1:62–63 *102*
1:63–64 *64*
1:67–79 *24, 59*
1:68 *65, 166, 321*
1:68–71 *65*
1:69 *227*
1:69–70 *65*
1:70 *65*
1:72–73 *65*
1:74 *65*
1:76 *66*
1:76–77 *66*
1:77 *65*
1:78 *66, 221, 256*
1:78–79 *66*
1:79 *66*
1:80 *59*
2:1 *125*
2:1–5 *124, 126*
2:1–7 *349*
2:1–20 *195*
2:2 *127*
2:4 *20, 41, 125*
2:4–7 *20*
2:5 *42*
2:5–6 *20*
2:6–7 *129–30*

2:7 *59, 129–30, 157, 359*
2:8–12 *140*
2:8–20 *349*
2:9–10 *63*
2:9a *141*
2:10 *11, 144*
2:11 *20, 142–43, 301, 321*
2:12 *287, 316*
2:13–14 *143*
2:14 *24, 144, 336–37*
2:15–20 *145*
2:16 *146*
2:17 *22*
2:18 *146*
2:19 *22, 146, 164*
2:20 *344*
2:21 *151, 195, 349*
2:21–24 *59, 150*
2:22–24 *153, 200, 357*
2:22–38 *195, 349*
2:23 *156*
2:25 *161–62*
2:25–35 *161*
2:27 *150*
2:28 *238*
2:28–32 *24*
2:29 *163*
2:29–32 *59, 163*
2:30–32 *167*
2:31 *163*
2:32 *163, 172*
2:34 *164*
2:35 *164*
2:36–38 *165*
2:37 *166*
2:38 *162*
2:39 *20, 199, 349*
2:39–40 *200, 350*
2:40 *59, 207*
2:41–51 *205*
2:41–52 *350*
2:46 *206*
2:47 *206*
2:48 *206*

2:51 *22, 146, 164, 207*
2:52 *59, 200, 207–8, 266, 323*
3 *36, 207*
3:1 *257*
3:4–6 *63*
3:19–20 *58*
3:21–22 *74*
3:22 *42, 167–68*
3:23 *41, 200, 218, 237*
3:23–38 *39–40*
3:29 *73*
3:31 *39*
3:38 *42, 237, 326*
4 *277*
4:1–13 *323*
4:22 *78, 102*
4:29 *198*
4:30 *198*
4:31 *257*
4:43 *26, 333*
6:1–11 *157*
6:20 *26*
7:27 *57*
7:28 *67, 233*
8:1 *26*
8:2 *71*
8:10 *26*
8:19 *359*
8:19–20 *165*
8:19–21 *361*
9:2 *26*
9:9 *58*
9:11 *26*
9:27 *26*
9:34 *76*
9:39 *144*
9:60 *26*
10:7 *232*
10:11 *26*
10:24 *7*
10:34 *130*
10:38–42 *71*
11:27–28 *90, 93*
12:32 *26*

12:49–53 *164*
13:10–17 *157*
16:16 *26, 62*
17:21 *334*
18:24 *26*
18:24–25 *334*
18:38–39 *227*
20:41–44 *221, 227*
21:16 *360*
21:31 *26*
22:12 *130*
22:18 *358*
22:30 *338*
22:37 *168*
22:42 *80, 211*
22:54–62 *65*
23:51 *162*
24:1–5 *63*
24:10 *71*
24:11 *147*
24:12 *146*
24:13–49 *7, 25*
24:25 *7*
24:27 *7, 150*
24:32 *10*
24:44 *150*
24:49 *358*
24:50–51 *246*

John

1:1–2 *219*
1:1–3 *291*
1:1–5 *219*
1:1–18 *219–20, 295*
1:3 *295, 314*
1:8 *67*
1:9 *172*
1:10–13 *222*
1:11 *33*
1:12 *289*
1:12–13 *289*
1:13 *222–24, 330*
1:14 *143, 221, 296, 314*
1:14a *220*

1:14b *220*
1:17 *158*
1:18 *220, 289, 291, 296*
1:29 *156, 329*
1:45 *102, 218*
1:46 *71, 226*
2:1–12 *98*
3:3 *223, 330*
3:3–8 *223*
3:5–8 *223*
3:6 *275*
3:13 *120, 291, 301*
3:16 *296*
3:18 *296*
3:24 *58*
3:29 *98*
3:31 *120*
4:22 *163*
5:39 *8*
6 *224*
6:1–15 *224*
6:22–59 *224*
6:27 *224*
6:33 *224*
6:35 *224*
6:38 *120, 224, 291, 301*
6:41 *120*
6:42 *78, 102, 218, 225*
6:51 *120*
7:1–4 *361*
7:1–7 *210*
7:2–5 *217*
7:3–5 *165, 359*
7:5 *359, 361*
7:40–44 *225*
7:41–42 *179*
7:42 *40, 226–27*
8:3–11 *98*
8:14 *225–26*
8:23 *225–26*
8:41 *99–100*
8:44 *289*
8:44–47 *243*
8:56 *34*

8:58 *221, 291*
8:59 *198*
9:38 *296*
9:39 *295*
10:14–15 *138*
10:31 *198*
11:1–43 *71*
12:23 *198*
12:27 *198*
13:1 *198*
13:38 *358*
14:18 *337*
14:26 *296*
14:26–27 *337*
15:26 *296*
16:5 *118*
16:7 *118*
17:1 *198*
17:3 *291*
17:4–5 *221*
17:5 *291*
19:25 *71*
19:25–27 *359*
19:30 *329*
19:41 *329*
20:19 *356*
20:22 *296*
20:25 *356*
20:29 *94, 340*
20:30 *219*
20:31 *17*
21:25 *219*

Acts

1:1–2 *232*
1:8 *139, 164*
1:9–10 *246*
1:9–11 *118*
1:11 *121, 286*
1:14 *21, 217*
2:1–11 *302*
2:14 *65*
2:17 *337*

2:17–18 *162, 296*
2:18 *86*
2:22–23 *329*
2:23 *198, 310*
2:30 *227*
2:32–33 *295*
2:41 *65*
3:21 *337*
3:22–26 *226*
3:25 *33*
5:3–4 *296*
5:31 *301*
7:19 *316*
7:55 *295*
8:9–23 *175*
8:30–31 *267*
8:30–35 *168*
9:3 *144*
10:36 *26*
12:12 *19, 71*
12:25 *19*
13:23 *78, 227, 301*
15:13 *217*
16 *18*
16:12b–13 *18*
17:24–27 *135*
17:28–29 *289*
17:31 *135*
19:1–7 *58*
19:4 *59*
20:6 *18*
20:8 *18*
20:13–16 *18*
21:1–25 *18*
21:26 *358*
22:6 *144*
23:12 *358*
23:21 *358*
25:21 *358*
27:1–8 *18*
27:13–44 *18*
28:1–16 *18*
28:30–31 *232*

Romans

1:1–4 *234*
1:3 *40, 42, 227, 230, 234–35*
1:3–4 *262*
1:4 *234–35, 329*
1:16 *142, 164*
3:11 *289*
3:23 *89, 156, 321*
3:25 *262*
4:16–17 *33*
4:24–25 *262*
5:1 *145*
5:5 *296*
5:6 *262*
5:8 *262*
5:10 *145, 321*
5:12 *323*
5:12–21 *237, 322, 326*
5:14 *326*
5:15b *327*
6:23 *321*
7:4 *262*
8:3 *323*
8:11 *262, 329*
8:20 *241*
8:29 *360*
8:32 *262*
9:3–4 *360*
9:4 *33*
9:4–5 *163*
9:5 *230, 295*
9:6 *164*
9:11 *233*
10:9 *262, 295*
10:9–13 *334*
10:13 *295*
15:6 *296*
15:8–9a *152*
16:6 *71*
16:20 *242, 248*

1 Corinthians

1:23 *164*
1:27 *135*
3:16–17 *296*
5:3–4 *119*
6:14 *262*
6:19–20 *296*
6:20 *157*
7:1 *367*
7:2 *367*
7:5 *367*
7:6 *368*
7:7 *368*
7:8 *368*
7:18 *152*
7:35 *368*
8:4–6 *295*
8:6 *262, 295*
8:11 *262*
9:5 *359*
11:17–26 *231*
11:23 *262*
12:3 *262*
12:4–6 *119*
12:4–11 *296*
12:12–30 *337*
13:12 *212*
15 *231, 327*
15:3–7 *262*
15:6 *215, 340*
15:7 *217*
15:12 *231*
15:12–19 *27*
15:19 *16*
15:22 *327*
15:24–28 *338*
15:25 *358*
15:28 *339*
15:35–49 *237*
15:45 *237*
15:47 *237*

2 Corinthians

3:17 *295*
3:17–18 *296*

4:6 *143*
4:14 *262*
5:10 *295*
5:14–15 *262*
5:16–21 *327*
5:17 *327, 330*
5:19 *145*
5:21 *156, 323, 327*
6:18 *295*
8:9 *156*
11:4 *231*

Galatians

1:1 *262*
1:6–9 *231*
1:19 *217, 359*
2:3 *152*
2:9 *217*
3:8 *183*
3:10 *158*
3:13 *158*
3:16 *33, 242*
3:19 *242*
4:4 *33, 124, 214, 327*
4:4–5 *151, 229, 233*
4:4a *123*
4:5 *262*
4:6 *296*
4:23 *233*
4:27 *316*
4:29 *233*
5:1–6 *231*
5:2 *152*

Ephesians

1:3 *295*
1:10 *261, 325*
1:22 *118*
2:1–10 *223*
2:3 *289*
2:13b–14a *145*
4:5 *262*
4:6 *295*

4:8 *246*
4:10 *120*
5:23 *118*

Philippians

2:5–11 *119, 262*
2:6 *238*
2:6–7 *298*
2:7 *119, 236, 238*
2:8 *238*
2:9–11 *238*
2:10–11 *340*
2:11 *295*
3:20 *301*

Colossians

1:3 *296*
1:12 *289*
1:13 *334*
1:13–14 *142*
1:15 *143, 289*
1:15–17 *291*
1:15–23 *231*
1:16 *295, 314*
1:17 *120*
1:18 *118*
2:4–23 *231*
2:5 *119*
2:6 *262*
2:9 *117, 143*
4:11 *73*
4:14 *18, 21, 231*

1 Thessalonians

1:10 *262*
4:3–8 *368*
4:14 *262*
5:10 *262*
5:23 *340*

2 Thessalonians

1:10 *337*
2:8 *248*
2:15 *253*

1 Timothy

1:1 *301*
1:15 *262, 329*
2:5–6 *295*
2:6 *262*
3:1–16 *236*
3:15 *236*
3:16 *235, 246, 330*
4:8–9 *262*
5:18 *232*

2 Timothy

2:8 *40, 227, 230*
2:11 *262*
3:1–9 *337*
3:16 *8, 301*
3:16–17 *351*
4:8 *337*
4:11 *18, 231*

Titus

2:1 *268*
2:13 *159, 338*
3:5–8 *262*
3:6 *296*

Philemon

1:24 *18, 231*

Hebrews

1:1–3 *67, 117*
1:2 *295, 314*
1:2–3 *291*
1:3 *143*
1:5 *75*
1:6 *296*
3:1–6 *67*
4:15 *277, 323*
5:7–8 *211*
5:9 *212*
7:3 *275*
7:14 *40, 227*

7:26 *323*
9:14 *296, 323*
9:15 *152*
9:22 *154*
9:23–28 *154*
9:28 *337*
10:5 *78, 301*
10:14–17 *193*
11:31 *52*
12:18–19 *145*
13:8 *120, 279, 286*
13:20 *138*

James

1:13 *277*
1:17 *311*
1:18 *223*
2:19 *295*
2:25 *52*
4:1–10 *91*
5:1–6 *337*

1 Peter

1:3b–4 *330*
1:11 *9*
1:18–19 *169*
1:23 *223*
2:8 *164*
2:21–24 *168*
2:22 *323*
2:25 *138*
3:18 *330*
5:4 *138*

2 Peter

1:1 *295*
1:16 *26*
1:19 *184*
1:20–21 *117*
1:21 *301*
3:3–7 *337*
3:16 *268*

1 John

2:28 *340*
3:2 *212*
3:5 *323*
3:8–15 *243*
3:9 *223*
4:1–6 *257*
4:9 *296*
5:4 *223*
5:20 *295*

2 John

1:7 *257*

Jude

1:3 *254, 261*
1:5 *9*
1:9 *247*
1:14–15 *236*

Revelation

1:4 *336*
1:6 *337*
1:7 *286, 340*
1:12–13 *118*
1:14 *248*
1:16 *118, 165*
1:16a *248*
1:16b *248*
1:20 *118*
2:20 *165*
3:7 *227*
4:4–10 *338*
4:11 *306*
5 *296*
5:5 *40, 227*
5:9 *103*

5:9–10 *337*
5:10 *103*
6:9–11 *248*
7:9 *181*
7:9–17 *248*
7:14 *248*
11:15 *245, 335*
12 *240, 243*
12:1–6 *243–44*
12:1–17 *243*
12:2 *244*
12:3 *244*
12:4 *245*
12:4b *185*
12:5 *246*
12:6 *246*
12:7–17 *246–47*
12:9 *242, 244*
12:10 *248*
12:11 *248*
12:12 *248*
12:13 *244*
12:15 *247*
12:17 *244, 248*
18:13 *181*
19:7 *337*
19:9 *338*
19:21 *165*
20 *240*
21 *240*
21:9 *337*
21–22 *168*
22 *240*
22:2 *240*
22:3 *240*
22:16 *40, 56, 66, 227*
22:21 *8*